Revised Form 990

Revised Form 990

A Line-by-Line Preparation Guide

Jody Blazek
Amanda Adams

WILEY

John Wiley & Sons, Inc.

Library of Congress Cataloging-in-Publication Data:

Blazek, Jody.
   Revised Form 990: a line-by-line preparation guide/Jody Blazek, Amanda Adams.
     p. cm.
   Includes bibliographical references and index.
   ISBN 978-0-470-44647-8 (paper/website)
1. Nonprofit organizations—Taxation—Law and legislation—United States—Forms. 2. Tax exemption—Law and legislation—United States—Forms. 3. Tax returns—United States. I. Adams, Amanda. II. Title.
   KF6449.B567 2009
   343-7305'26—dc22   2008052083

Printed in the United States of America

10 9 8 7 6 5 4 3 2 1

Contents

Preface

Forms 990 have traditionally provided a wealth of financial and programmatic information to enable government regulators, funders, journalists, and anybody else who is interested to measure a nonprofit's performance. Since 1987, the form must be provided to anyone who is willing to pay a modest fee for a copy of it. Charities, and an increasing number of non-(c)(3) organizations, have their returns posted on the Internet courtesy of Guidestar.org for the public to view. The forms are the most widely used tools for evaluating tax-exempt organizations. Schools, health and welfare organizations, business leagues, civic associations, museums, farmers' cooperatives, parent groups, garden clubs, private foundations, and the many other nonprofit organizations recognized under §501(c) of the Internal Revenue Code must file this form annually. Information on the return is the basis for IRS scrutiny in meeting its responsibility to allow continued exemption from income tax. Careful preparation of the form is therefore very important. This guide contains the three major forms filed by tax-exempt organizations: (1) Form 990 for §501(c) organizations that are not private foundations, (2) Form 990-T used by all to report taxable unrelated business income; and (3) Form 990-PF, filed by private foundations.

After 30 years of modest annual revisions, the IRS in June 2007 released a draft of an amazing and complex revision of the Form 990 for 2008. Thankfully, they invited input from the exempt sector, giving us a September 2007 deadline for comments. Hundreds of e-mails were posted on the IRS Web site throughout an incredible summer as professionals in firms like ours exchanged ideas and expressed suggestions for revisions. Again in April 2008 when the companion instructions were released, the ABA, AICPA, Independent Sector and many others weighed in. Many of the issues reviewers brought up concerning the form and instructions, were instituted by the IRS as improvements in its product. The final outcome is presented in this book.

The revised Form 990 reflects the IRS's intention to enhance the transparency of a tax-exempt organization's financial affairs and governance practices and procedures. The most controversial part of the new Core Form is Part VI, entitled "Governance, Management, and Disclosures." Readers will note the top of this part says that some sections "request information about policies not required by the Internal Revenue Code." Steven T. Miller, Commissioner, Tax Exempt and Government Entities, said in November 2005 that "we have seen the migration of the governance problems that surfaced a few years ago in the corporate world. Weak governance and the resulting problems appear in the sector, evidencing themselves in such things as excess compensation and poor Form 990 reporting." The evolution of the IRS's focus on governance can be found on its Web site at www.irs.gov/charities at Speeches on Governance.

The fact that the questions on governance in Part VI are answered according to practices in place as of the last day of the filing organization's fiscal year will be troubling for those who were unaware of the questions before year-end. IRS representatives have said that negative answers on this part will not necessarily result in examinations in the near future. However, those now required to file the return electronically because they file more than 250 W-2 and 1099-type returns otherwise should be careful. The IRS has already engaged programmers to design electronic auditing techniques. There is an Exempt Organizations Compliance Unit (EOCU) in Ogden, Utah, where physical returns are sent to use sampling techniques to identify issues to question.

The second most troublesome aspect of the revised return is the extraordinary increase in information requested throughout the schedules. Schedule M is a good example. Not only must 24 different types of noncash contributions received be quantified and described, but the method of valuation, the acceptance policy for such gifts, who sells such donated items, and the practice of making proper donor disclosures for such gifts are required. Similarly, the return previously made no distinction between domestic activities and those conducted outside the United States. A brief look at new Schedule F reveals the extensive details now to be submitted for off-shore activities, as distinguished from Schedule I, where grants paid to organizations, governments, and individuals located in the United States are reported.

Maybe the most important thought to convey is that the revised return will in most cases require more time and effort to adequately gather information for its completion despite Director of Exempt Organizations Lois Lerner's hope that the revision would minimize the burden on the filing organizations. For many, the work will fall on not only the accounting or finance department, but also the personnel and development departments and certain executive officials and board members. As the return data is prepared, the process should be evaluated to gather ideas to ease the burden. Questions like "Should the accounting system be improved to allow adequate tracking of details for costs and revenues?," "Should we identify a team of personnel to gather 990 data for 2009?," or "How can documentation systems be improved?" should be asked. Fortunately a transition period has been provided that will result in many former 990 filers being allowed to submit Form 990-EZ for 2008 and 2009, as shown on the chart in Chapter 1(§1.3).

What's good about the new return is the front page that presents an organizational snapshot with a brief description of mission, a bit of governance data, and a comparison of revenues and expenses for the current and past years. Second best may be the "reasonable effort" rule. An organization is only expected to do its best to send questionnaires to its board and staff members to obtain answers regarding relationships for Core Parts VI and Schedule L.

Part IV may be difficult for some as they navigate a long list of questions prompting attachment of one of the 16 new schedules based on an array of varying financial thresholds. Some of the questions don't mention the issue. One wishes the IRS had settled on $10,000 rather than the range of $5,000 to $25,000 that currently exists for the reporting thresholds. What is a very helpful list of other tax filing requirements is displayed in Part V.

Part VII for reporting compensation for officials has a good display by positions, a much clearer definition of key employees who must be reported, and a higher threshold for reporting. Only experienced 990 preparers, and the National Football League representatives who complained, will realize that this part now combines reporting of the compensation of those officials previously reported by §501(c)(3) charities on now-defunct Schedule A and non-(c)(3) personnel previously *not* reported unless they were an officer or a director.

Part VIII, "Statement of Revenue," combines the part that in the past identified revenue according to its character as related to exempt purposes, unrelated to exempt purposes and thereby reportable on Form 990-T, and unrelated revenue that is not taxed due to volunteer conduct, donated goods, irregularity, and other exceptions. Part IX, "Statement of Functional Expenses," expands categories of fees for services, adding lines for lobbying, investment management fees, advertising and promotion, information technology, payments to affiliates, and royalties. The relatively minor expense accounts previously listed have been combined to report "office expenses," including supplies, telephone, postage and shipping, and printing and publications. Part X presents the balance sheet in much the same fashion. Organizations with donor-advised funds, conservation easements, collections, endowments, and other types of assets must submit enhanced detailed, information in Schedule D.

The biggest impact of the new form may come to those §501(c)(3) organizations classified as public charities because the revenue to support their activities comes from many donors or participants in exempt function activities. The test for calculation of qualification now includes five rather than four years and can be prepared on either the cash or accrual basis, whichever method is normally followed for the organization's financial and 990 reporting purposes. Prior year calculations may need to be restated. A regulation change was required to implement the changes. Organizations with a support ratio below the $33\frac{1}{3}\%$ floor for the prior year are instructed to file Form 990-PF if the calculation for the current year is also below $33\frac{1}{3}\%$. Careful attention to support levels is critical for filers who must meet the test.

As readers go through the book, they will find schedules with significantly enhanced information for lobbying and electioneering activity (Schedule C) and fundraising and gaming (Schedule G). Again, thankfully, full completion of the amazingly detailed Schedule H for hospitals and Schedule K for tax exempt bonds has been delayed until 2009. Last, the form now contains a schedule that is virtually blank entitled Schedule O that undoubtedly will become the most viewed schedule of the form. Chapter 4, §15 lists the 45 different times the form and schedules require a comment in Schedule O either because the organization has to say "No" it has no policy for that issue or instead to explain its existing policies.

Even though they are classified as tax-exempt organizations, some nonprofits receive income through an activity that does not advance the mission and are therefore subject to the normal income tax. Chapter 5 considers the preparation of Form 990-T, which reports such unrelated income, and presents ideas for maximizing deductions and minimizing the resulting tax liability.

Issues that are key to maintaining exempt status are highlighted in this guide to alert readers to questions that deserve close attention. Specifically, the types of transactions that can endanger a nonprofit's tax-exempt status and/or result in an unexpected tax liability are explained. Footnotes provide references to the tax code and to the fourth edition of Blazek's *Tax Planning and Compliance for Tax-Exempt Organizations*, where extensive discussions of the criteria for obtaining and maintaining tax-exempt status can be found. In addition to using this book, return preparers might also find that the new "plain language" publications and training videos available on the IRS web site help explain the rules applicable to tax-exempt nonprofits.

We hope this line-by-line preparation guide will be a useful tool that enhances the quality of public reporting required for nonprofit organizations on Forms 990.

Jody Blazek
Amanda Adams

Houston, Texas
January 22, 2009

Acknowledgments

First and foremost, we acknowledge and thank the wonderful people who work with us at Blazek & Vetterling and our nonprofit clients who bring challenging tax and financial issues for us to solve. Next, we thank the folks at John Wiley & Sons who make the Wiley Nonprofit Series an invaluable collection of reference books for the nonprofit sector. Finally, Jody treasures all those who have joined her in serving the Texas Accountants and Lawyers for the Arts, the AICPA Tax-Exempt Organizations Resource Panel, the Volunteer Services Committee of the Houston Chapter of CPAs, and the Management Assistance Program of the United Way of Greater Houston over the years. Together, they have enhanced the body of knowledge available to the non-profit sector and improved the resulting delivery of valuable services to the constituents those nonprofits serve.

This book is dedicated to all the tireless volunteers who serve nonprofit organizations.

About the Authors

Jody Blazek is a partner in Blazek & Vetterling, a Houston, Texas, CPA firm providing tax compliance and auditing services to over 250 nonprofit, tax-exempt organization clients and tax consulting services to other lawyers and accountants who serve nonprofits.

Jody began her professional career at KPMG, then Peat, Marwick, Mitchell & Co. Her concentration on exempt organizations began in 1969, when she studied and advised clients about the Tax Reform Act, which completely revamped the taxation of charities and created private foundations. From 1972 to 1981, she gained nonprofit management experience as the treasurer of the Menil Interests where she worked with John and Dominique de Menil to plan the Menil Collection, The Rothko Chapel, and other projects of the Menil Foundation. She reentered public practice in 1981, to found the firm she now serves.

She is the author or co-author of five other books in the Wiley Nonprofit Series: *Tax Planning and Compliance for Tax-Exempt Organizations 4th Edition* (2004), *Nonprofit Financial Planning Made Easy* (2008), *IRS Form 1023 Tax Preparation Guide* (2005), and *Private Foundations: Tax Law and Compliance 3rd Edition* (2008) and *Private Foundation Legal Answer Book*, both co-authored with Bruce R. Hopkins.

Jody is the past chair of the American Institute of Certified Public Accountants' Tax-Exempt Organizations Resource Panel. She serves on the national editorial board of Tax Analysts' *The Exempt Organization Tax Review* and the AICPA *Tax Adviser*. She is a founding director of the Texas Accountants and Lawyers for the Arts and Houston Artists Fund. She is a frequent speaker at nonprofit symposia, including AICPA, TSCPA, and NYSSCPA Not-for-Profit Industry Conferences; the University of Texas School of Law Nonprofit Organizations Institute, among others.

Blazek received her BBA from the University of Texas at Austin in 1964, and took selected classes at the South Texas School of Law. She and her husband, David Crossley, nurture two sons, Austin and Jay Blazek Crossley.

Amanda Adams is a tax manager at Blazek & Vetterling, a Houston, Texas CPA firm providing tax compliance and auditing services to over 250 nonprofit, tax-exempt organization clients and tax consulting services to other lawyers and accountants who serve nonprofits.

Amanda joined Blazek & Vetterling in 2003, and currently serves a broad range of nonprofit clients, including social services agencies; civic, business, and cultural organizations; private foundations, and health-care-related organizations. In 2007, she co-authored an article entitled "Transfers Between Private Foundations" that appeared in *Trusts & Estates* magazine. Amanda received her Bachelor of Arts degree from the University of Texas at Austin in 1999, and is currently pursuing her Master's of Accountancy degree at the University of Houston, with an expected graduation date in the summer of 2009. She is a member of the American Institute of Certified Public Accountants, the Texas Society of Certified Public Accountants, and the Houston Chapter of CPAs. Amanda is also a member of The Woman's Club of Houston and serves as co-leader of Girl Scouts of the USA's Troop 21125. Her two children, Alexis and Major, are a continual source of inspiration and joy.

CHAPTER ONE

Redesigned Form 990

The responsibility of the IRS to grant, or approve, qualification for tax-exempt status for all §501(c) organizations, which includes charities designated as §501(c)(3)s, civic associations (c)(4)s, labor unions (c)(5)s, business leagues (c)(6)s, social clubs (c)(7)s, and more than 30 other types of tax-exempt organizations, is accompanied by the burden to evaluate continued qualification. The 990 series of tax returns serves this purpose. The challenge in designing a form suitable for overseeing and scrutinizing ongoing qualification for the diverse types of organizations qualifying under §501(c) is evidenced by the ever-expanding girth of the form, culminating with the 2008 version, which has a Core Form with 11 pages plus 16 schedules to be completed when applicable. The fact that the form has been available for inspection by anyone that asks to see it since 1987[1] has made this form the most accessible source of information about a tax-exempt organization. Form 990 for §501(c)(3) organizations (and others) is also available on the Internet at www.guidestar.org. Therefore, its redesign has an impact on all those involved in the nonprofit sector.

The various Forms 990 are designed to accomplish many purposes that go far beyond simply reporting to the Internal Revenue Service (referred to in this book as the IRS). Accurate and complete preparation of the forms should be given top priority by a nonprofit organization. The forms are part of the electronic age; many are accessible to one and all on the Internet. An organization's public reporting responsibilities are beyond the form's physical dimension and deserve careful attention. Since March 1997, when the IRS contracted with the Urban Institute of Washington, D.C., to receive and place the forms for the years 1996 through 2001 on CD-ROMs, the Forms 990 have been made available on the Internet. In a coordinated effort, Philanthropic Resources, Inc. began in 1998 to digitize the information so that it could be sorted and searched. Information from prior 990s of some 40,000 public charities was originally entered. The Guidestar site also provides an abstract of the information they glean from the forms, and it also posts the complete form;[2] the site can be accessed at http://www.guidestar.org. The IRS has also begun to implement an electronic filing system for 990s to eliminate the paperwork altogether and allow them to more effectively monitor exempts in a statistical and focused fashion. As of December 2008, the IRS has not yet worked out a system to transmit Forms 990 submitted electronically into a format suitable for posting on Guidestar's website, so organizations filing electronically may not see their returns on Guidestar for some years. Such organizations can voluntarily submit their return and other documents to Guidestar.

In essence, Form 990 is designed to be, and in fact, is a public document. Yet another reason for a tax-exempt organization to pay careful attention to completion of the forms is the requirement that copies of the three most recent year's returns, now including Forms 990-T of §501(c)(3) entities, must be given upon request to those that pay a modest fee. Between 1984 and 1997, an organization had to allow anyone who knocked on its door a look at its Forms 990 and 1023 or 1024 in its office. Beginning June 8, 1999, a copy of the forms must be furnished for a fee as discussed in §1.12. Forms 990 are also used for a wide variety of state and local purposes. In many states, an exempt organization can satisfy its annual filing requirement by furnishing a copy of Form 990 to the appropriate state authority. Many grant-making foundations request a copy of Form 990 in addition to, or in lieu of, audited financial statements, to verify an organization's fiscal activity. The open-records standards applicable in many states also require all financial reports and records to be open to the public.

Form 990 provides a wealth of information. An organization's basic financial information—revenues, expenses, assets, and liabilities—is classified into meaningful categories to allow the IRS to evaluate a nonprofit's ongoing qualification for federal tax exemption under Internal Revenue Code §501 (hereinafter code section numbers are simply identified with the symbol "§"). The revised 990 contains a wide range of questions and information regarding governance policies, other tax compliance filings, and for those that must file the new schedules, significantly enhanced details about activities and accomplishments. The returns are also used by funders, states, and other persons to evaluate the scope and type of a nonprofit's activity. Information pertaining to the accomplishment of the organization's mission is presented—how many persons are served, papers researched, reports completed, students enrolled, and the like. Extensive details are furnished for grants paid to support other organizations and disbursed as aid to the poor, sick, students, and others in need. Details are furnished to reflect overall compensation for services and loans (if any) to or from persons who run and control the organization. The program accomplishment reports should particularly be prepared with a view to presenting the organization to funders and other supporters. Some use the information to compare nonprofit organizations statistically.

A long list of questions and financial details fish for failures to comply with the federal and to some extent, state, requirements for donor and member disclosures, political and lobbying activity, transactions with nonexempt organizations, insider transactions, and more. In sum, the returns are designed to show that a nonprofit organization is entitled to maintain its tax-exempt status and also to provide a wealth of other information of interest to funders, constituents, and regulators. Questions that can be answered with information on the forms follow:

- Do the organization's activities focus on an exempt purpose as reflected on the first page of the Core Form and as detailed in Part III?

- Do the fundraising costs shown on Part IX, line 25 (with details in column (D)) equal too high a percentage of the total expenses indicating the nonprofit fails the commensurate test?[3] Notice input of professional fundraising expenses as a single item on the front page, line 16a.

- Does Part I, line 7 (on the Core front page) and column (c) of Part VIII show a high percentage of unrelated business revenues in relation to the total revenues, indicating the organization is devoted to business interests rather than exempt purposes?[4]

- Do amounts reported in Part VII and Schedule J reflect significant compensation payments to officials and related parties, particularly in relation to overall expenses?[5]

- Is the amount a public charity reported on Schedule C, Part II-A or B for lobbying expenditures excessive (private foundations can spend none and some nonprofits exempt in categories other than §501(c)(3) can spend an unlimited amount)?[6]

- Does the calculation of a public charity's sources of support shown on Schedule A indicate it receives at least $33\frac{1}{3}$ percent of its support from the public so it continues to be classified as a public charity under §509(a)(1) or (a)(2)?[7]

- Are there "No" answers to governance Questions 8, 10, 12, 13, 14, and 15 in Part VI indicating the organization has not adopted policies and procedures recommended by the IRS (though not technically required by the tax code)?

- Are "Yes" answers in Part V (a) questions followed by "Yes" answers for (b) indicating the organization has complied with the tax rule asked in the question? Some (but not all) "No" answers in this part indicate noncompliance).

It is extremely important by way of introduction to remind readers that tax-exempt organizations are taxpayers. Though certain types of revenues they collect may not be subject to income tax under §501(c), they are subject to all of the sections contained in the Internal Revenue Code and the tax rules imposed by the states in which they operate. Many of the problems nonprofits ask the authors to solve stem from lack of awareness of this fact. Matters that deserve attention include federal payroll taxes, gift and estate taxes, donor and dues deductibility rules that impact persons who provide the revenues, and other federal issues, such as labor laws and employee retirement plans (ERISA rules).

Lastly, representatives of federally tax-exempt organizations must also inform themselves of the wide variety of state and local tax collection, compliance, and filing requirements—beyond the scope of this guide—to which the nonprofit may be subject. Due to the increasing globalization of activity fostered by the Internet, readers must pay close attention for developments in this regard. Professional help should be sought; CPA and Bar Association referral services should be able to recommend persons with nonprofit-organization experience. For those organizations that cannot afford to pay, a nonprofit management assistance program can be found. Many civic-minded CPAs, lawyers, and business people volunteer their time through local Bar and CPA societies, United Ways, associations of retired executives, and others.

§1.1 HISTORY OF REDESIGN PROJECT

The Form 990 revision project was undertaken by the IRS in response to the changes in the tax-exempt sector over the quarter century since it was last overhauled. "We need a Form 990 that reflects the way this growing sector operates in the twenty-first century. The new 990 aims to give both the IRS and the public an improved window into the way tax-exempt organizations go about their vital mission."[8]

The forms have evolved slowly over the years through cooperative efforts between the IRS, the American Institute of Certified Public Accountants (AICPA), and the American Bar Association (ABA). Congress people, state officials, along with non-profit organizations such as Independent Sector, have also contributed to the effort to achieve adequate disclosure of the financial and program activities of tax-exempt organizations. The new Form 990 grew from a modest five pages in 1988 that was expanded in 1989 to add, in response to a Congressional mandate, page 6 to identify the related and unrelated nature of an organization's revenues. In 1995, parts were added to reconcile the numbers reported on the 990 to an organization's financial statements issued in accordance with reporting methods required by the Financial Accounting Standards Board. The form grew another two pages in 2005 when it first contained governance questions and disclosed compensation of former officials and key employees. In 2007, a page reflecting "information regarding transfers to and from controlled entities" brought the total to nine pages. Now, we have eleven pages resulting from a full page of governance questions (new Part VI) and other questions.

The draft of the revised Form 990 released by the Internal Revenue Service on June 14, 2007, materially expanded the information submitted annually by tax-exempt organizations. The initial draft inspired over 7,000 e-mails and letters, with some 3,000 pages of suggestions during a 90-day comment period. The authors were gratified that the IRS accepted several of our suggestions, particularly showing a synopsis of prior- and current-year financial data on the front page, removing metrics (many called for this change), and reordering of the compliance questions now contained in Parts IV and V.

The redesign has features intended to foster the enhanced transparency requested by Congress, the Independent Sector's Panel on the Nonprofit Sector, and many others. In order to achieve this goal, however, the job of gathering the information and preparing Form 990 for filing will be much harder for most. Lois G. Lerner, Director of the IRS's Exempt Organizations division, disagrees and, as the draft was released, said in the announcement of the draft, "Most organizations should not experience a change in burden. However, those with complicated compensation arrangements, related entity structures and activities that raise compliance concerns may have to spend more time providing meaningful information to the public."[9] The authors and those that submitted the more than 3,000 pages of e-mail comments respectfully disagreed.

The second, and final, draft issued December 20, 2007, reflected some changes in response to public comments. For history buffs, the June 2007, draft of the Core Form is illustrated in Appendix 1A. Our suggestion for redesign of the first page is shown in Appendix 1B. One will notice that the right-hand column reflecting metrics was removed and replaced with a column that displays prior year financial information for comparison purposes. Many objected to the metrics and agreed with the authors' comments to the IRS that "a comparison of functionally allocated expenses to total expenses without room for an explanation is prejudicial against organizations with special circumstances and should be eliminated. A more informative comparison would be between current year totals and last year's totals." Indeed this change was adopted in the final form.

When the final draft of new Form 990 was released, the Commissioner of Tax Exempt/Governmental Entities, said: "When we released the redesigned draft form this past June, we said we needed a Form 990 that reflects the way this growing sector operates in the 21st century. The public comments we received in response to our draft form helped us develop a final form consistent with our guiding principles of transparency, compliance and burden minimization. Tax-exempt organizations provide tremendous benefits to the people and the communities they serve, but their ability to do good work hinges upon the public's trust. The new Form 990 will foster this trust by greatly improving transparency and compliance in the tax-exempt sector."[10]

§1.2 HIGHLIGHTS OF REVISED FORM 990

The new Form 990 has been significantly redesigned and consists of an 11-page Core Form and a series of 16 schedules designed to require reporting of information only from those organizations that conduct particular activities. What the IRS calls the "Core Form" is in some respects similar to its predecessor, except for the new first page, Part IV, "Checklist of Required Schedules," and Part VI, "Governance, Management and Disclosure." Significantly, the form no longer asks for attachments that the filer is free to design. Instead, schedules with specific columns and directions must be submitted to provide required additional details. Schedule D, in its five pages as an example, illustrates both the extensive details that are requested in order to reveal an organization's type of assets and funds, but also the requirement that the information be submitted in the format provided by the IRS.

What may be the most challenging to the IRS in terms of reviewing the forms once they are all electronically filed is the new, unformatted, Schedule O. The form has many questions that require an explanation in Schedule O when the answer is "Yes." Schedule O may become the first page viewers go to in studying the forms in the future. The other features that will cause some confusion and mistakes are the dollar thresholds for submitting the schedules. Part IV, "Checklist of Required Schedules," contains an array of thresholds ranging from $5,000 to $100,000. To compound the matter, the attachment of some schedules has no threshold, but is simply prompted by the existence of, for example, donor-advised funds or conservation easements without regard to the associated dollar amounts.

The IRS worked long and hard to redesign the form and also to provide instructions and helpful information to aid in preparing the form. Indeed the Core Form instructions have 40 pages. An amazing 14-page glossary contains detailed definitions of terms used in the instructions and on the form. "TIP" suggestions and "NOTE" ideas appear throughout the instructions. A 19-page appendix rounds out the 75 pages of instructions for the core and contains the following information:

A. Exempt Organizations Reference Chart

B. How to Determine Whether an Organization's Gross Receipts Are Normally $25,000 (or $5,000) or Less

C. Special Gross Receipts Test for Determining Exempt Status of §501(c)(7) and §501(c)(15) Organizations

D. Public Inspection of Returns

E. Group Returns: Reporting Information on Behalf of the Group

F. Disregarded Entities and Joint Ventures; Inclusion of Activities and Items

G. Section 4958 Excess Benefit Transactions

H. Forms and Publications To File or Use

I. Use of Form 990, or Form 990-EZ, To Satisfy State Reporting Requirements

The distinguishing features and a brief description of the changes to the Core form and the new schedules follow:

Form 990, Part I. The front page of the Core Form presents a snapshot of the organization's mission and revenues, expenses and net assets for the year compared to the prior year. Boxes were added to list the name and address of the organization's principal officer, type of organization (corporation, trust, association, or other), year of formation, and state of legal domicile. With seven lines, what the IRS considers to be key organizational indicators are presented:

Line 1. First, a brief description of its mission or most significant activities (preparers will notice that essentially the same space is provided for this line and the opening description of the mission in Part III)

Line 2. A check box if operations were discontinued or >25 percent of assets disposed of

Line 3. Number of voting board members

Line 4. Number of independent voting members

Line 5. Number of employees

Line 6. Number of volunteers

Line 7a. Amount of gross unrelated business revenue

Line 7b. Amount of net unrelated business taxable income

Form 990, Part II. The signature block now appears at the bottom of the first page rather than the last page. A check box that practitioners will welcome was added to authorize the IRS to discuss the return with the preparer signing the return.

Form 990, Part III, "Statement of Program Service Accomplishments," essentially follows the format of the existing Part III with significant additions:

• Expanded space for input of mission description (may duplicate lines on front page)

• Check box to say "Yes" or "No" that there are (or are not) new program services

• Check box to say activities and program services have changed or been discontinued

• Blank to input revenue derived from conduct of each program service

• Blank for what will probably be NTEE (National Taxonomy of Exempt Entities) codes developed by the National Center for Charitable Statistics (input not required for 2008 as the IRS has not finalized what set of codes should be used)

Form 990, Part IV, "Checklist of Required Schedules," has 37 questions with thresholds that prompt completion of one of the 16 schedules.

Form 990, Part V, "Statements Regarding Other IRS Filings and Tax Compliance," has a very useful list of other federal tax filings that might be required and requests numbers of certain forms actually filed.

Form 990, Part VI, "Governance, Management and Disclosure," requests nonfinancial information about the filer's policies and procedures. It has been widely criticized since the draft was released because the information requested goes beyond what is required by the tax code and regulations setting forth standards for maintaining tax-exempt status.

Form 990, Part VII, "Compensation of Officers, Directors, Trustees, Key Employees, Highest Compensated Employees," presents organizational officials, highly compensated employees, and five top independent contractors receiving more than $100,000. For those reported, the amount shown on Form W-2 or 1099 for the calendar year corresponding with the filing year is presented, plus amounts paid by related organizations to any listed person. Thus for fiscal year filers, the amounts reported on Part VII will not agree with Part IX.

Form 990, Part VIII, "Statement of Revenue," combines the former front-page categories of revenue combined with columns from former Part VII, "Analysis of Income-Producing Activities." The revenue report now displays revenues in three categories: related or exempt function, unrelated business revenue, or unrelated revenue excluded from tax.

Form 990, Part IX, "Statement of Functional Expenses," retains the display of program service, management, and general and fundraising expenses in three columns. The expense categories have been expanded with new lines for six types of professional services, information technology, payments to affiliates, insurance, and royalties and combination of office-type expenses, such as telephone, supplies, repairs, and the like into one line.

Form 990, Part X, "Balance Sheet," has been streamlined to reflect receivables as net numbers and only one line for land, buildings, and equipment. Prior attachments are now replaced with Schedule D.

Form 990, Part XI, "Financial Statements and Reporting," asks three questions: What is the accounting method used? Were the organization's financial statements compiled, reviewed, or audited by an independent accountant, and if so, is there an audit committee? If the entity received a federal award, did it have the required A-133 single audit? Surprisngly, a filer included in consolidated audited statement is instructed to say they receive no audit.

Schedule A, "Public Charity Status and Public Support," is to be completed by organizations described in §501(c)(3) and §4947(a)(1) to provide information relevant to their status as public charities, including satisfaction of applicable public support tests on an ongoing five-year basis.

Schedule B, "Schedule of Contributors," is to be completed by organizations to provide information regarding contributions they report as revenues.

Schedule C, "Political Campaign and Lobbying Activities," is to be completed by organizations that conduct political campaign activities, organizations described in §501(c)(3) and §4947(a)(1) that conduct lobbying activities, and organizations subject to §6033(e) notice and reporting requirements and potential proxy tax on certain membership dues, assessments and similar amounts.

Schedule D, "Supplemental Financial Statements," is to be completed by organizations to supplement certain balance sheet information, as well as conservation organizations, museums, and other organizations maintaining collections, credit counseling organizations, and others holding funds in escrow or custodial arrangements, and organizations maintaining endowments or donor-advised funds and similar funds or accounts;

Schedule E, "Schools," is the private school questionnaire previously contained in former Schedule A.

Schedule F, "Statement of Activities Outside the United States," reports the organization's activities conducted outside the United States.

Schedule G, "Supplemental Information Regarding Fundraising or Gaming Activities," requires that details be provided by organizations that reported certain amounts of professional fundraising expenses, revenue from special events, and revenue from gaming activities.

Schedule H, "Hospitals," is to be completed by organizations that operate one or more facilities licensed or registered as a hospital under state law.

Schedule I, "Grants and Other Assistance to Organizations, Governments and Individuals in the U.S.," reports grants and other assistance provided by the organization to others within the United States.

Schedule J, "Compensation Information," is to be completed by organizations to provide detailed compensation information for certain current or former officers, directors, trustees, key employees, and highest compensated employees, and certain information regarding the organization's compensation practices and arrangements.

Schedule K, "Supplemental Information for Tax Exempt Bonds," is to be completed by organizations with outstanding tax-exempt bond liabilities.

Schedule L, "Transactions with Interested Persons," is to be completed by organizations that engage in certain types of relationships or transactions with interested persons, including excess benefit transactions, loans, grants or other financial assistance, and other financial or business transactions or arrangements.

Schedule M, "Non-Cash Contributions," reports contributions other than cash received by the organization.

Schedule N, "Liquidation, Termination, Dissolution or Significant Disposition of Assets," reports major financial contractions of the organization.

Schedule O, "Supplemental Information to Form 990," is to be used by organizations to provide supplemental information to describe or explain the organization's responses to questions contained in the Core Form or Schedules.

Schedule R, "Related Organizations and Unrelated Partnerships," is to provide information regarding the organization's relationships with other exempt and taxable organizations.

Another big change is elimination of the former 6-page Schedule A, which has grown in one leap for 2008 to 16 schedules, existing Schedule B plus 15 new ones devoted to specific topics. Little did author Blazek anticipate in 1989, when she suggested redesign of Schedule A to contain a summary page to prompt attachment of detailed attachments only by those public charities to which they apply, the resulting form and schedules and broad expanse of information that are now required of all 990 filers, not just public charities.

This significant change is troubling for business leagues and other non-(c)(3) organizations that have never been required to disclose the compensation of certain employees. New Schedule J provides names and details of compensation in excess of $150,000 for officials, key, and highly paid employees. Some business leagues and the American Society of Association Executives have requested a change in this requirement.[11] Many non-c3s are troubled to be required, for the first time, to disclose detailed information about lobbying and political activities (Schedule C), programs conducted in foreign countries (Schedule F), transactions with interested persons (Schedule L), and much more, which readers will see as they review the new schedules.

§1.3 FILING OF NEW FORM DELAYED FOR MANY

The IRS has provided for the phase-in of certain portions of the new form as described below. What will be most welcomed by some is a delay in filing the new Form 990. A new four-page Form 990-EZ was released with filing thresholds as follows:

May File 990-EZ for:	If Gross Receipts Are:	If Assets Are:
2008 tax year (filed in 2009)	> $25,000 and < $1 million	< $2.5 million
2009 tax year (filed in 2010)	> $25,000 and < $500,000	< $1.25 million
2010 and later tax years	> $50,000 and < $200,000	< $500,000

For 2008 returns, a large number of Form 990 filers will thereby have the option of filing a much simpler Form 990-EZ in which, for example, expenses are not reported in a functional fashion. The balance sheet will have 6, rather than 30, lines. There is no reconciliation to audited financials, no analysis of income-producing activities, and a reduced number of compliance questions.

It is important to study line L of the Form 990-EZ that addresses the calculation of gross receipts that determines eligibility to file the 990-EZ. The three items of cost (tax basis of assets sold, fundraising expense, and cost of inventory items sold) that reduce total revenue on the front page must be added back. In other words, the total proceeds from sale of investments (such as stock), special events, and inventory sales are counted as gross receipts.

See Appendix 1-C for Form 990-EZ. The basic format of Form 990-EZ was not redesigned for 2008. It did grow from three to four pages when the following were added:

- Prompt in bold on the front page that §501(c)(3) and §4947(a)(1) nonexempt charitable trusts must attach a completed Schedule A.

- 14 additional lines for reporting names, titles, and compensation of officials.

- New Question 36 prompts completion of Schedule N if the organization was liquidated, dissolved, terminated, or substantially contracted during the year.

- New Questions 38a and 40b ask whether the organization had any transactions with interested parties and requires completion of Schedule L if so.

- New Question 44 informs an organization that maintains donor-advised funds that it must file Form 990.

- New Question 45 similarly prompts filing of Form 990 if the filer has a §512(b)(13) related entity.

- New page 4 "For §501(c)(3) organizations only" requires filing of the following schedules:

  Schedule C if the organization has any political campaign activity

  Schedule C if the organization engaged in lobbying activity

  Schedule E if the organization is a school

Organizations that file Form 990-EZ (2008) must review the instructions for Schedules A, B, C, E, G, L, and N to determine whether they must report any of their activities or information on those Schedules. Form 990-EZ filers will not be required to complete any of the other 2008 Form 990 Schedules.

§1.4 FIND OUT WHY ORGANIZATION QUALIFIES FOR TAX EXEMPTION

The world of tax-exempt organizations includes a broad range of nonprofit institutions: churches, schools, charities, business leagues, political parties, schools, country clubs, and united giving campaigns conducting a wide variety of pursuits intended to serve the public good. For purposes of federal tax exemption, each category has its own distinct set of criteria for qualification.[12] It is also important to keep their nonprofit nature in mind in preparing the Form 990. All exempt organizations share the common attribute of being organized for the advancement of a group of persons, rather than particular individuals or businesses. Most exempt organizations are afforded special tax and legal status precisely because of the unselfish motivation behind their formation. The common thread running through the various types of exempt organizations is the lack of private ownership and profit motive. A broad definition of an exempt organization is a nonprofit entity operated without self-interest to serve a societal or group mission that pays none of the income or profit to private individuals.

Federal and state governments view nonprofits as relieving their burdens and performing certain functions of government. Thus, many nonprofits are exempted from the levies that finance government, including income, sales, ad valorem, and other local property taxes. This special status recognizes the work they perform essentially on behalf of the government. In addition, for charitable nonprofits, labor unions, business leagues, and other types of exempt organizations, the tax deductibility of dues and donations paid to them further evidences the government's willingness to forego money in their favor. At the same time, deductibility provides a major fund-raising tool. For complex reasons, some of which are not readily apparent, all nonprofits are not equal for tax deduction purposes, and not all "donations" are deductible.[13]

Form 990 return preparers should always familiarize themselves with the organization's proper exemption category and its past and current mission and activities conducted to accomplish its goals. To correctly answer the questions in Part III that ask if there are changes and to properly describe the organization, it is important that the preparer review, if available, the original IRS Application for Recognition of Exemption, Form 1023 or 1024, and any IRS correspondence pertaining to the organization's qualification to understand why the IRS originally approved exemption for the organization. For many reasons, it is important to know why the IRS granted exempt status. To identify revenues as related or unrelated to the nonprofit's mission necessitates an understanding of an entity's exempt functions. The starting point for evaluating whether a proposed program might in any way endanger the organization's exempt status is the rationale for their original qualification.

Scrutiny of the IRS determination letter is particularly important for §501(c)(3) organizations qualifying for public charity status under §509. Whether Form 990 or 990-EZ is filed, Schedule A must be completed to disclose the designated §509 category and to calculate satisfaction of the public support test, if applicable. The authors too often find that the returns disagree with the determination letter. As a result of enhanced rules placed on §509(a)(3) Supporting Organizations by the 2006 Pension Protection Act, it may be necessary for the organization to seek reclassification of its public status.[14]

§1.5 WHO IS REQUIRED TO FILE WHAT

The numerous categories of organizations exempt from income tax are reflected in the different types of returns to be filed. Not all organizations are required to file annual reports with the Internal Revenue Service. Churches, their affiliated organizations, and divisions of states or municipalities, in a manner similar to the Form 1023 rules, do not file Form 990, except churches must file 990-T. Modest-sized organizations may also be excused from filing. The different types of exempt organization annual reports and their basic requirements are as follows:

No Form Filed. Churches and certain of their affiliates, and other types of organizations listed below in §1.7 need not file.

Form 990-N. Organizations with gross annual receipts "normally" under $25,000 must now electronically file this brief report that contains only six items. A list of those that need not file appears in §1.7.

Form 990-EZ. All exempt organizations, except for private foundations, whose gross annual receipts equal between $25,000 and $1,000,000 and whose total assets are less than $2,500,000 (for 2008) file Form 990-EZ.[15]

Form 990. All exempt organizations, except private foundations, whose gross annual receipts are more than $1,000,000 or who have assets of more than $2,500,000 must file Form 990 (see Chapter 3). §501(c)(3) organizations that are public charities also file new Schedule A to reflect information about qualification as a public charity.

Form 990-PF. All private foundations (PFs) file Form 990-PF annually, regardless of annual receipts or asset levels (yes, even if the PF has no gross receipts). See Chapter 6.

Form 990-T. Any organization exempt under §501(a), including churches, state colleges, and universities,[16] and §401 pension plans (including individual retirement accounts) with $1,000 or more gross income from an unrelated trade or business must file Form 990-T. See Chapter 5.

Form 990-BL. Black lung trusts, §501(c)(21), file an annual Information and Initial Excise Tax Return for Black Lung Benefit Trusts and Certain Related Persons.

Form 4720. Form 4720 is filed to report excise taxes and to claim abatement of such taxes imposed on §501(c)(3) charities and their insiders for conducting prohibited activities.

Form 5500. One of several Forms 5500 may be due to be filed annually by pension, profit-sharing, and other employee welfare plans. Form 5500-EZ is filed for one-participant pension benefit plans.

Form 5768. The form is filed to elect or revoke an election by a public charity to measure its permissible lobbying expenditures under §501(h).[17]

Forms 941, 1099, W-2, W-3 and other federal and state compensation reporting forms are filed to report payments to workers that perform personal services for tax-exempt organizations.[18]

§ 1.6 FILING FOR NEW ORGANIZATIONS

An organization qualified for, and claiming exempt status under, §501(a) is entitled to file a Form 990 prior to receipt of formal IRS approval for its qualification. Even though Heading B on the front page of the Core Form contains a check box for "Application Pending," the revised instructions acknowledge that an exempt organization return, rather than Form 1120 or 1041, can be filed whether or not Form 1023 or 1024 seeking recognition of its qualification has been filed and whether or not, if filed, approval is still pending.[19]

This procedure stems from the fact that a properly organized §501(c) organization is recognized as exempt retroactively to date of its formation.[20] As a practical matter, the revenue of new organizations is often comprised of voluntary contributions that are gifts excluded from taxable income by §103 so that income tax returns may not technically be due to be filed. It is, therefore, reasonable for the IRS to accept Forms 990 filed by those organizations. If subsequently, exempt status is denied, normal income tax returns can be requested when denial is issued.

§ 1.7 WHO IS NOT REQUIRED TO FILE

The list of organizations not required to file is reproduced each year in the instructions to Form 990. The most recent version should be consulted if there is any question about filing requirements. The instructions for 2008 list the following organizations as being excused from filing:

- Churches and their affiliates, a convention or association of churches, an integrated auxiliary of a church (such as a men's or women's society, religious school, mission society, or youth group) or an internally supported, church-controlled organization.[21]

- Church-affiliated organizations that are exclusively engaged in managing funds or maintaining retirement programs.[22]

- Schools below college level affiliated with a church or operated by a religious order.

- Mission societies sponsored by or affiliated with one or more churches or church denominations, if more than half of the societies' activities are conducted in or directed at persons in foreign countries.

- Exclusively religious activities of any religious order.

- State institutions whose income is excluded from gross income under §115.

- §501(c)(1) organizations that are instrumentalities of the United States and organized under an act of Congress.[23]

- Governmental units and their affiliates granted exemption under §501(a).[24]

- Religious and apostolic organizations described in §501(d) that file Form 1065.

- An LLC or LLP that elects to be treated as a disregarded entity and the transactions of which are reported as the parent's information.[25]

§ 1.8 FILING DEADLINE AND FISCAL YEAR

The due date for Forms 990 gives tax practitioners and exempt organizations a reprieve. The forms are due to be filed within $4\frac{1}{2}$ months after the end of the organization's fiscal year, rather than the $2\frac{1}{2}$ allowed for Form 1120 (for-profit corporations) and the $3\frac{1}{2}$ months for Form 1041 (trusts). Thus, the filing due date for an organization reporting for a calendar year organization is May 15, and the return for an entity reporting on a July–June fiscal year period would be due November 15. An extension of time can be requested if the organization has not completed its year-end accounting soon enough to timely file. For Forms 990-T and 990-PF, an extension of time to file does not extend the time to pay the tax.

An automatic procedure for changing an organization's tax reporting year is available for an entity that has not made a change within the 10 years prior to the desired year of change. Advance IRS approval is not required. Assume a calendar year reporting entity wishes to change from a calendar year reporting cycle to a June 30 fiscal year ending. It has filed a full year return for the year 2007. A short-period 2008 return[26] reporting financial activity and information for the six months January through June 2008 would be filed in a timely manner by November 15 or the extended time frame for a June year end filer. For the period July 2008 through June 2009, it would file another 2008 return reporting on its new fiscal year. If permission is required, Form 1128 is filed.

The penalty for late filing is $20 a day (up from $10) for organizations with gross receipts under $1 million a year, not to exceed the greater of $10,000 or 5 percent of the annual gross receipts for the year of late filing.[27] The penalty can also be imposed if the form is incomplete as filed. The penalty for a large organization (>$1 million of annual gross receipts) is $100 a day up to a maximum penalty of $50,000. IRS officials have suggested an increase in penalties to encourage timely filing.

The annual Forms 990 are submitted, since 1997, to a processing center devoted exclusively to exempt return filings for Forms 990, 990-EZ, 990-PF, 990-T, 1041-A, 4720, 5227, 5578, and 5768 in the Ogden, Utah, Service Center. The centralization was planned to improve the speed and accuracy of return processing through a consolidation of expertise on exempt organization matters. In a similar fashion, the applications for recognition of initial qualification for tax-exempt status, Forms 1023 and 1024, are all filed with the Cincinnati, Ohio, Key District Office.[28] Examination of exempt organizations is the responsibility of the Dallas, Texas, Key District; technical advice and rulings continue to be issued by the Washington, D.C., office.

§ 1.9 NEW FORM 990-N (e-POSTCARD)

Modest tax-exempt organizations whose gross receipts are normally $25,000 or less may be required to electronically submit Form 990-N, also known as the e-Postcard. The Pension Protection Act of 2006 added this filing requirement to ensure that the

IRS and potential donors have current information about all recognized as tax-exempt organizations. The first e-Postcards are due in 2008 for tax years ending on or after December 31, 2007. The e-Postcard is due every year by the 15th day of the 5th month after the close of the tax year and can *only* be filed electronically on the IRS web site at http://epostcard.form990.org. A private foundation cannot file this form. There is no paper form. The following information is required:

- Employer identification number (EIN), or taxpayer identification number (TIN)
- Tax year
- Legal name and mailing address
- Any other names the organization uses
- Name and address of a principal officer
- Web site address, if the organization has one
- Confirmation that the organization's annual gross receipts are normally $25,000 or less
- If applicable, a statement that the organization has terminated or is terminating (going out of business)

Although there is no monetary penalty for filing Form 990-N late or not at all, after three consecutive years of failing to file the Form, the organization will have its exempt status revoked. Another important issue arises for the filer relying on its public support to qualify to file 990-N rather than form 990-PF. The filer should retain donor history and check its qualification using Schedule A. The following organizations are not required to file Form 990-N:

- Churches and their affiliates listed above in §1.7.
- Subordinates included in a group return

The following organization cannot file Form 990-N:

- Organizations with annual gross receipts that are normally greater than $25,000
- Private foundations (file Form 990-PF)
- §509(a)(3) supporting organizations
- §527 (political) organizations

§1.10 ELECTRONIC FILING OF RETURNS

Any organization can voluntarily file Form 990 and related forms, schedules, and attachments electronically. Electronic filing is required, however, for an organization that files at least 250 returns of any type during the calendar year and has total assets of $10 million or more at the end of the tax year. "Returns" for this purpose include information returns, for example, Forms W–2, Forms 1099, income tax returns, employment tax returns (including quarterly Forms 941), and excise tax returns. If an organization is required to file a return electronically but does not, the organization is considered not to have filed its return, even if a paper return is submitted.[29] For the most current information about this requirement, go to www.irs.gov/efile. The IRS may waive the requirements to file electronically in cases of undue hardship.[30]

§1.11   GROUP RETURNS AND ANNUAL AFFIDAVIT

A parent organization that is willing to be in "general supervision or control" of a group of subsidiary exempt organizations, once its own qualification for exemption is established, may apply for recognition of exemption for members of its group to be covered by a group exemption letter. The parent organization of the group may assume the burden of filing a consolidated Form 990 for its subordinate organizations. If the subordinate revenue is below the current filing level (for 2008 $25,000 of gross revenue), it need not be included in the group return or file a separate return. The group return reports an aggregate of financial information and data for all subordinates.

The 2008 Form 990 Instructions Appendix E contains a very useful listing of individual parts of the return that require special attention by group return filers. For example, if the answer to the Question in Part VI, line 4, is "Yes," the instruction says to report only changes to standardized organizational documents maintained by the central organization that subordinates are required to adopt. Group return filers should carefully use this resource as a guide to correct completion of the consolidated return.[31]

Rather than filing a consolidated return on their behalf, the parent can also require each subordinate to file its own return or only include some subordinates in the group return. The parent always separately files its own 990. The parent and the subordinates must each file separate 990-Ts. To be included in a group Form 990, there must be two or more consenting subordinate member organizations that possess all the following attributes:

- Affiliated with the central organization at the time its annual accounting period ends
- Subject to the central organization's general supervision or control
- Exempt from tax under a group exemption letter that is still in effect
- Use the same accounting period as the central organization

When the parent or controlling member of the group takes responsibility for filing a consolidated Form 990, each affiliate member covered by the group exemption must annually give written authority for its inclusion in the group return. A declaration, made under penalty of perjury, that the financial information to be combined into the group Form 990 is true and complete is included. An attachment showing the name, address, and employer identification number of included local organizations is attached to the group return. An affiliate choosing not to be included in the group return files a separate return and checks Block H(a) and enters the Group Exemption Number in Block H(c) on page 1 of Form 990. Each year, 90 days before the end of the fiscal year, the parent organization separately reports a current list of subsidiary organizations to the Ogden, Utah, Service Center.[32]

Appendix E of the IRS instructions contains five pages of specific instructions for "Reporting Information on Behalf of the Group" that should be studied by a parent filing a group Form 990. Special directions are also provided for attachment of

Schedule B for group returns. Again there is a choice, but importantly the instructions provide that once a method is adopted it cannot be changed without IRS consent. Any change must be reported on Schedule O. The alternative methods of reporting include:

- Parent includes Schedule B reporting on its donors.

- A consolidated Schedule B, including all subordinates is included in the group return (if one is filed).

- A consolidated Schedule B, including the parent and all subsidiaries, is included in the group return.

- The instructions are silent, but, one presumes, each subordinate submits its own Schedule B if no consolidated return is filed.

§1.12   PUBLIC INSPECTION OF FORMS 990 AND 1023/1024

An actual copy of Forms 990, 990-PF, and 990-EZ for the three most recent years and Form 1023 or 1024 must be given by tax-exempt organizations to anyone requesting one.[33] The names and addresses of the organization's contributors are not subject to public inspection and can be omitted from the copy made available to the public, except for private foundations and §527 organizations.

Form 990-T, Organization Business Income Tax Return, filed by a charity after August 17, 2006 must also be made available by §501(c)(3) organizations.[34] An exact copy of the return, plus any schedules, attachments, and supporting documents that relate to the imposition of tax on the unrelated business income of the charity, must be provided.

If the request is made in person at the organization's office, the copy must be provided immediately. In response to a written request, the copy must be mailed within 30 days. Between 1987 and 1997, the returns had to be made available for inspection in the organization's offices. Payment terms provided in the regulations say:

- An organization may charge $1.00 for the first page and $0.15 for each subsequent page.

- Payments must be accepted in cash, money orders, personal checks, or credit cards.

- Written requests can be transmitted by mail, electronic mail, facsimile, or private delivery service, or in person and must contain the address to which the copies can be mailed.

- Alternative methods an organization can use to make the forms widely available include through electronic media instead of furnishing copies.

If the organization that charges a fee for copying receives a request containing no payment, it must, within seven days of receipt of the request, notify the requester of its prepayment policy and the amount due. If the copy charge exceeds $20 and prepayment is not required, the organization must obtain the requester's consent to the charge. An organization can satisfy its public inspection requirement by making its returns available on the Internet either through its own site or a database of other exempt organizations on another site. The forms will be considered widely available only if they are posted in the same format used by the IRS to post forms and publication on the IRS website. The site must contain instructions to enable the user to download and print the forms without charge. The Guidestar.org posting is not mentioned in the statute and the 2008 instructions for Form 990 do not mention it as a source to satisfy this requirement.

If the Exempt Organization (EO) is the subject of a harassment campaign, the regulations contain procedures for applying to the key district office for relief. As an example, the regulation indicates the receipt of 200 requests following a national news report about the organization is not considered harassment. Receipt of 100 requests from known supporters of another organization opposed to the policies and positions the organization advocates are said to be disruptive to the organization's operations and to thereby constitute harassment.

An organization having more than one administrative office must have a copy available at each office where three or more full-time employees work. Service-providing facilities are not counted for this purpose if management functions are not performed there. A branch organization that does not file its own Form 990 because it is included in a group return must make the group return available.

A request to see a copy of the return can also be sent to the District Director of the Internal Revenue Service in the area in which the organization is located, or to the National Office of the IRS. Form 4506-A can also be used to request a copy of any return, and a photocopying fee will be imposed.

Up to a $10,000 penalty can be imposed against the person(s) responsible for a failure to disclose the returns. The penalty is $20 for each day the failure continues. An additional $10 per day, up to a maximum of $5,000, can also be imposed if the organization's manager(s) refuse to furnish the required information after a written request by the IRS. If more than one person is responsible, they are jointly and severally liable for the penalties.[35]

NOTES

1. IRC §6104 added by the Omnibus Budget Reconciliation Act of 1987.
2. In the authors' experience, some organizations are omitted.
3. See J. Blazek, *Tax Planning and Compliance for Tax-Exempt Organizations*, 4th edition, (Hoboken, N.J.: John Wiley & Sons, 2008), Ch. 2.2(d), and Ch. 20 for a discussion of factors indicating an organization is operated to benefit its founders, funders, fundraisers, or other private individuals rather than its exempt beneficiaries.
4. See Blazek, *Tax Planning and Compliance*, 4th edition, Ch. 21, for a discussion of the complicated array of definitions, exceptions, and modifications that cause certain types of business income to be taxed when the nonprofit is essentially operating a business in competition with for-profit businesses.
5. See Blazek, *Tax Planning and Compliance*, 4th edition, Ch. 20, for a discussion of penalties called Intermediate Sanctions imposed on public charities that pay excessive benefits to their insiders. The similar rules that are applicable to private foundations, called self-dealing, are discussed in Chapter 14.
6. Lobbying by public charities is limited by two different tests outlined in Blazek, *Tax Planning and Compliance*, 4th edition, Ch. 23.5. Private foundations are prohibited from making any expenditures for lobbying efforts but can support public charities that lobby so long as their grant is not designated for that purpose as discussed in Chapter 17.1.

7. See Blazek, *Tax Planning and Compliance*, 4th edition, Ch. 3, for a brief description of the labyrinth of rules applied to determine classification under the three very different types of public charities.

8. Lois G. Lerner, Director of Exempt Organizations Division, IR-2007–204, December 20, 2007.

9. IRS Announcement 2007–117, June 14, 2007.

10. Ibid. Note 8.

11. A 2008 article has revealed: "The National Football League, hard at work promoting its football season set to begin September 4, has another, less-public campaign afoot: asking Congress to redact the names and salary information of the league's highest-paid employees from the expanded Form 990 when it is made available to the public." F. Stokeld and A. Elliott, "NFL Wants to Withhold Salaries of Highly Paid Employees from Public," *Exempt Organization Tax Review*, August 18, 2008.

12. See Blazek, *Tax Planning and Compliance*, 4th edition, Chs. 2–10, for over 150 pages that discuss the requirements for the most common types, compare the categories, explain the attributes that distinguish them from each other, and consider instances in which they overlap.

13. See Blazek, *Tax Planning and Compliance*, 4th edition, Ch. 24, "Deductibility and Disclosures."

14. IRS Announcement 2006–03 provided guidance for seeking a change.

15. See §1.3 for phase–in amounts for 2009 and 2010.

16. IRC §511(a)(2)(B).

17. Discussed in Blazek, *Tax Planning and Compliance*, Ch. 3.5.

18. Penalties are imposed for failure to withhold and pay federal taxes from employees and failure to file other types of compensation reports. See Blazek, *Tax Planning and Compliance*, 4th edition, ch. 25, for checklists and guidance regarding this very important subject.

19. Treas. Reg. §1.6033–2(c).

20. IRC §508 provides this retroactive recognition for a §501(c)(3) only if it files Form 1023 within 27 months of its establishment.

21. See Blazek, *Tax Planning and Compliance*, 4th edition, Ch. 3.2, for a discussion of the criteria applied to define organizations qualifying as churches and their affiliates.

22. Rev. Proc. 96–11, 1996–1 C.B. 577.

23. IRC §6033(a)(2) and (3).

24. Defined in Rev. Proc. 95–48, 1995–47 I.R.B. 13.

25. Treas. Reg. §301.7701–2(c)(2).

26. The IRS has made an exception to this rule for short periods ending before December 31, 2008. It will allow those organizations to use the 2007 Form 990 to file their short-period return even if the short period begins in 2008.

27. IRC §6652(c)(1)(A) as amended by the Taxpayer Bill of Rights 2, H.R. 2670, §1314.

28. See Blazek, *Tax Planning and Compliance*, 4th edition, Ch. 18, for a thorough outline of the determination process.

29. Treas. Reg. §301.6033–4.

30. IRS Notice 2005–88, 2005–48 I.R.B. 1060.

31. IRS Publication 4573 (12–2006) expanded on the exemption and filing requirements for group exemptions and can be studied by prospective and existing Group Exemption holders. Helpful instructions on what to include in an application for recognition of exemption for the group and subsequent annual filings are outlined.

32. Rev. Proc. 96–40, 1996–32 I.R.B. 8.

33. Effective June 8, 1999; Taxpayer Bill of Rights 2, H.R. 2670, §1313, amending IRC §6104(e); applies to Forms 990-T filed with IRS after 8/17/2006; IRS Notice 2008–49, 2008–20 IRB 979.

34. Treas. Reg. § 301.6104(d)-1 and Notice 2007–45.

35. IRC §6652 amended by Taxpayer Bill of Rights 2, §1313.

APPENDIX 1A: 6/14/07 DRAFT OF CORE FORM

Form **990**	**Return of Organization Exempt From Income Tax**	OMB No. 1545-0047
	Under section 501(c), 527, or 4947(a)(1) of the Internal Revenue Code (except black lung benefit trust or private foundation)	**20XX**
Department of the Treasury Internal Revenue Service (77)	▶ The organization may have to use a copy of this return to satisfy state reporting requirements.	**Open to Public Inspection**

A For the 20XX calendar year, or tax year beginning _____ , 20XX, and ending _____ , 20

B Check if applicable:
- ☐ Address change
- ☐ Name change
- ☐ Initial return
- ☐ Termination
- ☐ Amended return
- ☐ Application pending

Please use IRS label or print or type. See Specific Instructions.

C Name of organization

Number and street (or P.O. box if mail is not delivered to street address) | Room/suite

City or town, state or country, and ZIP + 4

D Employer identification number

E Telephone number

F Name and address of Principal Officer:

G Website: ▶

H Enter amount of gross receipts $

I Accounting method:
- ☐ Cash
- ☐ Accrual ☐ Other ▶

J Books

In care of _____

Located at _____

K Organization type (check only one) ▶ ☐ 501(c) ( ) ◀ (insert no.) ☐ 4947(a)(1) or ☐ 527

Telephone number ( )

L Year of Formation:

M State of legal domicile ▶

Part I Summary

1 Briefly describe the organization's mission: ....

2 List the organization's three most significant activities and the activity codes (Part IX):
a _____ Code _____ b _____ Code _____ c _____ Code _____

3 Enter the number of members of the governing body (Part III, line 1a)	**3**	
4 Enter the number of independent members of the governing body (Part III, line 1b)	**4**	
5 Enter the total number of employees (Part VIII, line 9a)	**5**	
6 Enter the number of individuals receiving compensation in excess of $100,000 (Part II, line 2)	**6**	
7 Enter the highest compensation amount reported on Part II, Section A (sum of columns D and E)	**7**	
8a Enter officer, director, trustee, and other key employee compensation (Part V, line 5, column (B))	**8a**	
b Divide line 8a by line 17 _____ %		
9a Enter total gross unrelated business revenue from Part IV, line 14, column (C)	**9a**	
b Enter net unrelated business taxable income from Form 990-T, line 34	**b**	

10 Check this box ☐ if the organization discontinued its operations or disposed of more than 25% of its assets and attach Schedule N.

	Amount	% of Total
Revenues		
11 Contributions and grants (Part IV, line 1g, column (A))		
12 Program service revenue (Part IV, line 2g, column (A))		
13 Membership dues and assessments (Part IV, line 3, column (A))		
14 Investment income (Part IV lines 4, 5, 6, 8, 10d)		
15 Other revenue (Part IV, lines 3, 7, 9d, 11c, 12c, and 13e, column (A))		
16 Total revenue add lines 11 through 15 (must equal Part IV, line 14, column (A))		100%
Expenses		
17 Program service expense (Part V, line 24, column (B))		
18 Management and general expenses (Part V, line 24, column (C))		
19a Fundraising expenses (Part V, line 24, column (D))		
19b Percentage of contributions (divide line 19a by line 11) _____ %		
20 Total expenses (must equal Part V, line 24, column (A))		100%
21 Net income (line 16 minus line 20)		

Net Assets or Fund Balance	Beginning of Year	End of Year
22 Total assets (Part VI, line 17)		
23 Total liabilities (Part VI, line 27)		
24a Net assets or fund balances line 22 minus line 23		
24b Total expenses (line 20) as percentage of net assets (line 24a) _____ %)		

Gaming & Fundraising	**(i)** Gross Revenue	**(ii)** Expenses	**(iii)** Net to organization	**(iv)** Divide column (iii) by column (i)
25 Gaming	(Schedule G, Part III, line 1 column (d))	(Schedule G, Part III, line 7)	(Schedule G, Part III, line 6)	%
26 Fundraising (other than gaming)	(Schedule G, Part I, line 1b column (iii) total)	(Schedule G, Part I, line 1b column (iv) total)	(Schedule G, Part I, line 1b column (v) total)	%

For Privacy Act and Paperwork Reduction Act Notice, see the separate instructions.   Cat. No. 11282Y   Form **990** (20XX)

REDESIGNED FORM 990

Part II	Compensation and Other Financial Arrangements with Officers, Directors, Trustees, Key Employees, Highly Compensated Employees, and Independent Contractors

Section A   Complete this table for all persons required to be listed. Attach additional pages as needed.

1a* List all of the organization's current officers, directors, trustees (whether individuals or organizations) and key employees regardless of amount of compensation. Enter -0- if no compensation was paid.

* List the organization's five highest compensated employees (other than an officer, director, trustee or key employee) who received reportable compensation of more than $100,000 from the organization and any related organizations.

* List all of the organization's **former** officers, key employees or highest compensated employees who received more than $100,000 of reportable compensation from the organization and any related organizations.

* List all of the organization's **former** directors or trustees that received, in their capacity as a former director or trustee of the organization, more than $10,000 in reportable compensation from the organization and any related organizations.

(A) Name, City, and State of Residence	(B) Position (check all that apply)								(C) Check box if full-time officer or employee	(D) Reportable compensation from the organization	(E) Reportable compensation from related organizations	(F) Aggregate loans and other amounts owed to the organization	(G) Aggregate loans and other amounts owed to related organizations
	Individual Trustee or Director	Institutional Trustee	CEO or Executive Director	CFO or Treasurer	Other Officer	Key Employee	Other	Former					
1b Total													

2   Total number of individuals who received more than $100,000 in reportable compensation from the organization

Form 990 (20XX)   Page **3**

Part II   **(Continued)**

Section B

		Yes	No
3	For the CEO, Executive Director, Treasurer, and CFO listed in Section A, did the process for determining compensation include a review and approval by independent members of the governing body, comparability data, and contemporaneous substantiation of the deliberation and decision?.		
4	Did any current officer or employee listed in Section A earn or accrue more than $100,000 of non-qualified deferred compensation?		
5	During the tax year, did any person who is or was an officer, director, trustee, or key employee within the past 5 years:		
a	Have a family relationship with any other person listed in Section A?		
b	Have a business relationship with any other person listed in Section A?		
c	Have a business relationship with the organization (other than as an officer, director, trustee, or employee) directly or indirectly through ownership of more than 35% in another entity (individually or collectively with other person(s) listed in Section A)?		
d	Have a business relationship with the organization (other than as an officer, director, trustee, or employee) indirectly through a family member?		
e	Serve as an officer, director, trustee, key employee, partner or member of an entity (or a shareholder of a professional corporation), doing business with the organization?		

f Complete this table if the organization answered "Yes" to any of lines 5a–5e (for lines 5a and b, complete columns (i)–(iii) only).

(i) Name of Current or Former Officer, Director, Trustee, or Key Employee	(ii) Name of Individual or Entity	(iii) Relationship	(iv) Description of transaction	(v) Based on sharing of revenue or net earnings of organization? (Y/N)	(vi) Amount of the transaction

		Yes	No
6	Did the organization list any **former** officers, directors, trustees, key employees, or highest compensated employees in Section A? If yes, complete Schedule J		
7	For any individual listed in Section A, is the sum of columns (D) and (E) greater than $150,000? If yes, complete Schedule J		
8	Did any individual listed in Section A receive or accrue more than $250,000 of reportable or other compensation including deferred compensation, nontaxable fringe benefits and expense reimbursements? If yes, complete Schedule J		
9	Did any person listed in Section A receive or accrue compensation from any source other than the organization or a related organization for services rendered to the organization? If yes, complete Schedule J		

10a List the top five independent contractors that received more than $100,000 of compensation from the organization. Exclude those included in 5f.

(A) Name, City, and State of Residence	(B) Description of Services Provided	(C) Compensation

10b Total number of independent contractors (including those in 10a) that received more than $100,000 in compensation from the organization . . . .

Form **990** (20XX)

REDESIGNED FORM 990

Part III   Statements Regarding Governance, Management, and Financial Reporting

		Yes	No

1a Enter the number of members of the governing body **1a**

 b Enter the number of independent members of the governing body **1b**

2 Did the organization make any significant changes to its organizing or governing documents? If "Yes", briefly describe these changes. **2**

_____

_____

3a Does the organization have a written conflict of interest policy? **3a**

 b If "Yes," how many transactions did the organization review under this policy and related procedures during the year? **3b**

4 Does the organization have a written whistleblower policy? **4**

5 Does the organization have a written document retention and destruction policy? . . . **5**

6 Does the organization contemporaneously document the meetings of the governing body and related committees through the preparation of minutes or other similar documentation? **6**

7a Does the organization have local chapters, branches or affiliates? **7a**

 b If yes, does the organization have written policies and procedures governing the activities of such chapters, affiliates and branches to ensure their operations are consistent with the organization's? . . . **7b**

8 Does an officer, director, trustee, employee or volunteer prepare the organization's financial statements? **8**

Indicate whether an independent accountant provides any of the following services:

Compilation ☐   Review ☐   Audit ☐

9 Does the organization have an audit committee? **9**

10 Did the organization's governing body review this Form 990 before it was filed? **10**

11 How do you make the following available to the public? Check all that apply.

Organizing/Governing Documents	☐ n/a	☐ website	☐ other website	☐ office	☐ other _____
Conflict of Interest Policy	☐ n/a	☐ website	☐ other website	☐ office	☐ other _____
Form 990	☐ n/a	☐ website	☐ other website	☐ office	☐ other _____
Form 990-T	☐ n/a	☐ website	☐ other website	☐ office	☐ other _____
Financial Statements	☐ n/a	☐ website	☐ other website	☐ office	☐ other _____
Audit Report	☐ n/a	☐ website	☐ other website	☐ office	☐ other _____

12 List the states with which a copy of this return is filed:

Part IV Statement of Revenue

		(A) Total Revenue	(B) Related or Exempt Function Revenue	(C) Unrelated Business Revenue	(D) Revenue Excluded From Tax under IRC 512, 513, or 514
Contributions, gifts, grants and other similar amounts	**1a** Federated campaigns **1a**				
	b Outside fundraising or commercial co-ventures **1b**				
	c Fundraising events **1c**				
	d Related organizations **1d**				
	e Government grants (contributions) . . . **1e**				
	f All other contributions, gifts grants, and similar amounts not included above **1f**				
	g Noncash $ _____ Attach Schedule M.				
	h Total. . . . . ▶				
Program Service Revenue	Business Code				
	2a Medicare/Medicaid payments . . .				
	b Fees and contracts from government agencies				
	c Revenue from related investments . .				
	d _____				
	e _____				
	f _____				
	g Total . . . . ▶ $				
Other Revenue	**3** Membership dues and assessments . . . . ▶				
	4 Interest on savings and temporary cash investments . . . . . ▶				
	5 Dividends and interest from securities . . . . . . ▶				
	6 Income from investment of tax-exempt bond proceeds . . ▶				
	7 Royalties . . . . ▶				
	8 Other investment income . . . . ▶				

	(i) Real	(ii) Personal
9a Gross Rents		
b Less rental expenses		
c Rental income or (loss)		

d Net rental income or (loss) . . . . ▶

	(i) Securities	(ii) Other
10a Gross amount of sales of assets other than inventory		
b Less: Cost or other basis and sales expenses		
c Gain or (loss)		

d Net gain or (loss) from investments. *Combine line 10c, columns (i) and (ii)* . . . . ▶

11a Gross income from fundraising events (not including $ _____ of contributions reported on line 1c). *Attach Schedule G if total exceeds $10,000. If any amount is from gaming, check here* ☐ **a**

b Less direct expenses . . . . . **b**

c Net income from fundraising events . . . . . ▶

12a Gross sales of inventory, less returns and allowances . . . . **a**

b Less cost of goods sold . . . . . **b**

c Net income or loss from sales of inventory . . . .

Miscellaneous Revenue	Business Code
13a _____	
b _____	
c _____	
d _____	
e **Total** . . . . ▶ $ _____	

14 **Total Revenue.** Add lines 1g, 2g, 3–8, 9d, 10d, 11c, 12c, and 13c . . . .

REDESIGNED FORM 990

Part V	Statement of Functional Expense

501(c)(3) and (4) organizations must complete all columns.
All other organizations must complete column (A) but are not required to complete columns (B), (C), and (D).

Do not include amounts reported on lines 9b, 10b, 11b, and 12b of Part IV.	(A) Total expenses	(B) Program service expenses	(C) Management and general expenses	(D) Fundraising expenses
1 Grants to governments and organizations in the U.S. Complete Parts I and III of Schedule I if total exceeds $5,000				
2 Grants and other assistance to individuals in the U.S. Complete Parts II and III of Schedule I if total exceeds $5,000				
3 Grants and other assistance to governments, organizations and individuals outside the U.S.				
4 Benefits paid to or for members				
5 Compensation of current officers, directors, and key employees				
6 Compensation not included above, to disqualified persons (as defined under section 4958(f)(1)) and persons described in section 4958(c)(3)(B)				
7 Other salaries and wages				
8 Pension plan contributions (include section 401(k) and section 403(b) employer contributions)				
9 Other employee benefits				
10 Payroll taxes				
11 Fees for services (non-employees):				
a Management				
b Legal				
c Accounting				
d Lobbying				
e Professional fundraising (Complete Schedule G if total exceeds $10,000)				
f Investment management fees				
g Other				
12 Advertising				
13 Office expenses				
14 Information technology				
15 Royalties				
16 Occupancy				
17 Travel				
18 Payments of travel or entertainment expenses for any Federal, state or local public officials				
19 Conferences, conventions and meetings . . .				
20 Interest				
21 Payments to affiliates				
22 Depreciation, depletion, and amortization . . .				
23 Other expenses—Itemize expenses not covered above (Expenses grouped together and labeled miscellaneous may not exceed 5% of total expenses shown on line 24 below .				
a _____				
b _____				
c _____				
d _____				
e _____				
f _____				
24 **Total.** Functional expenses. Add lines 1 through 23f . . .				

Form **990** (20XX)

APPENDIX 1A: 6/14/07 DRAFT OF CORE FORM

Part VI   Balance Sheet

		(A) Beginning of year		(B) End of year
	Assets			
1	Cash—non-interest-bearing		1	
2	Savings and temporary cash investments		2	
3	Pledges and grants receivable, net		3	
4	Accounts receivable, net		4	
5	Receivables from current officers, directors, trustees, key employees or other related parties. Complete Schedule L		5	
6	Receivables from other disqualified persons (as defined under section 4958(f)(1)) and persons described in section 4958(c)(3)(B). Complete Schedule L		6	
7	Notes and loans receivable, net		7	
8	Inventories for sale or use		8	
9	Prepaid expenses and deferred charges		9	
10	Investments—publicly-traded securities ▶		10	
11	Investments—other securities. Complete Part I of Schedule D ▶		11	
12a	Investments-Land, buildings, and equipment: Cost basis. Complete Part II, Schedule D	12a		
12b	Less accumulated depreciation	12b	12c	
13	Investments—other. Complete Part III of Schedule D		13	
14	Investments-Program Related. Complete Part IV of Schedule D		14	
15a	Program Related-land, buildings, and equipment: cost basis. Complete Part V of Schedule D	15a		
15b	Less: accumulated depreciation	15b	15c	
16	Other assets. Complete Part VI of Schedule D		16	
17	**Total assets.** Add Columns A and B, lines 1 through 16 (must equal line 35)		17	
	Liabilities			
18	Accounts payable and accrued expenses		18	
19	Grants payable		19	
20	Deferred revenue		20	
21	Tax-exempt bond liabilities. Complete Schedule K		21	
22	Escrow account liability		22	
23	Payable to current and former officers, directors, trustees, or key employees (attach Schedule L)		23	
24	Mortgages and notes payable to unrelated third parties secured by:			
a	Investment property shown on lines 10, 13, and 14		24a	
b	Land, building, and equipment shown on lines 12 and 15		24b	
25	Unsecured notes and loans payable		25	
26	Other liabilities. Complete Part VII of Schedule D		26	
27	**Total liabilities.** Add lines 18 through 26		27	
	Net Assets or Fund Balances			
	Organizations that follow SFAS 117, check here ▶ ☐ and complete lines 28 through 30, and lines 34 and 35			
28	Unrestricted net assets		28	
29	Temporarily restricted net assets		29	
30	Permanently restricted net assets		30	
	Organizations that do not follow SFAS 117, check here ▶ ☐ and complete lines 31 through 35.			
31	Capital stock or trust principal, or current funds		31	
32	Paid-in or capital surplus, or land, building or equipment fund		32	
33	Retained earnings, endowment, accumulated income, or other funds		33	
34	Total net assets or fund balances		34	
35	Total liabilities and net assets/fund balances		35	

Form **990** (20XX)

Part VII	**Statements Regarding General Activities**			Yes	No

			Yes	No
1	Did the organization conduct any of the following outside the U.S.?	**1**		
a	grantmaking, fundraising, trade, business, or program service activities?	**1a**		
b	maintain an office, employees or agents?	**1b**		
c	maintain an interest in, or signature or other authority, over a financial account?	**1c**		
	If "yes" to any of these questions, complete Schedule F.			
2	Did the organization receive or hold a conservation easement, including easements to preserve open space, the environment, historic land areas or historic structures? If yes, complete Part VIII of Schedule D and Schedule M	**2**		
3	Did the organization provide credit counseling, debt management, credit repair, or debt negotiation services? If "yes", complete part XI of Schedule D.	**3**		
4	Did the organization maintain any donor advised funds or any accounts where donors have the right to provide advice on the distribution or investment of amounts in such funds or accounts? If "yes", complete Part IX of Schedule D and Schedule M	**4**		
5	Did the organization maintain collections of works of art, historical treasures, or other similar assets for public exhibition, education, or research in furtherance of public service rather than financial gain?. If "yes", complete part X of Schedule D.	**5**		
6a	Did the organization have any tax-exempt bonds outstanding at any time during the year? If yes, answer 6b–6d and complete Schedule K. If no, go to question 7.	**6a**		
6b	Did the organization invest any net proceeds of tax-exempt bonds beyond a temporary period exception?	**6b**		
6c	Did the organization maintain an escrow account other than an advance refunding escrow at any time during the year to defease any tax-exempt bonds?	**6c**		
6d	Did the organization act as an "on behalf of issuer" for bonds outstanding at any time during the year?	**6d**		
7	At any time during the year,			
a	Did the organization own 100% of an entity disregarded as separate from the organization under Regulations section 301.7701-2 and 301.7701-3? If yes, attach Schedule R	**7a**		
b	Was the organization related to any tax-exempt or taxable entity? If yes, attach Schedule R	**7b**		
8a	During the tax year, did the filing organization conduct all or a substantial part of its exempt activities through or using a partnership, LLC, or corporation?	**8a**		
b	If yes, identify below the name and primary activity of such partnership, LLC, or corporation in which the filing organization's ownership or control was 50% or less (attach additional pages if necessary):			

Name	Primary Activity	Ownership %	Type of Entity

			Yes	No
c	Is the organization a partner in a partnership, member of an LLC, or shareholder of a corporation that was managed by a company that was controlled by taxable partners, members or shareholders?	**8c**		
9	Did the organization operate, or maintain a facility to provide hospital or medical care? If yes, complete Schedule H	**9**		
10	Is the organization a school as described in section 170(b)(1)(A)(ii)? If yes, complete Schedule E	**10**		
11	Does the organization have a written policy or procedure to review the organization's investments or participation in disregarded entities, joint ventures, or other affiliated organizations (exempt or non-exempt)?	**11**		
12	Does the organization have a written policy that requires the organization to safeguard its exempt status with respect to its transactions and arrangements with related organizations?	**12**		
13	Is the organization filing Form 990 in lieu of Form 1041?.	**13**		
	Enter the amount of tax exempt interest received or accrued during the year ▶ _____			
14	*501(c)(7) Organizations.* Enter:			
a	Initiation fees and capital contributions included on Part IV, line 14	**14a**		
b	Gross receipts, included on Part IV, line 14, for public use of club facilities	**14b**		
15	*501(c)(12) Organization.* Enter:	**15**		
a	Gross income from members or shareholders	**15a**		
b	Gross income from other sources (Do not net amounts due or paid to other sources against amounts due or received from them).	**15b**		
16	Does the organization hold assets in term or permanent endowments? If yes, complete Schedule D, Part XII	**16**		
17	Is the organization required to attach Schedule B, Schedule of Contributors?	**17**		

Form **990** (20XX)

Form 990 (20XX)   Page **9**

Part VIII   Statements Regarding Other IRS Filings

		Yes	No
1	Did the organization engage in direct or indirect political campaign activities on behalf of or in opposition to candidates for public office? If"Yes", complete Schedule C, Political Campaign and Lobbying Activities.	**1**	
2	Did the organization engage in lobbying activities? If "Yes", complete Schedule C.	**2**	
3a	Was the organization a party to a prohibited tax shelter transaction at any time during the tax year?	**3a**	
b	Did any taxable party notify the organization that it was or is a party to a prohibited tax shelter transaction?	**3b**	
c	If "yes" to 3a, did the organization file Form 8886-T, *Disclosure by Tax-Exempt Entity Regarding Prohibited Tax Shelter Transaction?*	**3c**	
4a	Did the organization, during the year, receive any funds, directly or indirectly, to pay premiums on a personal benefit contract?	**4a**	
b	Did the organization, during the year, pay premiums, directly or indirectly, on a personal benefit contract?	**4b**	
5a	*501(c)(3) and 501(c)(4) Organizations.* Did the organization engage in an excess benefit transaction with a disqualified person during the year?	**5a**	
b	Did the organization become aware that it had engaged in an excess benefit transaction with a disqualified person during a prior year?	**5b**	
c	If "Yes," complete the table below.		

Name of Disqualified Person	Description of Transaction	Corrected? (Y/N)

		Yes	No
d	Enter the amount of tax imposed on the organization managers or disqualified persons during the year under section 4958 .	**5d**	
e	Enter the amount of tax on line 5d reimbursed by the organization	**5e**	
6	*501(c)(3) supporting organizations and sponsoring organizations maintaining donor advised funds.* Did the supporting organizations, or a fund maintained by a sponsoring organization, have excess business holdings at any time during the year?	**6**	
7	*501(c)(3) and other sponsoring organizations maintaining donor advised funds.*		
a	Did the organization make any taxable distributions under section 4966?	**7a**	
b	Did the organization make a distribution to a donor, donor advisor, or related person?	**7b**	
8a	Did the organization have unrelated business gross income of $1000 or more during the year covered by this return?	**8a**	
b	If "Yes," has it filed a Form 990-T for this year?	**8b**	
9a	Enter the number of employees reported on Form W-3, *Transmittal of Wage and Tax Statements* filed for the calendar year ending with or within the year covered by this return	**9a**	
b	If at least one, did the organization file all required employment tax returns?	**9b**	
10a	Did the organization provide Forms 1099 as required?	**10a**	
b	If "Yes", indicate the number filed	**10b**	
11a	Did the organization provide goods or services in exchange for any contribution of $75 or more?	**11a**	
b	If "Yes", did the organization notify the donor of the value of the goods or services provided?	**11b**	
12a	Did the organization solicit any contributions that were not tax deductible?	**12a**	
b	If "Yes", did the organization include with every solicitation an express statement that such contributions or gifts were not tax deductible?	**12b**	
13a	Did the organization sell, exchange, or otherwise dispose of tangible personal property for which it filed Form 8282?	**13a**	
b	If "Yes", how many Forms 8282 did the organization file during the tax year?	**13b**	
14	For all contributions of qualified intellectual property, did the organization file Form 8899 as required?	**14**	

Form **990** (20XX)

Part IX   **Statement of Program Service Accomplishments** (See the instructions.)

1 Did the organization make any significant changes in its activities or methods of conducting activities? ☐ Yes ☐ No
If "Yes," describe these changes.

....
....
....

2 Describe the organization's most significant program service accomplishment for the year:

....
....
....

**Total must equal Part V, line 24, column (B)	**(A)** Direct Revenue*	**(B)** Program Service Expenses** Required for 501(c)(3)and (4) orgs. and 4947 (a)(1) trusts; optional for others
3a .... Activity Code:		
....		
....		
....		
....		
(Grants and allocations $)		
b .... Activity Code:		
....		
....		
....		
....		
(Grants and allocations $)		
c .... Activity Code:		
....		
....		
....		
....		
(Grants and allocations $)		
d Other program services (attach schedule) (Grants and allocations $)		
e Total		

Part X   **Signature Block**

Please Sign Here

Under penalties of perjury, I declare that I have examined this return, including accompanying schedules and statements, and to the best of my knowledge and belief, it is true, correct, and complete. Declaration of preparer (other than officer) is based on all information of which preparer has any knowledge.

▶ _____   _____
Signature of officer   Date

▶ _____
Type or print name and title

Paid Preparer's Use Only	Preparer's signature ▶	Date	Check if self-employed ▶ ☐	Preparer's SSN or PTIN (See Gen. Inst.)
	Firm's name (or yours if self-employed), address, and ZIP + 4 ▶		EIN ▶	
			Phone no. ▶ ( )	

Third party designee   Do you want to allow another person to discuss this return with the IRS?   ☐ **Yes.** Complete the following. ☐ No

Designee's name ▶ _____   Phone no. ▶ (   )   Personal identification number (PIN) ▶ ☐☐☐☐☐

⊛ *Printed on recycled paper*   Form **990** (20XX)

APPENDIX 1B: BV SUGGESTED REVISIONS

Blazek & Vetterling Revision

OMB No. 1545-0047

Form 990

Return of Organization Exempt From Income Tax

Under section 501(c), 527, or 4947(a)(1) of the Internal Revenue Code (except black lung benefit trust or private foundation)

20XX

Open to Public Inspection

Department of the Treasury
Internal Revenue Service (77)

The organization may have to use a copy of this return to satisfy state reporting requirements.

A For the 20XX calendar year, or tax year beginning _____ , 20XX, and ending _____ , 20 _____

B	Check if applicable:	Please use IRS label or print or type. See Specific Instructions	C Name of organization	D Employer Identification number
☐	Address Change		Number and street (or P.O. box if mail is not delivered to street address). Room/suite	
☐	Name Change			E Telephone Number
☐	Initial Return		City or town, state or country, and ZIP + 4	( )
☐	Termination			
☐	Amended Return			
☐	Application pending			

F Website: _____

I Books
In care of _____
Located at _____

H Accounting Method: ☐ Cash ☐ Accrual ☐ Other

G Enter amount of gross receipts $ _____

J Organization type (check only one) ☐ 501(c) ( ) (insert no.) ☐ 4947 (a)(1) or ☐ 527

Telephone Number ( )

K Year of Formation: _____

L State of legal domicile _____

Part I	Summary

Activities

1 Briefly describe the organization's exempt purpose and accomplishments. (See Part IX for details). _____

2 Check this box ☐ if the organization discontinued its operations or disposed of more than 25% of its assets and attach Schedule N.

	Prior year	This year	See Att.
Revenues			
3 Contributions and grants (Part IV, line 1h, column (A))			☐
4 Program service revenue (Part IV, line 2g, column (A))			☐
5 Membership dues and assessments (Part IV, line 3, column (A))			☐
6 Investment income (Part IV, line 11, column (A))			☐
7 Other revenue (Part IV, line 15, column (A))			☐
8 Total revenue (add lines 4 through 8, must equal Part IV, line 16, column (A))			☐
(See Part IV for analysis of income-producing activities and Schedule G for Gaming and Fundraising Activity)			
Expenses			
9 Program service expenses (Part V, line 24, column (B))			☐
10 Management and general expenses (Part V, line 24, column (C))			☐
11 Fundraising expenses (Part V, line 24, column (D))			☐
12 Total expenses (must equal Part V, line 24, column (A)) See Part V.			☐
Net Assets or Fund Balances			
13 Excess/(Deficit) of revenue over expenses (line 8 minus line 12)			☐
14 Other changes in net assets:			☐
15 Net assets or fund balances at beginning of year (line 19, col (a))			☐
16 Net assets or fund balances at end of year (combine lines 13-15, should equal line 19 col(b))			☐

	(a) Beginning of Year	(b) End of Year	
17 Total assets (Part VI, line 17)			☐
18 Total liabilities (Part VI, line 27)			☐
19 Net assets or fund balances (line 17 minus line 18) See Part VI.			☐

More Information

20 Enter the number of members of the governing body (Part III, Line 1a)	**20**		☐
21 Enter the number of independent members of the governing body (Part III, Line 1b)	**21**		☐
22 Enter the total number of employees (Part VIII, Line 9a)	**22**		☐
23 Enter the estimated number of volunteers the organization had during the year	**23**		☐
24 Enter officer, director, trustee, and other key employee compensation (Part V, Line 5, column (A))	**24**		☐
25 Divide line 24 by line 12 (Also see Part II and Schedule J for details).	**25**	%	☐
26 Enter total gross unrelated business revenue (Part IV, Line 14, column (C))	**26**		☐
27 Enter net unrelated business taxable income (Form 990-T, Line 34)	**27**		☐
28 See Parts VII and VIII for listings of schedules and returns that may be required plus general information.			

For Privacy Act and Paperwork Reduction Act Notice, see the separate instructions.

Cat. No. 11282Y

Form **990** (20XX)

APPENDIX 1C: FORM 990-EZ

Form **990-EZ**	**Short Form** **Return of Organization Exempt From Income Tax**	OMB No. 1545-1150

Under section 501(c), 527, or 4947(a)(1) of the Internal Revenue Code
(except black lung benefit trust or private foundation)

▶ Sponsoring organizations of donor advised funds and controlling organizations as defined in section 512(b)(13) must file Form 990. All other organizations with gross receipts less than $1,000,000 and total assets less than $2,500,000 at the end of the year may use this form.

Department of the Treasury
Internal Revenue Service

▶ *The organization may have to use a copy of this return to satisfy state reporting requirements.*

2008

Open to Public Inspection

A For the 2008 calendar year, or tax year beginning _____, 2008, and ending _____, 20____

B Check if applicable:
- ☐ Address change
- ☐ Name change
- ☐ Initial return
- ☐ Termination
- ☐ Amended return
- ☐ Application pending

Please use IRS label or print or type. See Specific Instructions.

C Name of organization

Number and street (or P.O. box, if mail is not delivered to street address) | Room/suite

City or town, state or country, and ZIP + 4

D Employer identification number

E Telephone number
( )

F Group Exemption Number . . ▶

- • **Section 501(c)(3) organizations and 4947(a)(1) nonexempt charitable trusts must attach a completed Schedule A (Form 990 or 990-EZ).**

G Accounting method: ☐ Cash ☐ Accrual
Other (specify) ▶

I Website: ▶

H Check ▶ ☐ if the organization is **not** required to attach Schedule B (Form 990, 990-EZ, or 990-PF).

J Organization type (check only one)— ☐ 501(c) ( ) ◀ (insert no.) ☐ 4947(a)(1) or ☐ 527

K Check ▶ ☐ if the organization is not a section 509(a)(3) supporting organization **and** its gross receipts are normally **not** more than $25,000. A return is not required, but if the organization chooses to file a return, be sure to file a complete return.

L Add lines 5b, 6b, and 7b, to line 9 to determine gross receipts; if $1,000,000 or more, file Form 990 instead of Form 990-EZ ▶ $

Part I Revenue, Expenses, and Changes in Net Assets or Fund Balances (See the instructions for Part I.)

Revenue	**1**	Contributions, gifts, grants, and similar amounts received.	**1**	
	2	Program service revenue including government fees and contracts	**2**	
	3	Membership dues and assessments	**3**	
	4	Investment income	**4**	
	5a	Gross amount from sale of assets other than inventory	**5a**	
	b	Less: cost or other basis and sales expenses	**5b**	
	c	Gain or (loss) from sale of assets other than inventory (Subtract line 5b from line 5a) (attach schedule) .	**5c**	
	6	Special events and activities (complete applicable parts of Schedule G). If any amount is from **gaming**, check here ▶ ☐		
	a	Gross revenue (not including $ _____ of contributions reported on line 1)	**6a**	
	b	Less: direct expenses other than fundraising expenses	**6b**	
	c	Net income or (loss) from special events and activities (Subtract line 6b from line 6a) . . .	**6c**	
	7a	Gross sales of inventory, less returns and allowances	**7a**	
	b	Less: cost of goods sold	**7b**	
	c	Gross profit or (loss) from sales of inventory (Subtract line 7b from line 7a)	**7c**	
	8	Other revenue (describe ▶ _____)	**8**	
	9	**Total revenue.** Add lines 1, 2, 3, 4, 5c, 6c, 7c, and 8 . . . . ▶	**9**	
Expenses	**10**	Grants and similar amounts paid (attach schedule)	**10**	
	11	Benefits paid to or for members	**11**	
	12	Salaries, other compensation, and employee benefits	**12**	
	13	Professional fees and other payments to independent contractors	**13**	
	14	Occupancy, rent, utilities, and maintenance	**14**	
	15	Printing, publications, postage, and shipping	**15**	
	16	Other expenses (describe ▶ _____)	**16**	
	17	**Total expenses.** Add lines 10 through 16 . . . . ▶	**17**	
Net Assets	**18**	Excess or (deficit) for the year (Subtract line 17 from line 9)	**18**	
	19	Net assets or fund balances at beginning of year (from line 27, column (A)) (must agree with end-of-year figure reported on prior year's return)	**19**	
	20	Other changes in net assets or fund balances (attach explanation)	**20**	
	21	Net assets or fund balances at end of year. Combine lines 18 through 20 . . . . ▶	**21**	

Part II Balance Sheets. If Total assets on line 25, column (B) are $2,500,000 or more, file Form 990 instead of Form 990-EZ.

(See the instructions for Part II.)

		(A) Beginning of year		**(B)** End of year
22	Cash, savings, and investments		**22**	
23	Land and buildings		**23**	
24	Other assets (describe ▶ _____)		**24**	
25	**Total assets**		**25**	
26	**Total liabilities** (describe ▶ _____)		**26**	
27	**Net assets or fund balances** (line 27 of column (B) **must** agree with line 21) . .		**27**	

For Privacy Act and Paperwork Reduction Act Notice, see the Instruction for Form 990.   Cat. No. 10642I   Form **990-EZ** (2008)

APPENDIX 1C: FORM 990-EZ

Part III	Statement of Program Service Accomplishments (See the instructions for Part III.)	Expenses

What is the organization's primary exempt purpose? _____

Describe what was achieved in carrying out the organization's exempt purposes. In a clear and concise manner, describe the services provided, the number of persons benefited, or other relevant information for each program title.

(Expenses: Required for 501(c)(3) and (4) organizations and 4947(a)(1) trusts; optional for others.)

28 _____

(Grants \$ _____) If this amount includes foreign grants, check here ▶ ☐ | **28a** |

29 _____

(Grants \$ _____) If this amount includes foreign grants, check here ▶ ☐ | **29a** |

30 _____

(Grants \$ _____) If this amount includes foreign grants, check here ▶ ☐ | **30a** |

31 Other program services (attach schedule) . . . .

(Grants \$ _____) If this amount includes foreign grants, check here ▶ ☐ | **31a** |

32 Total program service expenses (add lines 28a through 31a) . . . . ▶ | **32** |

| Part IV | List of Officers, Directors, Trustees, and Key Employees. List each one even if not compensated. (See the instructions for Part IV.) |

(a) Name and address	(b) Title and average hours per week devoted to position	(c) Compensation (If not paid, enter -0-.)	(d) Contributions to employee benefit plans & deferred compensation	(e) Expense account and other allowances

REDESIGNED FORM 990

Part V	Other Information (Note the statement requirements in the instructions for Part VI.)		
		Yes	**No**

			Yes	No
33	Did the organization engage in any activity not previously reported to the IRS? If "Yes," attach a detailed description of each activity	33		
34	Were any changes made to the organizing or governing documents but not reported to the IRS? If "Yes," attach a conformed copy of the changes	34		
35	If the organization had income from business activities, such as those reported on lines 2, 6a, and 7a (among others), but **not** reported on Form 990-T, attach a statement explaining your reason for not reporting the income on Form 990-T.			
a	Did the organization have unrelated business gross income of $1,000 or more or section 6033(e) notice, reporting, and proxy tax requirements?	35a		
b	If "Yes," has it filed a tax return on **Form 990-T** for this year?	35b		
36	Was there a liquidation, dissolution, termination, or substantial contraction during the year? If "Yes," complete applicable parts of Schedule N	36		
37a	Enter amount of political expenditures, direct or indirect, as described in the instructions. ▶	37a			
b	Did the organization file **Form 1120-POL** for this year?	37b		
38a	Did the organization borrow from, or make any loans to, any officer, director, trustee, or key employee **or** were any such loans made in a prior year and still unpaid at the start of the period covered by this return? . . .	38a		
b	If "Yes," complete Schedule L, Part II and enter the total amount involved	38b			
39	Section 501(c)(7) organizations. Enter:			
a	Initiation fees and capital contributions included on line 9	39a			
b	Gross receipts, included on line 9, for public use of club facilities	39b			
40a	Section 501(c)(3) organizations. Enter amount of tax imposed on the organization during the year under: section 4911 ▶ _____ ; section 4912 ▶ _____ ; section 4955 ▶ _____			
b	Section 501(c)(3) and (4) organizations. Did the organization engage in any section 4958 excess benefit transaction during the year or did it become aware of an excess benefit transaction from a prior year? If "Yes," complete Schedule L, Part I	40b		
c	Enter amount of tax imposed on organization managers or disqualified persons during the year under sections 4912, 4955, and 4958 . . . . ▶ _____			
d	Enter amount of tax on line 40c reimbursed by the organization . . . . ▶ _____			
e	All organizations. At any time during the tax year, was the organization a party to a prohibited tax shelter transaction? If "Yes," complete Form 8886-T.	40e		
41	List the states with which a copy of this return is filed. ▶ _____			
42a	The books are in care of ▶ _____ Telephone no. ▶ (_____) _____			
	Located at ▶ _____ ZIP + 4 ▶ _____			

			Yes	No
b	At any time during the calendar year, did the organization have an interest in or a signature or other authority over a financial account in a foreign country (such as a bank account, securities account, or other financial account)?	42b		
	If "Yes," enter the name of the foreign country: ▶ _____			
	See the instructions for exceptions and filing requirements for **Form TD F 90-22.1, Report of Foreign Bank and Financial Accounts.**			
c	At any time during the calendar year, did the organization maintain an office outside of the U.S.?	42c		
	If "Yes," enter the name of the foreign country: ▶ _____			
43	Section 4947(a)(1) nonexempt charitable trusts filing Form 990-EZ in lieu of **Form 1041**—Check here . . . . ▶ ☐ and enter the amount of tax-exempt interest received or accrued during the tax year . . . . . ▶	43		

			Yes	No
44	Did the organization maintain any donor advised funds? If "Yes," Form 990 must be completed instead of Form 990-EZ	44		
45	Is any related organization a controlled entity of the organization within the meaning of section 512(b)(13)? If "Yes," Form 990 must be completed instead of Form 990-EZ	45		

Form **990-EZ** (2008)

Form 990-EZ (2008)   Page **4**

| **Part VI** | **Section 501(c)(3) organizations only.** All section 501(c)(3) organizations must answer questions 46–49 and complete the tables for lines 50 and 51. |

			Yes	No
46	Did the organization engage in direct or indirect political campaign activities on behalf of or in opposition to candidates for public office? If "Yes," complete Schedule C, Part I	**46**		
47	Did the organization engage in lobbying activities? If "Yes," complete Schedule C, Part II	**47**		
48	Is the organization operating a school as described in section 170(b)(1)(A)(ii)? If "Yes," complete Schedule E .	**48**		
49a	Did the organization make any transfers to an exempt non-charitable related organization?	**49a**		
b	If "Yes," was the related organization(s) a section 527 organization?	**49b**		

50 Complete this table for the five highest compensated employees (other than officers, directors, trustees and key employees) who each received more than $100,000 of compensation from the organization. If there is none, enter "None."

(a) Name and address of each employee paid more than $100,000	**(b)** Title and average hours per week devoted to position	**(c)** Compensation	**(d)** Contributions to employee benefit plans & deferred compensation	**(e)** Expense account and other allowances

Total number of other employees paid over $100,000 ▶

51 Complete this table for the five highest compensated independent contractors who each received more than $100,000 of compensation from the organization. If there is none, enter "None."

(a) Name and address of each independent contractor paid more than $100,000	**(b)** Type of service	**(c)** Compensation

Total number of other independent contractors each receiving over $100,000 . . ▶

Under penalties of perjury, I declare that I have examined this return, including accompanying schedules and statements, and to the best of my knowledge and belief, it is true, correct, and complete. Declaration of preparer (other than officer) is based on all information of which preparer has any knowledge.

| **Sign Here** | ▶ Signature of officer | Date |
| | ▶ Type or print name and title. | |

Paid Preparer's Use Only	Preparer's signature ▶	Date	Check if self-employed ▶ ☐	Preparer's Identifying Number (See instructions)
	Firm's name (or yours if self-employed), address, and ZIP + 4 ▶		EIN ▶	
			Phone no. ▶ ( )	

May the IRS discuss this return with the preparer shown above? See instructions . . . . ▶ ☐ Yes ☐ No

Form **990-EZ** (2008)

CHAPTER TWO

Good Accounting Makes
a Good 990

Good accounting is the key to successful preparation of federal information returns for a nonprofit organization.[1] The trick is to allocate and attribute revenues and expenses to the proper lines and columns on Forms 990. Both for those organizations that want to properly reflect activity costs and those that want to maximize deductions to offset unrelated business income,[2] proper identification of allocable expenses is an important goal. Direct costs are expenses that can be identified specifically with an organization's activity or project, and can be assigned to an activity or project with a high degree of accuracy. Indirect costs are costs that cannot be identified specifically with an activity or project. For example, a computer bought by a university specifically for a research project is a direct cost. In contrast, the costs of software licensing for programs that run on all the university's computers are indirect costs.

The accounting profession defines *accounting* as the art of recording, classifying, and summarizing in a significant manner and in terms of money, transactions, and events that are, in part at least, of a financial character, and interpreting the results thereof.[3] The United Way of America expands the definition and suggests that a nonprofit's accounting system records and summarizes the financial activities of the organization in a manner that:[4]

- Lends itself to revealing clearly and fully the organization's financial position, sources, and amounts of revenue, and nature and extent of expenditures, including per unit cost of the benefit, where feasible, and

- Complies with all legal and technical requirements of governmental and other authoritative organizations.

The functional expense display in Part IX on page 10 of the Core Form is the same as the reporting prescribed by generally accepted accounting standards. Three types, or categories, of expenses are reported—program service or exempt function, management and general, and fund-raising. As a rule, IRS standards allow use of any reasonable method of cost allocation.[5]

The Wise Giving Alliance/Better Business Bureau, National Center for Nonprofit Boards, regulatory agencies, and funders generally recommend that the sum of an organization's management and fund-raising costs equal no more than 25 percent of total expenditures. Thus the desired proportion for spending on programs and mission-related activities is 75 percent. The revised form no longer displays the functional expense totals on the front page. Instead, four expense totals that presumably evidence IRS concern—grants paid, benefits paid to members, salaries, other compensation and employee benefits, and professional fund-raising fees—are shown. Calculation of the expense ratios can still be derived from totals of line 25 on Part IX.

Documentation and cost accounting records must be designed to capture revenues and costs by function, including joint cost allocations. Direct costs are expenses that can be identified specifically with an organization's activity or project, and can be assigned to an activity or project with a high degree of accuracy. Indirect costs are costs that cannot be identified specifically with an activity or project. For example, a computer bought by a university specifically for a research project is a direct cost. In contrast, the costs of software licensing for programs that run on all the university's computers are indirect costs. When expenses are attributable to more than one function, organizations must develop techniques to have verifiable bases upon which expenses may be related to program or supporting service functions. The functional classification of expenses permits an organization to tell the reader of the financial statements not only the nature of its expenses, such as salary, supplies, and occupancy, but also the purpose for which the funds were expended. At a minimum, all 990 filing organizations need to maintain the following:

- A staff salary allocation system is essential for recording the time employees spend on tasks each day. The possibilities are endless. Each staff member should maintain an individual computer database or fill out a time sheet. The reports should be completed often enough to ensure accuracy, preferably weekly. In some cases, as when personnel perform repetitive tasks, preparing one week's report for each month or one month each year might be sufficient. Percentages of time spent on various functions can then be tabulated and used for accounting allocations.

- Office/program space utilization charts to assign occupancy costs can be prepared. All physical building space rented or owned must be allocated according to its usage. Floor plans must be tabulated to arrive at square footage of the space allocable to each activity center. In some cases, the allocation is made by using staff/time ratios, or the converse. For dual-use space, records must reflect the number of hours or days the space is used for each purpose.

- Direct program or activity costs should be captured whenever possible. The advantages include reduction of unrelated business income, proof of qualifying distributions for a private foundation, and insurance against an IRS challenge for low program expenditures. A minimal amount of additional time should be required by administrative staff to accumulate costs by programs. A departmental accounting system is imperative. Some long-distance telephone companies will assist in developing a coding system that quantifies the phone charges by department. As another example, the organization can establish separate accounts with vendors for different departments.

- Joint project allocations must be made on a reasonable and fair basis recognizing the cause and effect relationship between the cost incurred and where it is allocated. Four possible methods of allocating include: activity-based allocations (identifying departmental costs); equal sharing of costs (for instance, if three projects, divide by three); cost allocated relative to stand-alone cost (for instance, what it would cost if that department had to hire and buy independently); and cost allocated in proportion to cost savings.[6]

- Supporting, administrative, or other management costs should be allocated to departments to which the work is directly related. The organization's size and the scope of administrative staff involvement in actual programs determine the feasibility of such cost attributions. Staff salaries are most often allocable. Say, for example, the executive director is also the editor of the organization's journal. If a record of time spent is maintained, her salary and associated costs could be attributed partly to the publication. When allocating expenses to unrelated business income, an exploitation of the exempt functions rule may apply to limit such an allocation.[7]

- A computer-based fund accounting system, in which department codes are automatically recorded as moneys are expended, is preferable. The cost of the software is easily recouped in staff time saved, improved planning, and possibly tax savings due to a reduction in income and excise taxes.

§2.1 TAX ACCOUNTING METHODS

Plainly and simply, the instructions for Forms 990 say that an organization should generally use the same accounting method on the return to report revenue and expenses as it regularly uses to keep its books and records.[8] So long as the method clearly reflects income, either the cash, modified cash, or the accrual method may be used. For its simplicity, many organizations use the cash method in their early years, meaning only the actual cash received and expended is reported as the financial activity for the year. What is called the ''accrual method'' reports transactions when a binding obligation to pay or receive occurs. As discussed below, a promise to make a donation is counted under the accrual method when an unconditional pledge is received. Similarly an expense is recorded when the obligation to pay for the goods and services occurs, not when paid. There are a number of reasons, however, that a new nonprofit might instead select the accrual method.

Once an organization adopts either the cash or accrual method for 990 reporting purposes, it must file Form 3115 to change the method. A change from the cash to accrual method of accounting may need to be made, for example, by an organization that has, in its initial years or for whatever reason, not used the accrual method and chooses to begin to do so. Customarily this situation arises when the organization engages a CPA to issue audited reports of its financial condition.

An organization that changes its method of reporting contributions and grants to comply with a change required by the Financial Accounting Standards Board (''FASB'') standards, however, is not required to file Form 3115.[9] The prior year effect of such a change used to be reported on line 20 of Part I of Form 990[10] and still is reported on Part III of Form 990-PF, rather than on the beginning balance sheet. The many exempt organizations that adopted the new standards in 1996 and 1997 made significant changes in their financial reporting systems without permission.

Prior to the 2008 return, the cash method of accounting was required to be used by public charities for purposes of calculating public support percentages under §170 (b)(1)(A)(vi) and §509(a)(2) on Schedule A.[11] New Schedule A directs that the calculation be presented following the method the organization uses for completing Form 990. Private foundations must tally the §4942 minimum distribution requirements on a cash basis.[12]

§2.2 PROFESSIONAL ACCOUNTING STANDARDS

The FASB[13] issues the rules followed by CPAs in presenting financial information. The standards are referred to as generally accepted accounting principles, or GAAP. Though an organization is not required to follow GAAP, the accountant's report must make note of the exception in the covering opinion or say explicitly that the information is not presented according to GAAP. It is said that a "clean" accountant's opinion can only be issued for financials prepared according to GAAP. Thus, many nonprofit organizations apply these rules in maintaining and reporting financial information. The FASB continually studies and improves financial reporting by nonprofit organizations, and readers should be alert for changes. The rules are found in the periodically updated AICPA Audit and Accounting Guide for Not-For-Profit Organizations.[14] A brief introduction to the accounting concepts follows.

Statement of Financial Accounting Standards (SFAS) No. 116, "Accounting for Contributions Received and Contributions Made," affects the manner in which contributions are to be reported on GAAP financial statements. This SFAS defines a contribution as "an unconditional transfer of cash or other assets to an entity, or as a settlement or cancellation of its liabilities in a voluntary nonreciprocal transfer by another entity acting as other than an owner." FASB further provides that the following inflows of assets are *not* included in the definition of contributions:

- Transfers that are exchange transactions, in which both parties receive goods or services of commensurate value.

- Transfers in which the organization is acting as an agent, trustee, or intermediary for the donor (that is, the organization has little or no discretion concerning the use of the assets transferred).

- Tax exemptions, tax incentives, and tax abatements.

Contributions instead include volunteer payments motivated by detached and disinterested generosity with the desire to support a nonprofit organization's exempt activities, or what can be thought of as one-way street receipts (nothing is received in return), are classified as contributions. Intangible recognition, such as inclusion of a name on a sponsor list or on a church pew, of a gift is not valued and does not reduce the amount treated as a contribution. Gifts from corporations or other businesses are reported as direct public support when they represent a gift. Money raised by a business in a cause-related marketing campaign, also referred to as commercial co-ventures, are classified as donations following the agency theory. Typically, a business uses the charity's name in a sales promotion and promises to contribute a stated dollar amount for each item sold or upon the occurrence of some action on the public's part. Business sponsorships treated as acknowledgments are also reported as donations.

Gifts received in the form of charitable pledges are included in revenue when the pledge is unconditionally made or promised, rather than when paid in cash or other assets. A condition is a future and uncertain event. Thus, a pledge to match funding the organization raises from others is conditional and not reported until the matching gifts have been received. For the value of a pledge to be reported, there must be "sufficient evidence in the form of verifiable documentation that a promise was made and received." Restricted and unrestricted gifts of all kinds and in whatever form—cash, securities, other property, or in-kind—are subject to reporting as current revenue under this rule. Factors indicating a bookable pledge are compared in the following list to those indicating the gift is conditional and therefore not recordable (noted in parentheses):

- Written evidence exists (no written promise made).
- Documents contain language such as "promise," "agree," "will," or "binding" (no "hope," "intend," "may," or "expect").
- Pledge payments are scheduled for specific dates in the future (no specific payment dates indicated in documents).
- Donor's economic position indicates ability to pay pledged amount (collectibility of pledge is questionable).
- Donor has history of timely payment of pledged amounts (donor has no history).
- Donee has taken specific steps—signed contract to build the new building or sought matching pledges—in reliance on pledge (no action taken or obligation entered into as result of pledge).
- Pledge was made in response to solicitation of formal pledges (promise is unsolicited or funding request sought no pledge).
- Public recognition or announcement of pledge made (no announcement).

Pledges of donations to be received beyond the current year are discounted by applying an appropriate rate of interest (return the organization is currently earning on its investments or cash reserves). The increase (called accretion) in the value of the pledge each year is reported as a donation in that year. An allowance for uncollectible pledges must be provided to cover the inevitable uncollectible pledge (and reflected as a reduction of the revenue, not as an expense).

Contributed services provided by volunteers are recognized as income for financial purposes (but not for tax purposes) if one of two conditions exists when the services are received:

- The services create or enhance nonfinancial assets (volunteers construct a building or set for a theater performance).
- Or services are of a type that require specialized skills, are provided by individuals possessing those skills, and would typically have to be purchased if not provided by donations. SFAS No. 116 lists by example professions, such as doctors, lawyers, teachers, and carpenters.

Donated facilities produce recognizable income equal to the fair rental value of the facilities but not more than the organization would otherwise pay for its needed facilities. The present value of a binding multiyear lease is reported as income in the year the agreement is arranged. Again note that the value of such a donation is not reported as revenue on Form 990 or counted as support in calculating public charity status.[15] What are sometimes called in-kind donations of land, building, equipment, supplies, food, and other real and tangible property are recorded for both financial and tax reporting purposes.

Bequests: A testamentary bequest is recorded as income when the amount of the bequest can be accurately determined. A specific bequest of a sum certain amount or particular property is recorded when there is no uncertainty about its being subject to death taxes or other obligations of the decedent. The discounted present value of the organization's share of assets in a split-interest agreement is reported as a gift of current income in the year its ownership is made certain under the intention-to-give concepts defining unconditional gifts.

Unrealized Changes in Investment Value: Increases or decreases in an organization's investment in an affiliated entity are not reported as current revenue in Core Part VIII, line 3 (Core Part VIII), though they are reported as investment income for financial reporting purposes. The change in investment value is reported on Schedule D in Part XII to reconcile revenue reported for audit purposes to the tax revenue. For tax purposes, affiliated but legally independent exempt organizations must each file their own Forms 990, except for members of an affiliated association holding a group exemption.

Agency Transactions or Pass-Through grants are not recognized as revenue to the filing entity acting as an agent for another organization.[16] Such grants must be distinguished from indirect public support; contributions received from a fund-raising agency, such as a united giving campaign; or an affiliated or supporting organization. Pass-through contributions are those that are not the property of the reporting organization because the receiver, or agent, has no dominion or control over the ultimate distributions of the funds. Instead such funds represent a liability to the initial recipient because it is obligated to pay the funds to another organization—the designated donee. Because of the public and donor disclosure requirements and in some cases, public support test calculations, this distinction has far-reaching impact.

Contributions or grants paid out by the organization are recognized as an expense in the year the promise to pay is made, regardless of whether the cash or other asset is actually disbursed. Matching, conditional, or otherwise contingent promises to pay are booked at the time the uncertainty is removed because the condition is met.

SFAS No. 117, "Financial Statements for Not-For-Profit Organizations," redesigned financial statement presentation and made obsolete the different systems previously prescribed for hospitals, colleges, health and welfare, and all other not-for-profit organizations. Donations received are identified as subject to one of three types of restrictions:

- *Permanently restricted net assets,* such as moneys to be used to pay scholarships only, an endowment fund from which only the dividends and interest may be used, and long-lived assets, such as buildings or collections.

- *Temporarily restricted net assets* funds given to accomplish a particular program service or to buy certain assets over a period of time.

- *Unrestricted net assets* will identify all other resources of the not-for-profit organization freely available for use in accomplishing the organization's purposes and subject only to the control of the organization's board or officers.

A *Statement of Activity* for all organizational funds and programs replaces the statement of financial position and results of operations, also called statement of revenues and expenses. The statement is designed to help donors, creditors, and others assess an organization's service efforts functionally. In other words, the total cost of major program services is reported along with separate amounts for supporting services (management, fund-raising, and membership development expenses). Additionally, health and welfare organizations report total expenses in their natural categories—personnel, occupancy, interest, grants to others, and so on. For hospitals and all other nonprofits, this report is encouraged but not required. Current earnings on all funds, including those permanently restricted, are to be reported on the statement of activity. Revenues subject to restrictions, such as capital gains on endowment funds, are separately identified but still reported as current earnings.

SFAS No. 124, "Accounting for Certain Investments Held by Not-for-Profit Organizations," addresses the way in which nonprofit organizations account for equity securities, the value of which is readily determinable, and investments in debt securities. Investments in land, a partnership, a subsidiary corporation, or other investments are not addressed in this SFAS. Marketable equity and debt securities are reported at their fair market value. Such investments are initially reported at their acquisition cost (including brokerage and other transaction fees) if purchased and at fair value if they are received as donations or through an agency transaction. Changes in fair value of such investments are reflected in the statement of activity (income statement) as unrealized gain or loss and increase or decrease unrestricted net assets unless their use is temporarily or permanently restricted by donors to a specified purpose or future period. Such unrealized gains and losses are not recognized for tax purposes, but instead are reflected in Part III, line 3 or 5 (990-PF) as an item reconciling book to tax income. Consequently, the tax gain or loss reported upon sale or other disposition of such investments is different from that reflected for financial purposes. Similarly, the FASB permits investment revenues to be reported net of related expenses, such as custodial fees and investment advisory fees; such expenses are reported in Part IX of Form 990.

SFAS No. 136, "Transfers of Assets to a Not-for-Profit Organization or Charitable Trust That Raises or Holds Contributions for Others," sets forth the rules for "agency transactions." A nonprofit is an agent when it accepts a donation with the obligation to pay the money to another entity. Such a payment is recorded as a liability, rather than revenue, by the agent. If the agent, or collecting organization, possesses a "variance power," or some discretion and control over the regranting of the gift, it recognizes the payment as revenue. Also, if it receives the money on behalf of a financially interrelated organization over which it has the ability to influence the operating and financial decisions, and in which it has an ongoing economic interest, it reports revenue. This rule was effective for years beginning after December 15, 1999.

Statement of Position 94–3, "Reporting of Related Entities by Not-for-Profit Organizations," was proposed in February 1999 to be issued as an SFAS entitled "Consolidated Financial Statements: Purposes and Policy." Combined financial reports must be issued for organizations with interlocking control and economic interests. Federal tax returns must, however, be filed independently for each separate organization. Form 990 cannot be prepared from or readily compared to such financial statements.

Statement of Position 98–2, "Accounting for Costs of Activities of Not-for-Profit Organizations and State and Local Governmental Entities That Include Fund Raising," provides standards for reporting money spent for materials and activities that combine fund-raising activities with educational, or other, elements. Direct mail, telethons, special events, and a variety of methods are used by nonprofits to concurrently raise money and advance the mission. An athletic contest for handicapped persons or a cancer-warning signs brochure may embody requests for funding alongside the program content. Three rather complicated tests—purpose, audience, and content—are applied to determine whether any of the joint costs of such activities can be allocated to program or management, rather than all being treated as fund-raising costs. As described previously in the introduction to this section, allocation of expenses to the three functions displayed on page 10 of Form 990 (program, management, and fund-raising) requires cost accounting systems that capture people's time, space, and expenses devoted to each function. To make a joint cost allocation, the content of written materials and audience solicited are examined to find the primary motivation for an activity. The FASB suggests a test that asks, "Does the program component of the joint activity call for specific action by the recipient that will help accomplish the organization's mission?"

§2.3 CHART OF DIFFERENCES BETWEEN GAAP AND IRS RULES

SUBJECT	RULES		CITATIONS	
ACCOUNTING	GAAP	TAX	GAAP	TAX*
Donated services of volunteers	Must be recorded if specified criteria are met	May not be reported in Part VIII of Form 990	SFAS 116, para. 9	(I) page 17 (for line 1) bottom of right column, and page 28 (line 82)
Consolidated statements for affiliated entities	Must be prepared if certain criteria are met	May not be filed, except under a group exemption	SOP 94–3	(I) page 13 (GI–R)
Effects of accounting changes	Are sometimes reflected retroactively by restating prior years' data	Must be shown as a current year item	APB 20, and various new standards	(I) page 5 (GI–G) right column
Accrual basis	Required	Not required (Note 1)	(SAS 69, para. 5, 10; SAS 62, para. 4c)	(I) page 5 (GI–G) right column
Prepaid fund-raising costs	Must be expensed in the period incurred	May be reported as assets	Audit Guide, para. 13.06	(I) line 53
Investments	Most investments must be reported at fair value	May be reported at either cost or fair value	SFAS 124, para. 7	(F) line 54
Grants made to others	SFAS 116 is required	Not required	SFAS 116, para. 18	(I) line 22 (6th para.)

REPORTING FORMAT**

Net assets	3 classes required	Not required	SFAS 117, para. 13	(F) lines 67–69 vs. 70–72
Change in net assets	Total must be shown	Total is not shown	SFAS 117, para. 18	(F) lines 18 & 20
	must be shown by class	not shown by class	SFAS 117, para. 19	(F) line 18
Revenue from special fund-raising events	All event revenue may be reported together in one caption	Contribution portion is shown separately from purchase portion	Audit Guide, para. 13.24-.25	(I) page 18 (for line 1a) middle of middle column, and p. 20 (line 9)
Functional expenses	Required for all organizations	Required only for 501(c)(3) and (4) organizations	SFAS 117, para. 26	(I) lines 13–15, and part II
	Must be shown separately for major classes of program services	Are shown in total for all pro-grams together	SFAS 117, para. 26	(F) line 13, and part II
Statement of functional expenses	Required only for voluntary health & welfare organi-zations (VHWOs)	Required for all 501(c)(3) and (4) organizations	SFAS 117, para. 26	(F) part II, col. B, C,D
Natural expense categories	Required only for VHWOs	Required for all organizations	SFAS 117, para. 26	(F)—part II, col. A
Specific catego-ries of financial statement elements	Generally not specified	Specific catego-ries required	SFAS 117 gives example catego-ries only	(F) parts I, II, IV
Statement of cash flows; Footnotes	Required	Not required	SFAS 117, para. 6	(I) page 4 (GI—E) lower right column (under "Addi-tional informa-tion…")
Additional information	Not required	Various other schedules and questions are required	SFAS 117, para. 6	(F) heading; schedules sup-porting certain lines; parts III, IV-A, IV-B, V—X; Sch. A
Related party transactions	Disclosure of material items required (some exceptions)	Required only for transactions be-tween a 501(c) (3) and non-(c) (3)s or between and organization and its disquali-fied persons	SFAS 57, para. 2	(I) page 10 (GI–O); Schedule A—part VII

(Continued)

Subject	Rules		Citations	
Accounting	**GAAP**	**Tax**	**GAAP**	**Tax***
Number of fiscal years presented	Not specified (normally non-profits present the same number of years for all statements)	2 years' balance sheets; one year's revenues and expenses in detail (2 years in summary on the front page)	—	(F) parts I, II, IV
Other	**Financial Statements**	**Form 990**		
Public disclosure	Not required	Required, on request	—	(I) page 8 (GI –M)
Deadline for issuance; penalties	None specified by law (for non-SEC registrants)	Specified by IRS	—	(I) page 6 (GI–H & K)
If fiscal year is changed	May be prepared for either the "short" or the "long" period	Must be prepared for the "short" period	—	(I) page 5 (GI–G) top of right column
Audit	Although not a matter of GAAP, an audit is required only by some states, funders, and watchdog agencies	Not required	Various state rules; OMB Circular A-133; other requirements	(I) page 4 (GI–E) lower right column (under "Additional information…")
Applicability	No distinction by size or type of organization (except reporting of expenses by VHWOs, as noted above; also, some states exempt small organizations from filing)	Very small organizations, churches, and some others not required to file; small organizations may file a simplified form (990-EZ)	SFAS 117, para. 1, merely refers to "a not-for-profit organization."	(I) page 2 (GI–B); (GI–A as to Form 990-EZ)
Signature of an organization officer	Not required	Required	—(Note 2)	(I) page 14 (GI–W)

*References are to:
(I) the 2008 Instructions for Form 990; GI=General Instruction, or (F) the 2008 Form 990 and related instruction(s).
(Some references to Form 990-EZ are different; Form 990-PF is not covered by this summary.)

**-Because SFAS 117—beyond its basic requirements—is generally nonprescriptive as to precise classification and format, many of the specific requirements of Form 990 are *not contrary* to GAAP, even though they are not normally followed by most preparers of general-purpose financial statements, especially as to the degree of detail presented.

Note 1: The IRS instruction is to "generally use the same accounting method .. as it regularly uses to keep its books and records." However, some states require that copies of Form 990 filed with them be prepared on the accrual basis.

Note 2: However, some states and others may require nonprofit organizations to comply with the Sarbanes-Oxley Act, which does require signatures of organization officers.

NOTES

1. Chapter 6 of J. Blazek, *Nonprofit Financial Planning Made Easy* (Hoboken, N.J.: John Wiley & Sons, 2008) explains generally accepted accounting principles and provides sample financial reports and checklists to guide in design of the chart of accounts, internal (fiscal) control systems, and choice of software and accounting method (cash versus accrual).
2. See Blazek, *Nonprofit Financial Planning*, §1.14.
3. *Accounting Terminology Bulletin No. 1*, final ed. American Institute of Certified Public Accountants, 1941, p. 9.
4. *Accounting and Financial Reporting, A Guide for United Ways and Not-for-Profit Human-Service Organizations*, rev. 2d ed. United Way of America, 1989, p. 9.
5. See discussion for columnar display of functional expenses on Core Part IX and Reg. 1.512 (a)-1(b).
6. D. Tishlian, "Reasonable Joint Cost Allocations in Nonprofits." *Journal of Accountancy* (November 1992): 66.
7. Discussed in Chapter 5.
8. In accordance with IRC §446(a).
9. IRS Notice 96–30, I.R.B. 1996–20; still cited in Form 990 instructions.
10. The revised Form 990 no longer requires a "rollforward" of net assets from one year to the next, requiring explanation for a change in net assets other than income.
11. Discussed in Chapter 4, Schedule A.
12. Discussed in Chapter 6, Parts X-XIII.
13. The Governmental Accounting Standards Board ("GASB") is responsible for establishing the rules for financial reporting of state and local governmental organizations. Some nonprofit organizations are so closely linked to governmental organizations that they may be required to follow GASB rules in concert with FASB guidelines.
14. The following discussion follows the guide issued as of May 1, 2000.
15. Unless the donation comes from a governmental agency, then it counts 100 percent as public support in Schedule A.
16. FASB No. 135.

CHAPTER THREE

The Core

§3.1   2008 FORM 990 CORE

Form **990**	**Return of Organization Exempt From Income Tax**	OMB No. 1545-0047
	Under section 501(c), 527, or 4947(a)(1) of the Internal Revenue Code (except black lung benefit trust or private foundation)	**2008**
Department of the Treasury Internal Revenue Service	▶ The organization may have to use a copy of this return to satisfy state reporting requirements.	**Open to Public Inspection**

The front page of the 2008 Form 990 Core presents a snapshot of the organization's mission and revenues, expenses, and net assets for the year compared to the prior year. The intention is to provide a comprehensive overview of the organization to give a viewer that isn't interested in the details a picture. Preparers should, therefore, be particularly sensitive to the information in Part I. Though it looks deceptively simple and (for lines 8–17) reflects numbers from other parts, this page will be the basis for statistical analysis, metrics, and other comparisons between organizations and must be prepared with care.

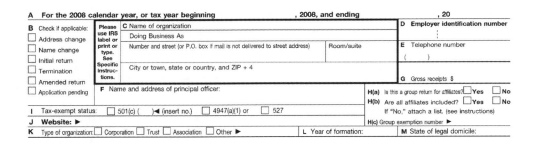

The top of the first page of this new version looks very much the same as the pre-2008 return but has new boxes.

Boxes A, D, E, G, H, I, and J remain the same.

Box F is new and may surprise some officials when it asks for the name and address of the principal officer, or the person who, regardless of title, has the ultimate responsibility for implementing the decisions of the organization's governing body, or for supervising the management, administration, or operation of the organization. When the officer prefers to be contacted at the organization's address listed in item C, the words "same as above" can be entered.

Box K asks that the type, or form, of organization (corporation, trust, association, or other), the year of formation, and the state of legal domicile be provided. Locating this information may be difficult for older organizations or organizations with frequent changes in leadership.

§3.2 PART I SUMMARY

Part I	Summary	
1	Briefly describe the organization's mission or most significant activities:	
	....	
	....	
2	Check this box ▶ ☐ if the organization discontinued its operations or disposed of more than 25% of its assets.	
3	Number of voting members of the governing body (Part VI, line 1a)	**3**
4	Number of independent voting members of the governing body (Part VI, line 1b)	**4**
5	Total number of employees (Part V, line 2a)	**5**
6	Total number of volunteers (estimate if necessary)	**6**
7a	Total gross unrelated business revenue from Part VIII, line 12, column (C)	**7a**
b	Net unrelated business taxable income from Form 990-T, line 34	**7b**

(left margin: Activities & Governance)

The Part I Summary requests seven items of information to illustrate the factors the IRS considers key organizational indicators that should be readily available on the front page. An IRS TIP recommends preparers consider General Instruction C, "Sequencing List to Complete the Form," prior to preparing Part I in saying, "Part I generally reports information reported elsewhere on the form. Completion of Part I should be deferred until after the other parts of the form are completed."

Line 1. Mission or Chief Activity: Three lines are provided to allow the organization to describe either its mission or its most significant activity for the year. Preparers will notice that essentially the same space is provided for this line and the opening description of the mission in Part III. The IRS instructions ask for "whichever the organization wishes to highlight on the summary page." The mission and much more information about activities is also provided in Part III.

Line 2. A check box is marked if operations were discontinued or more than 25 percent of assets were disposed of during the year. In addition, if an organization checks the box on this line, it must answer "Yes" to question 31 or 32 in Part IV, and complete Schedule N.

Line 3. Number of voting board members of the governing body, or that group of persons authorized under state law to make governance decisions on behalf of the organization. This number should be the same as that reported on line 1a of Part VI following instructions for that line.

Line 4. Number of independent voting members of the governing body as of the end of the organization's tax year is displayed. This number should agree with line 1b of Part VI and be determined following instructions and standards provided for that part.

Line 5. Number of employees reported in Part V, Line 2a, which is the number on Form W-3 filed for the calendar year ending with or within the year covered by the return. An organization filing Form 990 for the fiscal year ending June 30, 2009, would use the number on the Form W-3 filed for 2008. Fortunately a metric appearing on the June 2007 draft of the return, compensation of highest paid employee, was removed as a result of public comments.

Line 6. Number of volunteers, full- and part-time, who provided volunteer services to the organization during the reporting year is entered. An organization that does not maintain a record of volunteer hours is told to use a "reasonable basis" for determining an estimate of the number. The instructions suggest the method for estimating the number and the types of services or benefits provided by the organization's volunteers may, but is not required to, be provided in Schedule O.

Line 7a. Amount of gross unrelated business revenue that appears on line 12 of Part VIII is entered. If more than $1,000 is reported here, Question 3a in Part V must be answered "Yes" and Form 990-T filed to report the income.

Line 7b. Amount of the actual or estimated net unrelated business taxable income (or loss) from line 34 of Form 990-T is requested. If the Form 990-T is not filed, a "0" is entered. This metric will give the IRS an interesting scanning tool for potential examinations.

		Prior Year	Current Year
Revenue	8 Contributions and grants (Part VIII, line 1h)		
	9 Program service revenue (Part VIII, line 2g)		
	10 Investment income (Part VIII, column (A), lines 3, 4, and 7d)		
	11 Other revenue (Part VIII, column (A), lines 5, 6d, 8c, 9c, 10c, and 11e) . .		
	12 Total revenue—add lines 8 through 11 (must equal Part VIII, column (A), line 12)		
Expenses	13 Grants and similar amounts paid (Part IX, column (A), lines 1–3)		
	14 Benefits paid to or for members (Part IX, column (A), line 4)		
	15 Salaries, other compensation, employee benefits (Part IX, column (A), lines 5–10)		
	16a Professional fundraising fees (Part IX, column (A), line 11e)		
	b Total fundraising expenses (Part IX, column (D), line 25) ▶		
	17 Other expenses (Part IX, column (A), lines 11a–11d, 11f–24f)		
	18 Total expenses. Add lines 13–17 (must equal Part IX, column (A), line 25).		
	19 Revenue less expenses. Subtract line 18 from line 12		
		Beginning of Year	End of Year
Net Assets or Fund Balances	20 Total assets (Part X, line 16)		
	21 Total liabilities (Part X, line 26)		
	22 Net assets or fund balances. Subtract line 21 from line 20		

Total revenue and expenses from Core Parts VIII and IX for 2008 are entered on these lines. For comparison, amounts from Parts I and II of the 2007 Form 990 are entered. The instructions contain a guide for transferring the information reported on the 2007 return to the appropriate 2008 categories.

Line 16a. The isolation of *professional fundraising fees* illustrates the IRS's desire to draw attention to this type of expenditure. Other reviewers of the Form 990 are also concerned about the ratio of fundraising expenses. Some confusion may arise because the title for lines from which this line is referred (called professional fundraising services) uses a different name. Part II, line 30, for 2007 is entitled "professional fundraising fees" and Part IX, line 11, for 2008, is simply entitled "professional fundraising services." Since this line refers to a line for reporting only "fees," it would be logical to assume that no other expenses associated with fundraising efforts be reported. The instructions for Part IX indicate that if such expenses (other than fees for services) can be isolated, they should be reported separately on the lines to which they relate (that is, printing). The filer is prompted in Part IV, Question 17 to complete Part I of Schedule G if line 11e of Part IX exceeds $15,000. Schedule G itself seeks information regarding agreements with individuals in connection with professional fundraising activities and requires details for each individual compensated at least $5,000 for professional fundraising services.

§ 3.3   PART II SIGNATURE BLOCK

Part II	Signature Block

Under penalties of perjury, I declare that I have examined this return, including accompanying schedules and statements, and to the best of my knowledge and belief, it is true, correct, and complete. Declaration of preparer (other than officer) is based on all information of which preparer has any knowledge.

Sign Here

▶ _____ | _____
Signature of officer   Date

▶ _____
Type or print name and title

Paid Preparer's Use Only

Preparer's signature ▶		Date	Check if self-employed ▶ ☐	Preparer's identifying number (see instructions)
Firm's name (or yours if self-employed), address, and ZIP + 4 ▶			EIN ▶	
			Phone no. ▶ ( )	

May the IRS discuss this return with the preparer shown above? (see instructions) . . . .   ☐ Yes   ☐ No

For Privacy Act and Paperwork Reduction Act Notice, see the separate instructions.   Cat. No. 11282Y   Form **990** (2008)

The signature block now appears at the bottom of the first page rather than the last page. A check box that practitioners will welcome was added to authorize the IRS to contact and discuss the return with the preparer that signs the return. The organization is authorizing the paid preparer to:

- Give the IRS any information that is missing from the return
- Call the IRS for information about the processing of the return
- Respond to certain IRS notices about math errors, offsets, and return preparation

The organization is not authorizing the paid preparer to bind the organization to anything or otherwise represent the organization before the IRS. Somewhat illogically, the authorization will automatically end one year from the due date (excluding extensions) for filing the organization's 2008 Form 990. If the organization wants to expand the paid preparer's authorization, or revoke the authorization before it ends, Form 2848 should be filed.

To make a return complete, an officer of the organization authorized to sign it must sign in the space provided. For a corporation or association, this may be the president, vice president, treasurer, assistant treasurer, chief accounting officer, or other corporate or association officer, such as a tax officer. A receiver, trustee or assignee must sign any return he or she, files for a corporation or association. For a trust, the authorized trustee(s) must sign.

One who is paid to prepare the return must sign the return and fill in identifying information requested. The EIN or Social Security Number (or Preparer's Tax Identification Number, ''PTIN'') is only required when return is being filed for a §4947(a)(1) nonexempt charitable trust. A volunteer who prepares the return *gratis,* or on a *pro bono* basis, should also sign as return preparer. An employee of the filing organization is not a paid preparer. A copy of the return must be provided by the preparer to the organization.

§ 3.4   PART III STATEMENT OF PROGRAM
SERVICE ACCOMPLISHMENTS

Form 990 (2008)   Page **2**

Part III	Statement of Program Service Accomplishments (see instructions)

This Statement of Program Service Accomplishments is perhaps the most important part of the return because the organization provides information that paints (or doesn't) a picture of its worth to its supporters and exempt constituents. Disclosure of expenses and, new for 2008, revenue by program service continues to be required only for §501(c)(3) and (4) organizations and §4947(a)(1) trusts.

1	Briefly describe the organization's mission:	

2	Did the organization undertake any significant program services during the year which were not listed on the prior Form 990 or 990-EZ? . . . . If "Yes," describe these new services on Schedule O.	☐ **Yes** ☐ **No**
3	Did the organization cease conducting, or make significant changes in how it conducts, any program services? . . . . If "Yes," describe these changes on Schedule O.	☐ **Yes** ☐ **No**

This part follows the format of the existing Part III with the addition of questions pertaining to any changes in mission or activities. The space to input the mission description is the same space allotted on line 1 on the front page. The instructions suggest some may wish to feature a significant activity or accomplishment of the year on the front page and present the mission in this part appearing on the second page. When the organization runs out of space on the one page provided, the instructions suggest use of Schedule O if more space is needed.

Similar to the governance questions in Part VI, the instructions to this part appear designed to influence organizational behavior. The mission "as articulated in its mission statement or as otherwise adopted by the organization's governing body" is to be described in this part. The mission should address why the charity exists, what it hopes to accomplish, and what activities it will undertake, where, and for whom.[1] "If the organization does not have a mission that has been adopted by its governing body, state None." Undoubtedly no filer will want to put "None" in this part. On a positive note, it is appreciated that the space for describing the mission was expanded six-fold. When possible, organizations should craft descriptions that fit entirely on the page without the need for additional reporting in Schedule O to enhance the flow for the reader.

Lines 2 and 3. Questions asking if there are (or are not) new, expanded, discontinued, or changed program services and activities have logically been moved to this part. Two check boxes ask the filer to say whether:

- Significant program services were undertaken during the year that were not listed on the prior Form 990 or 990-EZ

- The organization ceased to conduct, or made significant changes in how it conducts, any program services

A "Yes" answer requires that the changes be described in Schedule O. Based on past lack of response to such information submitted on a return, it is reasonable to assume the IRS will not acknowledge the information with an actual statement that the activity has no negative impact on the organization's exempt status. A response will be provided, however, if the description is sent to the Cincinnati Service Center. The fact that the changes were disclosed and available for IRS evaluation may, however, protect against any retroactive impact of the conduct if the organization is challenged regarding the exempt nature of the activity. These questions should remind the preparer why it is important to consider the reasons the organization was originally found to qualify for tax-exemption.[2]

---

4 Describe the exempt purpose achievements for each of the organization's three largest program services by expenses. Section 501(c)(3) and 501(c)(4) organizations and section 4947(a)(1) trusts are required to report the amount of grants and allocations to others, the total expenses, and revenue, if any, for each program service reported.

4a (Code: _____) (Expenses $ _____ including grants of $_____) (Revenue $_____)

4b (Code: _____) (Expenses $ _____ including grants of $_____) (Revenue $_____)

4c (Code: _____) (Expenses $ _____ including grants of $_____) (Revenue $_____)

4d Other program services. (Describe in Schedule O.)
(Expenses $ _____ including grants of $_____) (Revenue $ _____)

4e **Total program service expenses ▶ $** _____ *(Must equal Part IX, Line 25, column (B).)*

Form **990** (2008)

Lines 4a-4e are similar to the pre-2008 990s in most respects. Three differences exist:

Revenue: Importantly for those that may not be prepared, there is a new space to disclose the revenue derived directly from the activity, including fees for services and sale of goods or materials. Such revenue is called program service revenue and is reported in Part VIII, in column (B). Though these amounts will most often appear on line 2, amounts on lines 3–11 of Part VIII that are related to a program would also be reported. Unrelated business income generated by a program must also be reported, such as advertising in a journal. Contributions and gifts are not included even if they are received to fund a specific program.

Code: Another new item for this part is the blank entitled "Code." Input of a code is not required for 2008. The IRS is uncertain, and is studying, whether the NTEE (National Taxonomy of Exempt Entities) codes developed by the National Center for Charitable Statistics will be used. The Background Paper to the changes in the instructions from the April draft also say, "Contrary to the intent expressed in the Highlights document released on April 7, 2008 with the draft instructions, the instructions do not contain specific indicators of program service accomplishments for particular sub-sectors such as nursing homes, hospitals, colleges and universities, social clubs, and trade associations. The IRS expects to continue to work with the sector to develop these lists for various sub-sectors, and to develop activity codes for use in 2009 or later tax years."

No Foreign Check box: Lastly, the check box to indicate that foreign grant amounts were included has been removed. Details about foreign activity are now separately presented in Schedule F.

Part III continues to provide (with more space than 2007) an opportunity for the organization to describe its program services. The organization is encouraged to include accomplishments with specific measurements, such as clients served, days of care provided, number of sessions or events held, or publications issued. For research, or other intangible activity, the objective, for both this time period and the longer-term goal, should be described. Reasonable estimates for any statistical information may be provided if exact figures are not readily available.

Donated services and use of materials, equipment, or facilities quantified and reported for financial statement purposes, but not permitted to be included in the financial information in Parts VIII and IX for tax purposes, can be disclosed in this part in the narrative description. For organizations that have volunteers performing significant services, such as a pro bono legal clinic or income tax preparation or physician services for the poor, the omission of the value of such services can significantly understate the financial accomplishments of an organization.

§3.5 PART IV CHECKLIST OF REQUIRED SCHEDULES

Form 990 (2008)   Page **3**

Part IV	**Checklist of Required Schedules**

This Checklist of Required Schedules has 37 questions with thresholds that prompt the completion of 16 different schedules. The questions flow in the alphabetical order of the schedules. Some questions have dollar thresholds that must be met for completion of certain schedules to be required.[3] An inexperienced preparer unfamiliar with exempt organization tax matters will certainly find this part challenging. The instructions that say, "See Glossary and instructions for pertinent schedules for definition of terms and explanations that are relevant to questions in this part," will ring very true as one tries to correctly answer the questions. The following chart provides a guide to the new schedules, the matters reported, the thresholds, and importantly the period covered by the response.

(a) Part IV Chart of Amount/Time Sensitive Answers

Question	Schedule	Title	Threshold	At Any Time During Year	At Year-End
1	A	Public charity status	n/a		X
2	B	Contributions received	$5,000 or 2%	X	
3	C	Political campaign activity	Any amount	X	
4	C	Lobbying activity	Any amount	X	
5	C	Lobby disclosure/proxy tax	Any amount	X	
6	D	Donor-advised fund	Any amount	X	
7	D	Conservation easements	Any amount	X	
8	D	Art & collectibles	Any amount	X	
9	D	Credit counseling/escrows	Any amount	X	
10	D	Endowment funds	Any amount	X	
11	D	Investments/other assets	Any amount*		X
12	D	Audited statements	n/a**		X
13	E	School	n/a	X	
14b	F	Foreign revenue/expense	$10,000	X	
15	F	Foreign grants-organizations	$5,000	X	
16	F	Foreign grants-individuals	$5,000	X	
17	G	Prof. fundraising fees	$15,000	X	
18	G	Fundraising revenue/events	$15,000	X	
19	G	Gaming revenue	$15,000	X	
20	H	Operate hospital	n/a	X	
21	I	Grants to U.S. organizations	$5,000	X	
22	I	Grants to U.S. individuals	$5,000	X	
23	J	Comp-former officials	Any amount	X	
		Officials/highly paid	$150,000	X	
24	K	Tax-Exempt bonds	$100,000		X
25	L	Excess benefit transactions	Any amount	X	
26	L	Loans to officials	Any amount	X	
27	L	Grant to related party	Any amount	X	
28	L	Business relationships	n/a	X	
29	M	Noncash contributions	$25,000	X	
30	M	Gifts of art/collectibles	Any amount	X	
31	N	Liquidate or terminate org.	n/a	X	
32	N	Dispose/sell >25% assets	n/a	X	
33	R	Disregarded entity	Owned 100%	X	
34	R	List related entities	n/a	X	
35	R	Controlled business entity	n/a	X	
36	R	Transfers to noncharity	Of any amount	X	
37	R	Unrelated partnerships	> 5% of activities	X	

*For certain lines, only if amount exceeds 5% of assets or liabilities.
**The answer is "No" if the organization's financials were included in a consolidated audit report.

§3.5 PART IV CHECKLIST OF REQUIRED SCHEDULES

			Yes	No
1	Is the organization described in section 501(c)(3) or 4947(a)(1) (other than a private foundation)? *If "Yes," complete Schedule A*	1		
2	Is the organization required to complete Schedule B, Schedule of Contributors?.	2		
3	Did the organization engage in direct or indirect political campaign activities on behalf of or in opposition to candidates for public office? *If "Yes," complete Schedule C, Part I*	3		
4	**Section 501(c)(3) organizations.** Did the organization engage in lobbying activities? *If "Yes," complete Schedule C, Part II*	4		
5	**Section 501(c)(4), 501(c)(5), and 501(c)(6) organizations.** Is the organization subject to the section 6033(e) notice and reporting requirement and proxy tax? *If "Yes," complete Schedule C, Part III*	5		
6	Did the organization maintain any donor advised funds or any accounts where donors have the right to provide advice on the distribution or investment of amounts in such funds or accounts? *If "Yes," complete Schedule D, Part I*	6		
7	Did the organization receive or hold a conservation easement, including easements to preserve open space, the environment, historic land areas, or historic structures? *If "Yes," complete Schedule D, Part II* . . .	7		
8	Did the organization maintain collections of works of art, historical treasures, or other similar assets? *If "Yes," complete Schedule D, Part III*	8		
9	Did the organization report an amount in Part X, line 21; serve as a custodian for amounts not listed in Part X; or provide credit counseling, debt management, credit repair, or debt negotiation services? *If "Yes," complete Schedule D, Part IV*	9		
10	Did the organization hold assets in term, permanent, or quasi-endowments? *If "Yes," complete Schedule D, Part V*	10		
11	Did the organization report an amount in Part X, lines 10, 12, 13, 15, or 25? *If "Yes," complete Schedule D, Parts VI, VII, VIII, IX, or X as applicable*	11		
12	Did the organization receive an audited financial statement for the year for which it is completing this return that was prepared in accordance with GAAP? *If "Yes," complete Schedule D, Parts XI, XII, and XIII* . .	12		
13	Is the organization a school described in section 170(b)(1)(A)(ii)? *If "Yes," complete Schedule E*	13		
14a	Did the organization maintain an office, employees, or agents outside of the U.S.?	14a		
b	Did the organization have aggregate revenues or expenses of more than $10,000 from grantmaking, fundraising, business, and program service activities outside the U.S.? *If "Yes," complete Schedule F, Part I*	14b		
15	Did the organization report on Part IX, column (A), line 3, more than $5,000 of grants or assistance to any organization or entity located outside the United States? *If "Yes," complete Schedule F, Part II*. . . .	15		
16	Did the organization report on Part IX, column (A), line 3, more than $5,000 of aggregate grants or assistance to individuals located outside the United States? *If "Yes," complete Schedule F, Part III*	16		
17	Did the organization report more than $15,000 on Part IX, column (A), line 11e? *If "Yes," complete Schedule G, Part I*	17		
18	Did the organization report more than $15,000 total on Part VIII, lines 1c and 8a? *If "Yes," complete Schedule G, Part II*	18		
19	Did the organization report more than $15,000 on Part VIII, line 9a? *If "Yes," complete Schedule G, Part III*	19		
20	Did the organization operate one or more hospitals? *If "Yes," complete Schedule H*	20		
21	Did the organization report more than $5,000 on Part IX, column (A), line 1? *If "Yes," complete Schedule I, Parts I and II*	21		
22	Did the organization report more than $5,000 on Part IX, column (A), line 2? *If "Yes," complete Schedule I, Parts I and III*	22		
23	Did the organization answer "Yes" to Part VII, Section A, questions 3, 4, or 5? *If "Yes," complete Schedule J*	23		
24a	Did the organization have a tax-exempt bond issue with an outstanding principal amount of more than $100,000 as of the last day of the year, that was issued after December 31, 2002? *If "Yes," answer questions 24b–24d and complete Schedule K. If "No," go to question 25.*	24a		
b	Did the organization invest any proceeds of tax-exempt bonds beyond a temporary period exception? . .	24b		
c	Did the organization maintain an escrow account other than a refunding escrow at any time during the year to defease any tax-exempt bonds?	24c		
d	Did the organization act as an "on behalf of" issuer for bonds outstanding at any time during the year?	24d		
25a	**Section 501(c)(3) and 501(c)(4) organizations.** Did the organization engage in an excess benefit transaction with a disqualified person during the year? *If "Yes," complete Schedule L, Part I*	25a		
b	Did the organization become aware that it had engaged in an excess benefit transaction with a disqualified person from a prior year? *If "Yes," complete Schedule L, Part I*	25b		
26	Was a loan to or by a current or former officer, director, trustee, key employee, highly compensated employee, or disqualified person outstanding as of the end of the organization's tax year? *If "Yes," complete Schedule L, Part II*	26		
27	Did the organization provide a grant or other assistance to an officer, director, trustee, key employee, or substantial contributor, or to a person related to such an individual? *If "Yes," complete Schedule L, Part III*	27		
28	During the tax year, did any person who is a current or former officer, director, trustee, or key employee:			
a	Have a direct business relationship with the organization (other than as an officer, director, trustee, or employee), or an indirect business relationship through ownership of more than 35% in another entity (individually or collectively with other person(s) listed in Part VII, Section A)? *If "Yes," complete Schedule L, Part IV*	28a		
b	Have a family member who had a direct or indirect business relationship with the organization? *If "Yes," complete Schedule L, Part IV*	28b		
c	Serve as an officer, director, trustee, key employee, partner, or member of an entity (or a shareholder of a professional corporation) doing business with the organization? *If "Yes," complete Schedule L, Part IV* . .	28c		
29	Did the organization receive more than $25,000 in non-cash contributions? *If "Yes," complete Schedule M*	29		

Form **990** (2008)

(Continued)

■ 55 ■

Form 990 (2008) Page **4**

Part IV   **Checklist of Required Schedules** *(continued)*

			Yes	No
30	Did the organization receive contributions of art, historical treasures, or other similar assets, or qualified conservation contributions? *If "Yes," complete Schedule M*	**30**		
31	Did the organization liquidate, terminate, or dissolve and cease operations? *If "Yes," complete Schedule N, Part I*	**31**		
32	Did the organization sell, exchange, dispose of, or transfer more than 25% of its net assets? *If "Yes," complete Schedule N, Part II*	**32**		
33	Did the organization own 100% of an entity disregarded as separate from the organization under Regulations sections 301.7701-2 and 301.7701-3? *If "Yes," complete Schedule R, Part I*	**33**		
34	Was the organization related to any tax-exempt or taxable entity? *If "Yes," complete Schedule R, Parts II, III, IV, and V, line 1*	**34**		
35	Is any related organization a controlled entity within the meaning of section 512(b)(13)? *If "Yes," complete Schedule R, Part V, line 2*	**35**		
36	**Section 501(c)(3) organizations.** Did the organization make any transfers to an exempt non-charitable related organization? *If "Yes," complete Schedule R, Part V, line 2*	**36**		
37	Did the organization conduct more than 5% of its activities through an entity that is not a related organization and that is treated as a partnership for federal income tax purposes? *If "Yes," complete Schedule R, Part VI*	**37**		

Form **990** (2008)

§3.6   PART V STATEMENTS REGARDING OTHER IRS FILINGS AND TAX COMPLIANCE

Form 990 (2008) Page **5**

Part V   Statements Regarding Other IRS Filings and Tax Compliance

Part V, "Statements Regarding Other IRS Filings and Tax Compliance," seeks to determine whether the organization is in compliance with various tax rules and whether it has filed other forms that may be required. These questions serve several purposes, first as an instruction or reminder to the organization of other forms it may be required to file, second as a reminder that, though exempt, the organization is subject to the entire Internal Revenue Code, and lastly, as an evaluation of whether the organization is in compliance with those requirements. The questions have been segregated into two types:

1. Data Questions asking for data about the forms filed (that is, number of forms filed or whether the form was filed).

2. Compliance Questions asking whether the organization violated a tax rule.

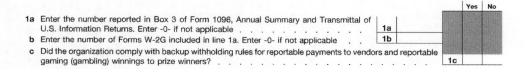

Q. 1a: Form 1096 is used as a cover sheet to transmit Forms W-2G, 1098, 1099, and 5498. The most common forms filed by exempt organizations are W-2G (to report gambling winnings such as raffle prizes at special events) and 1099-MISC (to report payments to independent contractors for personal services). A separate Form 1096 is used for each type of information return so the organization will need to add up the amounts reported in Box 3 of all Forms 1096 it filed.

Q. 1b: Form W-2G differs from other information returns in that it requires the signature of the recipient of the winnings. Therefore, it is prudent to have the forms prepared before awarding the prize so that receiving the prize is contingent upon signing the form. It may be difficult to track down someone to get a signature months after the prize was awarded.

Q 1c: For prize winnings valued at more than $5,000, organizations are required to withhold 25 percent of the prize (if it is cash) or ask the winner to furnish 25 percent of the value of the prize (if it is noncash) as tax withholding and deposit it with the IRS. Alternatively, the organization can pay the tax on behalf of the winner (at 33 percent of the prize) but the amount paid is added to the value of the prize to total the reportable income for the winner. If the winner does not provide a tax identification number, then the withholding rate increases from 25 percent to 28 percent.

Similarly, organizations making payments to independent contractors that do not obtain a signed Form W-9 (Request for TIN and Certification) are required to withhold tax at 28 percent on such payments except in special circumstances.

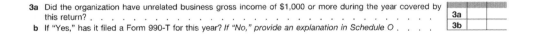

Q 2a: Form W-3 is used as a cover sheet to transmit Forms W-2 which report employee compensation for the calendar year.

Q 2b: Other filings include Form 941 (filed quarterly to report employee earnings and payroll taxes) and Form 940 (filed annually to report Federal Unemployment Tax paid on employee earnings). §501(c)(3) organizations are exempt from FUTA, but other exempt organizations are subject to FUTA.

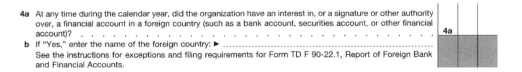

Q 3a: The answer to this question should be coordinated with the amount of unrelated income reported on Core Part I, line 7 and Core Part VIII, Line 12, Column (C).

Q 3b: Form 990-T is filed to report unrelated business income and deductions and to calculate income tax due.

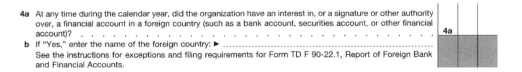

Q 4a: Here, the IRS instructs the preparer to look at the filing requirements for Form TD F 90–22.1, but does not ask whether the organization filed the form. The TD

F 90–22.1 states the form must be filed by "each United States person, who has a financial interest in or signature authority, or other authority over any financial accounts, including bank, securities, or other types of financial accounts in a foreign country, if the aggregate value of these financial accounts exceeds $10,000 at any time during the calendar year." The form is due on June 30 and is filed separately from the organization's Form 990.

Q 4b: The name of each foreign country in which a foreign account is located is listed.

5a Was the organization a party to a prohibited tax shelter transaction at any time during the tax year? . .	**5a**	
b Did any taxable party notify the organization that it was or is a party to a prohibited tax shelter transaction?	**5b**	
c If "Yes," to question 5a or 5b, did the organization file Form 8886-T, Disclosure by Tax-Exempt Entity Regarding Prohibited Tax Shelter Transaction?	**5c**	

Q 5a: The instructions provide the following clarification: "a prohibited tax shelter transaction is any listed transaction,[4] within the meaning of §6707A(c)(2), and any prohibited reportable transaction. A prohibited reportable transaction is a confidential transaction within the meaning of Regulations §1.6011–4(b)(3), and a transaction with contractual protection within the meaning of Regulations §1.6011–4(b)(4)." Exempt organizations are most likely to encounter the potential for being a party to a prohibited tax shelter transaction through alternative investments, such as partnerships or hedge funds.

Q 5b: Typically, the method by which a partnership would notify an organization with an interest in it that it was or is a party to a prohibited tax shelter transaction is through the annual Form K-1 supplied to report tax information.

Q 5c: Form 8886-T is a new form issued in 2007 for use by an exempt organization to report information about any prohibited tax shelter to which it was a party during the year. Some organizations may also need to file Form 8886.

6a Did the organization solicit any contributions that were not tax deductible?	**6a**	
b If "Yes," did the organization include with every solicitation an express statement that such contributions or gifts were not tax deductible?.	**6b**	

Q 6a: §501(c)(3) organizations that "test for public safety" and are classified as a public charity under §509(a)(4) and organizations exempt under other categories of §501(c) or §527 are not eligible to receive tax-deductible contributions. Dues and similar payments to such organizations may be eligible for deduction as business expenses to the extent the funds were not used for lobbying purposes.

Q 6b: §6113 requires the organizations mentioned above to include "an express statement (in a conspicuous and easily recognizable format) that contributions to the organization are not deductible for federal income tax purposes as charitable contributions." This requirement does not apply to organizations whose gross receipts do not normally exceed $100,000.[5] The instructions indicate that such organizations that are exempt from this requirement should answer "No" to question 6a.

7	Organizations that may receive deductible contributions under section 170(c).		
a	Did the organization provide goods or services in exchange for any quid pro quo contribution of more than $75?	7a	
b	If "Yes," did the organization notify the donor of the value of the goods or services provided?	7b	
c	Did the organization sell, exchange, or otherwise dispose of tangible personal property for which it was required to file Form 8282?	7c	
d	If "Yes," indicate the number of Forms 8282 filed during the year . . . . `7d`		
e	Did the organization, during the year, receive any funds, directly or indirectly, to pay premiums on a personal benefit contract?	7e	
f	Did the organization, during the year, pay premiums, directly or indirectly, on a personal benefit contract? .	7f	
g	For all contributions of qualified intellectual property, did the organization file Form 8899 as required? .	7g	
h	For contributions of cars, boats, airplanes, and other vehicles, did the organization file a Form 1098-C as required?.	7h	

Q7a: This type of transaction is generally referred to as a *"quid pro quo* contribution." Such a transaction is a payment partly for goods and services and partly intended to be a contribution. The typical example is a gala event ticket. A transaction in which goods or services are furnished to the contributor in exchange for their payment is presumed not to be a gift—to lack donative intent. To overcome the presumption, the donor must prove that he or she intended the payment to charity to exceed the value of benefits received. The burden of making such valuations has shifted to the charity where +$75 is paid. Intangible benefits—having one's name placed on a building or donor listing—are treated as having incidental or tenuous benefit and are not valued. "Intangible religious benefits not generally sold in a commercial transaction outside of the donative context" are also not valued and such payments are treated as gifts.

Q. 7b: If a charitable organization receives a *quid pro quo* contribution, the organization shall, "in connection with the solicitation or receipt" of the contribution do the following:

- "Inform the donor that the amount of the contribution that is deductible for Federal income tax purposes is limited to the excess of the amount of any money and the value of any property other than money contributed by the donor over the value of the goods or services provided by the organization, and

- Provide donor with a good faith estimate of the value of such goods or services."

An organization failing to meet the disclosure requirement with respect to a *quid pro quo* contribution is penalized $10 for each contribution in respect of which the organization fails to make the required disclosure. The total penalty for a particular fundraising event or mailing can be no more than $5,000. If the charity can prove to the IRS that the failure is due to reasonable causes, such as "our CPA misinformed us," the penalty may be abated. It is not reasonable to expect the IRS to be lenient in cases of intentional disregard of the rules.

Many organizations find the most difficult part of meeting the requirement is calculating the fair market value of the goods/services provided. Technically the IRS says, "the fair market value (FMV) is that amount a willing buyer under no extraordinary compulsion to buy would pay a willing seller also not required to sell in the normal market place for the property being valued." The unique nature of most charitable fundraising events means the benefits often have no commercial counterpart. The cost of rendering a service or providing a benefit to members and/or attendees is not the prescribed measure of value. The cost, however, may be determinative absent a comparable market. The concept can be illustrated with examples. The object or service to be valued is shown below on the left with suggested valuation method on the right.

BENEFIT	VALUE ASSIGNED
Objects or services sold normally in stores and by service providers.	Price at which good or services normally sell.
Discounts on purchases.	Amount of discount given.
Benefit dinner dance in the nonprofit's facility.	Cost of event, including donated goods and services.
Benefit golf tournament.	Normal cost of playing golf on course.
Chance to play with pro.	Price of the chance.
Raffle or door prize ticket.	Price paid for ticket.
Participation in educational tour.	Price of similar commercial tour.
Attendance at performance or movie or admission to facility.	Normal ticket or admission price.
Posters, buttons, bumper sticks, books, and publications.	Comparable market price unless *de minimis* rules apply.
Goods/services purchased at auction.	Normal commercial price.
Name printed in program or on a building.	None.
Noncommercial quality publication.	None.

Q 7c: Presumably the IRS wants this information to compare with noncash contribution details reported in Schedule M and, possibly, the Forms 8283 filed with income tax returns of donors of noncash gifts. This form reports the proceeds of sale of noncash donated items if sold within three years of the date of the gift.

Q 7d: The number of Forms 8282 filed during the year is entered.

Q 7e: A personal benefit contract is defined as "any life insurance, annuity, or endowment contract if any direct or indirect beneficiary under such contract is the transferor, any member of the transferor's family, or any other person (other than an organization described in subsection (c)) designated by the transferor."[6] The import of this question is that a contribution deduction is denied for a payment made by an individual to an organization to pay a premium on his (or his family member's) life insurance contract (or similar).

Q 7f: If an organization makes such a payment, it must pay a penalty in the form of an excise tax on the amount of the payment. In this case, the excise tax is 100 percent of the premium payment.

Q 7g: Form 8899 reports income earned during the year from donated intellectual property held by a charitable organization. The information is used to enable the donor of the intellectual property to take charitable contribution deductions as the property earns income in the hands of the donee organization.

Q 7h: Form 1098-C reports information about cars, boats, and so on donated to a charitable organization that informs the IRS (and the donor) whether the donor of the property is enabled to take a deduction equal to the FMV of the property donated (if the organization uses the property in carrying out its exempt purposes) or equal to the sales proceeds of the property (if the organization does not use the property and sells it instead).

For §501(c)(3) and Other Sponsoring Organizations Maintaining Donor Advised Funds and §509(a)(3) Supporting Organizations Only.

8 **Section 501(c)(3) and other sponsoring organizations maintaining donor advised funds and section 509(a)(3) supporting organizations.** Did the supporting organization, or a fund maintained by a sponsoring organization, have excess business holdings at any time during the year?	**8**

Q 8: One of the methods by which the Congress, Treasury Department and IRS is leveling the playing field between supporting organizations ("SOs"), donor-advised funds ("DAFs"), and private foundations ("PFs") is by making certain SOs and all DAFs subject to the excess business holdings rules[7] that PFs have been subject to since 1970. The only types of SOs that are currently subject to the excess business holdings limitation are (1) Type I, II, or III—Functionally Integrated organizations if they accept a donation from a person that controls the supported organization[8] and (2) Type III, Non-Functionally Integrated organizations.

Excess business holdings are defined as "with respect to the holdings of any private foundation (now also certain SOs or DAFs) in any business enterprise, the amount of stock or other interest in the enterprise which the foundation would have to dispose of to a person other than a disqualified person in order for the remaining holdings of the foundation in such enterprise to be permitted holdings."[9] Generally, permitted holdings are 20 percent reduced by the percentage owned by disqualified persons; 35 percent can be substituted for the 20 percent if an unrelated third party controls the enterprise. However, if the organization owns less than 2 percent of the enterprise, it will not be considered to have excess business holdings regardless of the amount owned by disqualified persons.

Disqualified persons for DAFs include:[10]

- Donor advisor(s)
- Family members of the above individuals
- An entity owned at least 35 percent by individuals mentioned above

Disqualified persons for SOs include:[11]

- Any person "in a position to exercise substantial influence over the affairs of the organization"
- Substantial contributor (one whose cumulative donations exceed 2 percent of the organization's cumulative donations)
- Family members of the above individuals
- An entity owned at least 35 percent by individuals mentioned above
- Any organization "which is effectively controlled (directly or indirectly) by the same person or persons who control the organization in question"
- Any organization substantially all of the contributions to which were made by substantial contributors, officers, directors, or trustees of the organization, or an

individual having similar powers or responsibilities, or an owner of more than 20 percent of an entity that is a substantial contributor to the organization.

Business holdings do not include:

- Functionally related businesses[12]
- A business that earns 95 percent or more of its income from passive sources[13]

An organization deemed to have excess business holdings must file Form 4720 to report such holdings and is subject to a 10 percent excise tax on the highest value of the holdings during the year. In order to remedy the situation, the organization must dispose of the holdings to unrelated parties.[14]

For §501(c)(3) and Other Sponsoring Organizations Maintaining Donor Advised Funds Only.

9 Section 501(c)(3) and other sponsoring organizations maintaining donor advised funds.		
a Did the organization make any taxable distributions under section 4966?	9a	
b Did the organization make a distribution to a donor, donor advisor, or related person?.	9b	

Q 9a: The term "taxable distribution" means: (1) any distribution to an individual, (2) any distribution to an organization if it is for any purpose other than "religious, charitable, scientific, literary, or educational purposes, or to foster national or international amateur sports competition (but only if no part of its activities involve the provision of athletic facilities or equipment), or for the prevention of cruelty to children or animals,"[15] and (3) any distribution for which the sponsoring organization was required to, but did not, exercise expenditure responsibility ("ER") with respect to such distribution in accordance with §4945(h). The organization would be required to exercise ER for a gift to an organization other than the ones mentioned below:[16]

- An organization described in §170(b)(1)(A) (other than a disqualified supporting organization),[17]
- The sponsoring organization of such donor advised fund, or
- Any other donor advised fund.

Q 9b: New IRC §4967 imposes a 125 percent penalty on any of the above individuals who advise the organization to make a distribution that results in "more than incidental benefit" to any of the above individuals. But, what is an incidental benefit? The legislative history states that a benefit is more than incidental if the fact that the donor receives it "would have reduced (or eliminated) a charitable contribution deduction if the benefit was received as part of the contribution to the sponsoring organization." As an example, the committee reports states that a grant from a DAF to the Girl Scouts of America will not result in impermissible benefit to the donor advisor merely because the person's daughter is a Girl Scout. It may be difficult to determine where the line between an incidental benefit and a prohibited benefit lies.

Token Gifts: Under the token exception rules for contributions to charities, insubstantial goods or services received do not reduce the amount of the donor's deduction. Goods or services are insubstantial if the payment occurs in the context of a fundraising campaign and:[18]

- The fair market value of the benefit does not exceed 2 percent of the payment or $95* (whichever is lower), or

- The payment is at least $47.50* and the only items provided bear the organization's name or logo (e.g. calendars, mugs, posters) and the cost of these items is within the limit for "low cost articles"—currently $9.50.*

Fundraising Events: It is unclear whether having a DAF make a payment equal to the deductible portion of a sponsorship and the donor pay the noncharitable portion individually results in a prohibited benefit. In interpreting the self-dealing rules for private foundations (which also prohibit all but incidental benefits), the IRS has stated that splitting payments (or bifurcation) is not permitted. Therefore, it seems inadvisable to make such distributions from a DAF without further IRS guidance.

Personal Pledges: Under existing law, the IRS has taken the position that using DAF funds to satisfy legally binding personal pledges of an individual results in an impermissible benefit to that individual.

For §501(c)(7) Organizations Only

10	Section 501(c)(7) organizations. Enter:		
a	Initiation fees and capital contributions included on Part VIII, line 12	10a	
b	Gross receipts, included on Form 990, Part VIII, line 12, for public use of club facilities	10b	

Q 10a: Enter initiation fees and capital contributions included on Part VIII, line 12.

Q 10b: The purpose of the above two questions is to determine whether the organization meets the IRS requirement for a social club to maintain its exempt status that no more than 35 percent of its gross receipts are derived from nonmembers. (This includes investment income.) As part of the 35 percent permitted amount, no more than 15 percent of its gross receipts may be derived from the use of the club's facilities or services by the general public or from other activities not furthering social or recreational purposes for members. Additionally, all nonmember income is considered to be unrelated business income and subject to tax. In making the percentage calculations, initiation fees and capital contributions are excluded from gross receipts.

For §501(c)(12) Organizations Only

11	Section 501(c)(12) organizations. Enter:		
a	Gross income from members or shareholders	11a	
b	Gross income from other sources (Do not net amounts due or paid to other sources against amounts due or received from them.)	11b	

Q 11a: Enter gross income from members or shareholders.

Q 11b: IRC §501(c)(12) organizations include "benevolent life insurance associations of a purely local character, mutual ditch or irrigation companies, mutual or cooperative telephone companies, or like organizations." At least 85 percent of its gross income must consist of amounts collected from members for the purpose of meeting losses and expenses. Again, we have a comparison to determine whether the requirements are met. The instructions provide details regarding which types of income are excluded from this test.

---

*These figures are adjusted annually for inflation.

> 12a **Section 4947(a)(1) non-exempt charitable trusts.** Is the organization filing Form 990 in lieu of Form 1041? | 12a | |
>   b If "Yes," enter the amount of tax-exempt interest received or accrued during the year. | 12b | |
>
> Form **990** (2008)

Q 12a: Generally, nonexempt charitable trusts must file Form 1041 and Form 990 (if they qualify as public charities) or Form 990-PF (if they are treated as private foundations). However, if they do not have taxable income for the year, they are not required to file Form 1041.

Q 12b: Enter the amount of tax-exempt interest earned during the year.

§3.7 PART VI GOVERNANCE, MANAGEMENT, AND DISCLOSURE

> Form 990 (2008)   Page **6**
>
> **Part VI**   **Governance, Management, and Disclosure** *(Sections A, B, and C request information about policies not required by the Internal Revenue Code.)*

(a) Background

Those that were unaware of the new questions asked in this part until after their year ended as they began to prepare this return may not be able to answer "Yes" to certain questions that they expect the IRS would like the answer to be "Yes." Those that like to plan ahead will be relieved to know the answer can be "Yes" if the organization had the policy in place as of the last day of the organization's tax year.

Part VI of the revised Form 990 asks 20 nonfinancial questions related to the organization's governing body, management, policies, and return disclosure. The extent of the IRS's interest in this information is evidenced by the fact, announced in italics at the top of the page, that the majority of the lines ask for submission of explanations on Schedule O. Only lines 1b, 9a, 13, 14, 17, and 20 request no explanation. Return filers and their accountants will undoubtedly need additional time to compose the responses. Organizational officials who may not have been involved in IRS reporting in the past will certainly need to evaluate policies and procedures and consider changes that may be indicated from the answers their organization must provide in this part. One can imagine that Schedule O may be the first part of the return a reader goes to in reviewing Form 990 in the future.

Six of the questions have appeared in previous versions of the 990, but the rest are new. In studying the questions, it becomes apparent that the preferred answer for some is "Yes" and for others "No." It is easy to imagine designing an audit program to choose candidates for examination based on the answers. Although the IRS admits that the tax law does not require the policies and procedures it asks about in the new form, the instructions say, "every organization is required to answer each (and every) question in Part VI." For example, all organizations must answer line 10, which asks about the organization's process, if any, it uses to review the Form 990, even though the governing body is not required by federal tax law to review the Form 990."

This part has been widely criticized since the draft was released because the information requested goes beyond what is required by the tax code and regulations setting forth standards for maintaining tax-exempt status as noted in the parenthetical phrase at the top of the page. The IRS designed this part to meet the mandate from Congress and others that information reporting foster "transparency" for tax-exempt organizations. The instructions say, "The IRS considers such policies and procedures to generally improve tax compliance." They also say, "Whether a particular policy, procedure, or practice should be adopted by an organization may depend on the organization's size, type, and culture."

The concern about governance of tax-exempt organizations actually began in 2002, with news of extravagant expenditures of the chief executive of the United Ways of America. The Sarbanes-Oxley Act was enacted later that year. The *Boston Globe* investigative reporters uncovered multiple examples of the use of funds for personal reasons in 2003.

The IRS added its first governance queries, contained in Question 75, to the 2005 Form 990. In February 2007, a discussion draft proposing policies and procedures the IRS recommended organizations should adopt, entitled *Good Governance Practices for 501(c)(3) Organizations,* was issued.[19] The practices the IRS recommends organizations follow to achieve appropriate oversight of activities are now embodied in Part VI. Information about governance provided in the Life Cycle of a Public Charity presented on the IRS website mirrors the questions in Part VI with one exception—it also recommends that charities "adopt and monitor policies to ensure that fundraising solicitations meet federal and state law requirements and solicitation materials are accurate, truthful, and candid."

Most would agree that it is appropriate for a nonprofit organization—the very essence of which is to operate to benefit its constituents rather than those that control it—to have a conflict-of-interest policy. But the form implies that such a policy, plus other governance practices, is required. Though the IRS instructions reassure filers that "No" answers will not necessarily lead to examinations, some worry. It is important that each nonprofit required to file the new 990 study this part to consider its existing policies in view of those the IRS considers necessary for governing a tax-exempt organization.

Section A. Governing Body and Management

		Yes	No
	For each "Yes" response to lines 2–7b below, and for a "No" response to lines 8 or 9b below, describe the circumstances, processes, or changes in Schedule O. See instructions.		
1a	Enter the number of voting members of the governing body **1a**		
b	Enter the number of voting members that are independent **1b**		
2	Did any officer, director, trustee, or key employee have a family relationship or a business relationship with any other officer, director, trustee, or key employee? **2**		
3	Did the organization delegate control over management duties customarily performed by or under the direct supervision of officers, directors or trustees, or key employees to a management company or other person? . **3**		
4	Did the organization make any significant changes to its organizational documents since the prior Form 990 was filed? **4**		
5	Did the organization become aware during the year of a material diversion of the organization's assets? **5**		
6	Does the organization have members or stockholders? **6**		
7a	Does the organization have members, stockholders, or other persons who may elect one or more members of the governing body? **7a**		
b	Are any decisions of the governing body subject to approval by members, stockholders, or other persons? . . **7b**		
8	Did the organization contemporaneously document the meetings held or written actions undertaken during the year by the following:		
a	The governing body? **8a**		
b	Each committee with authority to act on behalf of the governing body? **8b**		
9a	Does the organization have local chapters, branches, or affiliates? **9a**		
b	If "Yes," does the organization have written policies and procedures governing the activities of such chapters, affiliates, and branches to ensure their operations are consistent with those of the organization? **9b**		
10	Was a copy of the Form 990 provided to the organization's governing body before it was filed? All organizations must describe in Schedule O the process, if any, the organization uses to review the Form 990 . . . . **10**		
11	Is there any officer, director or trustee, or key employee listed in Part VII, Section A, who cannot be reached at the organization's mailing address? *If "Yes," provide the names and addresses in Schedule O* **11**		

Line 1 displays both the total number of members of the governing body that, at year-end, are entitled to vote and the number of that group that are independent. The numbers on this line should agree with the Core Part I, lines 3 and 4 numbers. A voting member possesses the power to vote on all matters that may come before the governing body (other than when a conflict of interest disqualifies the member from voting).

Independent Board Members

A member of the governing body is considered "independent" only if all three of the following circumstances applied at all times during the organization's tax year:

1. Member was not compensated as an officer or other employee of the organization or of a related organization (see Schedule R instructions), except as provided in the religious exception discussed below.

2. Member did not receive total compensation or other payments exceeding $10,000 during the organization's tax year from the organization or from related organizations as an independent contractor, other than reimbursement of expenses under an accountable plan or reasonable compensation for services provided in the capacity as a member of the governing body. For example, a person who receives reasonable expense reimbursements and reasonable compensation as a director of the organization does not cease to be independent merely because he or she also receives payments of $7,500 from the organization for other arrangements.

3. Neither the member, nor any family member of the member, was involved in a transaction with the organization (whether directly or indirectly through affiliation with another organization) that is required to be reported in Schedule L for the organization's tax year, or in a transaction with a related organization of a type and amount that would be reportable on Schedule L if required to be filed by the related organization.

Factors *Not* Causing Lack of Independence
A member of the governing body is not considered to lack independence merely because of the following circumstances:

1. Member is a donor to the organization, regardless of the amount of the contribution;

2. Member has taken a bona fide vow of poverty and either (A) receives compensation as an agent of a religious order or a §501(d) religious or apostolic organization, but only under circumstances in which the member does not receive taxable income;[20] or

3. Member receives financial benefits from the organization solely in the capacity of being a member of the charitable or other class served by the organization in the exercise of its exempt function, such as being a member of a §501(c)(6) organization, so long as the financial benefits comply with the organization's terms of membership.

A Schedule O explanation is requested when there are material differences in voting rights among the members of the governing body. An explanation is also requested when authority has been delegated to an executive or similar committee with broad authority to act on behalf of the governing body. The explanation should include the committee composition, whether any of the committee's members are not on the governing body, and the scope of its authority. Limited scope delegation of authority to an audit, investment or compensation committee need not be explained.

▶ Some organizations will lack the information regarding an official's independence and relationships needed to correctly respond to lines 1 and 2. Such an organization "need not engage in more than a reasonable effort to obtain the necessary information to determine the independence of members of the governing body and may rely on information provided by such members. For instance, the organization may rely on information it obtains in response to a questionnaire sent annually to each member of the governing body that includes the name, title, date, and signature of each person reporting information and contains the pertinent instructions and definitions for lines 1b and 2 to determine whether the member is or is not independent." This relationship information can be requested along with the annual conflict-of-interest disclosures recommended on line 12.

Line 2 asks if there were any family or business relationships among the officials at any time during the year. The question presumes, similar to a nonindependent official, that a person's vote is compromised by such relationships. For a "Yes" answer, the names of family members and business-related persons are submitted on Schedule O. Family members[21] include spouse, brothers or sisters (whole or half-blood), spouses of those siblings, ancestors, children, grandchildren, great-grandchildren, and their spouses. Business relationships between two persons include any of the following:

- One person is employed by the other in a sole proprietorship or by an organization with which the other is associated as a trustee, director, officer, key employee, or greater-than-35 percent owner;

- One person is transacting business with the other (other than in the ordinary course of either party's business on the same terms as are generally offered to the public), directly or indirectly, in one or more contracts of sale, lease, license, loan, performance of services, or other transaction involving transfers of cash or property valued in excess of $10,000 in the aggregate during the organization's tax year (indirect transactions are transactions with an organization with which the one person is associated as a trustee, director, officer, key employee, or greater-than-35 percent owner); and

- The two persons are each a director, trustee, officer, or greater than 10 percent owner in the same business or investment entity. Ownership is measured by stock ownership (either voting power or value) of a corporation, profits or capital interest in a partnership or limited liability company, membership interest in a nonprofit organization, or beneficial interest in a trust. Ownership includes indirect ownership (e.g., ownership in an entity that has ownership in the entity in question); there may be ownership through multiple tiers of entities.

See the IRS instructions for examples of family and business relationships.

Line 3 asks if management of the organization has been outsourced to a company or person who performs the duties customarily conducted by or under the direct supervision of officers, directors or trustees, or key employees. Management duties include, but are not limited to, hiring, firing, and supervising personnel, planning or executing budgets or financial operations, or supervising exempt operations or unrelated trades or businesses of the organization. Management duties do not include purely administrative functions such as bookkeeping or payroll processing. Although the form indicates that a "Yes" answer to this question requires a description in Schedule O, the instructions do not indicate precisely what is to be described. Perhaps a description of the duties outsourced will be sufficient.

Line 4 asks whether the organization made any significant changes to its organizing or enabling documents by which it was created or the rules governing its affairs (commonly known as bylaws) since the prior Form 990 was filed or that were not reported on a prior Form 990. Examples of significant changes include changes to:

- Exempt purposes or mission

- Number, composition, qualifications, authority, or duties of the governing body's voting members

- Number, composition, qualifications, authority, or duties of the organization's officers or key employees

- Role of the stockholders or membership in governance

- Distribution of assets upon dissolution

- Provisions to amend the organizing or enabling document or bylaws

- Quorum, voting rights, or voting approval requirements of the governing body members or the organization's stockholders or membership

- Policies or procedures contained within the organizing document or bylaws regarding compensation of officers, directors, trustees, or key employees, conflicts of interest, whistleblowers, or document retention and destruction

- Composition or procedures contained within the organizing document or bylaws of an audit committee

Examples of insignificant changes made to organizing or enabling documents or bylaws that are not required to be reported here include changes to:

- Registered agent with the State

- Required or permitted number or frequency of governing body or member meetings

- Conflict of interest or investment policy not embodied in bylaws

The significant changes are to be described in Schedule O, but a copy of the amendments is not attached to the return. An IRS response that indicates the changes have no impact on the organization's tax-exempt status should not be expected.[22] The point of the question is to simply update the documents originally submitted in seeking recognition of exemption. An exception is provided for documents reflecting a change of name. For corporations, a copy of the amended articles of incorporation along with state approval for the change is attached, and the box in item B on the front page should be checked.

▶ Change in legal structure, such as from a nonprofit corporation to a trust, is treated as creation of a new entity that requires seeking tax-exemption recognition with the filing of Form 1023.

Line 5 asks if the organization became aware during the year of a material diversion of the organization's assets by any person (volunteer, employee, officer, and so on) regardless of his or her relationship to the organization. A diversion of assets includes any unauthorized conversion or use of the organization's assets, including embezzlement or theft. A material diversion exceeds the lesser of $250,000 or 5 percent of the lesser of the entity's gross receipts for the tax year or total assets at the end of the tax year. A Schedule O report that does not name names is requested. The nature of the diversion, amounts or property involved, corrective actions taken to address the matter, and pertinent circumstances surrounding the diversion should be explained.

Line 6 may be troubling for some because a thorough reading of the instructions is required to understand the use of the term ''members.'' The answer is ''No'' if the organization is a trust for federal tax purposes. The answer is ''Yes'' under two situations:

Filing entity is organized as a stock corporation, joint-stock company, partnership,[23] joint venture, or limited liability company or

Filing entity is a nonstock, nonprofit, or not-for-profit corporation or association with members.

Importantly for this purpose, a member is one who under the governing documents or applicable state law has the following rights:

- Members elect the members of the governing body (but not if the persons in the body are the organization's only members) or their delegates;

- Members approve significant decisions of the governing body; or

- Members may receive a share of the organization's profits or excess dues, or a share of the organization's net assets upon the organization's dissolution.

A §501(c)(3) or (4) organization that answers this question ''Yes'' will want to carefully describe in Schedule O the rights of its members to evidence that it is not operating to provide them private benefits or allowing the organization's assets and income to inure to their benefit as is required for maintaining tax exemption.

Line 7 asks first if the members, stockholders, or others may elect one or more members of the governing body and, then, if decisions of the governing body are subject to the approval of those persons. Instructions ask for a Schedule O description of the classes of such persons, decisions requiring their approval, and the nature of their rights if at any time during the year one or more persons had the following rights:

- To approve or ratify decisions of the governing body, such as election or removal of members, or

- To approve of the governing body's decision to dissolve the organization;

- To elect or appoint one or more members of the organization's governing body.

Line 8 encourages the filer to contemporaneously document, by any means permitted by state law, every meeting held or written action undertaken during the year by the governing body, and each committee with authority to act on behalf of the governing body. Documentation may include minutes, strings of e-mails, or similar writings that explain the action taken, when it was taken, and who made the decision. *Contemporaneous* means, according to the IRS, by the later of the next meeting of the governing body or committee, or 60 days after the date of the meeting or written action. A "No" answer requires an explanation of the type of documentation that is maintained in Schedule O.

Line 9 asks if an organization has local chapters, branches, or affiliates, and if so, whether the organization has written policies and procedures governing the activities of these chapters, branches, and affiliates to ensure their operations are consistent with the reporting organization. Such policies and procedures may include required provisions in the chapter's articles of organization or bylaws, a manual provided to chapters, a constitution, or similar documents. If the answer is "No," explain in Schedule O how the organization ensures that the local unit's activities are consistent with its own. The central organization (parent organization) of a group exemption ruling is required to exercise oversight over its subordinate organizations as a condition of the group exemption.[24]

Line 10 asks whether the organization's Form 990 was provided to (not necessarily reviewed by) the organization's governing body before it was filed. The instructions add the stipulation: "provided to each voting member of the governing body whether in paper or electronic form." A Schedule O description of the process, if any, by which any of the organization's officers, directors, trustees, board committee members, or management reviewed the prepared Form 990, whether before or after it was filed with the IRS, including specifics regarding who conducted the review, when they conducted it, and the extent of any such review must be provided. Note that the list of persons to review the return includes "management." The Schedule O description for this line asks who conducted the review, when they conducted it, and the extent of any such review. If no review was or will be conducted, the organization must state: "No review was or will be conducted." In its "Governance and Related Topics—501(c)(3) organizations," the IRS includes in its section on Form 990 reporting: "The Internal Revenue Service encourages the board, either directly, or through a board-authorized committee, to ensure that financial resources are used to further charitable purposes and that the organization's funds are appropriately accounted for by regularly receiving and reviewing up-to-date financial statements and any auditor's letters or finance and audit committee reports."

It is customary in our practice to provide a draft of the Form 990 to the client for approval before the return is signed and finalized. The reviewer has, however, often been the chief financial officer or executive director. This new question recommends the approval come from the board. As a practical matter, some tax returns are filed near to an extended deadline. Preparation of schedules from both the organization's and the accountant's standpoint may need to be accelerated to accommodate this extra level of review.

Line 11 suggests the names and addresses of any officer, director or trustee, or key employee listed in Part VII, Section A, that cannot be reached at the reporting organization's mailing address be listed in Schedule O.

Section B. Policies

			Yes	No
12a	Does the organization have a written conflict of interest policy? *If "No," go to line 13*	12a		
b	Are officers, directors or trustees, and key employees required to disclose annually interests that could give rise to conflicts?	12b		
c	Does the organization regularly and consistently monitor and enforce compliance with the policy? *If "Yes," describe in Schedule O how this is done*	12c		
13	Does the organization have a written whistleblower policy?	13		
14	Does the organization have a written document retention and destruction policy?	14		
15	Did the process for determining compensation of the following persons include a review and approval by independent persons, comparability data, and contemporaneous substantiation of the deliberation and decision:			
a	The organization's CEO, Executive Director, or top management official?	15a		
b	Other officers or key employees of the organization? . . . . Describe the process in Schedule O. (see instructions)	15b		
16a	Did the organization invest in, contribute assets to, or participate in a joint venture or similar arrangement with a taxable entity during the year?	16a		
b	If "Yes," has the organization adopted a written policy or procedure requiring the organization to evaluate its participation in joint venture arrangements under applicable federal tax law, and taken steps to safeguard the organization's exempt status with respect to such arrangements?	16b		

Line 12a regarding whether the organization has a conflict-of-interest policy was added to Form 990 in 2005 and to the extensively revised Form 1023 in 2004. Therefore many filers will be able to answer this question "Yes." If not, the IRS encourages organizations to tailor the sample policy provided in the Form 1023 instructions to their own particular situations and needs and use the help of counsel if necessary.

Line 12b asks if officials are required to annually disclose any conflicts that exist, and

Line 12c asks for the following details of enforcement procedures in Schedule O:

- Practices for monitoring conflicts in proposed or ongoing transactions and for dealing with potential or actual conflicts, whether discovered before or after the transaction has occurred

- Explanation of which persons are covered under the policy, the level at which determinations of whether a conflict exists are made, and the level at which actual conflicts are reviewed

- Any restrictions imposed on persons with a conflict, such as prohibiting them from participating in the governing body's deliberation and decision in the transaction

Line 13 asks if the organization has a written whistleblower policy that encourages staff and volunteers to come forward with credible information on illegal practices or violations of adopted policies of the organization, specifies that the organization will protect the individual from retaliation, and identifies those staff or board members or outside parties to whom such information can be reported. Sarbanes-Oxley imposes criminal liability on tax-exempt organizations for retaliation against whistleblowers that report federal offenses. Further, the IRS encourages organizations to consider adopting and regularly evaluating a code of ethics that describes behavior it wants to encourage and behavior it wants to discourage. A code of ethics is thought to serve to communicate a strong culture of the importance of legal compliance and ethical integrity to all persons associated with the organization.

Line 14 asks if the organization has a written document retention and destruction policy that identifies the record retention responsibilities of staff, volunteers, board members, and outsiders for maintaining and documenting the storage and destruction of the organization's documents and records. Sarbanes-Oxley imposes criminal liability on tax-exempt organizations for destruction of records with the intent to obstruct a federal investigation. At a minimum, the organization must keep books and records relevant to its tax-exemption and its filings with the IRS.

Line 15 essentially asks whether the information gathered in determining the compensation of top management officials meets the rebuttable presumption test for Intermediate Sanction purposes.[25] Note that line 15b asks if the same process is followed for other officers or key employees of the organization. Those required factors include:

- Review and approval by independent persons
- Comparability data (amount paid to persons with similar qualification, experience, in similar location for organization of similar size)[26]
- Contemporaneous (written) substantiation of the deliberation and decision

Again, if "Yes," the process followed in setting compensation is described in Schedule O. The instructions ask for the identity of the offices or positions for which the recommended compensation process was used and to state the year in which this process was undertaken.

▶ See comments at beginning of Part VII for a discussion of the rules that require no excessive compensation be paid by the organization.

Line 16 asks if, at any time during the year, the organization invested in, contributed assets to, or participated in a joint venture, co-ownership, or contractual arrangement with a taxable entity. Reportable arrangements can include a specific business enterprise, investment or exempt-purpose activity without regard to whether or not the organization does or does not have control of the legal form of the venture. If the primary purpose of the venture is for the production of income or appreciation of the property and 95 percent of the income from the venture is passive income in the form of dividends, interest, rents, royalties, it is disregarded for this purpose.

If the organization says "Yes" it has invested in a reportable venture, a description of the written policy or procedure it follows to evaluate the investment to assure its assets are protected and exempt status is maintained is requested in Schedule O. "Safeguards" suggested include retaining control over the venture, a requirement that the venture give priority to exempt purposes over maximizing profits for other participants, and a requirement that the venture not conduct any activity that would jeopardize its exempt status.[27]

Section C. Disclosure

17 List the states with which a copy of this Form 990 is required to be filed ▶ -

18 Section 6104 requires an organization to make its Forms 1023 (or 1024 if applicable), 990, and 990-T (501(c)(3)s only) available for public inspection. Indicate how you make these available. Check all that apply.
☐ Own website   ☐ Another's website   ☐ Upon request

19 Describe in Schedule O whether (and if so, how), the organization makes its governing documents, conflict of interest policy, and financial statements available to the public.

20 State the name, physical address, and telephone number of the person who possesses the books and records of the organization: ▶ -

---

Form **990** (2008)

Line 17 requests a list of the states in which a copy of this Form 990 is filed to satisfy state requirements. Tax-exempt organizations are not required under the Internal Revenue Code to file a copy of the Form 990 with the states in which they conduct their activities, although a private foundation must file a copy of its Form 990-PF with the attorney general of each state in which it is registered or conducts activity.

Line 18 asks how the organization makes the required public disclosure of its *Application for Recognition of Exemption* (Form 1023 or 1024), Form 990, and if a §501(c)(3) organization, its Form 990-T. The check boxes indicate how the organization makes public disclosure by posting them on a public website maintained by the organization, posting them on another publicly available website, or providing them on request, checking all methods that apply. If the organization does not make these documents publicly available, it should provide an explanation in Schedule O. See Chapter 1.12 for a description of methods that satisfy this statutory requirement. The posting on Guidestar.org does not satisfy this requirement.

Line 19 prompts the organization to describe in Schedule O whether, and if so, how, its governing documents, conflict-of-interest policy, and financial statements are made available to the public. If the documents are not made available, the filer is to "so state." Examples of methods include posting on its website, providing copies on request, or inspection at an office of the organization. This disclosure is not required by the Internal Revenue Code, but the Panel on the Nonprofit Sector and the BBB Wise Giving Alliance agree with the IRS and also suggest this practice prompts good governance.

Line 20 requests contact information for the "person who possesses" the organization's books and records. If the records are maintained at a personal residence, the organization's information is acceptable. Information for the person responsible for coordinating the recordkeeping is requested if records are maintained in more than one location.

§3.8 PART VII COMPENSATION OF OFFICERS, DIRECTORS, TRUSTEES, KEY EMPLOYEES, HIGHEST COMPENSATED EMPLOYEES, AND INDEPENDENT CONTRACTORS

Form 990 (2008)   Page **7**

| **Part VII** | Compensation of Officers, Directors, Trustees, Key Employees, Highest Compensated Employees, and Independent Contractors |

(a) Background

Organizations exempt under most categories of §501 must meet two separate tests in order to retain exemption. The first test, called the organizational test, ensures that no one owns a proprietary interest in an exempt organization.[28] No dividends are paid; shareholders exist only in certain membership organizations; and the circumstances under which funds can be returned to the members in the business league, social club, or other category are very limited. When recognizing an organization's exempt status, the Internal Revenue Service ("IRS") applies this test to review the charter, bylaws, and other organizational documents.

The second test, though, is an ongoing one. Exempt organizations of all categories must continually operate *exclusively* for their particular exempt purposes, whether charitable, agricultural, or advancement of a line of business. An exempt organization ("EO") must not devote itself to benefiting private individuals. To describe the requirements of tax-exempt status, §501 uses the word *inures* to limit the activities of §501(c)(3), (4), (6), (7), (9), (10), (13), and (19) organizations. All are subject to the rule that "no part of the net earnings inure to the benefit of any private shareholder or individual." Previously only §501(c)(3) organizations, on prior Schedule A, had to report the top five highly-paid employees and contractors that were not officers or directors. Now all 990 filers must provide expanded compensation information, much to the displeasure of some non(c)(3) entities.

A tax-exempt organization may pay compensation and have other financial transactions with members of its board and key employees, so long as the amounts paid are reasonable. The tax code has *Intermediate Sanctions* to impose penalties on *disqualified* persons that receive payments that are beyond reason.[29] A penalty equal to 25 percent of the excess payments can be imposed, and any excessive pay must be returned by a person receiving such payments from a §501(c)(3) or (4) entity. A brief test for reasonableness is referred to as the *like, like, like* rule. For compensation, the question to ask is whether the compensation paid is similar to that a person with comparable experience and training doing a job with similar responsibilities for an organization with equivalent resources located in the same area. For asset sales or usage, the test would be based on appraisals of value or normal rental for use of like assets. It is very important that all organizations providing compensation of $100,000 or more study the rules for protecting personnel with a *rebuttable presumption of reasonableness.*[30]

The most common way in which private inurement is found to occur is the payment of excessive compensation. This core part, therefore, requests the amount of compensation for those that control and manage the organization. More details are reported for those persons with compensation >$150,000 in Schedule J. All persons shown in the first chart that follows are to be listed regardless of whether or not they are compensated, even if there are more than the 34 persons for which lines are provided in Section A. Additional persons are reported in Schedule J-2.

With this part, the IRS seeks information to allow itself and other authorities to identify organizations that pay compensation amounts that are excessive and could therefore result in inurement. Since 1995, the tax code has contained Intermediate Sanctions to impose penalties if excess benefits are paid by §501(c)(3) or (4) organizations.[31]

The information requested in this part is purely statistical. It is in Core Part VI, Question 14, and Schedule J that the procedures for gathering documentation of the appropriateness of salary levels and policies for approving compensation are described. A prudent organization will review its policies, procedures, and information retained to document the absence of impermissible private benefit in its compensation structure and to protect its officials and employees from penalties.

§3.8 PART VII COMPENSATION OF OFFICERS, DIRECTORS, TRUSTEES

Section A. Officers, Directors, Trustees, Key Employees, and Highest Compensated Employees

1a Complete this table for all persons required to be listed. Use Schedule J-2 if additional space is needed.

- List all of the organization's **current** officers, directors, trustees (whether individuals or organizations), regardless of amount of compensation, and **current** key employees. Enter -0- in columns (D), (E), and (F) if no compensation was paid.

- List the organization's five **current** highest compensated employees (other than an officer, director, trustee, or key employee) who received reportable compensation (Box 5 of Form W-2 and/or Box 7 of Form 1099-MISC) of more than $100,000 from the organization and any related organizations.

- List all of the organization's **former** officers, key employees, and highest compensated employees who received more than $100,000 of reportable compensation from the organization and any related organizations.

- List all of the organization's **former directors or trustees** that received, in the capacity as a former director or trustee of the organization, more than $10,000 of reportable compensation from the organization and any related organizations.

List persons in the following order: individual trustees or directors; institutional trustees; officers; key employees; highest compensated employees; and former such persons.

☐ Check this box if the organization did not compensate any officer, director, trustee, or key employee.

(A) Name and Title	(B) Average hours per week	(C) Position (check all that apply)						(D) Reportable compensation from the organization (W-2/1099-MISC)	(E) Reportable compensation from related organizations (W-2/1099-MISC)	(F) Estimated amount of other compensation from the organization and related organizations
		Individual trustee or director	Institutional trustee	Officer	Key employee	Highest compensated employee	Former			

Form **990** (2008)

(Continued)

■ 75 ■

Part VII	Section A. Officers, Directors, Trustees, Key Employees, and Highest Compensated Employees *(continued)*									
(A) Name and title	**(B)** Average hours per week	**(C)** Position (check all that apply)						**(D)** Reportable compensation from the organization (W-2/1099-MISC)	**(E)** Reportable compensation from related organizations (W-2/1099-MISC)	**(F)** Estimated amount of other compensation from the organization and related organizations
		Individual trustee or director	Institutional trustee	Officer	Key employee	Highest compensated employee	Former			

1b Total . . . . ▶

2 Total number of individuals (including those in 1a) who received more than $100,000 in reportable compensation from the organization ▶

		Yes	No
3	Did the organization list any **former** officer, director or trustee, key employee, or highest compensated employee on line 1a? *If "Yes," complete Schedule J for such individual* **3**		
4	For any individual listed on line 1a, is the sum of reportable compensation and other compensation from the organization and related organizations greater than $150,000? *If "Yes," complete Schedule J for such individual.* **4**		
5	Did any person listed on line 1a receive or accrue compensation from any unrelated organization for services rendered to the organization? *If "Yes," complete Schedule J for such person* **5**		

Column A reflects the names and titles of officials and reportable employees, but their addresses are no longer requested. The first box below displays persons treated as officials whose names and compensation are reported regardless of any compensation threshold. **Importantly, the form is wrong** when it says all key employees are included without regard to the amount of compensation they receive. The final instructions clarify that a $150,000 threshold applies for classifying individuals as key employees. Persons that meet the definition described below "at any time during organization's tax year" are reported on this schedule.

Officials Reported in Section A

Member of board of directors or trustees

Elected Officers, such as president, vice president, secretary, treasurer, and without regard to their title

Top management official. The person who has ultimate responsibility for implementing the decisions of the governing body or for supervising the management, administration, or operation of the organization

Top financial official. The person who has ultimate responsibility for managing the organization's finances

---

Three Factors Required for a Key Employee

$150,000 Test: Receives reportable compensation from the organization and all related organizations in excess of $150,000 for the calendar year ending with or within the organization's tax year.

Responsibility Test: (a) has responsibilities, powers or influence over the organization as a whole that is similar to those of officers, directors, or trustees;

(b) manages a discrete segment or activity of the organization that represents 10 percent [originally 5 percent] or more of the activities, assets, income, or expenses of the organization, as compared to the organization as a whole; or (c) has or shares authority to control or determine 10 percent or more of the organization's capital expenditures, operating budget, or compensation for employees.

Top 20 Test: Only the top 20 employees that satisfy the $150,000 Test and Responsibility Test are reported starting with those that receive the highest compensation.

Comp Thresholds for Reporting Persons

Current officers, directors/trustees	$ -0- Report ALL
Current key employees	$150,000
Current five highest (nonkey) compensated employees	$100,000
Independent contractors	$100,000
Former officers, key and five highest employees	$100,000
Former directors/trustees (in capacity as a former)	$10,000

Column B asks for the "average hours per week" devoted to the position. The IRS wants real hours and deems "as needed" or "40+" not acceptable. Often, officials serve as volunteers and do not keep a record of time they spend in carrying out the position. If the persons are uncompensated, it is sufficient to give an estimate such as "4 to 6 hours." For compensated persons (particularly highly paid ones), records substantiating actual time spent are appropriate.

Column C displays the positions of officials in a neat checkbox fashion.

Column D reflects a new term: **reportable compensation**. Without regard to the amount of compensation a person receives during the organization's fiscal year, the amount of each person's reportable compensation is equal to the amount reported on a calendar year basis in Box 5 of Form W-2 or Box 7 of Form 1099-MISC. A June 30, 2009, reporting entity, for example, filing the 2008 return would input amounts from the 2008 W-2s or 1099s. Essentially this column includes benefits not taxable for income tax purposes (but still subject to FICA) of the sort displayed on the table on pages 78 and 79 that are included in annual IRS compensation reported as Medicare wages.

Column E contains reportable compensation from related entities, including those controlled by the filing organization, a commonly controlled entity, a supported or supporting organization, or a partnership or corporation owned >50 percent by the organization.[32] The reporting organization may not necessarily be informed about the relationships of its officials. To obtain the information, the instructions suggest that the "use of a completed and signed questionnaire provided to and returned by all board members" is acceptable. This step is deemed a "reasonable effort to identify related-entity compensation" that excuses the filer of any responsibility for the accuracy of the related-entity information. See Appendix 3A for a sample board questionnaire that could be used to identify this information and also whether any transactions required to be reported in Schedule L occurred.

A payment of less than $10,000 from a single related entity can be omitted unless paid to a former director or trustee of the organization for services provided to it. Compensation paid to a volunteer by a noncontrolled or owned for-profit entity is not reported in this column.

IRS Guide for Columnar Reporting of Compensation

Type of Compensation	Form 990, Part VII, Sect. A, Col. (D) or (E)			Form 990, Part VII, Sect. A, Col. (F)	
	Schedule J, Part II, Column				
	B(i)	B(ii)	B(iii)	C	D
Base salary/wages/fees paid	X				
Base salary/wages/fees deferred (taxable)	X				
Base salary/wages/fees deferred (nontaxable)				X	
Bonus paid (including signing bonus)		X			
Bonus deferred (taxable in current year)		X			
Bonus deferred (not taxable in current year)				X	
Incentive compensation paid		X			
Incentive compensation deferred (taxable in current year)		X			
Incentive compensation deferred (not taxable in current year)				X	
Severance or change of control payments made			X		
Sick pay paid by employer	X				
Third party sick pay			X		
Other compensation amounts deferred (taxable in current year)		X			
Other compensation amounts deferred (not taxable in current year)				X	
Tax gross-ups paid			X		
Vacation/sick leave cashed out			X		
Stock options at time of grant				X	
Stock options at time of exercise			X		
Stock awards paid by taxable organizations substantially vested			X		
Stock awards paid by taxable organizations not vested				X	
Stock equivalents paid by taxable organizations substantially vested			X		
Stock equivalents paid by taxable organizations not vested				X	
Loans—forgone interest or debt forgiveness			X		
Contributions (employer) to qualified retirement plan				X	
Contributions (employee deferrals) to 401(k) plan			X		
Contributions (employee deferrals) to 403(b) plan			X		
Qualified or nonqualified retirement plan defined benefit accruals (reasonable estimate of increase in actuarial value)				X	

(Continued)

Qualified or nonqualified retirement defined contribution plan investment earnings (no reportable or other compensation)					
Taxable distributions from qualified retirement plan (reported on Form 1099-R) – no reportable or other compensation					
Distributions from nongovernmental 457(b) plan – no reportable or other compensation					
Amounts includible in income under 457(f)			X		
Amounts deferred (plus earnings) under 457(b) plan (vested)			X		
Amounts deferred (plus earnings) under 457(b) plan (nonvested)				X	
Contributions to nonqualified plans (vested)			X		
Contributions to nonqualified plans (nonvested)				X	
Increase in earnings of nonqualified plan			X		
Scholarships and fellowship grants (taxable)			X		
Health benefit plan premiums (taxable)			X		
Health benefit plan premiums (nontaxable)					X
Medical reimbursement and flexible spending programs (taxable)			X		
Medical reimbursement and flexible spending programs (nontaxable)					X
Other health benefits (taxable)			X		
Other health benefits (nontaxable)					X
Life, disability, or long-term-care insurance (taxable)			X		
Life, disability, or long-term-care insurance (nontaxable)					*
Split-dollar life insurance (see Notice 2002-8)			X		
Housing provided by employer (taxable)			X		
Housing provided by employer (nontaxable)					*
Personal legal services (taxable)			X		
Personal legal services (nontaxable)					*
Personal financial services (taxable)			X		
Personal financial services (nontaxable)					*
Dependent care assistance (taxable)			X		
Dependent care assistance (nontaxable)					*
Adoption assistance (taxable)			X		
Adoption assistance (nontaxable)					*
Tuition assistance for family (taxable)			X		
Tuition assistance for family (nontaxable)					*
Cafeteria plans (taxable)			X		
Cafeteria plans (nontaxable health benefit)					X
Cafeteria plans (nontaxable benefit other than health)					*
Liability insurance (taxable)			X		
Employer-provided automobile (taxable)			X		
Employer-subsidized parking (taxable)			X		
Travel (taxable)			X		
Moving (taxable)			X		
Meals and entertainment (taxable)			X		
Social club dues (taxable)			X		
Spending account (taxable)			X		

*Items are excludible from Form 990, Part VII, Section A, column (F) if below $10,000.

Column F reflects "other compensation," representing nontaxable benefits not reportable on W-2 or 1099 from both the organization itself and related entities. Some benefits are only reported if they exceed the somewhat confusing **$10,000-per-item exception** illustrated in the box below. The items that must be included regardless of amount are the following:

- Tax-deferred payments by employer to retirement plan
- Increase in actuarial value of qualified defined-benefit plan
- Value of health insurance and reimbursement plans that are not included in reportable compensation
- Employer contributions to nonqualified plans
- Increase in actuarial value of nonqualified defined-benefit plan

---

$10,000-per-Item Exception

Neither the organization nor a related organization is to report in Form 990, Part VII, Section A certain items of other compensation if their value is less than $10,000 per item for the calendar year ending with or within the organization's tax year. Amounts excluded under the two separate $10,000 exceptions (the $10,000-per-related organization and $10,000-per-item exceptions) are to be excluded from compensation in determining whether an individual's total reportable compensation and other compensation exceeds the thresholds set forth in Form 990, Part VII, Section A, line 4. If the individual's total compensation exceeds the relevant threshold, then the amounts excluded under the $10,000 exceptions are included in the individual's compensation reported in Schedule J. Thus the total amount of compensation reported in Schedule J may be higher than the amount reported in Form 990, Part VII, Section A. The $10,000 exceptions apply separately with respect to each item of other compensation from the organization and from each related organization.

Example. Organization X provides the following compensation to its current officer:

- $110,000 reportable compensation (including $5,000 pretax employee contribution to qualified defined-contribution retirement plan)
- $5,000 tax-deferred employer contribution to qualified defined-contribution retirement plan,
- $5,000 nontaxable employer contribution to health benefit plan,
- $4,000 nontaxable dependent care assistance,
- $500 nontaxable group life insurance premium,
- $8,000 moving expense (nontaxable as qualified under §132).

Organization Y, a related organization, also provides compensation to the officer as follows:

- $21,000 reportable compensation (including $1,000 pretax employee contribution to qualified defined-contribution retirement plan)
- $1,000 tax-deferred employer contribution to qualified defined-contribution retirement plan,
- $5,000 nontaxable tuition assistance.

The organization may disregard as other compensation (a) the $4,500 dependent care and group life payments from the organization, under the $10,000-per-item exception, (b) the $8,000 moving expense from the organization, because such amount is excluded from reportable and other comp under §132 (in both Form 990, Part VII and Schedule J, Part II), and (c) the $5,000 tuition from the related organization, under the $10,000-per-item exception, in determining whether the officer's total reportable and other compensation from the organization and related organizations exceeds $150,000. In this case, total reportable comp is $131,000, and total other compensation (excluding the excludible items below $10,000) is

$11,000. Under these circumstances, the officer's dependent care, group life, moving expense, and tuition items need not be reported as other comp in Form 990, Part VII, Section A, column (F), and the officer's total reportable and other compensation ($142,000) is not reportable in Schedule J. If instead, the officer's reportable comp from Y were $30,000 rather than $21,000, then the officer's total reportable and other compensation ($151,000) would be reportable in Schedule J, including the dependent care, group life, and tuition items, even though these items would not have to be reported as other comp in Form 990, Part VII.

Section B. Independent Contractors

1   Complete this table for your five highest compensated independent contractors that received more than $100,000 of compensation from the organization.

(A) Name and business address	(B) Description of services	(C) Compensation

2   Total number of independent contractors (including those in 1) who received more than $100,000 in compensation from the organization ▶

Form **990** (2008)

Section B is similar to prior Schedule A, Part II-A and II-B except that the separate sections to distinguish between professional and other independent service providers have been removed and the threshold has increased to a level of >$100,000 of compensation, up from the former $50,000. Organizations exempt under sections other than §501(c)(3) previously did not have to disclose this information because they were not required to file the prior Schedule A which requested this information. Similarly, they did not have to report information about highly compensated employees that were not key employees.

§3.9   PART VIII STATEMENT OF REVENUE

Form 990 (2008)   Page **9**

Part VIII   **Statement of Revenue**

(a)   Background

Those who have prepared prior 990s may find it disconcerting that the 2008 version of Form 990 does not contain the concise report of Revenue, Expenses, and Changes in Net Assets similar to that found in the accountants' financial statements as former 990s did. Revenues are still reported in keeping with the system used by the organization to maintain its accounting records and report to its constituents.[33] Though there is a prior and current year comparison of major revenues, expenses, assets, and liabilities on the front page, there is no visible connection, or reconciliation, between the years. In other words, this year's increase or decrease in net assets resulting from an excess of revenue over expenses or vice versa is not shown except in Schedule D, Part XI if the amounts are being tied to audited financial statements. A careful return preparer will do this tally to assure that the numbers reported are correct. Hopefully, software providers will add a diagnostic for this purpose.

The new Statement of Revenue presents the "Analysis of Income-Producing Activities," which was presented separately in Part VII of prior returns. All filers, except for §527 (political) organizations must complete all columns. The amount on each line of revenue, other than contributions shown on line 1, is entered in column (A) plus one of three additional columns that identify its character for unrelated business income (UBI) tax purposes. Preparers familiar with the pre-2008 version of the columnar display may welcome the removal of the exclusion codes and the part in which the relationship of activities to the accomplishment of exempt purposes was described to prove an entry in column E (now D) was correct.

This revenue display has not been the focus of an IRS compliance audit check to date. The display now asks for business codes pertaining to the revenue listed on lines 2 and 11. However, the instructions say, "Use of these codes [in lines 2a–2f and 11a–11d] does not imply that the business activity is unrelated to the organization's exempt purpose." Careful entry of revenues into the columns is important nonetheless because column C revenues must also be reported on Form 990-T. An understanding of the terms *regularly carried on, member convenience, related* and *unrelated,* and *fragmented* is absolutely necessary for correct completion of this page. The complex distinctions are presented in Chapter 5.1.and deserve careful study in choosing which one or more of the following columns correctly identifies each line of revenue:

- Column B—Related or Exempt Function Revenue, or those fees and charges paid by those that participate in or benefit from the organization's exempt activities.

- Column C—Unrelated Business Revenue from activities that do not accomplish the organization's mission and are not otherwise excluded from taxation.

- Column D—Unrelated Business Revenue Excluded from Tax, including investment income, fundraising events, and business activities statutorily excluded from tax.

Revenue Reporting Concepts: Contributions reported on line 1 of this part represent money given to the organization with the intention to make a gift for which the donor receives nothing in return. Payments for which the payer expects something specific in return (school tuition, patient fees, publication sales, and so on), called *exchange transactions,* are not line 1 revenue and instead are reported on other lines. Fundraising event proceeds are fragmented on line 8 to extract the contributed portion that is included on line 1 from the exchange portion attributable to raffles, dinners, auctions, and the like, that is reported on line 8.

Exchange revenues, however, may be treated as support for Schedule A purposes in determining qualification as a §509(a)(2) public charity. A labor union or a business league that provides benefits to its members reports dues on line 2 instead of line 1. A §501(c)(3) organization reports its member dues payments either on line 1 or line 2, depending on whether the dues are a charitable contribution, rather than a purchase of services.[34]

Sales of tangible or intangible objects can be troublesome because they can be reported on line 2, 8, 9, or 10. Hospitals and colleges using special accounting procedures are allowed to report in accordance with their prescribed categories.

The primary goal in classifying an exempt organization's revenues depends on the exemption category. For a charitable exempt organization, donations that enable it to satisfy the public support tests may be of utmost importance. A labor union is more concerned about distinguishing between member purchases of goods and services that might be treated as taxable business income and those that are dues in support of the league's activities that benefit the group as a whole. The accounting profession defines those payments that are treated as donations in Statement of Financial Accounting Standards (SFAS) No. 116.[35] Contributions pledged to be unconditionally paid in the future, thereby treated as current-year revenue by FASB, are also reported by an accrual-basis exempt organization and also on Schedule A, which is no longer required to be prepared on a cash basis.

			(A) Total revenue	(B) Related or exempt function revenue	(C) Unrelated business revenue	(D) Revenue excluded from tax under sections 512, 513, or 514
Contributions, gifts, grants and other similar amounts	1a	Federated campaigns ...	1a			
	b	Membership dues	1b			
	c	Fundraising events	1c			
	d	Related organizations . . .	1d			
	e	Government grants (contributions).	1e			
	f	All other contributions, gifts, grants, and similar amounts not included above	1f			
	g	Noncash contributions included in lines 1a-1f: $				
	h	**Total.** Add lines 1a–1f . . . . ▶				
Program Service Revenue			Business Code			
	2a	--------------				
	b	--------------				
	c	--------------				
	d	--------------				
	e	--------------				
	f	All other program service revenue .				
	g	**Total.** Add lines 2a–2f . . . . ▶				

Line 1a. Federated Campaigns. Contributions received indirectly from the public through solicitation campaigns conducted by federated fundraising agencies and similar fundraising organizations, such as a United Way, Earth Share, Combined Federal, or other organizations that conduct fundraising campaigns within a city or state for a targeted cause for allocation to participating organizations on the basis of the donors' individual designations and other factors.

Line 1b. Membership Dues may represent a charitable donation or fee for services depending on "commensurate rights and privileges" provided to members. A donation occurs when the benefit is only the personal satisfaction of being of service to others and furthering the charitable cause in which the members have a common interest. Otherwise, an exchange transaction occurs, and service revenue is realized. Membership dues representing service revenue should be reported on line 2 rather than line 1. Due to the difficulty of valuing certain member privileges, the IRS in 1995, significantly eased the disclosure requirements by extending the token item *de minimis* rules to apply to member benefits. Benefits provided to members can be disregarded, and the full payment treated as a contribution, if they are given as a part of a basic annual membership of $75 or less.[36] The IRS reasoned that it was "often difficult to value membership benefits, especially rights or privileges that are not limited as to use, such as free or discounted admission or parking, and gift shop discounts" and decided to allow "limited relief."

Line 1c. Fundraising Events. Such fundraising efforts—gala balls, fun runs, spaghetti suppers—produce both contributions and exchange revenues. The donation portion of a payment received in connection with an event is reported on line 1.

Essentially, the total payment less the amount attributable to the value of dinner, merchandise, raffle ticket, or other benefits provided to the donor is reported as a contribution. When token items are given to donors, their value can be ignored, and the entire payment reported as a donation on line 1.[37] The portion of an event payment not treated as a contribution is reported on lines 8 or 9. If more than $15,000 is reported on this line and lines 8/9, Schedule G must be completed. Donations solicited on behalf of the organization must be reported gross, not net, of any fees or expenses paid to persons who raised the funds on behalf of the entity and the fees reported as expenses in Part IX.

Line 1d. Related Organizations. Support received from a parent or subordinate organization, supporting organization, or other group that raises or holds funds on behalf of the organization is reported here. Money collected by a professional society whose members voluntarily add designated donations to their dues payments and transferred to its charitable arm go here. Grants received from other charitable organizations for support in operating the organization's programs, building its facilities, conducting its research, and the like are also reported.

Line 1e. Government Grants reportable on line 1e are those awards that represent support for the recipient organization to carry on programs and activities that further its organizational objectives.[38] Such grants are said to give a direct benefit primarily to the general public rather than an economic or physical benefit to the payor of the grant. Instead, some grants are payments in exchange for services and not treated as contributions. When a sale of goods, performance of service, or admission to or use of a facility must be delivered or provided specifically to the governmental grantor, program service revenue reported on line 2 is received; what GAAP calls an *exchange transaction* occurs. For example, Medicare funding a health care provider receives for treatment of patients is reported on line 2. The terms of the grant agreement indicating gross receipts from a service contract, as contrasted to (terms identifying a contribution), might include the following:

- Specific delivery of services is required within specific time frame (time for performance at discretion of grantee).

- Penalties beyond the amount of the grant can be imposed for failure to perform (only penalty is return of grant for not conducting specific program or other restriction).

- Goods or services furnished or delivered only to grantor (program benefits, or services provided to recipients other than grantor).

A government grant that is treated as program service revenue for financial purposes may, for tax purposes, be treated as a contribution if the parenthetical conditions above exist. For public support purposes, the distinction can be very important as illustrated in Schedule A.

Line 1e. All other contributions are reported on this line, including payments from donor-advised funds and gifts to endowment and annual giving campaigns. Business sponsorship payments in return for which the organization provides acknowledgment without quantitative or qualitative information promoting the business go here.[39] Agency transactions or pass-through gifts are not reported as revenue to the filing entity acting as an agent for another organization.[40]

Line 1g. The value of gifts of marketable securities, real estate, and other noncash property such as food, clothing, or medical supplies included on lines 12–1f is reported in this blank.[41] Details about such gifts are reported on Schedule M when total noncash contributions exceed $25,000. See discussion for Core Part V for reporting requirements for noncash gifts.

Line 2. Program service revenues are those received by a nonprofit in return for carrying out the mission for which it was granted tax exemption, also referred to as *exempt function revenues*. Examples are many, including student tuition, hospital patient fees, testing fees, golf course green fees, trade show admission, ticket sales for cultural events, and convention registrations. Revenue from program-related investments, such as interest on student or credit union loans or low-cost housing rent goes here. Royalties received from publication of a school's educational materials go here, but royalty from a donated mineral interest is reported on line 5. Payments a voluntary employees' beneficiary association[42] receives for voluntary member health, life, and other welfare benefits are reported as program revenue as well as rents and interest from investments the nonprofit makes to accomplish an exempt purpose.

Grants that represent payments for services rendered on behalf of the donor are reported here, such as membership fees when benefits are provided to members. A grant received by a scientific laboratory testing automobile emissions for a state under the standards described above for government grants would be service revenue. Sales of inventory, such as books, posters, reproductions, or other items sold in a bookstore; crafts produced by the handicapped; or tennis balls sold in the country club shop, even though they are related to exempt function activities, are not reported here but on line 10. Hospitals and colleges whose accounting systems do not allow them to readily extract the cost of goods sold attributable solely to inventory are permitted to report inventory sales on line 2. Line 2 revenues are counted as public support for those (c)(3) organizations qualifying as public charities under §509(a)(2) but not under §509(a)(1).[43]

Fees for services generated in an exempt activity but taxed as unrelated business income, such as advertising revenues from an exempt publication, are reported on this line. A social club reports all revenues from use of club facilities here, although the portion received from nonmembers will also be reported on Form 990-T.

Other Revenue		(i) Real	(ii) Personal				
3 Investment income (including dividends, interest, and other similar amounts) . . . . ▶							
4 Income from investment of tax-exempt bond proceeds ▶							
5 Royalties . . . . ▶							
6a Gross Rents . .							
b Less: rental expenses							
c Rental income or (loss)							
d Net rental income or (loss) . . . . ▶							
		(i) Securities	(ii) Other				
7a Gross amount from sales of assets other than inventory							
b Less: cost or other basis and sales expenses .							
c Gain or (loss) . .							
d Net gain or (loss) . . . . ▶							

Line 3. Investment income, including dividends, interest, and other similar amounts. This line is mostly self-explanatory. Clearly, interest earned on the non-profit's accumulated funds is reported on this line. Interest earned on program-related loans that serve an exempt purpose, such as money lent to build a low-income housing project or as student loans, is reported on line 2. The prior confusion regarding where to report dividends earned on money market accounts was removed by the combination of income now included on this line.

Interest on a note receivable that is not an investment or program related, such as an employee loan, is reported on line 11. Interest on a note receivable from the sale of an exempt function asset would also be reported as other income on line 11. A labor union loaning funds to a faltering company to protect the jobs of its worker members, however, would report the interest on line 2 as program related.

Line 4. Income from investment of tax-exempt bond proceeds under the control of the organization. Proceeds held on deposit in a defeasance escrow that is irrevocably pledged to pay the debt services on a bond issue are not under the control of the organization. Schedule K must be attached when the organization has an outstanding bond issue that had principal due of more than $100,000 as of the last day of the year and was issued after December 31, 2002.

Line 5. Royalties. Report royalties received by the organization from licensing the use of its property to others on this line. Typically, royalties are received for the use of intellectual property, such as patents and trademarks. Royalties also include payments to the owner of property for the right to exploit natural resources on the property, such as oil, natural gas, or minerals. Royalties from educational publications or research patents might be classed as program service revenue and reported on line 2 instead.

Line 6. Gross Rents. Rents from real estate and personal property not used for exempt purposes are reported on this line. Rents produced through exempt programs, such as low-income housing, are included on line 2. Rental of office space to unaffiliated exempt organizations is reportable as rent here. Such rents are reported only on line 2 as exempt function income, if the rental rate is well below the fair rental value of the property, and if the rental itself serves the lessor exempt organization's mission.

Expenses directly connected with obtaining and maintaining the property producing the rental income are deducted on line 6b but need not be itemized. Repairs, interest on mortgages, depreciation, and other direct costs are placed here and are not included on Part IX. Those costs associated with program-related rental properties (whose income is reported on line 2) are reported on Part IX.

Line 7. Gains or losses from sales of assets other than inventory. All types of capital assets, except goods held in inventory for regular sale, including those held for investment, those held for exempt purposes, and those that produce UBI, are reported on line 7. Details are no longer requested for this line. Though the instructions are silent, capital gains distributed from partnerships, trusts, and S corporations should be reported here as well. Unrealized gains or losses reported for financial statement purposes are not reported on this line or any other line in Part VIII. The number only appears on Schedule D, Part XII, to reconcile revenue for Form 990 purposes to financial statements.

Form **990** (2008)

Line 8, Gross income from fundraising events. A popular funding tool for non-profits is an event at which food, drink, and entertainment are provided to partici-pants. The ticket price for such an event often embodies both a donation and a purchase of the goods and services—called a *quid pro quo*. When an organization pro-vides *quid pro quo* benefits in connection with a solicitation of a payment of more than $75, the value of the benefits must be disclosed on the invitation or receipt for pay-ment.[44] Penalties are imposed for failure to disclose. Services or goods received are to be valued at their fair market value, which is often difficult to determine. The cost of the event is not necessarily determinative of its value. Technically, a payment of less than $75 must also be reduced by benefits (unless *de minimis*[45]) for tax deductibility purposes; the helpful nonprofit makes a valuation disclosure in connection with all solicitations.

This line fragments event proceeds into two parts:

1. That amount equal to the value of the goods or services provided in connection with payments for tickets or admission is reported on this line.

2. The excess, if any, of the payment over the value of services or goods received is reported as a donation on line 1 and noted in parentheses on line 8a.

Proceeds of an auction, car wash, cookie sale, dinner, or other event are included here. When the cost of the goods provided in connection with fundraising efforts—a T-shirt, coffee cup, or poster, for example—is less than a *de minimis* amount, the item or benefit is treated as having no value. The total payment made to the organization is then treated as a gift and reported on line 1, with no amount reported on line 8. Also, the expenses associated with purchase of the *de minimis* items are reported on page 10 as fundraising expenses, and not on line 8.

Fundraising campaign contributions for which donors receive nothing in return for their gifts are totally reported on line 1. The instructions direct §501(c)(3) organiza-tions to keep both their solicitations and the receipts they furnish to participants in events, as well as proof of the method used to determine the noncontribution portion of the proceeds. Schedule G, Part II displaying details of the two largest events sponsored during the year is required when total revenue from fundraising events exceeds $15,000. The cost of direct benefits (the food, drink, prizes, and so on) provided during the event is deducted on line 8b to arrive at the net income. The portion of the administrative and fundraising department expenses attributable to management of and solicitation for the event is not reported on this line but on the applicable line of Part IX.

Line 9. Gross Income from Gaming Activities. The IRS instructions list more than 20 types of gaming and caution that revenue from "many games of chance are taxable," including pull tabs and instant bingo. Income from games that meet the legal definition of bingo are not subject to the tax on unrelated business income. Direct expenses associated with the games, including prizes, compensation, rental of equipment, and supplies are reported on line 9b. Schedule G, Part III is required if the gross revenue is more than $15,000.

Line 10. Gross Sales of Inventory, Less Returns and Allowances. Sales of inventory property made or purchased for resale (not including sales of capital assets or items sold during a fundraising event) and both items related and unrelated to exempt functions are reported here. An educational center's or school's books, a retirement home's or a hospital's pharmaceuticals, a thrift shop's used clothing, or other objects purchased for resale constitute inventory items. Cost of goods sold includes direct and indirect labor, materials and supplies consumed, freight, and a portion of overhead expenses. Marketing and distribution expenses are reported in Part IX.

Line 11. Other Revenue. Revenues not reported on the first 10 lines are reported here, including interest earned on loans not made for investment or program purposes, such as an employee advance or officer loan, advertising revenues not treated as sponsorships, increase in cash surrender value of life insurance, and certain partnership distributions.

§3.10 PART IX STATEMENT OF FUNCTIONAL EXPENSES

Form 990 (2008)   Page **10**

Part IX   **Statement of Functional Expenses**

(a) Background

In this part, all 990 filers report operating expenses in column A by object classification, such as salaries, occupancy, and so on, according to the accounting method used for the nonprofit's financial reporting purposes. Only §501(c)(3) and (4) organizations and §4947(a)(1) nonexempt charitable trusts complete all four columns. Those filers might find it useful to review the introductory materials about cost allocations and accounting theory in Chapter 2 before completion of this part. Organizing the accounting system to parallel the display of expense accounts in this part and to quantify the cost of programs described in Part III is also appropriate. The listing is common to that suggested by many national organizations; its use can facilitate comparison of a nonprofit's financial reports to other nonprofits using the standard display.

While it may seem wrong, expenses associated with unrelated business activities are reported in this part in combination with expenses of conducting program services and managing the organization. It is important to remember that certain grants reported on line 1 may qualify as a charitable deduction in calculating the unrelated business income (UBI) tax. Chapter 5.8 discusses unrelated income and associated deductions and defines direct and indirect costs—an accounting concept that applies in preparing this part.

The challenge in this part is to divide the expenses into functional categories of program service, management and general (M&G), and fundraising. The column totals allow the IRS and others to evaluate the proportion of costs devoted to exempt activities—optimally, a high proportion. Conversely, fundraising costs should be low; some recommend limiting them to 20 percent to 25 percent of total expenses. The administrative (M&G) expense level depends on the nature of the organization. Some say the combined management and fundraising costs should be less than 25 percent of the total.

Program services are those activities performed to accomplish the purposes for which the organization is exempt (its exempt function). Direct expenses specifically incurred in association with a project are included, along with an allocable part of indirect costs, such as salaries of employees directly involved in the project, occupancy cost for space utilized, and the cost of printing the reports. Colleges and hospitals whose internal accounting systems allocate indirect costs into cost centers have options for reporting such costs and should read the IRS instructions carefully.

Management and general expenses include overhead and administration—those expenses that are not allocable to programs or fundraising. The executive director or controller and her or his staff and expenses, personnel and accounting departments, auditors, and lawyers are reported in column C. The administrative staff of a modest organization might perform all three functions so that their compensation and associated costs are allocated. The cost of organizational meetings, such as the annual membership meeting; monthly board, staff, and committee meetings; and other meetings unrelated to a specific program or fundraising are reported in column C. The investment or cash management function, budgeting, auditing, personnel, and staff cafeteria operations typify the costs reported here. Organizational and officer and director liability coverage is a management expense.

Fundraising includes expenses incurred in soliciting donations, memberships, and grants voluntarily given to the exempt organization, including

- Annual giving campaign costs of printing, publicity, mailing, staffing, and the like
- Professional fees to plan and execute the campaign or to draw up documents for planned giving
- Development or grant-writing department
- Costs of collecting fund campaign pledges
- Portion of event costs not reported on line 8b
- Advertisements soliciting support

Fundraising expenses do not include

- Expenses of an unrelated business (these go in column B or C, or possibly only on page 9 if directly related to rents or inventory items)

- Fundraising event, rental, and direct inventory expenses and other direct do-nor benefit costs deducted directly from the gross receipts on page 9 (lines 6b, 8b, 9b, or 10b)

- Costs associated with collecting exempt income, such as student tuition or seminar registration fees (report these in column B)

The key changes to the revised functional expenses include

- New lines to separately report grants and assistance, isolate foreign activity, and prompt completion of Schedules I (domestic) and F (foreign).

- New fees for services lines double the number of identified professional ser-vices, including not only legal, accounting and fundraising, but now also man-agement, lobbying, investments and other.

- Advertising and promotion and information technology added.

- Supplies, telephone, postage and shipping, equipment rental and maintenance, and printing and publications replaced with a single line for Office Expenses.

- Depreciation detail listing of asset cost, life, and calculation method for expense was eliminated. A summary on Schedule D simply discloses five cate-gories of assets (land, buildings, leasehold improvements, equipment, and other) with their cost, accumulated depreciation, and resulting book value.

Section 501(c)(3) and 501(c)(4) organizations must complete all columns.
All other organizations must complete column (A) but are not required to complete columns (B), (C), and (D).

Do not include amounts reported on lines 6b, 7b, 8b, 9b, and 10b of Part VIII.	(A) Total expenses	(B) Program service expenses	(C) Management and general expenses	(D) Fundraising expenses
1 Grants and other assistance to governments and organizations in the U.S. See Part IV, line 21				
2 Grants and other assistance to individuals in the U.S. See Part IV, line 22				
3 Grants and other assistance to governments, organizations, and individuals outside the U.S. See Part IV, lines 15 and 16 . . .				
4 Benefits paid to or for members				

Line 1. Grants to U.S. Organizations. Grants to governments and organizations located in the United States are reported on line 1. The information requested on an attachment in the past has been expanded by the new Schedule I required when the line reflects more than $5,000 in grants. Not only is the name, address, amount, and purpose of each grant requested, but the following details for any recipient that received more than $5,000:

- IRC Code section of the recipient, if applicable

- Cash and noncash grant amount in separate columns

- Method of valuation of property granted

- Description of noncash assistance

Grants are reported in keeping with the amounts expensed per books. Pledges of grants accrued according to GAAP rules are reported as current-year grants by accrual-basis organizations. Cash-basis organizations would not report pledges, simi-lar to private foundations, which are only allowed to report grants actually paid as qualifying distributions.

Only the grant award amounts are reported; the cost of administering the grant program, such as selection of recipients and monitoring compliance, are included on lines 5–24.

Line 2. Grants and other assistance to individuals in the U.S. Scholarships, medical care, food, clothing, and cash and other aid given to members of a charitable class are reported on this line. When the total amount is more than $5,000, Schedule I requests the following details:

- Type of grant or assistance
- Number of recipients
- Amount, valuation method, and description of noncash assistance

The individual names are not reported. A (c)(3) organization must be alert to defining its charitable class and avoiding challenges that it benefits particular individuals or families—a condition that prevents tax exemption. A grant to another organization that operates a homeless shelter to buy food and clothes is reported on line 1, but a direct purchase of food and clothing to give out to homeless individuals is reported on this line.

Line 3. Grants and Other Assistance to Governments, Organizations, and Individuals Outside the U.S. Expenses paid for programs directly conducted by the filing entity and grants paid to organizations outside of the United States are reported on this line. In response to comments on the June 2007 draft of the return, the details requested on Schedule F, when the total amount exceeds $10,000, is reported by "regions" rather than specific country. Essentially the same types of details for grants described above for line 1 are requested. When programs are directly conducted, the number of offices and employees and type of activity is requested.

Line 4. Benefits Paid to or for Members. Payment of member benefits is usually antithetical to the purposes of an organization classified as exempt under §501(c)(3) or (c)(4). As charities and social welfare organizations, they must operate to benefit the public rather than particular individuals. This line is suited to labor unions, fraternal benefit societies, voluntary employee beneficiary associations, unemployment benefit trusts, and other nonprofit associations formed to benefit their members in a nonprofit mode. They set aside and spend monies for member benefits as a part of their underlying exempt function. Similar payments and the insurance premiums associated with such protection paid on behalf of a nonprofit's employees are reported on lines 8 and 9.

5	Compensation of current officers, directors, trustees, and key employees			
6	Compensation not included above, to disqualified persons (as defined under section 4958(f)(1)) and persons described in section 4958(c)(3)(B) . .			
7	Other salaries and wages			
8	Pension plan contributions (include section 401(k) and section 403(b) employer contributions) . .			
9	Other employee benefits			
10	Payroll taxes			

Line 5. Compensation of Current Officers, Directors, and Key Employees. Compensation for lines 5–7 is to be reported based on the accounting method and reporting period used by the organization for the Form 990 reporting year, rather than the definitions and calendar year used to complete Part VII or Schedule J regarding compensation of certain officers, directors, trustees, and other employees. Compensation includes all forms of income and other benefits earned or received in return for services rendered, including pension plan contributions and other employee benefits (taxable and nontaxable), but does not include noncompensatory expense reimbursements or allowances. Report all compensation amounts relating to such an individual, including those related to services performed in a capacity other than service as a director, officer, or key employee. Amounts earned by directors in their capacity as directors and/or as staff or management, compensation of an officer treated as an independent contractor, amounts paid on behalf of leased employees who are officers and key employees are also reported on this line. The IRS has settled the argument with the requirement that Part VII and Schedule J be reported on a calendar year basis, but in the past there were some who recommended the amounts reported on this line agree with Forms 941 for fiscal year filers.

Line 6. Compensation, Not Included Above, to Disqualified. Total compensation and other distributions provided to disqualified persons such as substantial contributors and related parties of officials,[46] must be reported on this line by §501(c)(3) and (4) organizations. The compensation categories to be reported follow the instructions for line 5.

Lines 7–10: Other Salaries and Wages, Pension Contributions, Employee Benefits, and Payroll Taxes. The compensation paid during the entity's 990 reporting year for all employees not reported on lines 5 and 6 is reported on these lines. Other reporting requirements are signaled to the IRS by the numbers on these lines. Entries here should be coordinated with responses in Part V, lines 1 and 2. In addition to payroll taxes, unemployment taxes may be due, and Form 5500 may be due for pension plans. Section 501(c)(3) organizations are exempt from all federal, as well as some state, unemployment taxes. To properly report personnel costs by function, the organization's employees customarily must maintain time reports or other evidence of the portion of their efforts devoted to programs, management, and fundraising.[47]

Do not include amounts reported on lines 6b, 7b, 8b, 9b, and 10b of Part VIII.	(A) Total expenses	(B) Program service expenses	(C) Management and general expenses	(D) Fundraising expenses
11 Fees for services (non-employees):				
a Management				
b Legal				
c Accounting				
d Lobbying				
e Professional fundraising services. See Part IV, line 17				
f Investment management fees				
g Other				
12 Advertising and promotion				
13 Office expenses				
14 Information technology				
15 Royalties				
16 Occupancy				
17 Travel				
18 Payments of travel or entertainment expenses for any federal, state, or local public officials				
19 Conferences, conventions, and meetings				
20 Interest				

Lines 11a–g. Fees for Services Paid to Non-Employees. These new lines are a welcome addition to describe independent contractors (not including amounts paid to employees) that provide services indicated in the titles. The prior return only listed professional fundraisers, lawyers and accountants. Special suggestions provided in the instructions include the following:

Line 11b reflects legal fees, but any penalties, fines, settlements or judgments imposed against the organization as a result of legal proceedings on line 24.

Line 11d. Legal fees for any direct or grassroots lobbying services intended to influence foreign, national, state, or local legislation are reported on this line. Fees for matters not treated as lobbying, such as work to influence actions by executive, judicial, or administrative officials or bodies, or other advocacy services are reported on line 11g.

Line 11e. Professional fundraising services could include solicitation campaigns and advice or other consulting services supporting in-house fundraising campaigns. If they can be distinguished, printing, paper, envelopes, postage, mailing list rental, and equipment rental associated with fundraising services should be separated and reported on line 24 as other expenses.

Line 11f. Investment counseling, portfolio management, and monthly account service fees are considered portfolio management expenses. Do not include transaction costs. Brokerage fees are considered sales expenses reportable on Part VIII, line 7b.

Line 12. Advertising and Promotion. Amounts for print and electronic media advertising, Internet site link costs, signage costs, and advertising costs for the organization's in-house fundraising campaigns go here. Do not include fees paid to independent contractors for conducting professional fundraising services or campaigns (these amounts must be reported on line 11e).

Line 13. Office Expenses. This new line combines and replaces five lines from the former expense display. Amounts paid for supplies, telephone, fax, postage, delivery expenses, shipping materials, equipment rental, bank fees and other similar costs, such as printing costs of a general nature are reported on this line. Printing costs that relate to conferences or conventions are reported on line 19. Similarly printing of promotional materials would be reported on line 12.

Line 14. Information Technology. Include costs for hardware, software, and support services, such as maintenance, help desk, and other technical support services here. Also include expenses for infrastructure support, such as website design and operations, and virus protection and other information security programs and services to keep the organization's website operational and secured.

Line 15. Royalties. Enter amounts for royalties, license fees, and similar amounts paid to use intellectual property such as patents and copyrights here.

Line 16. Occupancy. Enter amounts for the use of office space or other facilities, including utilities, property insurance, real estate taxes, mortgage interest, and similar occupancy-related expenses here. Do not net any rental income received from leasing or subletting rented space against the amount reported on line 16 for occupancy expenses. If rental income is reported as program-service revenue on Part VIII, line 2, report allocable occupancy expenses on this line. However, if the rental income is not program-related, report related rental expenses on Part VIII, line 6b. Do not include depreciation as an occupancy expense because it is reported separately on line 22.

Line 17. Travel. The total travel expenses, including transportation costs, meals and lodging, and per diem payments are entered here. Travel costs include the expenses of purchasing, leasing, operating, and repairing any vehicles owned by the organization and used for the organization's activities. However, if the organization leases vehicles on behalf of its executives or other employees as part of an executive or employee compensation program, the leasing costs are considered employee compensation, and are reported on lines 5 through 7. The boxes in Line 1 of Schedule J indicate IRS concern for first class travel and other perks for the highly compensated that are not necessarily reported as compensation.

Line 18. Payments of Travel or Entertainment Expenses for any Federal, State, or Local Public Officials. Enter total amounts for travel or entertainment expenses for any federal, state, or local public officials and their family members on this line.[48]

Line 19. Conferences, Conventions, and Meetings. Include such expenses as facility rentals, speakers' fees and expenses, and printed materials related to conducting meetings related to the organization's activities here. Include the registration fees (but not travel expenses reportable on line 17) paid for sending any of the organization's staff to conferences, conventions, and meetings conducted by other organizations.

Line 20. Interest. The total interest expense for the year is entered. Do not include any interest attributable to rental property (reported on Part VIII, line 6b) or any mortgage interest (reported as occupancy expense on line 16).

Do not include amounts reported on lines 6b, 7b, 8b, 9b, and 10b of Part VIII.	(A) Total expenses	(B) Program service expenses	(C) Management and general expenses	(D) Fundraising expenses
21 Payments to affiliates				
22 Depreciation, depletion, and amortization .				
23 Insurance				
24 Other expenses. Itemize expenses not covered above. (Expenses grouped together and labeled miscellaneous may not exceed 5% of total expenses shown on line 25 below.)				
a				
b				
c				
d				
e				
f All other expenses				
25 **Total functional expenses.** Add lines 1 through 24f				
26 **Joint Costs.** Check here ▶ ☐ if following SOP 98-2. Complete this line only if the organization reported in column (B) joint costs from a combined educational campaign and fundraising solicitation				

Form **990** (2008)

Line 21. Payments to Affiliates. Certain types of payments to organizations closely related to the filing organization, such as dues paid by a local organization to its affiliated state or national (parent) organization are reported here. Also reportable on this line are predetermined quota support and dues by local agencies to their state or national organizations for unspecified purposes; that is, general use of funds for the national organization's own program and support services. Purchases of goods or services from affiliates are not reported on line 21 but are reported as expenses in the usual manner.

Line 22. Depreciation, Depletion, and Amortization. An organization is not required to use the Modified Accelerated Cost Recovery System (MACRS) to compute depreciation reported here. If an amount is reported on this line, the organization is required to maintain books and records to substantiate the amount reported but no longer has to attach a schedule to the 990. Certainly, Form 4562 used to report depreciation expense for income tax paying filers should not be attached as some have in the past.

Line 23. Insurance. This line should not include insurance attributable to rental property, employment-related benefits, or occupancy-related property. The cost of general liability, policies to cover assets owned, and key-person insurance payable to the organization are examples for inclusion on this line. The instructions do not clarify the ongoing discussion of where to report worker's compensation insurance premiums, but the authors' recommend the cost belongs on this line because it insures an obligation of the organization.

Line 24. Other Expenses. Enter the description and amount for the 5 largest expense categories (not listed above) on lines 24a through 24e and the total of all remaining expenses on line 24f. Due to this restriction, organizations that previously had a long list of "other expenses" will want to scrutinize their expense classifications in order to avoid having an inordinately large amount reported on line 24f (and therefore not described at all). Unrelated business income taxes must be reported as a separate line item. An amount labeled "other" or "miscellaneous" cannot exceed 5 percent of the total expenses reported on line 25.

Line 26. Joint Costs. An organization that has costs associated with a combined educational campaign and fundraising solicitation included in program costs is asked to explain how it allocates costs. To allocate costs that are of benefit to more than one function of the organization's operations, the IRS suggests, "Use an appropriate basis for each kind of cost." Some expenses, such as salaries, are allocated based on time expended. Occupancy can be based on space assigned or people using it (and may be partly based on their time allocation). The accounting profession provides some guidance for allocating materials that serve both an educational and informational purpose.[49]

§ 3.11   PART X BALANCE SHEET

Form 990 (2008)   Page **11**

Part X   Balance Sheet

(a)   Background

An exempt organization's beginning and ending assets, liabilities, and fund balances or net assets are reported in Part X, using the same method it uses for maintaining its normal accounting books and records. Beginning in 1995, this part of Form 990 reflects fund balances two ways. For organizations not following SFAS No. 117, lines 30 through 32 retain their former titles.

Fair market value of the assets may be reported if the organization's normal accounting method adjusts (referred to as "mark-to-market") asset carrying value to the current value. The amounts are often reported at original cost, or "book value." If so, there is no requirement that current value be reported. The only detailed information requested pertains to the end-of-year figures and is reported on Schedule D. The instructions for this part are quite good and need not be repeated here.

This part contains a particular trouble spot. Lines for loans between the organization, its officials, and other disqualified persons alert the IRS to potential inurement issues, and in those cases detailed reporting of the terms in Schedule L is requested. Loans to and from officers, directors, trustees, key employees, and other disqualified persons are presented as separate totals on lines 5, 6, and 22. Significant amounts on these lines, particularly if high in relation to the overall asset amounts, might indicate impermissible private benefit to insiders and should be very carefully disclosed. A $10,000 loan for purchase of a residence to a new vice president may not cause additional scrutiny, but a $100,000 loan to refinance his credit cards might.

What's new for this part follows:

- Separate lines for land, building, and equipment held for investment versus exempt functions have been eliminated here and instead are disclosed on Schedule D, Part VI with the misleading title *Investments*.

- Program-related investment line has been added.

- Schedule D replaces attachments with preformatted display.

			(A) Beginning of year		(B) End of year
Assets	1	Cash—non-interest-bearing		1	
	2	Savings and temporary cash investments		2	
	3	Pledges and grants receivable, net		3	
	4	Accounts receivable, net		4	
	5	Receivables from current and former officers, directors, trustees, key employees, or other related parties. Complete Part II of Schedule L		5	
	6	Receivables from other disqualified persons (as defined under section 4958(f)(1)) and persons described in section 4958(c)(3)(B). Complete Part II of Schedule L		6	
	7	Notes and loans receivable, net		7	
	8	Inventories for sale or use		8	
	9	Prepaid expenses and deferred charges		9	
	10a	Land, buildings, and equipment: cost basis 10a			
	b	Less: accumulated depreciation. Complete Part VI of Schedule D 10b		10c	
	11	Investments—publicly traded securities		11	
	12	Investments—other securities. See Part IV, line 11		12	
	13	Investments—program-related. See Part IV, line 11		13	
	14	Intangible assets		14	
	15	Other assets. See Part IV, line 11		15	
	16	**Total assets.** Add lines 1 through 15 (must equal line 34)		16	
Liabilities	17	Accounts payable and accrued expenses		17	
	18	Grants payable		18	
	19	Deferred revenue		19	
	20	Tax-exempt bond liabilities		20	
	21	Escrow account liability. Complete Part IV of Schedule D		21	
	22	Payables to current and former officers, directors, trustees, key employees, highest compensated employees, and disqualified persons. Complete Part II of Schedule L		22	
	23	Secured mortgages and notes payable to unrelated third parties		23	
	24	Unsecured notes and loans payable		24	
	25	Other liabilities. Complete Part X of Schedule D		25	
	26	**Total liabilities.** Add lines 17 through 25		26	
Net Assets or Fund Balances		**Organizations that follow SFAS 117, check here ▶ ☐ and complete lines 27 through 29, and lines 33 and 34.**			
	27	Unrestricted net assets		27	
	28	Temporarily restricted net assets		28	
	29	Permanently restricted net assets		29	
		Organizations that do not follow SFAS 117, check here ▶ ☐ and complete lines 30 through 34.			
	30	Capital stock or trust principal, or current funds		30	
	31	Paid-in or capital surplus, or land, building, or equipment fund		31	
	32	Retained earnings, endowment, accumulated income, or other funds		32	
	33	Total net assets or fund balances		33	
	34	Total liabilities and net assets/fund balances		34	

§3.12 PART XI FINANCIAL STATEMENTS AND REPORTING

Part XI	Financial Statements and Reporting		Yes	No
1	Accounting method used to prepare the Form 990: ☐ Cash ☐ Accrual ☐ Other			
2a	Were the organization's financial statements compiled or reviewed by an independent accountant? . .	**2a**		
b	Were the organization's financial statements audited by an independent accountant?	**2b**		
c	If "Yes" to lines 2a or 2b, does the organization have a committee that assumes responsibility for oversight of the audit, review, or compilation of its financial statements and selection of an independent accountant? . .	**2c**		
3a	As a result of a federal award, was the organization required to undergo an audit or audits as set forth in the Single Audit Act and OMB Circular A-133?	**3a**		
b	If "Yes," did the organization undergo the required audit or audits?	**3b**		

Form **990** (2008)

This portion of the revised 990 is new, but starts with information about the type of accounting method the organization uses to prepare the Form 990 that was previously displayed at the top of the front page. Showing again IRS concern for enhanced oversight over financial affairs of nonprofit organizations, this part asks for the type of services obtained in connection with its financial reporting. New Question 2a asks if the organization's financial statements were compiled or reviewed by an independent accountant.

New Question 2b asks if the organization's financial statements were audited by independent accountants. In what many think is a significant mistake, an entity whose financials are included in a consolidated audit report must answer "No" to the question. The same negative response is to be provided for Question 12 of Core Part IV. It is an amazing notion to say there was no audit when in fact the organization engaged independent accountants to perform audit services. The IRS instruction to say no stems from the difficulty some found in preparing former Parts IV-A and IV B, now Part XI and XII of Schedule D, to reconcile the numbers appearing on the audit report to the tax return. The author's firm has provided the IRS a suggested revision for the reconciliation that begins with the consolidated audit numbers and has lines to eliminate revenue and expenses of the other organizations included in the audited report.

Question 2c, similar to other questions asked in Part VI, asks about procedures for organizational oversight of the financial reporting process. Two separate issues are expected to be addressed by the committee: Is the committee responsible for *both* the oversight of the independent accountants and their selection? Though the form itself does not say so, a Schedule O explanation is requested by the instructions if the process of meeting this responsibility changes during the year. Lastly, Question 3 asks if the organization received federal awards, and if so, whether it underwent audit(s) required by Circular A-133.

NOTES

1. http://www.irs.gov/pub/irs-tege/governance_practices.pdf.
2. See discussion in Chapter 1.4.
3. On the June 2007 version of this part, 17 questions appeared in random order without the thresholds.
4. Go to www.irs.gov/businesses/corporations/article/0,,id=120633,00.html for details regarding current transactions listed by the IRS.

5. See Notice 88–120, 1988–2 C.B. 454.
6. IRC §170(f)(10)(B).
7. Newly added IRC §4943(e) for donor-advised funds and IRC §4943(f) for supporting organizations.
8. See IRC §509(f)(2)(B) for complete definition.
9. IRC §4943(c)(1).
10. IRC §4943(e)(2).
11. IRC §4943(f)(4).
12. As defined in IRC §4942(j)(4).
13. IRC §4043(d)(3)(B).
14. See J. Blazek, *Tax Planning and Compliance* (Hoboken, N.J.: John Wiley & Sons, 2008), Ch. 16.
15. IRC §170(c)(2)(B).
16. IRC §4966(c)(2).
17. Disqualified supporting organizations include any Type III supporting organization that is not functionally integrated and any Type I, Type II, or functionally integrated Type III supporting organization where the donor or donor advisor (and any related parties) directly or indirectly controls a supported organization of the supporting organization.
18. Rev. Proc. 2008–66, 2008–45 IRB 1107, updating Rev. Proc. 90–12, deems 2009 de minimis amounts to be $9.50, $47.50, and $95.
19. A year later, on February 14, 2008, the IRS withdrew the memo and said, ''The public comments received by the IRS, and the continued discussions within the sector regarding the respective roles of the IRS, the states and the sector regarding nonprofit governance, ultimately contributed to a revised governance section of the new Form 990 that the IRS released on December 20, 2007. The IRS also took these comments and discussions into account in making enhancements to our educational tool, Life Cycle, which we first made available in 2004.''
20. Rev. Ruls. 77–290, 80–332.
21. Reg. §53.4958–3(b).
22. See Chapter 1§4, ''Find Out Why Organization Qualifies for Tax Exemption.''
23. One wonders why partnership is mentioned here, since the IRS currently does not permit an organization formed as a partnership to qualify for recognition of exempt status.
24. See Publication 4573 for more information about group exemptions.
25. See Part VI Background discussion and Blazek, *Tax Planning and Compliance*, Ch. 20.10.
26. An Urban Institute report updated periodically is available at www.urbaninstitute.org entitled ''Foundation Expenses and Compensation.'' The Association for Small Foundations annually publishes Foundation Operations and Management Survey, a comprehensive survey of salaries and benefits by size of organization, by region of the country, and by positions (executive director, controller, clerical assistant, program manager, and the like). The Nonprofit Times and The Chronicles of Philanthropy publish annual salary surveys. Abbott, Langer & Associates publishes and sells an annual survey entitled ''Compensation in Nonprofit Organizations,'' which includes a variety of statistical information.
27. See Rev. Rul. 98–15 for ''good'' and ''bad'' examples of terms the IRS considers safeguards.
28. See Blazek, *Tax Planning and Compliance*, Ch. 2.1.
29. IRC §4958; see Blazek, *Tax Planning and Compliance*, Ch. 20.10.
30. See description of process used to approve compensation in answer to Question 15 of Core Part VI.
31. Ibid., note 29.
32. See definition provided for Schedule R.
33. See Chapter 2.
34. Deductibility information must be disclosed by many nonprofits. See comments for line 7 of Core Part V and Blazek, *Tax Planning and Compliance*, Ch. 24.

35. Readers should review the Professional Accounting Standards discussion in Chapter 2.2 for additional concepts and rules for reporting revenue.
36. Reg. §1.170–13(f)(8); see IRS Publication 1771, *Charitable Contributions—Substantiation and Disclosure Requirements*.
37. Ibid., See note 19.
38. Regs. §1.170A-9(e)(8) and §1.509(a)-3(g). Note that the definitions are somewhat different under these regulations so that a nonprofit should study the one pertaining to its category of public charity.
39. See Blazek, *Tax Planning and Compliance*, Ch. 21§8(e). A sponsorship is treated as a contribution when the words used to recognize the sponsor in print and by broadcast contain no quantitative or qualitative words promoting the sponsor according to IRC §513-(i). A thank-you displaying the sponsor's name and logo is permitted. Saying the sponsor sells the best product in the world is an advertisement.
40. FASB No. 135; see Chapter 2.2.
41. The estate tax rules of Treas. Reg. §20.2031 prescribe valuation methods; also see IRS Publication 56, *Determining the Value of Donated Property*.
42. IRC §501(c)(9) referred to as a VEBA.
43. The public support tests are considered for Schedule A.
44. IRC §6115; Part V, Question 7 asks whether the nonprofit has made this disclosure.
45. See Blazek, *Tax Planning and Compliance*, Ch. 24.
46. As defined by §4958(f)(1)) and §4958(c)(3)(B).
47. See introduction to Chapter 2.
48. IRC §4946(d).
49. See explanation of Statement of Position 98–2 in Chapter 2.2.

APPENDIX 3A

Transactions with Interested Parties Questionnaire

Name of organization _____

Name of interested party _____

This annual questionnaire must be completed and signed by our directors, officers, key employees, and other persons with substantial influence over financial decisions in accordance with the Conflict of Interest Policy. The responses include not only a description of relationships that could result in reportable transactions, but also the amount(s,) if any occurred.

FUTURE BUSINESS TRANSACTIONS: The following is a list of all entities:

(1) in which I have a financial interest (directly or indirectly) through business, family members, or investment, which, during the year, may have a transaction or arrangement for the purchase of goods and services or payment of compensation, with the Organization or with any entity or individual with which the Organization has an interest.

(2) in which I am an officer, director, manager or influential person, if I anticipate that such organizations will do business with the Organization in the coming fiscal year.

Please describe the nature, dates, and amounts of each business transaction that I anticipate will occur: Respond N/A if you have no transactions to disclose:

_____

_____

LOANS, GRANTS OR AWARDS: Describe any loan(s) to or from you or an entity in which you or your family have a financial interest and the Organization. Include the purpose of the loan, original principal amount and balance due. Enter N/A, if none.

_____

_____

List the name of any person related to you (including you) that did or will receive a grant or award or other assistance from the Organization during the year. Enter N/A if none.

_____

_____

OTHER TRANSACTIONS: The following is a description of all business transactions involving the Organization in the past fiscal year (1) in which I had a financial interest (direct or indirect) or (2) that involved an entity or organization in which I hold a position as an officer, director, manager or other influential person.

Provide a brief description of each transaction and a description of your interest in the transaction. Enter N/A if you have no transactions to disclose.

_____

_____

In completing this questionnaire, I have reviewed the Organization's conflicts of interest policy and hereby agree to comply with the policy to assure that our organization maintains its qualification as a Federal tax-exempt organization.

_____   _____

Signature of interested party   Date

CHAPTER FOUR

Form 990, Schedules A through R

§4.1 SCHEDULE A

SCHEDULE A (Form 990 or 990-EZ) Department of the Treasury Internal Revenue Service	**Public Charity Status and Public Support** To be completed by all section 501(c)(3) organizations and section 4947(a)(1) nonexempt charitable trusts. ▶ Attach to Form 990 or Form 990-EZ. ▶ See separate instructions.	OMB No. 1545-0047 Open to Public Inspection

Organizations that qualify as charities under Internal Revenue Code (IRC) §501(c)(3) and §501(a), (e), (f), (k), and (n), and nonexempt wholly charitable trusts furnish information to enable the IRS to review their ongoing qualification for public charity status on Schedule A. The issues addressed in this form are complex, and an adequate explanation of the genesis of the questions is beyond this book. The IRS, however, provides rather complete instructions, and preparers will be well informed by studying them. The chapters in J. Blazek, *Tax Planning and Compliance for Tax-Exempt Organizations* where additional information can be found are also referenced.

New Rules for 2008

To implement what readers will see is a five-year, rather than a four-year, public support test, effective October 9, 2008, new regulations were issued.[1] The public support test was previously based on the four years preceding the current year. As seen in Parts II and III, the test now includes those four years plus the current year. The mathematical tests are now calculated following the organization's regular accounting method—either cash or accrual.

A major challenge may face those organizations that report on an accrual basis for tax purposes. To correctly report revenue for 2004–2007, the cash-basis numbers reported on the prior return cannot be used, but instead must be restated.[2] A reasonable effort should be made to make a conversion, but for some the data may not be available.

In another significant change intended to streamline the IRS approval processes, the advance ruling period system under which new organizations were issued a tentative five-year period of classification as a public charity was eliminated. If information in the initial application for exemption, Form 1023, establishes to the satisfaction of the IRS that the organization can reasonably be expected to meet a public support test during its first five years, the organization qualifies as publicly supported for its first five years as a §501(c)(3) organization. The IRS will issue a determination letter stating that the organization is

(Continued)

---

exempt under §501(c)(3) and is classified as a public charity. The organization will be a public charity for its first five years, regardless of the level of public support it in fact receives during this period. The filing of Form 8734 is no longer required. Instead, information provided in Schedule A will demonstrate the support information to determine ongoing qualification as a public charity. The organization will not owe any §4940 tax or §507 termination tax with respect to its first five years. Beginning with the organization's sixth year, if the organization cannot establish that it is not a private foundation (as shown on lines 14 and 15 of Schedule A Part II or lines 15–16 of Schedule A Part III) as a public charity or a supporting organization under §509(a)(3), it will become a private foundation.

The form now provides a line for organizations to check during their first five years when no support percentages will be reflected. Organizations with advance ruling periods ending on or after June 9, 2008, will not receive a new determination letter. Those entities should carefully study the FAQs issued in connection with the announcement of the new regulations. The IRS admits that donors may not be willing to accept a determination letter reflecting an advance ruling period, but advises such donors should refer to IRS Publication 78. It is the authors' experience that this database is not updated in a timely manner. Alternatively, the FAQ advises donors should call the Customer Account Services at 1–877–829–5500 to verify public charity status.

Part I   **Reason for Public Charity Status** (All organizations must complete this part.) (see instructions)

(a) Background

The "reason for public charity status" rests on the organization's ability to qualify as a public charity and to fit into one of the 11 boxes on page 1 of Schedule A. These distinctly different categories of public charity are described in IRC §509(a)(1), (2), and (3), and are briefly discussed below.[3] The authors apologize for the extensive use of code citations in this subchapter but recommend that 990 preparers become conversant with them due to their extreme importance.

A wide variety of organizations qualify as public charities under §509(a)(1) (boxes 1 through 8). The (a)(1) category includes all §501(c)(3) tax-exempt organizations that are described in IRC §170(b)(1)(A)(i)–(vi), the tax code section that lists organizations eligible to receive deductible charitable contributions. The definition is complicated and rather unwieldy because it includes six distinct types of exempt entities. Following- the code design, the categories are labeled with numerical letters.

The first four categories include those organizations that perform what is called *inherently public activity*. They achieve public status because of the nature of their activities without regard to sources of funds with which they pay their bills—even if they are privately supported. The fifth and sixth are closely connected with governmental support and activities. Last, but certainly not least, because of the large variety of charities included, the seventh and eighth categories embody those organizations balancing their budgets with donations from a sizeable group of supporters, such as the United Way or the American Red Cross. These organizations must meet a mathematically measured contribution base formula and are referred to as *donative public charities*. A consideration of the rules that pertain to both donative public charities and service provider entities[4] is important in understanding public charities.

Box 9 is checked by organizations qualifying under §509(a)(2), which are referred to as *service-providing public charities*. Box 10 is checked by organizations that test for public safety that qualify under §509(a)(4). Box 11 is checked by organizations qualifying under §509(a)(3), which are referred to as *supporting organizations* because they derive their public charity status from supporting another public charity.

1   ☐   A church, convention of churches, or association of churches described in **section 170(b)(1)(A)(i).**

The first category of IRC §509(a)(1) includes a ''church, convention, or association of churches.'' Churches are narrowly defined, and not all religious organizations are regarded as churches.[5] Perhaps due to the need to separate church and state, neither the Internal Revenue Code nor the IRS regulations define a church. The fact that churches are not required to file Form 990 makes checking of this box a rarity. The IRS uses a 14-point test to allow qualification as a church. Most importantly a church must have a congregation of persons who worship together sharing belief in spiritual liturgy.

2   ☐   A school described in **section 170(b)(1)(A)(ii).** (Attach Schedule E.)

IRC §170(b)(1)(A)(ii), the second category, includes formal schools. A school is an ''educational organization that normally maintains a regular faculty and curriculum and normally has a regularly enrolled body of pupils or students in attendance at the place where its educational activities are regularly carried on.'' The presentation of formal instruction must be the primary function of a school. The term *school* includes primary, secondary, preparatory, high schools, colleges, and universities. Schools publicly supported by federal, state, and local governments qualify for this category, and in some cases also qualify as governmental units under (e), discussed below.

What the regulations call *noneducational* activities must be incidental. A recognized university can operate a museum or sponsor concerts and remain a school. A museum's art school, however, does not make the museum a school. All four elements must be present to achieve recognition as a school: regular faculty, students, curriculum, and facility. A home-tutoring entity providing private tutoring was held not to be an educational organization for this purpose. Likewise, a correspondence school was not approved under this section because it lacked a physical site where classes were conducted.

What constitutes a ''regular curriculum'' was loosely construed in one case, permitting an elementary school to qualify despite the fact that it had no ''formal course program'' and espoused an open learning concept. However, leisure learning classes, in the eyes of the IRS, do not present a sufficiently formal course of instruction to qualify as a school. Lectures and short courses on a variety of general subjects not leading to a degree or accreditation do not constitute a curriculum. Also, invited authorities and personalities recognized in the field are not considered to be members of a regular faculty. The duration of the courses was not considered a barrier to qualification for a particular outside survival school. Though classes lasted only 26 days and part of the facilities it used were wide open spaces, regular teachers, students, and a regular course study existed.[6]

3   ☐   A hospital or a cooperative hospital service organization described in **section 170(b)(1)(A)(iii).** (Attach Schedule H.)
4   ☐   A medical research organization operated in conjunction with a hospital described in **section 170(b)(1)(A)(iii).** Enter the hospital's name, city, and state: ---

This class of public charity includes hospitals, the principal purpose or function of which is providing medical or hospital care, medical education, or medical research. An organization directly engaged in continuous, active medical research in conjunction with a hospital may also qualify if, during the year in which the contribution is made to the organization, the funds are committed to be spent within five years.

Medical care includes the treatment of any physical or mental disability or condition on an inpatient or outpatient basis. A rehabilitation institution, outpatient clinic, or community mental health or drug treatment center may qualify. Convalescent homes, homes for children or the aged, handicapped vocational training centers, and medical schools are not considered to be hospitals. An animal clinic was also found not to be a hospital. The issues involved in qualifying for exemption as a hospital are evolving, and close attention must be paid to the latest information.

Medical research is the conduct of investigations, experiments, and studies to discover, develop, or verify knowledge relating to the causes, diagnosis, treatment, prevention, or control of physical or mental diseases and impairments of man. "Appropriate equipment and qualified personnel necessary to carry out its principal function must be regularly used." The disciplines spanning the biological, social, and behavioral sciences, such as chemistry, psychiatry, biomedical engineering, virology, immunology, biophysics, and associated medical fields, can be studied. Such organizations must conduct research directly. Granting funds to other organizations, while possible, may not be a primary purpose. The rules governing medical research organizations' expenditure of funds and endowment levels are complicated, and the regulations must be studied to understand this type of public organization.[7]

5 ☐ An organization operated for the benefit of a college or university owned or operated by a governmental unit described in **section 170(b)(1)(A)(iv).** (Complete Part II.)

Entities operating to receive, hold, invest, and administer property and to make expenditures to or for the benefit of a college or university qualifying under §170(b)(1)(A)(ii) are public charities. Such entities may normally receive a substantial part of their support from governmental grants as well as contributions from the general public, rather than exempt function revenue.

6 ☐ A federal, state, or local government or governmental unit described in **section 170(b)(1)(A)(v).**

The United States, District of Columbia, states, possessions of the United States, and their political subdivisions are classified as governmental units. They are listed as qualifying as public charities although they are not actually tax exempt under IRC §501(c)(3). In essence, they are public charities because they are responsive to all citizens. The regulations contain no additional definition or explanation of the meaning of this term, but IRS rulings and procedures and the courts have provided some guidance.[8]

7 ☐ An organization that normally receives a substantial part of its support from a governmental unit or from the general public described in **section 170(b)(1)(A)(vi).** (Complete Part II.)
8 ☐ A community trust described in **section 170(b)(1)(A)(vi).** (Complete Part II.)

Public charities in this category are organizations that normally receive at least 33⅓ percent of their annual support in the form of donations from members of the general public (not including fees and charges for performing exempt functions). *Normally* is based on an aggregation of the four years preceding the year in question and the current year; for example, the basis for qualification as a public charity for the tax year 2008 and 2009 is the revenue received during the five years 2004 through 2008. This calculation is made in Part II of Schedule A, lines 1 through 18. The revenue is reported for this test following the accounting method used by the organization for tax reporting purposes—either cash or accrual. Previously, only the cash basis was used.[9]

What's New: Organizations completing the public support tests for Form 990, Schedule A, previously were required to report revenues on a cash basis using income from the four years prior to the current year. On September 9, 2008, the IRS issued temporary regulations to implement the change shown in this Schedule for 2008 that calculates the public support test on a five-year basis. The five-year base applies to both §509(a)(1) and (2) public charities.

---

[9] ☐ An organization that normally receives: (1) more than 33⅓ % of its support from contributions, membership fees, and gross receipts from activities related to its exempt functions—subject to certain exceptions, and (2) no more than 33⅓ % of its support from gross investment income and unrelated business taxable income (less section 511 tax) from businesses acquired by the organization after June 30, 1975. See **section 509(a)(2).** (Complete Part III.)

Like those organizations said to conduct "inherently public" activities—churches, schools, and hospitals—the second major category of public charity includes entities that also provide services to the public—museums, libraries, low-income housing projects, and the like. Unlike churches, schools, and hospitals that qualify without regard to their sources of support, §509(a)(2) service providers must meet public support tests. Also unlike donative public charities that disregard fee-for-service revenue in calculating public support, service providers count exempt function revenues as support when their qualification is calculated on line 15 of Part III. Thus, this type of public charity usually includes organizations receiving a major portion of their support from fees and charges for activity participation such as day care centers, animal shelters, theaters, and educational publishers. Just like the §509(a)(1) test shown in Part II, the §509(a)(2) test is now calculated on a five-year basis using the accounting method for reporting revenue used for completing the Form 990, either cash or accrual.[10] A two-part support test must be met to qualify under this category:

1. Investment income cannot exceed one-third of the total support (all revenue except capital gains). Gifts from supporting organizations and split-interest trusts retain their character as investment income for purposes of calculating this limitation. A qualifying service provider cannot receive over one-third of its revenue from investment income. Dividends, interest, payments with respect to security loans, rents, royalties, and net unrelated business income (less the unrelated business income tax [UBIT]) are treated as investment income for this purpose. Program-related investments, such as low-income housing loans, do not produce investment income but rather exempt function gross receipts.

2. Over one-third of the total support must be received from exempt function sources made up of a combination of the following:

   • Gifts, grants, contributions, and membership dues received from nondisqualified persons. Unusual grants can be excluded.

- Admission to exempt function facilities or performances, such as theater or ballet performance tickets, museum or historic site admission fees, movie or video tickets, seminar or lecture fees, and athletic event charges.

- Fees for performance of services, such as school tuition, day care fees, hospital room and laboratory charges, psychiatric counseling, testing, scientific laboratory fees, library fines, animal neutering charges, athletic facility fees, and so on.

- Merchandise sales of goods related to the organization's activities, including books and educational literature, pharmaceuticals and medical devices, handicrafts, reproductions and copies of original works of art, byproducts of a blood bank, and goods produced by handicapped workers.

- Exempt function revenues received from one source are not counted to the extent they exceed $5,000 or 1 percent of the organization's support, whichever is higher.

10 ☐ An organization organized and operated exclusively to test for public safety. See **section 509(a)(4).** (see instructions)

Although organizations operated to test for public safety are exempt under §501 (c)(3), they are not eligible to receive tax-deductible contributions because they are not operated for purposes described in §170. In order to check Box 10, the organization must have received a letter from the IRS demonstrating recognition of this status. It does not have to complete any further tests to prove public charity status.

11 ☐ An organization organized and operated exclusively for the benefit of, to perform the functions of, or to carry out the purposes of one or more publicly supported organizations described in section 509(a)(1) or section 509(a)(2). See **section 509(a)(3).** Check the box that describes the type of supporting organization and complete lines 11e through 11h.

    a ☐ Type I   **b** ☐ Type II   **c** ☐ Type III–Functionally integrated   **d** ☐ Type III–Other

e ☐ By checking this box, I certify that the organization is not controlled directly or indirectly by one or more disqualified persons other than foundation managers and other than one or more publicly supported organizations described in section 509(a)(1) or section 509(a)(2).

f   If the organization received a written determination from the IRS that it is a Type I, Type II, or Type III supporting organization, check this box . . . . ☐

g   Since August 17, 2006, has the organization accepted any gift or contribution from any of the following persons?

		Yes	No
(i) A person who directly or indirectly controls, either alone or together with persons described in (ii) and (iii) below, the governing body of the supported organization?	11g(i)		
(ii) A family member of a person described in (i) above?	11g(ii)		
(iii) A 35% controlled entity of a person described in (i) or (ii) above?	11g(iii)		

h   Provide the following information about the organizations the organization supports.

(i) Name of supported organization	(ii) EIN	(iii) Type of organization (described on lines 1–9 above or IRC section (see instructions))	(iv) Is the organization in col. (i) listed in your governing document?		(v) Did you notify the organization in col. (i) of your support?		(vi) Is the organization in col. (i) organized in the U.S.?		(vii) Amount of support
			Yes	No	Yes	No	Yes	No	
Total									

For Privacy Act and Paperwork Reduction Act Notice, see the Instructions for Form 990.   Cat. No. 11285F   **Schedule A (Form 990 or 990-EZ) 2008**

The last category of organizations that escape the requirements placed on private foundations is a *supporting organization* ("SO"). If such organizations are sufficiently responsive to, controlled or supervised by, or operated in connection with one or more public charities, they are classified as public charities themselves, even if they are privately funded.

Basically, SOs dedicate all of their assets to one or more public charities that need not necessarily control them (except an SO cannot be controlled by disqualified persons). Beneficiary organization(s) must be specified, but can be changed under certain conditions. This flexibility makes SOs popular with benefactors that want neither to create a private foundation nor to make an outright gift to an established charity. The rules are not entirely logical, and the regulations are quite detailed and extensive.[11] The questions that must be answered on Form 1023, Schedule D, for organizations seeking this classification are also instructive. An SO must meet three unique organizational and operational tests as follows:

1. It must be organized, and at all times thereafter, operated exclusively for the benefit of, to perform the functions of, or to carry out the purposes of one or more specified public charities (*purpose*).

2. It must be operated, supervised, controlled by, or in connection with, one or more public charities (*organizational test*).

3. It cannot be controlled, directly or indirectly, by one or more disqualified persons.

The Pension Protection Act has placed many new restrictions on supporting organizations and those that fund them. First, it is now important to know the supporting organization's Type. The Type depends on the degree of control and organizational oversight the supported public charity(ies) exercises over the SO as listed below. The original IRS letter designating qualification as a §501(c)(3) tax-exempt entity most likely does not specify the SO Type. However, an organization may now request (free of charge) a determination letter that specifies its Type except that, until final regulations are released, the IRS will not issue a determination letter as to whether a Type III supporting organization qualifies as a Type III-Other (nonfunctionally integrated).[12]

A Type I supporting organization is operated, supervised, or controlled by one or more supported organizations.[13] This characteristic exists if a majority of the governing board or officers are elected or appointed by the supported organization(s).

A Type II supporting organization is supervised or controlled in connection with the supported organization.[14] This characteristic exists if a majority of the governing board consists of individuals who also serve on the governing board of the supported organization(s).

A Type III supporting organization is operated in connection with one or more publicly supported organizations.[15] Qualification as a Type III can be evaluated using the following list of criteria:

- Do the officers, directors, trustees, or members of the supported organization (s) elect or appoint one or more of your officers, directors, or trustees?

- Do one or more members of the governing body of the supported organization(s) also serve as your officers, directors, or trustees or hold other important offices with respect to you?

- Do your officers, directors, or trustees maintain a close and continuous working relationship with the officers, directors, or trustees of the supported organization(s)?

- Does the supported organization(s) have a significant voice in your investment policies, in the making and timing of grants, and in otherwise directing the use of your income or assets?

- Do you conduct activities that would otherwise be carried out by the supported organization(s)?

- Do you ensure that the supported organization(s) is attentive to your operations?

- Does your organizing document specify the supported organization(s) by name?

- Has there been an historic and continuing relationship between you and the supported organization(s)?

Type III organizations are further classified as to whether they are *functionally integrated* with their SO or not. The term *functionally integrated* means "a Type III SO which is not required to make payments to supported organizations due to the activities of the organization related to performing the functions of, or carrying out the purposes of, such SOs."[16] For example, a disaster aid society, created by and operated in affiliation with, a church, but not controlled by the church, might be treated as functionally related. Private foundations may not count grants to a non-functionally integrated Type III SO as qualifying distributions and must exercise expenditure responsibility in regard to such grants.

On line 11, the SO checks one of the boxes a–d to identify what type of supporting organization it is. On line 11e, all SOs must certify that they are not controlled by disqualified persons (a criterion for classification as an SO). Line 11g seeks to determine whether the organization has accepted contributions from certain persons. If the organization answers "Yes" to any of those items, it becomes subject to restrictions imposed on Type III—Other organizations such as excess business holdings and penalties imposed on private foundations that make grants to them without exercising expenditure responsibility. Line 11h provides information about the supported organization(s). Only Type III organizations are required to complete column (v), which points to the requirement that the SO must notify its supported organization of its support to demonstrate "responsiveness."

(b) Understanding the Calculation

Revenues are reported for public support purposes differently from the way they are reported in Part VIII of Form 990. For many organizations, there will not be a simple transposition of numbers from one line to another. The classification of revenue as related or unrelated (and why the revenue is not UBI) is critical to determining the correct placement on Schedule A and impacts the public support percentage. Donative public charities check the box for line 7 on Form 990 Schedule A, Part I, "Reason for Public Charity Status" and complete Schedule A, Part II, "Support Schedule for Organizations Described in IRC 170(b)(1)(A)(iv) and 170(b)(1)(A)(vi). The formula used to calculate the public support percentage follows:

Public Support Percentage

Total support (not counting exempt function revenue from line 12)
    Less: Gifts (five years worth) from any donor that exceed 2 percent of total donations
for the five year period
    Interest and dividends
    Unrelated business income and other income.
    =Public support
    ./. Divided by Total support = public support percentage (must be $33\frac{1}{3}$ or higher)

Schedule A (Form 990 or 990-EZ) 2008   Page **2**

| **Part II** | **Support Schedule for Organizations Described in Sections 170(b)(1)(A)(iv) and 170(b)(1)(A)(vi)** (Complete only if you checked the box on line 5, 7, or 8 of Part I.) |

Section A. Public Support

Calendar year (or fiscal year beginning in) ▶	(a) 2004	(b) 2005	(c) 2006	(d) 2007	(e) 2008	(f) Total
1 Gifts, grants, contributions, and membership fees received. (Do not include any "unusual grants.") . . .						
2 Tax revenues levied for the organization's benefit and either paid to or expended on its behalf						
3 The value of services or facilities furnished by a governmental unit to the organization without charge . . .						
4 **Total.** Add lines 1-3						
5 The portion of total contributions by each person (other than a governmental unit or publicly supported organization) included on line 1 that exceeds 2% of the amount shown on line 11, column (f)						
6 **Public support.** Subtract line 5 from line 4.						

Section B. Total Support

Calendar year (or fiscal year beginning in) ▶	(a) 2004	(b) 2005	(c) 2006	(d) 2007	(e) 2008	(f) Total
7 Amounts from line 4						
8 Gross income from interest, dividends, payments received on securities loans, rents, royalties and income from similar sources						
9 Net income from unrelated business activities, whether or not the business is regularly carried on						
10 Other income. Do not include gain or loss from the sale of capital assets (Explain in Part IV.)						
11 **Total support.** Add lines 7 through 10 .						

12 Gross receipts from related activities, etc. (see instructions)	**12**

13 **First five years.** If the Form 990 is for the organization's first, second, third, fourth, or fifth tax year as a section 501(c)(3) organization, check this box and **stop here** . . . . ▶ ☐

Section C. Computation of Public Support Percentage

14 Public support percentage for 2008 (line 6, column (f) divided by line 11, column (f))	**14**	%
15 Public support percentage from 2007 Schedule A, Part IV-A, line 26f	**15**	%

16a **$33\frac{1}{3}$ % support test—2008.** If the organization did not check the box on line 13, and line 14 is $33\frac{1}{3}$ % or more, check this box and **stop here.** The organization qualifies as a publicly supported organization . . . . ▶ ☐

  b **$33\frac{1}{3}$ % support test—2007.** If the organization did not check a box on line 13 or 16a, and line 15 is $33\frac{1}{3}$ % or more, check this box and **stop here.** The organization qualifies as a publicly supported organization . . . . ▶ ☐

17a **10%-facts-and-circumstances test—2008.** If the organization did not check a box on line 13, 16a, or 16b, and line 14 is 10% or more, and if the organization meets the "facts-and-circumstances" test, check this box and **stop here.** Explain in Part IV how the organization meets the "facts-and-circumstances" test. The organization qualifies as a publicly supported organization . . . . . ▶ ☐

  b **10%-facts-and-circumstances test—2007.** If the organization did not check a box on line 13, 16a, 16b, or 17a, and line 15 is 10% or more, and if the organization meets the "facts-and-circumstances" test, check this box and **stop here.** Explain in Part IV how the organization meets the "facts-and-circumstances" test. The organization qualifies as a publicly supported organization . . . . . ▶ ☐

18 **Private foundation.** If the organization did not check a box on line 13, 16a, 16b, 17a, or 17b, check this box and see instructions ▶ ☐

Schedule A (Form 990 or 990-EZ) 2008

Line 5 seeks to determine amounts received from substantial contributors that should be treated as private support. A list needs to be prepared that includes the name and amounts given by those individuals or organizations (other than a §509(a)(1) public charity or governmental unit) during the five-year period that gave more than 2 percent of line 11f of Sch. A, Part II (the total revenue received by the organization during the period covered by the support schedule *except* amounts reported on line 12). These people/organizations are considered to be substantial contributors, and any amounts they gave over the 2 percent are added together and reported on line 5 of Sch. A, Part II as nonpublic support. During the first five years of the organization's existence it completes lines 1–12, but stops at a check box on line 13 and does not make the percentage calculations.

The 33⅓ percent support formula for donative public charities does not include revenues the organization receives from performing its exempt activities—student tuition or patient fees, for example—as does the formula for service providers.[17] Donations of services for which a contribution deduction is not allowed[18] are also excluded unless they are from a governmental entity—then, they are reported on line 3. An organization that is primarily dependent on exempt function revenues (receives a minimum amount of donations) cannot qualify as a donative public charity.[19]

There is a 2 percent of total support ceiling for donations included as public support. Contributions from each donor, whether an individual, corporation, trust, private foundation, or other type of entity (after combining related parties), during each five-year period are counted only up to the 2 percent ceiling. Voluntary grants and donations received by a donative public charity from other charities listed in §170(b)(1)(A) and governmental units, including foreign governments,[20] are not subject to the 2 percent limit and instead are fully counted as donations from the general public (unless the gift was passed through as a donor-designated grant).[21] Grants from a service-providing entity[22] and from a supporting organization are subject to the 2 percent inclusion limitation.[23]

For example, say an organization receives total support during the five-year test period of $1 million. In such a case, contributions from each donor up to $20,000 could be counted as public donations. If one person gave $20,000 each year for a total of $100,000 for five years, only $20,000 is counted as public support. The $1 million organization must receive at least $333,333 in public donations of $20,000 or less from each donor. It could receive $666,666 from one source and $10,000 from 33 sources or $20,000 from 17 sources, for example.

> A public donation = Up to and no more than 2 percent of total support
> $20,000 = 2% of $1 million

A guide for transferring page 1 lines follows:

SCH. A, PART II	DESCRIPTION
Line 1	Gifts, grants, and contributions reported on Part VIII, line 1h of Form 990.
Line 2	Tax revenues levied for your benefit. This amount may be reported on Part VIII, line 11 of Form 990.
Line 3	The value of services furnished by a governmental unit without charge. This amount may not be reported on 990 because the instructions explicitly indicate donated services are not to be reported as revenue or expense.

Line 8	*Gross* income from interest, dividends, payments received on securities loans (990 Part VIII, line 3), rents (990 Part VIII, line 6a), royalties (990 Part VIII, line 5), and income from similar sources (990 Part VIII, line 4 and possibly 11).
Line 9	Net income from unrelated business activities not reported on line 12. Examples include income from special events (990 Part VIII, lines 8a and 9a), advertising (Part VIII, line 11), and rents from debt-financed property (Part VIII, line 6d).
Line 10	Other income.
Line 12	*Gross* receipts from merchandise sold (990 Part VIII, line 10a), services performed (990 Part VIII, line 2) are reported, and certain other income excluded from UBI under §513—(1) activity conducted by volunteers (990 Part VIII, line 10a or 11), (2) activity conducted for the convenience of members (990 Part VIII, line 2, 10a, or 11), selling of donated merchandise (990 Part VIII, line 10a), income from trade show/ qualified public entertainment activity (990 Part VIII, line 2), bingo (990 Part VIII, line 9a), rental of member list (990 Part VIII, line 5 or 11).

(c) Facts and Circumstances

When the percentage of an organization's public donations falls below the precise 33⅓ percent test, it may be able to sustain public charity status by applying the *facts and circumstances test*.[24] The history of the organization's fund-raising efforts and other factors are considered as an alternative method to the strict mathematical formula for qualifying for public support under §509(a)(1). This test is not available for charities qualifying as publicly supported under §509(a)(2).

An organization may need to apply this test at different times during its life. It can seek such qualification when it originally files Form 1023. In that instance, the IRS will scrutinize the facts and issue its approval or disapproval. The test may also be applied later in its life if support falls below the 33⅓ percent level.

The information evidencing qualification must be submitted in Part IV of Schedule A of the annual Form 990. The box for either 17a or 17b (or both) should be checked when "Facts and Circumstances Apply" and Box 14 or 15 (or both) show an amount less than 33⅓ percent. The IRS does not customarily respond to an organization checking this box for the first time.

Though prior IRS approval is not required, an organization might choose to seek approval by submitting the information to the Cincinnati office responsible for determinations.[25] For the facts and circumstances test to apply, the following factors must be present:

- Public support must be at least 10 percent of total support, and the higher the better.
- The organization must have an active "continuous and bona fide" fund-raising program designed to attract new and additional public and governmental support. Consideration will be given to the fact that, in its early years of existence, it limits the scope of its solicitations to those persons deemed most likely to provide seed money in an amount sufficient to enable it to commence its charitable activities and to expand its solicitation program.

Other favorable factors must be present, such as:

- The composition of the board is representative of broad public interests (rather than those of major contributors).

- Some support comes from governmental and other sources representative of the general public (rather than a few major contributors).

- Facilities and programs are made available to the general public, such as a museum or symphonic society.

- Programs appeal to a broadly based public (and in fact the public participates).

(d) Unusual Grants

When inclusion of a substantial donation(s) causes an organization to fail the 33⅓ percent public support test, public charity status may still be sustained by excluding such gift(s). A qualifying *unusual grant* can be excluded from gross revenue in calculating total support for both (a)(1) and (a)(2) purposes.[26] A grant is unusual if it is an unexpected and substantial gift attracted by the public nature of the organization *and* received from a disinterested party. A number of factors are taken into account; no single factor is determinative, and not all factors need be present. The positive factors are shown below, along with their opposites in parentheses:

1. The contribution is received from a party with no connection to the organization. (The gift is received from a person who is a substantial contributor, board member, or manager, or related to a board member or manager of the organization.)

2. The gift is in the form of cash, marketable securities, or property that furthers the organization's exempt purposes. (The property is illiquid, difficult to dispose of, and not pertinent to the organization's activities—useless, in other words.) A gift of a painting to a museum, or a gift of wetlands to a nature preservation society would be useful and appropriate property.

3. No material restrictions are placed on the gift. (Strings are attached.)

4. The organization attracts a significant amount of support to pay its operating expenses on a regular basis, and the gift adds to an endowment or pays for capital items. (The gift pays for operating expenses for several years and is not added to an endowment.)

5. The gift is a bequest. (The gift is an *inter vivos* transfer.)

6. An active fund-raising program exists and attracts significant public support. (Fund solicitation programs are unsuccessful.)

7. A representative and broadly based governing body controls the organization. (Related parties control the organization.)

8. Prior to the receipt of the unusual grant, the organization qualified as publicly supported. (The unusual grant exclusion was relied on in the past to satisfy the test.)

If the grant is payable over a period of years, it can be excluded each year, but any income earned on the sums would be included. The IRS has provided a set of safe harbor reliance factors to identify unusual grants. If the first four factors listed above are present, unusual grant status can automatically be claimed and relied on. As to item 4, the terms of the grant cannot provide for more than one year's operating expense.

In previous versions of Schedule A, the IRS provided the following instruction on the form itself: "for an organization . . . that received any unusual grants during [the public support test period], prepare a list for your records to show, for each year, the name of the contributor, the date and amount of the grant, and a brief description of the nature of the grant. Do not file this list with your return.'' For 2008, this directive has been relegated to the instructions to the form. As a new requirement, the IRS now asks organizations who received unusual grants during the five-year period to report in Part IV of Schedule A the list showing the *amount* (but not the donor's name) of each unusual grant excluded from the support test.

Schedule A (Form 990 or 990-EZ) 2008   Page **3**

Part III   **Support Schedule for Organizations Described in Section 509(a)(2)**
(Complete only if you checked the box on line 9 of Part I.)

Section A. Public Support

Calendar year (or fiscal year beginning in) ▶	(a) 2004	(b) 2005	(c) 2006	(d) 2007	(e) 2008	(f) Total
1 Gifts, grants, contributions, and membership fees received. (Do not include any "unusual grants.")						
2 Gross receipts from admissions, merchandise sold or services performed, or facilities furnished in any activity that is related to the organization's tax-exempt purpose						
3 Gross receipts from activities that are not an unrelated trade or business under section 513						
4 Tax revenues levied for the organization's benefit and either paid to or expended on its behalf						
5 The value of services or facilities furnished by a governmental unit to the organization without charge						
6 **Total.** Add lines 1-5						
7a Amounts included on lines 1, 2, and 3 received from disqualified persons						
b Amounts included on lines 2 and 3 received from other than disqualified persons that exceed the greater of 1% of the total of lines 9, 10c, 11, and 12 for the year or $5,000						
c Add lines 7a and 7b						
8 **Public support** (Subtract line 7c from line 6.)						

Section B. Total Support

Calendar year (or fiscal year beginning in) ▶	(a) 2004	(b) 2005	(c) 2006	(d) 2007	(e) 2008	(f) Total
9 Amounts from line 6						
10a Gross income from interest, dividends, payments received on securities loans, rents, royalties and income from similar sources						
b Unrelated business taxable income (less section 511 taxes) from businesses acquired after June 30, 1975						
c Add lines 10a and 10b						
11 Net income from unrelated business activities not included in line 10b, whether or not the business is regularly carried on						
12 Other income. Do not include gain or loss from the sale of capital assets (Explain in Part IV.)						
13 **Total support.** (Add lines 9, 10c, 11, and 12.)						

14 **First five years.** If the Form 990 is for the organization's first, second, third, fourth, or fifth tax year as a section 501(c)(3) organization, check this box and **stop here**   ▶ ☐

Section C. Computation of Public Support Percentage

15 Public support percentage for 2008 (line 8, column (f) divided by line 13, column (f))	**15**	%
16 Public support percentage from 2007 Schedule A, Part IV-A, line 27g	**16**	%

Section D. Computation of Investment Income Percentage

17 Investment income percentage for **2008** (line 10c, column (f) divided by line 13, column (f))	**17**	%
18 Investment income percentage from **2007** Schedule A, Part IV-A, line 27h	**18**	%

19a **33⅓ % support tests—2008.** If the organization did not check the box on line 14, and line 15 is more than 33⅓ %, and line 17 is not more than 33⅓ %, check this box and **stop here.** The organization qualifies as a publicly supported organization   ▶ ☐

b **33⅓ % support tests—2007.** If the organization did not check a box on line 14 or line 19a, and line 16 is more than 33⅓ %, and line 18 is not more than 33⅓ %, check this box and **stop here.** The organization qualifies as a publicly supported organization   ▶ ☐

20 **Private foundation.** If the organization did not check a box on line 14, 19a, or 19b, check this box and see instructions ▶ ☐

Schedule A (Form 990 or 990-EZ) 2008

Service-providing public charities check the box for line 9 on Schedule A, Part I, and complete Sch. A, Part III. To fulfill the requirements of this test, the organization must receive more than 33⅓ percent of its support from revenue reported on lines 1–6 and not more than 33⅓ percent of its support from revenues reported on lines 9–10b. During the first five years of the organization's existence, it submits support information, but stops at a check box on line 14 and does not make the percentage calculations. Two types of support are considered to be private under this test:

- Donations from Disqualified Persons

    The first type is donations received from disqualified persons—the board members, key employees, substantial contributors, and their family members. A substantial contributor is one that has donated more than 2 percent of the total contributions the organization has received over its entire life. All amounts received from disqualified persons are reported on line 7a of Sch. A, Part III and treated as private support.

- Major Vendors

    The second type of potentially private support relates to income reported on lines 2 and 3 of Sch. A, Part III. Any individual or organization that purchased the larger of $5,000 or 1 percent of the total of such revenue for the year. The amount given in *excess* of the 1 percent (or $5,000) is treated as private and reported on line 7b of Sch. A, Part III. The formula used to calculate the public support percentage first determines the total amount of public support by subtracting what is considered to be private support—excess amounts calculated above, interest and dividends, unrelated business income, and other income. Then, public support is divided by total considered support and the percentage is obtained. This percentage needs to be 33⅓ or higher to maintain public charity status.

A guide for transferring page 1 lines follows:

Sch. A, Part III	Description
Line 1	Gifts, grants, and contributions reported on Part VIII, line 1h of Form 990.
Line 2	Gross receipts from merchandise sold (990 Part VIII, line 10a), services performed (990 Part VIII, line 2), and any other income derived from activities related to the organization's exempt purpose (990 Part VIII, line 11) are reported.
Line 3	Gross receipts from other activities excluded from UBI under 513: (1) activity conducted by volunteers (990 Part VIII, line 10a or 11), (2) activity conducted for the convenience of members (990 Part VIII, line 2, 10a, or 11), selling of donated merchandise (990 Part VIII, line 10a), income from trade show/qualified public entertainment activity (990 Part VIII, line 2), bingo (990 Part VIII, line 9a), rental of member list (990 Part VIII, line 5 or 11), qualified sponsorship payments (990 Part VIII, line 11).
Line 4	Tax revenues levied for your benefit. This amount may be reported on Part VIII, line 11 of Form 990.

Line 5	The value of services furnished by a governmental unit without charge. This amount may not be reported on 990 because the instructions explicitly indicate donated services are not to be reported as revenue or expense.
Line 10a	Gross income from interest, dividends, payments received on securities loans, (990 Part VIII, line 3), rents (990 Part VIII, line 6a), royalties (990 Part VIII, line 5), and income from similar sources (990 Part VIII, line 4 and possibly 11).
Line 10b	Unrelated business taxable income less any tax paid (990-T Line 13 Column (A).
Line 11	Net income from unrelated business activities not reported on lines 3 or 10b. Examples include income from special events (990 Part VIII, lines 8a and 9a) and research (Part VIII, line 11).
Line 12	Other income.

(e) Differences Between §509(a)(1) and §509(a)(2)

Some organizations, including most churches, schools, and hospitals, can qualify for public status under both §509(a)(1) and (a)(2). The (a)(1) class is the preferred public charity category. For purposes of annual reporting, unrelated business income, limits on deductions for donors, and most other tax purposes, the two categories are virtually the same, with one important exception: To receive a terminating distribution from a private foundation upon its dissolution, the charity must be an (a)(1) organization.

(i) Definition of Support. The items of gross income included in the requisite ''support'' are different for each category and do not equal total revenue under either class. ''Support'' forms the basis of public status for both categories, and the calculations are made on a five-year moving average basis using the organization's normal method of accounting. For (a)(1) purposes, certain revenue is not counted as support and is not included in the numerator or the denominator:

- Exempt function revenue, or that amount earned through charges for the exercise or performance of exempt activities, such as admission tickets, patient fees, and so on
- Capital gains or losses
- Unusual grants
- Donations of in-kind services and facilities (although facility and service donations from governmental units are counted)

For (a)(2) purposes, total revenue less capital gains or losses, unusual grants, and plus in-kind service and facility donations equals total support.

(ii) Major Gifts. Contributions received are counted as public support differently for each category.[27] Under the (a)(1) category, a particular giver's donations (including grants from supporting organizations and §509(a)(2) organizations) are counted only up to an amount equal to 2 percent of the total "support" for the five-year period. Gifts from other public charities and governmental entities are not subject to this 2 percent floor.

For (a)(2) purposes, all gifts, grants, and contributions are counted as public support, except those received from disqualified persons. Such a person may be a substantial contributor (or one who gives over $5,000 if such amount is more than 2 percent of the organization's aggregate contributions for its life), a board member, trustee, or officer, a business controlled by a disqualified person, or a relative of such a person. For (a)(2) purposes, gifts from these insiders are not counted at all. Subject to the 2 percent ceiling, their gifts are partially counted for (a)(1) purposes.

(iii) Membership Fees. For both categories, this may represent donations or charges for services rendered. In some cases, a combined gift and payment for services may be present. The facts in each circumstance must be examined to properly classify the revenue. A membership fee is a donation if it is paid by persons to support the goals and interests they have in common with the organization rather than to purchase admission, merchandise, services, or the use of facilities.[28] The charitable deduction rules also provide that members provided *de minimis* benefits may treat the entire dues payment as a donation. Particularly for (a)(1) purposes, this distinction is very important because dues treated as exempt function fees are not included in the public support calculations.

(iv) Grants for Services. These grants, to be rendered for the granting organization, such as a state government's funding for home health or prisoner care, are treated under both categories as exempt function income, not donations or grants. The accounting rules call such revenue *exchange function* when the recipient organization performs a service or provides a facility or product to serve the needs of the grantor. A grant is instead treated as a contribution when the payment is made to encourage the grantee organization to carry on certain programs or activities in furtherance of its own exempt purposes; no economic or physical benefit accrues to the grant maker.

Under both categories, this distinction is important to determine amounts qualifying as contributions. For (a)(2) status, the distinction has yet another dimension: Only the first $5,000 of fees, or 1 percent of the total revenue (whichever is higher), for such services received from a particular grantor or vendor is includible in public support. Government payments made on behalf of a third-party payor, such as Medicare or Medicaid patient receipts or blood bank charges collected by a hospital as agent for a blood bank, are treated as revenue from the individual patients.[29]

Pass-through grants received from another public charity are totally counted toward public support unless the gift represents an indirect grant expressly or implicitly earmarked by a donor to be paid to a subgrantee organization. In that case, the donor is the individual. *Donor-designated* grants, therefore, require careful scrutiny. The basic question is whether the intermediary organization received the gift as an agent or whether it can freely choose to regrant the funds. Donations received under a donor designation and donor-advised funds ("DAFs") should qualify as public support to the initial recipient organization (and again to the ultimate recipient) because it retains ultimate authority to approve the regrants.

(v) In-Kind Gifts. These are counted differently for each category. For (a)(1) purposes, the regulation specifically says support does not include "contributions of services for which a deduction is not allowable." For (a)(2) purposes, the regulation says support includes the fair market or rental value of gifts, grants, or contributions of property or use of such property on the date of the gift. Back to (a)(1), the regulations and the IRS instructions to Form 990 are silent about gifts of property that are deductible. It is not stated whether the full fair market value of property for which the contribution deduction is limited to basis, such as a gift of clothing to the charity resale shop, is counted at full value or at basis. The organization, for accounting purposes, would count such gifts at their full value.

(f) Solving Troublesome Public Status Problems

To secure one of its major sources of funding, a public charity must carefully guard its status to be sure it can continue to receive grants from private foundations (PFs). One PF can give a grant to another PF only if it exercises expenditure responsibility, a paperwork requirement that many refuse to undertake. The test is based on revenues the charity *normally* receives. The normal period is the four years preceding the year in question and the current year. The basis for qualification as a public charity for the tax years 2008 and 2009 is the revenue received during 2004 through 2008. That means an organization that falls below 33⅓ percent for 2008 must be very careful to seek funding needed to achieve that level for 2009 (based on 2005–2009). Those unprepared for the new five-year calculation may face unexpected loss of status. Indeed a cautious organization with a support ratio below 50 percent will maintain ongoing projections of support levels. A few problems that might arise and suggested solutions include:

- Change of public charity category. Sometimes, the sources of a public charity's revenue change, causing it to fail to qualify under one category or another. Simply reporting the financial information on Schedule A is sufficient to allow an organization to continue its public status; the issue is whether to seek a new determination letter to reflect the new category. Funders and other interested parties who compare Schedule A to the determination letter may want an explanation. The IRS Exempt Business Master File in the past has sometimes shown a category differing from the determination letter and the Form 990 as well. The instructions to the form acknowledge that a new letter is not required though a request for one can be sent to the Exempt Organization Division with information described in Rev. Proc. 2008–4.[30]

- An organization could conceivably change annually, depending on the category into which it fits. The consequence is minimal, except that §509(a)(2) organizations are not qualified recipients for a PF's terminating distribution, and grants received by a §509(a)(1) public charity from an (a)(2) public charity are subject to the 2 percent limit. Only loss of public status is truly harmful.

- Loss of public status. A more serious situation arises when the changes in support cause the organization to lose its public charity status. Important to note here is that the loss of status is not immediate; if the financial tally submitted with the organization's 2008 return reflects support for the years 2004 through 2008 was less than the requisite one-third, public status continues through the year 2009. Special rules apply for new organizations. Until a change of status is announced in the Internal Revenue Bulletin, contributors are entitled to rely on the latest IRS letter. A donor who is responsible for or otherwise aware of the changes is not entitled to such reliance.[31]

- *Timing* can be extremely important for an organization that inadvertently loses its public status and becomes a private foundation. The organization can make an application to terminate PF status under a plan to raise an appropriate level of public donations during the following five years, referred to as a *60-month termination*. However, a notice of such a conversion plan must be filed for IRS approval prior to the period for which it is effective. An inattentive organization may not realize its need to file until after the end of the year in which the failure occurs.[32]

  ○ Change of operation. An organization that has qualified as a public charity for reasons of its activity, such as a school or a hospital, loses its public status at the end of a year, if not technically on the day, when it ceases to conduct the activity. Commonly, such an organization sells its assets, invests the proceeds, and converts to a grant-making private foundation. Because of the excise tax on investment income, mandatory payout, and other rules that begin to apply, delaying the conversion date may be desirable. Due to its revenue sources during the time it operated as a hospital or school, it is likely it can qualify as a public charity for at least one, if not two, years after the sale of its assets.[33]

Coordination of the reporting functions between the accounting and development departments is particularly important for an organization the public status of which is dependent upon revenues from major contributors. Schedule A, Part II, line 5, asks §509(a)(1) organizations for the total amount received for the past five years from donors in excess of 2 percent of line 11f. For §509(a)(2) organizations, similar details for its disqualified persons[34] (major donors, board members, and their families) are shown on Part III, line 7a. To complete this report, each disqualified person's total annual gifts and exempt function purchases for five years must be available. An organization does not necessarily know in any one year which donors will, over the succeeding five-year period, fall into this special reporting.

§4.2 SCHEDULE B

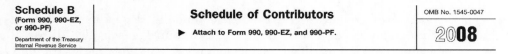

Schedule B	Schedule of Contributors	OMB No. 1545-0047
(Form 990, 990-EZ, or 990-PF)	► Attach to Form 990, 990-EZ, and 990-PF.	2008
Department of the Treasury Internal Revenue Service		

Schedule B is required to be completed by organizations receiving a contribution of $5,000 or more from any one contributor. Organizations that complete Part II of Schedule A and display a public support percentage of at least 33⅓ percent for the year can substitute 2 percent of Part VIII, line 1h for the $5,000 figure if it is larger. For example, an organization showing $1,000,000 for total contributions received on Part VIII, line 1h would only need to complete Schedule B for contributors of $20,000 (2 percent of $1,000,000) or more. When completing Schedule B, the organization must follow the same accounting method it has indicated it uses in Part XI, line 1.

The entire Schedule B is only open to public inspection for private foundations and §527 organizations. For all other organizations, the names and addresses of the contributors are not open to inspection but all other information (amount of contributions and description of noncash contributions) is open unless it clearly identifies the contributor. When filing a copy of the return with a state, one should not include Schedule B unless specifically required because the state may inadvertently make the information publicly available.

In previous years, organizations completing Schedule B were not required to report contributions from governmental entities of any amount. Now the instructions indicate that organizations qualified as public charities by meeting a mechanical support test (i.e., §170(b)(1)(A)(iv), §170(b)(1)(A)(vi), and §509(a)(2) organizations) must treat government entities as contributors for Schedule B purposes.

Name of the organization | **Employer identification number**

Organization type (check one):

Filers of: | **Section:**

Form 990 or 990-EZ | ☐ 501(c)(   ) (enter number) organization

☐ 4947(a)(1) nonexempt charitable trust **not** treated as a private foundation

☐ 527 political organization

Form 990-PF | ☐ 501(c)(3) exempt private foundation

☐ 4947(a)(1) nonexempt charitable trust treated as a private foundation

☐ 501(c)(3) taxable private foundation

Check if your organization is covered by the **General Rule** or a **Special Rule**. (**Note.** Only a section 501(c)(7), (8), or (10) organization can check boxes for both the General Rule and a Special Rule. See instructions.)

General Rule

☐ For organizations filing Form 990, 990-EZ, or 990-PF that received, during the year, $5,000 or more (in money or property) from any one contributor. Complete Parts I and II.

Special Rules

☐ For a section 501(c)(3) organization filing Form 990, or Form 990-EZ, that met the 33⅓ % support test of the regulations under sections 509(a)(1)/170(b)(1)(A)(vi), and received from any one contributor, during the year, a contribution of the greater of **(1)** $5,000 or **(2)** 2% of the amount on Form 990, Part VIII, line 1h or 2% of the amount on Form 990-EZ, line 1. Complete Parts I and II.

☐ For a section 501(c)(7), (8), or (10) organization filing Form 990, or Form 990-EZ, that received from any one contributor, during the year, aggregate contributions or bequests of more than $1,000 for use *exclusively* for religious, charitable, scientific, literary, or educational purposes, or the prevention of cruelty to children or animals. Complete Parts I, II, and III.

☐ For a section 501(c)(7), (8), or (10) organization filing Form 990, or Form 990-EZ, that received from any one contributor, during the year, some contributions for use *exclusively* for religious, charitable, etc., purposes, but these contributions did not aggregate to more than $1,000. (If this box is checked, enter here the total contributions that were received during the year for an *exclusively* religious, charitable, etc., purpose. Do not complete any of the parts unless the **General Rule** applies to this organization because it received nonexclusively religious, charitable, etc., contributions of $5,000 or more during the year.)   . . . . ▶ $ ....

Caution. Organizations that are not covered by the General Rule and/or the Special Rules do not file Schedule B (Form 990, 990-EZ, or 990-PF), but they **must** answer "No" on Part IV, line 2 of their Form 990, or check the box in the heading of their Form 990-EZ, or on line 2 of their Form 990-PF, to certify that they do not meet the filing requirements of Schedule B (Form 990, 990-EZ, or 990-PF).

For Privacy Act and Paperwork Reduction Act Notice, see the Instructions for Form 990. These instructions will be issued separately. | Cat. No. 30613X | Schedule B (Form 990, 990-EZ, or 990-PF) (2008)

Most organizations will check the General Rule box and report information about contributors of $5,000 or more. Organizations meeting the 33⅓ percent public support test under §170(b)(1)(A)(vi) will check the first Special Rule box and report information about contributors of the greater of $5,000 or 2 percent of total contributions received during the year. The second and third boxes pertain only to §501(c)(7), (8), and (10) organizations who typically do not receive substantial contributions.

Schedule B (Form 990, 990-EZ, or 990-PF) (2008)   Page _____ of _____ of **Part I**

Name of organization	Employer identification number

Part I   **Contributors** (see instructions)

(a) No.	(b) Name, address, and ZIP + 4	(c) Aggregate contributions	(d) Type of contribution
....	....	$	Person ☐ Payroll ☐ Noncash ☐ (Complete Part II if there is a noncash contribution.)
....	....	$	Person ☐ Payroll ☐ Noncash ☐ (Complete Part II if there is a noncash contribution.)
....	....	$	Person ☐ Payroll ☐ Noncash ☐ (Complete Part II if there is a noncash contribution.)
....	....	$	Person ☐ Payroll ☐ Noncash ☐ (Complete Part II if there is a noncash contribution.)
....	....	$	Person ☐ Payroll ☐ Noncash ☐ (Complete Part II if there is a noncash contribution.)
....	....	$	Person ☐ Payroll ☐ Noncash ☐ (Complete Part II if there is a noncash contribution.)

Schedule B (Form 990, 990-EZ, or 990-PF) (2008)

The completion of this part is pretty straightforward. The name, address, and amount given are reported for each contributor required to be listed here. Additionally, a box must be checked to identify whether the contributions were (1) noncash, (2) made by payroll deduction, or (3) if neither (1) nor (2) applies, the box for "person" is used. If any of the listed contributors made noncash contributions, then Part II of Schedule B must be completed to provide further information.

Schedule B (Form 990, 990-EZ, or 990-PF) (2008)   Page ____ of ____ of Part II

Name of organization

Employer identification number

Part II   **Noncash Property** (see instructions)

(a) No. from Part I	(b) Description of noncash property given	(c) FMV (or estimate) (see instructions)	(d) Date received
....	....	$	...../....../......
....	....	$	...../....../......
....	....	$	...../....../......
....	....	$	...../....../......
....	....	$	...../....../......
....	....	$	...../....../......

Schedule B (Form 990, 990-EZ, or 990-PF) (2008)

Here a description of the noncash property donated, the fair market value of the donation (equivalent to amount recorded as contribution), and the date of the donation is provided. If the property is immediately sold upon receipt by the organization, the instructions say to report the proceeds amount as the value of the contribution similar to the method followed under GAAP. For marketable securities not immediately sold, use the average of the high and low price on the contribution date to determine the value. For all other property gifts, an appraised or estimated value is used. See IRS Publication 561, *Determining the Value of Donated Property*, for more information. For gifts where the donor has provided a completed Form 8283 to the organization, it is important to make an effort to coordinate the information presented by the donor on that form (date and value of gift) with the information presented here unless they are materially different. Also, the organization will need to determine whether it needs to file Form 8282 as a result of the gift.

Schedule B (Form 990, 990-EZ, or 990-PF) (2008)   Page ____ of ____ of Part III

Name of organization	Employer identification number

Part III   *Exclusively* religious, charitable, etc., individual contributions to section 501(c)(7), (8), or (10) organizations aggregating **more than $1,000 for the year.** Complete columns **(a)** through **(e)** and the following line entry.

For organizations completing Part III, enter the total of *exclusively* religious, charitable, etc., contributions of **$1,000 or less** for the year. (Enter this information once. See instructions.) ► $

(a) No. from Part I	(b) Purpose of gift	(c) Use of gift	(d) Description of how gift is held

(e) Transfer of gift	
Transferee's name, address, and ZIP + 4	Relationship of transferor to transferee

(a) No. from Part I	(b) Purpose of gift	(c) Use of gift	(d) Description of how gift is held

(e) Transfer of gift	
Transferee's name, address, and ZIP + 4	Relationship of transferor to transferee

(a) No. from Part I	(b) Purpose of gift	(c) Use of gift	(d) Description of how gift is held

(e) Transfer of gift	
Transferee's name, address, and ZIP + 4	Relationship of transferor to transferee

(a) No. from Part I	(b) Purpose of gift	(c) Use of gift	(d) Description of how gift is held

(Continued)

	(e) Transfer of gift	
Transferee's name, address, and ZIP + 4	Relationship of transferor to transferee	

Schedule B (Form 990, 990-EZ, or 990-PF) (2008)

This part is completed by §501(c)(7), (8), or (10) organizations who have received contributions exclusively for charitable purposes aggregating more than $1,000 during the year from a single donor. Information is requested about how the organization tracks the gift and the intended purpose and use of the gift. Generally, §501(c)(7), (8), and (10) organizations are not eligible to receive tax-deductible donations, however, an exception exists in §170(c)(4) which provides deductibility for income tax purposes "in the case of a contribution or gift by an individual, a domestic fraternal society, order, or association, operating under the lodge system, but only if such contribution or gift is to be used exclusively for religious, charitable, scientific, literary, or educational purposes, or for the prevention of cruelty to children or animals."

§4.3 SCHEDULE C

SCHEDULE C (Form 990 or 990-EZ) Department of the Treasury Internal Revenue Service	**Political Campaign and Lobbying Activities** For Organizations Exempt From Income Tax Under section 501(c) and section 527 ▶ To be completed by organizations described below. ▶ Attach to Form 990 or Form 990-EZ.	OMB No. 1545-0047 **2008** **Open to Public Inspection**

If the organization answered "Yes," to Form 990, Part IV, line 3, or Form 990-EZ, Part VI, line 46 (Political Campaign Activities), then
- Section 501(c)(3) organizations: Complete Parts I-A and B. Do not complete Part I-C.
- Section 501(c) (other than section 501(c)(3)) organizations: Complete Parts I-A and C below. Do not complete Part I-B.
- Section 527 organizations: Complete Part I-A only.

If the organization answered "Yes," to Form 990, Part IV, line 4, or Form 990-EZ, Part VI, line 47 (Lobbying Activities), then
- Section 501(c)(3) organizations that have filed Form 5768 (election under section 501(h)): Complete Part II-A. Do not complete Part II-B.
- Section 501(c)(3) organizations that have NOT filed Form 5768 (election under section 501(h)): Complete Part II-B. Do not complete Part II-A.

If the organization answered "Yes," to Form 990, Part IV, line 5 (Proxy Tax), then
- Section 501(c)(4), (5), or (6) organizations: Complete Part III.

(a) Background

Schedule C allows the IRS to evaluate potential violations of the limitations on electioneering and lobbying activities of tax-exempt organizations.[35] The limits differ for the various types of §501(c) entities that complete one or more of the eight parts of the schedule. From the outset it is important to emphasize that charities (including private foundations) are permitted to conduct voter registration and education programs, but cannot electioneer or conduct efforts to influence legislation, referred to as lobbying. A public charity is similarly not allowed to electioneer, but can conduct some lobbying activities. The portion of a public charity's total effort spent on lobbying, however, is limited and governed by one of two very different sets of rules. One test, called the *expenditure test*, is based on money spent with separate limits for direct and grassroots efforts as described below (the "§501(h) election"). The limitations on lobbying expenses for all other types of exempt organizations are not specified with a particular amount or percentage. The complex nature of the rules is reflected in the length of the extensive instructions provided for this schedule.

Importantly, §501(c)(3) organizations are absolutely prohibited from conducting any efforts to influence the election of a person to public office. As a general rule, §501(c)(4) organizations should not spend more than 50 percent of their budget on attempts to influence an election. Lastly, other §501(c) and §527 entities may spend an unlimited amount. The IRS conducted examinations of charities that allegedly intervened in elections in 2004, and 2006, and issued guidelines that contain 20 helpful examples contrasting activity that was or was not electioneering.[36] Examples describe circumstances when an organizational official is speaking as an individual rather than on behalf of the entity, what constitutes voter education, and the consequence of certain Internet links.

DEFINITIONS

Political Campaign Activities include all activities that support or oppose candidates for elective federal, state, or local public office. Candidates are people who offer themselves or are proposed by others for public office. An activity to encourage participation in the electoral process, such as voter registration or voter education that does not directly or indirectly support or oppose a candidate is not political campaign activity.

Section 527 Exempt Function Activities: All functions that influence or attempt to influence the selection, nomination, election, or appointment of any individual to any federal, state, or local public office or office in a political organization, or the election of presidential or vice-presidential electors, whether or not such individual or electors are selected, nominated, elected, or appointed.

Political Expenditures include any expenditure for political campaign activities, such as a payment, distribution, loan, advance, deposit, or gift of money, or anything of value to advance a campaign. It also includes a contract, promise, or agreement to make an expenditure, whether or not legally enforceable.

Lobbying Activities include activities intended to influence foreign, national, state, or local legislation, and can be either *direct* (attempting to influence the legislators) or *grassroots* (attempting to influence legislation by influencing the general public).

Legislation includes action by Congress, any state legislature, any local council, or similar governing body with respect to acts, bills, resolutions, or similar items or by the public in referenda, ballot initiatives, constitutional amendments, or similar procedures. It does not include actions by executive, judicial, or administrative bodies.

Specific Legislation includes (1) legislation that has already been introduced in a legislative body and (2) specific legislative proposals that an organization either supports or opposes.

Part I-A   **To be completed by all organizations exempt under section 501(c) and section 527 organizations.** See the instructions for Schedule C for details.

1	Provide a description of the organization's direct and indirect political campaign activities in Part IV.
2	Political expenditures . . . . ▶ $
3	Volunteer hours . . . .

Compliance with other filing requirements and tax issues is surveyed in the questions of this schedule, some of which are designated for completion by different types of exempt organizations to reflect the different limitations applicable to each. It is important to read the headnotes on each part.

The request to provide a description of direct and indirect political campaign activities in Part IV and the blanks that reflect amounts spent on line 2 and volunteer hours on line 3 *must be blank* for §501(c)(3) organizations, which are not allowed to conduct such activities. Unfortunately, the instructions do not make this point.

Non-(c)(3) organizations report the amount of political campaign (also referred to as Section 527 Exempt Function Activity) expenses on line 2 and explain the campaign activity in Part IV. The number of either actual, or reasonably estimated, hours volunteers spent working on political campaign activity is reported on line 3. Those entities that have established a §527(f)(3) segregated fund (a PAC) to engage in political activity do not report the funds they collect on behalf of and disburse to the PAC. Those amounts are reported on line 5, column (e) of Part I-C.

Part I-B	**To be completed by all organizations exempt under section 501(c)(3).**
	See the instructions for Schedule C for details.

1	Enter the amount of any excise tax incurred by the organization under section 4955 . . . . ▶	$	
2	Enter the amount of any excise tax incurred by organization managers under section 4955 . ▶	$	
3	If the organization incurred a section 4955 tax, did it file Form 4720 for this year?	☐ Yes	☐ No
4a	Was a correction made?	☐ Yes	☐ No
b	If "Yes," describe in Part IV.		

(b) Background

A charitable organization exempt under §501(c)(3) does not necessarily lose its exempt status if it participates in election activity.[37] The tax code was revised in 1976, to provide a tool, short of revocation of exemption, to penalize charities for impermissible electioneering activity. This part discloses the amount of such penalties both on the organization and its managers. In addition to the penalty, a charity that spends money to influence an election is also expected to correct the problem as described below.

A detailed description is requested in Part IV to describe the steps the organization has taken to correct the activity which subjected the organization to the §4955 tax. Correction of a political expenditure means recovering the expenditure to the extent possible and establishing safeguards to prevent future political expenditures. Recovery of the expenditure means recovering part or all of the expenditure to the extent possible, and, where full recovery cannot be accomplished, by any additional corrective action that is necessary. The instructions, however, say that the organization that made the political expenditure is not under any obligation to attempt to recover the expenditure by legal action if the action would in all probability not result in the satisfaction of execution on a judgment.

Part I-C	**To be completed by all organizations exempt under section 501(c), except section 501(c)(3).**
	See the instructions for Schedule C for details.

1	Enter the amount directly expended by the filing organization for section 527 exempt function activities . . . . ▶	$	
2	Enter the amount of the filing organization's funds contributed to other organizations for section 527 exempt function activities . . . . ▶	$	
3	Total of direct and indirect exempt function expenditures. Add lines 1 and 2 and enter here and on Form 1120-POL, line 17b . . . . ▶	$	
4	Did the filing organization file **Form 1120-POL** for this year?	☐ Yes	☐ No
5	State the names, addresses and employer identification number (EIN) of all section 527 political organizations to which payments were made. Enter the amount paid and indicate if the amount was paid from the filing organization's funds or were political contributions received and promptly and directly delivered to a separate political organization, such as a separate segregated fund or a political action committee (PAC). If additional space is needed, provide information in Part IV.		

(Continued)

Part I-C — To be completed by all organizations exempt under section 501(c), except section 501(c)(3).
See the instructions for Schedule C for details.

(a) Name	(b) Address	(c) EIN	(d) Amount paid from filing organization's funds. If none, enter -0-.	(e) Amount of political contributions received and promptly and directly delivered to a separate political organization. If none, enter -0-.

For Privacy Act and Paperwork Reduction Act Notice, see the Instructions for Form 990.　Cat. No. 50084S　Schedule C (Form 990 or 990-EZ) 2008

(c) Background

Section 527 is entitled "Political Organizations" and outlines rules that designate funds received by such entities as "exempt function," meaning they were spent on qualifying election activity and therefore exempt from income tax. Taxable income for a §527 entity is typically interest income earned on account balances that is taxed with the filing of Form 1120-POL. The "exempt function" of a §527 organization is defined as "amounts spent to influence or attempt to influence the selection, nomination, election, or appointment of any individual to any Federal, State, or public office, or office in a political organization, or election of Presidential or Vice-Presidential electors."

Non-§501(c)(3) organizations that collect political contributions or member dues earmarked for a separate segregated fund, and promptly and directly transfer them to that fund[38] should not report them on lines 1 or 2. Such amounts should be reported on line 5e.

Schedule C (Form 990 or 990-EZ) 2008　　　　　　　　　　　　　　　　　　　Page 2

Part II-A — To be completed by organizations exempt under section 501(c)(3) that filed Form 5768 (election under section 501(h)). See the instructions for Schedule C for details.

A　Check ▶ ☐ if the filing organization belongs to an affiliated group.
B　Check ▶ ☐ if the filing organization checked box A and "limited control" provisions apply.

Limits on Lobbying Expenditures (The term "expenditures" means amounts paid or incurred.)	(a) Filing organization's totals	(b) Affiliated group totals
1a　Total lobbying expenditures to influence public opinion (grass roots lobbying) . . .		
b　Total lobbying expenditures to influence a legislative body (direct lobbying)		
c　Total lobbying expenditures (add lines 1a and 1b)		
d　Other exempt purpose expenditures		
e　Total exempt purpose expenditures (add lines 1c and 1d)		
f　Lobbying nontaxable amount. Enter the amount from the following table in both columns.		

If the amount on line 1e, column (a) or (b) is:	The lobbying nontaxable amount is:
Not over $500,000	20% of the amount on line 1e.
Over $500,000 but not over $1,000,000	$100,000 plus 15% of the excess over $500,000.
Over $1,000,000 but not over $1,500,000	$175,000 plus 10% of the excess over $1,000,000.
Over $1,500,000 but not over $17,000,000	$225,000 plus 5% of the excess over $1,500,000.
Over $17,000,000	$1,000,000.

	(a)	(b)
g　Grassroots nontaxable amount (enter 25% of line 1f)		
h　Subtract line 1g from line 1a. Enter -0- if line g is more than line a		
i　Subtract line 1f from line 1c. Enter -0- if line f is more than line c		
j　If there is an amount other than zero on either line 1h or line 1i, did the organization file Form 4720 reporting section 4911 tax for this year? . . . . ☐ Yes ☐ No		

(d) Background

Those charities that elect the mathematical lobbying limitations under §501(h) complete Part II-A, which reflects the specific numerical test that is applied. Successful completion of this part depends on good accounting and an ability to identify direct expenses and to allocate indirect ones.[39] A public charity that makes the election may spend up to a relatively high percentage of its exempt purpose expenditures to influence legislation without incurring tax or losing its tax-exempt status. The election can be adopted or revoked for any tax year by filing Form 5768 within the year for which it is to be effective. Both the IRS and most advisors to exempt organizations recommend making the election for a public charity that engages in any efforts to influence legislation. There are two advantages of making the election:

1. The allowable spending for lobbying is based on a precise mathematical percentage of the organization's overall expenditures.

2. The definition of what constitutes lobbying is both specific and broad.

Under §501(h), the "expenditure test" measures permissible lobbying activities. For example, to constitute lobbying under §501(h), any communication with legislators or the general public must include a "call-to-action" that

- Refers to specific legislation and
- Reflects a view on such legislation.

Absent the election, a "substantial part test," said by most to be a vague and imprecise test subject to interpretation is applied.[40]

Once the direct and indirect lobbying expenses are identified and entered on lines 1a and 1b of this part, it is important that line 1d and resulting line 1e be quantified. An organization's "Exempt Purpose Expenditures" include most of its expenses, including fund-raising, management, and depreciation, but excludes expenses "paid for the production of income,"[41] not including revenues from performance of exempt functions such as tuition, counseling fees, or operation of low-income housing. Line 1e, therefore, should be equal to total expenses shown on line 25 of Core Part IX column (A) less investment management and custody expenses of endowment or other funds held.

The lobbying spending limits are imposed in a consolidated fashion for affiliated organizations. Such a group exists when one organization is "bound by the other organization's decisions on legislative issues (control) or if enough representatives of one belong to the other organization's governing board to cause or prevent action on legislative issues (interlocking directorate)." The affiliate enters its own lobbying and exempt function expenses in column (a) and the entire total for all affiliates in column (b). A list showing each affiliated group member's name, address, EIN, and expenses, plus identity of those members that made the election under §501(h) and those that did not should be provided in Part IV. Each electing member's share of the excess lobbying expenditures is also requested.

The nontaxable lobbying amount calculated for line 1f is well illustrated on the form. A graduated percentage of total expenses is allowed beginning with 20 percent of an organization's first $500,000 of expenses and rising to 5 percent of those expenses over $17,000,000 with a maximum of $1,000,000 allowed. A separate grassroots limit on line g equals 25 percent of the permissible direct lobbying. Importantly, any amount other than zero on lines h and i indicates excessive lobbying expenses. An excess in any one year results in an excise tax under §4911 of 25 percent of the excess expenditures. Additionally, if the four-year average described below indicates excess expenditures, the organization will have its exempt status revoked.

4-Year Averaging Period Under Section 501(h)
(Some organizations that made a section 501(h) election do not have to complete all of the five columns below. See the instructions for lines 2a through 2f of the instructions.)

Lobbying Expenditures During 4-Year Averaging Period					
Calendar year (or fiscal year beginning in)	(a) 2005	(b) 2006	(c) 2007	(d) 2008	(e) Total
2a Lobbying non-taxable amount					
b Lobbying ceiling amount (150% of line 2a, column(e))					
c Total lobbying expenditures					
d Grassroots non-taxable amount					
e Grassroots ceiling amount (150% of line 2d, column (e))					
f Grassroots lobbying expenditures					

Schedule C (Form 990 or 990-EZ) 2008

This chart compares the permissible direct lobbying from line 1f, called "lobbying non-taxable amount," to the "ceiling" of 150 percent of line 1f for all four years. Similarly, the permissible grassroots lobbying expenses from line 1g (25 percent of line 1f) is compared to a ceiling amount.

For organizations who did not have the §501(h) election in place for all of the years shown in Part II-A, only the columns pertaining to the years in which the election was effective are required to be completed. However, if the test is not satisfied based on that information, the organization should complete all columns for which it is in existence as a §501(c)(3) organization. Additionally, if the organization is not required to complete all columns, it should explain why in Part IV.

Schedule C (Form 990 or 990-EZ) 2008 · Page **3**

Part II-B	To be completed by organizations exempt under section 501(c)(3) that have NOT filed Form 5768 (election under section 501(h)). See the instructions for Schedule C for details.	(a)		(b)
		Yes	No	Amount
1	During the year, did the filing organization attempt to influence foreign, national, state or local legislation, including any attempt to influence public opinion on a legislative matter or referendum, through the use of:			
a	Volunteers?			
b	Paid staff or management (include compensation in expenses reported on lines 1c through 1i)?			
c	Media advertisements?			
d	Mailings to members, legislators, or the public?			
e	Publications, or published or broadcast statements?			
f	Grants to other organizations for lobbying purposes?			
g	Direct contact with legislators, their staffs, government officials, or a legislative body?			
h	Rallies, demonstrations, seminars, conventions, speeches, lectures, or any other means?			
i	Other activities? If "Yes," describe in Part IV			
j	Total lines 1c through 1i			
2a	Did the activities in line 1 cause the organization to be not described in section 501(c)(3)?			
b	If "Yes," enter the amount of any tax incurred under section 4912			
c	If "Yes," enter the amount of any tax incurred by organization managers under section 4912			
d	If the filing organization incurred a section 4912 tax, did it file Form 4720 for this year?			

A "substantial part" test is instead applied to those public charities that do not make the §501(h) election to measure their permissible lobbying expenditures. Such organizations face a subjective and qualitative measure to ascertain if the lobbying comprises a substantial part of their activities. This test is embodied in the regulations that require a §501(c)(3) organization to operate exclusively for charitable purposes. While some would argue lobbying advances their mission, lobbying is not considered an exempt function activity for a tax-exempt organization. The big disadvantage of this test is that the permissible amount of lobbying for organizations that do not elect is not specified. Instead, all of the facts and circumstances are taken into account to determine whether the overarching "exclusively for charitable purposes" (c)(3) test is satisfied. Overall lobbying efforts are not only evidenced by spending, but also by involvement of volunteers and board members, by use of the organization's name to promote an effort, and a host of similar intangible factors that may be taken into account if the IRS wants to challenge an organization's tax-exempt status. The nationwide organization, Independent Sector, conducted a public information campaign in recent years to encourage charities to participate in public affairs and to inform public charities about the advantages of making the election.

The information displayed in this part on line 1 is fairly self-explanatory. Again, a good accounting system capable of capturing the information is critical for a charity that conducts lobbying. Great care must be taken *not* to answer the question on line 2a "Yes." If so, the organization is saying its lobbying activity was of such an excessive amount that its exemption should be revoked. Lines 2a and 2b ask for the amount of §4912 penalty[42] imposed on the organization and its managers as a result of the excessive expenditures. Line 2d reminds such an organization to file Form 4720 to report the excess and associated penalty.

Part III-A	**To be completed by all organizations exempt under section 501(c)(4), section 501(c)(5), or section 501(c)(6).** See the instructions for Schedule C for details.		Yes	No
1	Were substantially all (90% or more) dues received nondeductible by members?	1		
2	Did the organization make only in-house lobbying expenditures of $2,000 or less?	2		
3	Did the organization agree to carryover lobbying and political expenditures from the prior year?	3		
Part III-B	**To be completed by all organizations exempt under section 501(c)(4), section 501(c)(5), or section 501(c)(6) if BOTH Part III-A, questions 1 and 2 are answered "No" OR if Part III-A, question 3 is answered "Yes."** See Schedule C instructions for details.			
1	Dues, assessments and similar amounts from members	1		
2	Section 162(e) non-deductible lobbying and political expenditures **(do not include amounts of political expenses for which the section 527(f) tax was paid).**			
a	Current year	2a		
b	Carryover from last year	2b		
c	Total	2c		
3	Aggregate amount reported in section 6033(e)(1)(A) notices of nondeductible section 162(e) dues . . .	3		
4	If notices were sent and the amount on line 2c exceeds the amount on line 3, what portion of the excess does the organization agree to carryover to the reasonable estimate of nondeductible lobbying and political expenditure next year?	4		
5	Taxable amount of lobbying and political expenditures (line 2c total minus 3 and 4)	5		

§501(c)(4), (5), and (6) organizations that conduct lobbying are required to disclose to their members, the percentage of dues paid by members that are nondeductible as business expenses as a result of the funds being used for lobbying. Three exceptions to this rule apply: (1) if more than 90 percent of the dues are not deductible by members, or (2) the organization's lobbying expenses were in-house (not paid to an outside consultant) and less than $2,000, or (3) the organization pays a proxy tax on its lobbying expenses. The answers to the questions in Part III-A indicate whether an analysis in Part III-B is required to determine whether the organization has allocated a sufficient nondeductibility percentage to dues to cover actual expenses or the amount subject to the proxy tax. If the organization has used too high a percentage (that is, lobbying expenses are lower than anticipated), it is allowed to carryover the excess to future years. Conversely, if the organization has not used a high enough percentage (that is, lobbying expenses are more than anticipated), it is allowed to carryover the shortfall to the next year only. The instructions provide good examples for this part.

Part IV	**Supplemental Information**

Complete this part to provide the descriptions required for Part I-A, line 1; Part I-B, line 4; Part I-C, line 5; and Part II-B, line 1i. Also, complete this part for any additional information.

Schedule C (Form 990 or 990-EZ) 2008

The following lines request description of activities in Part IV:

Part I-A asks for a detailed description of political campaign activities. A §501(c)(3) organization MUST not have such activity or a penalty results.

Part I-B describes correction steps a §501(c)(3) organization took if it did have impermissible political campaign activity.

Part I-C suggests using this part as a continuation for the list of PACs supported by the organization if necessary.

Part II-A asks for details regarding affiliated group members and an explanation if all columns of line 2 are not completed.

Part II-B requires a description of all lobbying activities checked "Yes" on line 1.

§4.4 SCHEDULE D

SCHEDULE D **(Form 990)**	**Supplemental Financial Statements**	OMB No. 1545-0047
Department of the Treasury Internal Revenue Service	► Attach to Form 990. To be completed by organizations that answered "Yes," to Form 990, Part IV, line 6, 7, 8, 9, 10, 11, or 12.	Open to Public Inspection

Schedule D is a hodgepodge of parts required for an organization filing Form 990 to report information about its donor-advised funds, conservation easements, certain art and museum collections, escrow accounts and custodial arrangements, endowment funds, and other supplemental financial information. Many organizations will not be required to complete all of the parts. Several of the parts provide a standard format for reporting information that was previously requested as an unformatted attachment to the 990. Presumably, this will enhance the comparability and completeness of those statements because the return preparer will not have much latitude to decide what information to include and how to display it.

Part I	Organizations Maintaining Donor Advised Funds or Other Similar Funds or Accounts. Complete if the organization answered "Yes" to Form 990, Part IV, line 6.

(a) Background

Prior to the passage of the Pension Protection Act in 2006, the Internal Revenue Code did not define the term *donor-advised fund*. However, the term was generally understood to refer to either component funds of certain community trusts or to an account established by one or more donors but owned and controlled by a public charity to which such donors (or other individuals designated by the donors) could make recommendations regarding distributions from the account or investment of the assets in the account. In 2004, the IRS gathered testimony regarding perceived charitable giving problems and misuse of tax-exempt organizations. The portion pertaining to donor-advised funds ("DAFs") follows below:

> In operation these funds allow considerable input from the donor but are not classified as private foundations. Again, in a legitimate donor-advised fund, the charity must have legal control over the donated funds and must have the right to disregard the donor's advice. We have seen abuses in this area, both in examinations and in applications for exemption from new organizations. A case in which the IRS denied exemption is pending in the Court of Federal Claims. In addition, we are aware that some promoters encourage clients to donate funds and then use those funds to pay personal expenses, which might include school expenses for the donor's children, payments for the donor's own 'volunteer work,' and loans back to the donor. We have over 100 individuals under audit in connection with such cases.[43]

In Notice 2007–21, the IRS described the new requirements for DAFs enacted by the PPA as an effort to improve the accountability of such funds and to eliminate some of their advantages relative to private foundations. The notice also called for comments about the following 10 issues:

1. Whether charitable contribution deductions are appropriate in light of the use of assets contributed to these organizations;

2. Whether DAFs should be required to distribute a specified amount for charitable purposes;

3. Whether retaining certain rights with respect to transferred assets (including advisory rights with respect to making grants or investing assets) is consistent with treating the transfers as completed gifts;

4. Whether issues identified in paragraphs 1–3 are also issues for other forms of charities or charitable donations;

5. The advantages and disadvantages of these organizations, compared to other charitable giving arrangements;

6. How to determine the amount of a charitable contribution deduction for transfers to these organizations if the transferor retains certain rights, receives certain benefits, or the property is not readily convertible to cash;

7. The effects of new legislative provisions (including applying excess benefit transaction taxes) on the practices of these organizations and their donors;

8. Appropriate payout requirements for these organizations;

9. Advantages and disadvantages of perpetual existence for these organizations;

10. Whether issues identified in paragraphs 5–9 are also issues for other types of charitable giving arrangements.

The IRS has not yet shared the information received in response to this request.

In addition, the IRS sent out its "Community Foundations Questionnaire" in August of 2007, to approximately 2,000 exempt organizations classified as community foundations. They maintained that the purpose of the check was due to the significant increase in the number, size, and complexity of these organizations as a whole during the last decade and was intended to gather information on how they operate and allow them to follow up with organizations that may have compliance issues. Many of the questions pertained to DAFs and policies applicable to donor advisors.

Although the new restrictions on DAFs have not removed all of their advantages, it seems clear that the IRS intends to scrutinize them closely over the coming years.

DEFINITIONS

A Donor-advised fund or account is one:

   That is separately identified by reference to contributions of a donor or donors;

   That is owned and controlled by a **sponsoring organization**; and

   For which the donor or **donor advisor** has or reasonably expects to have advisory privileges in the distribution or investment of amounts held in the donor-advised funds or accounts because of the donor's status as a donor.[44]

   Sponsoring organization: any organization which is described in §170(c), except for governmental entities or organizations described in §170(c)(1) or §170(c)(2)(A); is not a private foundation as defined in §509(a); and maintains one or more DAFs.[45]

   Donor advisor: Any person appointed or designated by a donor to advise a sponsoring organization on the distribution or investment of amounts held in the donor's DAF or similar account.

	(a) Donor advised funds	(b) Funds and other accounts
1 Total number at end of year		
2 Aggregate contributions to (during year)		
3 Aggregate grants from (during year) .		
4 Aggregate value at end of year . . .		

5 Did the organization inform all donors and donor advisors in writing that the assets held in donor advised funds are the organization's property, subject to the organization's exclusive legal control? . . . . . ☐ Yes ☐ No

6 Did the organization inform all grantees, donors, and donor advisors in writing that grant funds may be used only for charitable purposes and not for the benefit of the donor or donor advisor or other impermissible private benefit? . . . . ☐ Yes ☐ No

The questions in this part fall into two categories. The first consists of data regarding DAFs maintained by the organization (Questions 1–4)—the number of DAFs at year-end, the amount of contributions to DAFs, grants from DAFs, and total value of DAFs at year-end. The second category consists of questions seeking to determine compliance with IRS standards established for DAFs (Questions 5 & 6). Although one of the criteria for qualification as a DAF is that the donor must be allowed to give advice as to distributions or investments of the amounts in the fund, the ultimate control of the funds and responsibility to be certain that funds are used only for charitable purposes belongs to the sponsoring organization.[46]

Part V of the 990 also asks Questions (8 & 9) concerning whether the organization's DAFs are in compliance with other potentially penalty-causing rules.[47]

Part II **Conservation Easements.** Complete if the organization answered "Yes" to Form 990, Part IV, line 7.

(b)   Background

On May 12, 2008, the IRS released the following information on its website regarding its position on conservation easements:[48]

> In recognition of our need to preserve our heritage, Congress allowed an income tax deduction for owners of significant property who give up certain rights of ownership to preserve their land or buildings for future generations. The IRS has seen abuses of this tax provision that compromise the policy Congress intended to promote. We have seen taxpayers, often encouraged by promoters and armed with questionable appraisals, take inappropriately large deductions for easements. In some cases, taxpayers claim deductions when they are not entitled to any deduction at all (for example, when taxpayers fail to comply with the law and regulations governing deductions for contributions of conservation easements). Also, taxpayers have sometimes used or developed these properties in manner inconsistent with section 501(c)(3). In other cases, the charity has allowed property owners to modify the easement or develop the land in a manner inconsistent with the easement's restrictions. Another problem arises in connection with historic easements, particularly façade easements. Here again, some taxpayers are taking improperly large deductions. They agree not to modify the façade of their historic house and they give an easement to this effect to a charity. However, if the façade was already subject to restrictions under local zoning ordinances, the taxpayers may, in fact, be giving up nothing, or very little. A taxpayer cannot give up a right that he or she does not have.

The IRS first began to require the disclosure of information about conservation easements with the 2005 Form 990, when it asked whether the organization had received a contribution of qualified real property interest under §170(h). However, a "Yes" answer did not prompt the attachment of any information. The 2006 Form 990 greatly expanded the question and required the attachment of a detailed statement similar to Part II. For the most part, the IRS has refined the questions to take into account the concerns of Land Trust Alliance and other similar organizations that provided comments to the IRS after the first draft of the revised 990 was released. However, contrary to what was suggested by those groups, the questions are not restricted merely to conservation easements that were contributed to the organization and for which a charitable deduction was claimed but, in fact, concern all conservation easements, whether donated or purchased (except for line 2).

DEFINITIONS

Conservation easement is a restriction on the use that may be made of, or changes made to, real property that is granted in perpetuity to a qualified organization exclusively for conservation purposes. Conservation purposes include protection of natural habitat, the preservation of open space; or the preservation of property for historic, educational, or recreational purposes. Qualified organizations include governmental units and certain tax-exempt organizations described in §501(c)(3) that have a commitment to protect the conservation purposes of the easement and the resources to enforce the restrictions.[49]

Qualified conservation contribution: Any contribution of a qualified real property interest exclusively for conservation purposes. A "qualified real property interest" means any of the following interests in real property:

- The entire interest of the donor,

- A remainder interest,

- A restriction (e.g., an easement), granted in perpetuity, on the use which may be made of the real property.[50]

Conservation purpose means:

- The preservation of land areas for outdoor recreation by, or the education of, the general public,

- The protection of a relatively natural habitat of fish, wildlife, plants, or similar ecosystems,

- The preservation of open space (including farmland and forest land) where such preservation is for the scenic enjoyment of the general public or is in accordance with governmental conservation policy, or

- The preservation of an historically important land area or a certified historic structure.[51]

---

1 Purpose(s) of conservation easements held by the organization (check all that apply).
   ☐ Preservation of land for public use (e.g., recreation or pleasure)   ☐ Preservation of an historically important land area
   ☐ Protection of natural habitat   ☐ Preservation of certified historic structure
   ☐ Preservation of open space
2 Complete lines 2a–2d if the organization held a qualified conservation contribution in the form of a conservation easement on the last day of the tax year.

		Held at the End of the Year
a	Total number of conservation easements	2a	
b	Total acreage restricted by conservation easements	2b	
c	Number of conservation easements on a certified historic structure included in (a)	2c	
d	Number of conservation easements included in (c) acquired after 8/17/06	2d	

Part II, line 2 must be completed by organizations that held conservation easements that are also qualified conservation contributions on the last day of the tax year. These questions focus on quantitative measurements only.

3 Number of conservation easements modified, transferred, released, extinguished, or terminated by the organization during the taxable year ▶ ....

Part II, line 3 concerns all conservation easements held by the organization, not merely those that are also qualified conservation contributions. Here the organization is asked not only to provide a number but also to describe the modification, transfer, release, extinguishment, and/or termination in Part XIV of this Schedule.

The instructions provide the following clarifications:

- *An easement is modified* when the terms of easement are amended. For example, if the deed of easement is amended to increase or decrease the amount of land subject to the easement and/or to add or remove restrictions regarding the use of the property subject to the easement, the easement is modified.

- *An easement is transferred* when the organization assigns the deed of easement whether with or without consideration.

- *An easement is released or terminated* when it is condemned, extinguished by court order, transferred to the land owner, or in any way rendered void and unenforceable.

4 Number of states where property subject to conservation easement is located ▶ ....
5 Does the organization have a written policy regarding the periodic monitoring, inspection, violations, and enforcement of the conservation easements it holds?   .   .   .   .   ☐ **Yes** ☐ **No**
6 Staff or volunteer hours devoted to monitoring, inspecting, and enforcing easements during the year ▶ ....
7 Amount of expenses incurred in monitoring, inspecting, and enforcing easements during the year ▶ $ ....

The organization must have a commitment to protect the conservation purposes of the easement, and the resources to enforce the restrictions. Questions 4–7 are intended to request information that will demonstrate the organization's commitment to its easement(s) and any difficulty it expects to face in honoring that commitment. For example, if an organization has easements in 12 states and devotes less than 20 volunteer/staff hours per year to monitor or enforce the easements, the IRS may consider that to evidence lack of sufficient commitment.

If the organization has a written policy or policies regarding how the organization will monitor, inspect, respond to violations, and enforce conservation easements, it must briefly summarize such policy or policies in Part XIV of this Schedule and indicate whether such policy or policies are reflected in the organization's easement documents.

The instructions provide the following clarifications:

- *Monitoring* means that the organization investigates the use or condition of the real property restricted by the easement to determine if the property owner is adhering to the restrictions imposed by the terms of the easement to ensure that the conservation purpose of the easement is being achieved.

- *Inspection* means an onsite visit to observe the property to carry out a monitoring purpose.

- *Enforcement* of an easement means action taken by the organization after it discovers a violation to compel a property owner to adhere to the terms of the conservation easement. Such activities may include communications with the property owner explaining his or her obligations with respect to the easement, arbitration, or litigation.

8 Does each conservation easement reported on line 2(d) above satisfy the requirements of section
170(h)(4)(B)(i) and section 170(h)(4)(B)(ii)? . . . . ☐ **Yes** ☐ **No**

Question 8 seeks to determine compliance with new rules regarding façade easements acquired after August 17, 2006. The tax code requires each façade easement to include a restriction that preserves the entire exterior of the building, including the front, sides, rear, and height of the building, and to prohibit any change in the exterior of the building that is inconsistent with the historical character of such exterior and also requires the donor and donee to enter into a written agreement certifying, among other things, that the donee organization has the resources to manage the historic preservation property and a commitment to do so.[52]

9 In Part XIV, describe how the organization reports conservation easements in its revenue and expense statement, and balance sheet, and include, if applicable, the text of the footnote to the organization's financial statements that describes the organization's accounting for conservation easements.

Line 9 asks for a description of how the organization reports conservation easements in its financial statements and, if so, to input the text of the footnote that describes the organization's accounting for conservation easements and the basis for its reporting position in Part XIV of this schedule.

Part III   **Organizations Maintaining Collections of Art, Historical Treasures, or Other Similar Assets.**
        Complete if the organization answered "Yes" to Form 990, Part IV, line 8.

(c) Background

The instructions refer to SFAS (Statement of Financial Accounting Standards)[53] 116 for meanings of the various terms. Pursuant to SFAS 116, nonprofit organizations may choose one of two methods to report collections of works of art, historical treasures, or other similar assets held for public exhibition, education, or research in furtherance of public service. An organization may recognize and capitalize its collections for financial statement purposes and report its collections as assets and revenues based upon its fair value measurement. An organization may instead disclose that it has collections on the face of its statement of activities without amounts, separately from revenues, expenses, gains, losses, and assets. In that situation, SFAS 116 requires (and in Question 1a of Part III the IRS asks for) the disclosure of the following information as a footnote to the organization's financial statements:

> A description of its collections, including their relative significance, and its accounting and stewardship policies for collections. If collection items not capitalized are deaccessed during the period, it also shall (a) describe the items given away, damaged, destroyed, lost, or otherwise deaccessed during the period or (b) disclose their fair value.

1a If the organization elected, as permitted under SFAS 116, not to report in its revenue statement and balance sheet works of art, historical treasures, or other similar assets held for public exhibition, education, or research in furtherance of public service, provide, in Part XIV, the text of the footnote to its financial statements that describes these items.

b If the organization elected, as permitted under SFAS 116, to report in its revenue statement and balance sheet works of art, historical treasures, or other similar assets held for public exhibition, education, or research in furtherance of public service, provide the following amounts relating to these items:
  (i) Revenues included in Form 990, Part VIII, line 1 . . . . ▶ $ _____
  (ii) Assets included in Form 990, Part X . . . . ▶ $ _____

2 If the organization received or held works of art, historical treasures, or other similar assets for financial gain, provide the following amounts required to be reported under SFAS 116 relating to these items:
a Revenues included in Form 990, Part VIII, line 1 . . . . ▶ $ _____
b Assets included in Form 990, Part X . . . . ▶ $ _____

For Privacy Act and Paperwork Reduction Act Notice, see the Instructions for Form 990.   Cat. No. 52283D   Schedule D (Form 990) 2008

■ **138** ■

If the organization holds the assets for financial gain, rather than for public exhibition, education, or research in furtherance of public service, items received as assets and contribution revenue are recorded for financial purposes. Line 2 asks the organization to disclose that information.

3 Using the organization's accession and other records, check any of the following that are a significant use of its collection items (check all that apply):

a ☐ Public exhibition   d ☐ Loan or exchange programs

b ☐ Scholarly research   e ☐ Other _____

c ☐ Preservation for future generations

4 Provide a description of the organization's collections and explain how they further the organization's exempt purpose in Part XIV.

5 During the year, did the organization solicit or receive donations of art, historical treasures, or other similar assets to be sold to raise funds rather than to be maintained as part of the organization's collection? . . . ☐ Yes ☐ No

Line 5 asks whether the organization received a donation for which the donor's deduction should be limited. The deduction for a donation of tangible personal property that the donee uses in a manner unrelated to its exempt purposes or that is sold, exchanged, or disposed of within three years of receipt is limited to the donor's basis in the property.[54] A good example of this type of donation is the gift of an antique for sale in a charity auction. There should be a coordination of the response to this question with information presented in Form 8283 completed by the donor, Form 8282 completed by the donee organization, if applicable, and the answer to Question 7c in Core Part V.

Part IV   **Trust, Escrow and Custodial Arrangements.** Complete if organization answered "Yes" to Form 990, Part IV, line 9, or reported an amount on Form 990, Part X, line 21.

(d) Background

The instructions mention two types of organizations who may potentially enter into escrow or custodial arrangements—credit counseling and down payment assistance organizations. Both types have been the focus of IRS scrutiny in recent years.

(i) Credit Counseling Organizations. The IRS launched a credit counseling compliance project with "both an aggressive examination program to halt abuses within the credit counseling industry and a rigorous determination process to prevent abusive organizations from receiving tax exemption." Most existing credit counseling organizations were examined resulting in revocation of exempt status of nearly all the organizations. The IRS affirmed that "the revocations result[ed] from these organizations failing to provide the level of public benefit required to qualify for tax exemption. Many of these agencies offered little or no counseling or education and appeared to be primarily motivated by profit. In many instances, these agencies also served the private interests of related for-profit businesses, officers and directors."[55] Not only did the IRS revoke the exempt status of existing organizations, it also closely scrutinized applications for exemption submitted by similar organizations. Out of the approximately 100 applications submitted from 2003 to 2006, only three were approved.

(ii) Down Payment Assistance Organizations. Around the same time, the IRS also released information about a certain kind of down payment assistance program that did not qualify as exempt—a "seller-funded program." "Increasingly, the IRS has found that organizations claiming to be charities are being used to funnel down-payment assistance from sellers to buyers through self-serving, circular-financing arrangements. In a typical scheme, there is a direct correlation between the amount of the down-payment assistance provided to the buyer and the payment received from the seller. Moreover, the seller pays the organization only if the sale closes, and the organization usually charges an additional fee for its services."[56] The IRS examined 185 organizations in connection with this compliance initiative. The specific number of revocations related to those examinations has not yet been announced by the IRS.

			Amount
1a Is the organization an agent, trustee, custodian or other intermediary for contributions or other assets not included on Form 990, Part X?			☐ Yes ☐ No
b If "Yes," explain the arrangement in Part XIV and complete the following table:			
c Beginning balance	1c		
d Additions during the year	1d		
e Distributions during the year	1e		
f Ending balance	1f		
2a Did the organization include an amount on Form 990, Part X, line 21?			☐ Yes ☐ No
b If "Yes," explain the arrangement in Part XIV.			

Part V   **Endowment Funds.** Complete if organization answered "Yes" to Form 990, Part IV, line 10.

(e) Background

The instructions refer to SFAS 117 as the source for meanings of the various terms. SFAS 117 emphasizes that the main purpose for reporting on endowment funds as a separate part of net assets is to disclose information to financial statement users about the organization's "liquidity and financial flexibility." Under these standards, funds held by the reporting entity on behalf of others, either related or unrelated organizations, are reported. Correspondingly, the obligation reflected as a liability for "funds held for others" will be reported as an Other Liability in Part X discussed below. When the reporting organization's endowment funds are held by others on its behalf, it would also report its funds here. The instructions to Core Part IV, Question 10,[57] and this part do not clearly address what would seem like double reporting by both the beneficiary of the endowment funds and the entity that holds them on its behalf.

Restrictions imposed by donors limit how the organization may spend the contributions it receives, and the impact may be considerable. The further information now required by the IRS will provide even more details about what makes up the change in endowment funds from year to year, what the purposes of the funds are, and whether endowment funds are held by a related organization rather than by the organization itself.

DEFINITIONS

Permanent endowment funds are funds that are maintained to provide a permanent source of income, with the stipulation that principal must be invested and kept intact in perpetuity, while only the income generated can be used by the organization.

Term endowment funds are maintained to provide a source of income for either a specified period of time or until a specific event occurs.

Quasi-endowment (board-designated) funds are funds functioning as an endowment that are established by the organization itself, either from donor or institutional funds, and that must retain the purpose and intent as specified by the donor or source of the original funds.

	(a) Current year	(b) Prior year	(c) Two years back	(d) Three years back	(e) Four years back
1a Beginning of year balance . . .					
b Contributions					
c Investment earnings or losses .					
d Grants or scholarships					
e Other expenditures for facilities and programs					
f Administrative expenses . . .					
g End of year balance					

2 Provide the estimated percentage of the year end balance held as:
a Board designated or quasi-endowment ▶ -------------%
b Permanent endowment ▶ -------------%
c Term endowment ▶ ------------- %
3a Are there endowment funds not in the possession of the organization that are held and administered for the organization by:

		Yes	No
(i) unrelated organizations	3a(i)		
(ii) related organizations	3a(ii)		
b If "Yes" to 3a(ii), are the related organizations listed as required on Schedule R?	3b		

4 Describe in Part XIV the intended uses of the organization's endowment funds.

This section is to be completed using the market value of the funds. Therefore, line 1c will include both realized and unrealized gains. In order to phase in this new reporting requirement, only the current year column is required to be completed. However, in future years, the organization will also have to report past information up to four years old.

Part VI Investments—Land, Buildings, and Equipment. See Form 990, Part X, line 10.

Description of investment	(a) Cost or other basis (investment)	(b) Cost or other basis (other)	(c) Depreciation	(d) Book value
1a Land				
b Buildings				
c Leasehold improvements				
d Equipment				
e Other				
Total. Add lines 1a–1e. (Column (d) should equal Form 990, Part X, column (B), line 10(c).) . . . . ▶				

Schedule D (Form 990) 2008

This part is completed by organizations answering, "Yes" to Part IV, Question 11 and reporting an amount for land, buildings, and equipment on the Core Part X. This information was previously provided as an attachment to Form 990, not as part of the form itself. Preparers were instructed to "attach a schedule listing these fixed assets held at the end of the year showing, for each item or category listed, the cost or other basis, accumulated depreciation, and book value." Some preparers listed each item held by the organization (making for a very long list) while others provided a total for each category (such as buildings). The new chart to display the information by preformatted columns will facilitate statistical analysis. Core Part X does not use the term "Investments—Land, Buildings, and Equipment" as this schedule does, instead, it omits the term "Investments." Previous Forms 990 distinguished between the two types of assets and had a separate line for each rather than combining them. Here the distinction is provided in the columns of the Schedule.

Schedule D (Form 990) 2008   Page **3**

Part VII Investments—Other Securities. See Form 990, Part X, line 12.

(a) Description of security or category (including name of security)	(b) Book value	(c) Method of valuation: Cost or end-of-year market value
Financial derivatives and other financial products . .		
Closely-held equity interests		
Other -------------------------------		

(Continued)

Part VII	Investments—Other Securities. See Form 990, Part X, line 12.	
(a) Description of security or category (including name of security)	**(b)** Book value	**(c)** Method of valuation: Cost or end-of-year market value
Total. *(Column (b) should equal Form 990, Part X, col. (B) line 12.)* ▶		

This part is completed by organizations answering, "Yes" to Part IV, Question 11 and reporting an amount for "Other securities" on Form 990, Part X, line 12. Responding to comments made following the draft form released in June 2007, the IRS has provided two sample types of other investments on the form as a guide, presumably ones it thinks will be the most common. Although the glossary provides a definition for "closely-held stock," it is silent on the term "financial derivatives." Wikipedia defines the term to include "financial instruments whose value changes in response to the changes in underlying variables," including futures, forwards, options, and swaps.[58] Strangely, the term *partnership* was not provided since it is a fairly common type of investment for all kinds of investors. Investors holding 5 percent or more of the outstanding shares of the same class of publicly traded stock are asked to list each separate class of publicly traded stock held by the organization that meets the 5 percent ownership test in this section. Program-related investments are now reported in the following separate part.

Part VIII	Investments—Program Related. See Form 990, Part X, line 13.	
(a) Description of investment type	**(b)** Book value	**(c)** Method of valuation: Cost or end-of-year market value
Total. *(Column (b) should equal Form 990, Part X, col. (B) line 13.)* ▶		

This part is completed by organizations answering "Yes" to Part IV, Question 11 and reporting an amount for program-related investments on Form 990, Part X, line 13 that is 5 percent or more of the amount reported for total assets on Form 990, Part X, line 16. Program-related investments are those made primarily to accomplish the organization's exempt purposes rather than to produce income, though income may be produced by them. Illustrations of program-related investments include:

- Low-interest or interest-free loans to needy students
- High-risk investments in nonprofit low-income housing projects
- Low-interest loans to small businesses owned by members of economically disadvantaged groups, where commercial funds at reasonable interest rates are not readily available
- Investments in businesses in deteriorated urban areas under a plan to improve the economy of the area by providing employment or training for unemployed residents
- Investments in nonprofit organizations combating community deterioration

Part IX	Other Assets. See Form 990, Part X, line 15.	
	(a) Description	**(b)** Book value
Total. *(Column (b) should equal Form 990, Part X, col. (B) line 15.)* . . . . ▶		

Part IX is completed by organizations answering "Yes" to Part IV, Question 11 and reporting an amount for other assets on Form 990, Part X, line 15 that is 5 percent or more of the amount reported for total assets on Form 990, Part X, line 16. The instructions do not provide examples of other assets, but the following are good examples of entries on this schedule: amounts due from related organizations, surrender value of life insurance policies, and artwork collections (if capitalized).

Part X	Other Liabilities. See Form 990, Part X, line 25.		
	(a) Description of liability	**(b)** Amount	
Federal income taxes			
Total. *(Column (b) should equal Form 990, Part X, col. (B) line 25.)* ▶			

In Part XIV, provide the text of the footnote to the organization's financial statements that reports the organization's liability for uncertain tax positions under FIN 48.

Schedule D (Form 990) 2008

Part X is completed by organizations answering, "Yes" to Part IV, Question 11 and reporting an amount for other liabilities on Form 990, Part X, line 25. The amount reported for "Federal Income Taxes" will be those taxes imposed on unrelated business income signaling a need for other reporting. An input here for income tax indicates an entry should be made on Core Part I, line 7 where the gross amount of unrelated business revenue and corresponding net unrelated taxable income is entered on the front page. Core Part V, Question 3 also asks if the organization has more than $1,000 of such income and whether Form 990-T has been filed.

The FIN 48 footnote this part requests will alert the IRS that the organization has a potential unreported tax liability on its financial statements. FIN 48 requires an explanation of a tax position that is "more likely than not" unsustainable upon examination[59] For this purpose, "tax position" includes the following: "A decision not to file an income tax return, an allocation or a shift of income between jurisdictions, the characterization of income or a decision to exclude reporting taxable income in a tax return, or a decision to classify a transaction, entity, or other position in a tax return as tax exempt."[60] If an organization's financial statements contain a footnote disclosing a liability for an uncertain tax position, the text of the footnote *verbatim* goes in Part XIV.

The instructions also indicate that each liability owed to a related organization should be listed separately on this schedule. Other liabilities that could potentially be listed here are "funds held for others." Many schools hold bank accounts for parent-teacher organizations and booster clubs and report the amounts held on behalf of them as assets and liabilities for financial statement purposes.

Schedule D (Form 990) 2008   Page **4**

Part XI Reconciliation of Change in Net Assets from Form 990 to Financial Statements

1	Total revenue (Form 990, Part VIII, column (A), line 12)	1
2	Total expenses (Form 990, Part IX, column (A), line 25)	2
3	Excess or (deficit) for the year. Subtract line 2 from line 1	3
4	Net unrealized gains (losses) on investments	4
5	Donated services and use of facilities	5
6	Investment expenses	6
7	Prior period adjustments	7
8	Other (Describe in Part XIV)	8
9	Total adjustments (net). Add lines 4–8	9
10	Excess or (deficit) for the year per financial statements. Combine lines 3 and 9	10

Parts XI–XIII are completed by organizations receiving an audited financial statement prepared in accordance with Generally Accepted Accounting Principles (GAAP) for the filing year. An organization included in a consolidated financial statement that includes activity of other organizations is not required, but can choose, to complete these parts. It will be disconcerting to organizations included in a consolidated report to follow the instruction to say No, they did not receive an audit in accordance with GAAP in response to Core Part IV Question 12. The IRS has indicated it expects to revisit that question for the 2009 return. Amounts needed to remove amounts attributable to other organizations included in the consolidated statements could be presented on line 8.

Part XI reconciles tax-reportable net income (revenue less expenses) and resulting increase or decrease in fund balance to the change in the organization's net assets reported in its audited financial statements. This part previously appeared on the front page as lines 18–21 and was completed by all organizations regardless of whether they received an audit. Lines 5 and 6 may confuse some, and typically will be blank. Following long-standing IRS policy, donated services are typically excluded from both revenue and expense, thereby creating a net effect of zero on the change in net assets. Similarly, investment expenses, other than those that are donated services, would be reported as an expense for tax and financial statement purposes. These two items are likely a holdover from the reconciliation of revenue/expense per audited financial statements with revenue/expense per return. It will be normal for them to appear in Parts XII and XIII.

Part XII Reconciliation of Revenue per Audited Financial Statements With Revenue per Return

1	Total revenue, gains, and other support per audited financial statements		1
2	Amounts included on line 1 but not on Form 990, Part VIII, line 12:		
a	Net unrealized gains on investments	2a	
b	Donated services and use of facilities	2b	
c	Recoveries of prior year grants	2c	
d	Other (Describe in Part XIV)	2d	
e	Add lines **2a** through **2d**		2e
3	Subtract line **2e** from line 1		3
4	Amounts included on Form 990, Part VIII, line 12, but not on line **1**:		
a	Investment expenses not included on Form 990, Part VIII, line 7b .	4a	
b	Other (Describe in Part XIV)	4b	
c	Add lines **4a** and **4b**		4c
5	Total revenue. Add lines **3** and **4c**. (This should equal Form 990, Part I, line 12.)		5

This section is identical to the previous Form 990, Part IV-A, which was added in 1995, to clarify items for which there are reporting differences for tax and financial purposes similar to Schedule M on Form 1120. A common reconciling item is revenue from donated services or use of facilities. This part reminds organizations that such revenues are not deductible contributions for tax purposes.[61] Unrealized gains or losses on investments recognized for financial reporting purposes are not shown as revenue in Part VIII, but if Schedule D, Part XI is completed, may be shown as a reconciling item in that part.

Part XIII	Reconciliation of Expenses per Audited Financial Statements With Expenses per Return		
1	Total expenses and losses per audited financial statements		1
2	Amounts included on line 1 but not on Form 990, Part IX, line 25:		
a	Donated services and use of facilities	2a	
b	Prior year adjustments	2b	
c	Losses reported on Form 990, Part IX, line 25	2c	
d	Other (Describe in Part XIV)	2d	
e	Add lines 2a through 2d		2e
3	Subtract line 2e from line 1		3
4	Amounts included on Form 990, Part IX, line 25, but not on line 1:		
a	Investment expenses not included on Form 990, Part VIII, line 7b	4a	
b	Other (Describe in Part XIV)	4b	
c	Add lines 4a and 4b		4c
5	Total expenses. Add lines 3 and 4c. (This should equal Form 990, Part I, line 18.)		5

This section is identical to the previous Form 990, Part IV-B. A common reconciling item is expense from donated services or use of facilities.

Part XIV	Supplemental Information

Part XIV is used by organizations to report additional narrative information requested in other parts of the schedule as follows:

RELEVANT SECTION	WHAT TO DESCRIBE
Part II, line 5 (if answered "Yes")	The organization's written policy regarding monitoring, inspection, and enforcement of conservation easements
Part II, line 9	How the organization reports conservation easements in its financial statements and, if applicable, the text of the footnote to the organization's financial statements that describes the organization's accounting for conservation easements
Part III, line 1a (if answered "Yes")	The text of the footnote to the organization's financial statements that describes how the organization has elected not to report in its financial statements its works of art, historical treasures, and so on.
Part III, line 4	The organization's collections and how they further the organization's exempt purposes
Part IV, line 1a (if answered "Yes")	Why the organization is an agent, trustee, custodian, or other intermediary for assets not included in Form 990, Part X
Part IV, line 2a (if answered "Yes")	The arrangements under which the amounts reported in Form 990, Part X, line 21 are held, including any obligations the organization has to other persons under such arrangements
Part V, line 4	The intended uses of the organization's endowment funds
Part X	FIN 48 footnote text

(Continued)

RELEVANT SECTION	WHAT TO DESCRIBE
Part XI, line 8	Type of other adjustment to net assets
Part XII, line 2d	Type of other adjustment to revenue included in audited financial statements but not in return
Part XII, line 4b	Type of other adjustment to revenue included in return but not in audited financial statements
Part XIII, line 2d	Type of other adjustment to expenses included in audited financial statements but not in return
Part XIII, line 4b	Type of other adjustment to expenses included in return but not in audited financial statements

Part XIV may also be used to provide additional narrative explanations and descriptions, even though not explicitly required. The specific part and line number that the information relates to should be identified. Responses should be entered in the order that the part it relates to appears in Schedule D. Part XIV may be duplicated to the extent space is needed.

§4.5 SCHEDULE E

SCHEDULE E (Form 990 or 990-EZ) Department of the Treasury Internal Revenue Service	**Schools** ▶ To be completed by organizations that answer "Yes" to Form 990, Part IV, line 13, or Form 990-EZ, Part VI, line 48. ▶ Attach to Form 990 or Form 990-EZ.	OMB No. 1545-0047 Open to Public Inspection

(a) Background

A statement that a school has a racially nondiscriminatory policy must be included in the charter, bylaws, or other governing instrument, or be effective by resolution of its governing body in order to meet the organization requirements of the tax code to qualify as an exempt organization. School brochures, catalogs, and other printed matter used to inform prospective students of the school's programs must state the policy as it relates to admission applications, scholarships, and program participation. A reference to its policy must be included in other written advertising that it uses as a means of informing prospective students of its program. The following example is provided in the instructions.

> The (name) school admits students of any race, color, national and ethnic origin to all the rights, privileges, programs, and activities generally accorded or made available to students at the school. It does not discriminate on the basis of race, color, national and ethnic origin in administration of its educational policies, admissions policies, scholarship and loan programs, and athletic and other school-administered programs.

A school must also make its racially nondiscriminatory policy known to all segments of the general community served by the school using one of the methods outlined on page 147. The answer to Questions 1, 2, 3, 4a–4h, and 7 *must be "Yes."* The answer to Questions 5a–5h and 6b *must be "No."* It is only Question 6a that can be either "Yes" or "No."

Schedule E asks questions to allow the IRS to evaluate the school's continued qualification for tax-exemption based on the racial nondiscriminatory policies and practices schools are required to adopt and follow. Specific words to use in communicating the policy are recommended by the IRS, "The (name) school admits students of any race, color, and national or ethnic origin." The questions concern the school's organizational and operating documents and information disseminated by the school to its staff, students, applicants, and the general public that evidence its satisfaction with the very strict rules that prohibit racial discrimination.[62] Actions taken to publicize the school's antidiscrimination policies to its constituency are reported in this part. Form 5578 can be used to furnish the requested information, but is not specifically required. Form 5578 is designed to be separately submitted to the IRS by schools that are not required to file Form 990, including primarily government schools and church schools that qualify as an integrated auxiliary of a church.

		YES	NO
1	Does the organization have a racially nondiscriminatory policy toward students by statement in its charter, bylaws, other governing instrument, or in a resolution of its governing body? **1**		
2	Does the organization include a statement of its racially nondiscriminatory policy toward students in all its brochures, catalogues, and other written communications with the public dealing with student admissions, programs, and scholarships? **2**		
3	Has the organization publicized its racially nondiscriminatory policy through newspaper or broadcast media during the period of solicitation for students, or during the registration period if it has no solicitation program, in a way that makes the policy known to all parts of the general community it serves? If "Yes," please describe. If "No," please explain **3**		

Lines 1 and 2 are relatively self-explanatory.

Line 3 concerns the school's procedures for making "all segments of the general community served by the school" aware of the school's nondiscriminatory policy. This requirement can be satisfied in the following ways:

Method 1. A school that customarily draws its students from local communities, follows a racially nondiscriminatory policy, and enrolls students of racial minority groups in meaningful numbers may satisfy the publicity requirement under a facts and circumstances test. The most meaningful fact demonstrating compliance is the actual racial composition of the students. The instructions say the IRS recognizes that a low number of racial minority students may not necessarily indicate the absence of a suitable policy when there are relatively few or no such students in the community. If so, the test is met if the school's promotional activities and recruiting efforts are reasonably designed to inform students of all racial segments in the general communities within the area of the availability of the school.

Method 2. A statement of a school's policy can be published each year in an area newspaper during the period of the school's solicitation of students. The notice should appear in a section of the newspaper likely to be read by prospective students and their families and must occupy at least three column inches and be captioned in at least 12 point boldface type. Where more than one community is served by a school, the school may publish its notice in those newspapers that are reasonably likely to be read by all racial segments of the communities that it serves. The instructions contain an example of an acceptable notice that should be used as a guide.

Method 3. The school may instead use broadcast media to make its non-discriminatory policy known to the general community the school serves. A tape of the announcement must be maintained, as well as evidence that there were an adequate number of announcements broadcast during a time when all segments of the general community audience could be reached. Proof the announcements were broadcast on radio or television stations likely to be listened to by substantial numbers of members of all racial segments of the general community should be kept. Announcements must be made during the period of the school's solicitation for students or, in the absence of a solicitation program, during the school's registration period.

Method 4. A parochial or other church-related school the student body (75 percent in preceding three years) of which consists of members of the sponsoring religious denomination may publish its notice in newspapers or circulars of the particular religious organization serving the same community the school serves or an association that represents a number of religious organizations of the same denomination. If, however, the school advertises in newspapers of general circulation in the community or communities from which its students are drawn, it must meet the requirements of Method 1.

Method 5. A school that customarily draws a substantial percentage of its students nationally or worldwide, or from a large geographic section of the United States, and actually follows a racially nondiscriminatory policy, can simply announce its policy in its brochures and catalogs dealing with student admissions, programs, and scholarships. Such a school may demonstrate its policy by showing that it currently enrolls students of racial minority groups in meaningful numbers or, if not, that its promotional activities and recruiting efforts in each graphic area were reasonably designed to inform students of all racial segments in the general communities within the area of the availability of the school.

4	Does the organization maintain the following?		
a	Records indicating the racial composition of the student body, faculty, and administrative staff? . . .	**4a**	
b	Records documenting that scholarships and other financial assistance are awarded on a racially nondiscriminatory basis?	**4b**	
c	Copies of all catalogues, brochures, announcements, and other written communications to the public dealing with student admissions, programs, and scholarships?	**4c**	
d	Copies of all material used by the organization or on its behalf to solicit contributions?	**4d**	
	If you answered "No" to any of the above, please explain. (If you need more space, attach a separate statement.)		

Records to support the school's answers to the four questions in this part must be kept and maintained for a minimum period of at least three years to evidence compliance with the nondiscrimination rules. The statistical information can be estimated based on the best information available to the school each year. There is no requirement for verification from students and school staff that might not otherwise be in school records. A record of the method used when estimating should be maintained.

5	Does the organization discriminate by race in any way with respect to:		
a	Students' rights or privileges?	**5a**	
b	Admissions policies?	**5b**	
c	Employment of faculty or administrative staff?	**5c**	

(Continued)

d	Scholarships or other financial assistance?	**5d**	
e	Educational policies?	**5e**	
f	Use of facilities?	**5f**	
g	Athletic programs?	**5g**	
h	Other extracurricular activities?	**5h**	

If you answered "Yes" to any of the above, please explain. (If you need more space, attach a separate statement.)

The answers to questions 5a–5h *must be "No."*

6a	Does the organization receive any financial aid or assistance from a governmental agency?	**6a**	
b	Has the organization's right to such aid ever been revoked or suspended?	**6b**	
	If you answered "Yes" to either line 6a or line 6b, please explain using an attached statement.		
7	Does the organization certify that it has complied with the applicable requirements of sections 4.01 through 4.05 of Rev. Proc. 75-50, 1975-2 C.B. 587, covering racial nondiscrimination? If "No," attach an explanation.	**7**	

For Privacy Act and Paperwork Reduction Act Notice, see the Instructions for Form 990.　　Cat. No. 50085D　　Schedule E (Form 990 or 990-EZ) 2008

Line 6a instructions say copies of reports provided to governmental agencies need not necessarily be maintained. It does, however, seem prudent to keep them for IRS inspection if there is challenge to exempt status.

Line 6b needs to be answered with, if possible, a "No." A "Yes," to either Question 6a or 6b requires an explanation. Extreme care, however, should be taken in preparing the information to describe a negative answer. Suspension or loss of funding due to inadequate records or lack of audited financial statements should not necessarily cause the school to lose its exempt status.

Line 7 again should be "Yes." If the return signer cannot "certify that it has complied with the applicable requirements" of a nondiscriminatory admission policy, the IRS is certainly signaled that exempt status should be removed or at the very least, the school should be examined. The IRS 2008–09 Work Plan includes an intention to revise Rev. Proc. 75–50 cited in this question.

§4.6 SCHEDULE F

Schedule F **(Form 990)**	**Statement of Activities Outside the United States**	OMB No. 1545-0047
Department of the Treasury Internal Revenue Service	▶ **Attach to Form 990. Complete if the organization answered "Yes" to** **Form 990, Part IV, line 14b, line 15, or line 16.**	**Open to Public Inspection**

(a) Background

A distinction between programs conducted in the United States and those conducted outside the United States was not requested and not necessarily illustrated in prior Form 990s. There is no geographic limit placed on the place where programs qualifying for exemption can be operated. In former 990s, the type and extent of activities conducted outside the United States was sometimes identified in the activity description in prior Part III and foreign addresses appearing on the attachment listing grantees. The only information requested pertained to foreign bank accounts, now Question 4 in Part V.

Since the events of September 11, 2001, the IRS has more carefully scrutinized programs conducted internationally and revoked exemptions of some organizations it found to be supporting terrorists. The 2004 revision of Form 1023 added three questions to seek information similar to that now requested in this schedule. Details about programs and money spent are presented here by regions, rather than by name of particular country within each region as the original design of the form released in the June 2007 draft requested. Out of concern for the safety of their volunteers and employees, international aid organizations and others asked for removal of specific country names.

It is recommended that a preparer study the IRS instructions in detail to ensure accurate completion of this schedule. Importantly, the IRS prompts reporting of activity by one of the nine regions delineated by the World Bank. Other concepts for reporting foreign activity may be confusing to some, including the following examples:

- Question 14b in Core Part IV asks if the organization had "aggregate revenue or expenses" from activities outside the United States. There is, however, no line or column to report such revenues nor any instructions regarding revenues provided for this part. In most instances, it would be unusual to generate revenues without expenditures, but this factor may be confusing for an organization that sells educational materials to entities in foreign countries.

- No mention is made on the schedule itself, but for Part I, Columns (a) and (d), the instructions say conduct of an unrelated trade or business ("UBI") is an activity included in determining what should be reported. Filers that don't read the instructions will be unaware of this request. Filers who invest in partnerships that distribute UBI may not necessarily receive information that fragments the reportable revenue between domestic and outside of the U.S. sources.[63]

U.S. organizations that conduct activities outside the United States must keep sufficient records to evidence they control the decision to make grants and funds to foreign entities and individuals. Under IRC §170, a gift by a U.S. taxpayer to a non-U.S. organization does not qualify for the charitable donation deduction.[64] A designated, or restricted, gift to a U.S. charity that had no control or power to spend the gift for any other purpose is similarly not deductible. Conceptually, when the U.S. entity simply serves as a conduit, the gift is not to it but rather to the ultimate recipient.

DEFINITIONS

United States is defined as the 50 States and the District of Columbia, the Commonwealths of Puerto Rico and Northern Mariana Islands, Guam, American Samoa, and the United States Virgin Islands. A foreign country is any sovereignty that is not the United States.

Grant making includes awards, prizes, cash allocations, stipends, scholarships, fellowships, research grants, and similar payments and distributions made by the organization at any time during the tax year to foreign organizations, foreign governments, or foreign individuals. It does not include salaries or other compensation to employees.

Fund-raising activity essentially precedes grant making and involves seeking contributions, gifts, grants, or sponsoring events intended to generate gifts or contributions, outside the United States.

Program services encompass those activities conducted outside the United States that accomplish the exempt organization's mission, such as operating a school or health care clinic, building shelters, teaching agricultural methods, grant making, distributing food, clothing, medical supplies, pharmaceuticals, and the like.

Foreign organizations include a foreign estate or trust, nonprofits or other nongovernmental organizations, partnerships, corporations, or other entities that are not created or organized in the United States or under the laws of the United States, as defined above. For purposes of defining grant making for Schedule F, a foreign organization includes an affiliate that is organized as a legal entity separate from the filing organization, but does not include any branch office, account, or employee of the filing organization located outside the United States.

Foreign governments include political subdivisions thereof. Foreign governments do not include a U.S. government agency regardless of where it is located or operated.

Foreign individuals are persons who live or reside outside the United States at the time the grant is paid or distributed, including U.S. citizens or residents.

Maintaining offices, employees, or agents includes principal, regional, district, or branch offices, such offices maintained by agents, and persons situated at those offices paid wages for services performed. An agent is one formally authorized to act on the organization's behalf or essentially a person or organization entrusted to conduct the organization's affairs. When the filing organization cooperates with a local organization under an agreement or understanding, but does not control the operation, the office, its volunteers, and employees are allowed to work it should not be treated as the office of the U.S. entity.

Geographic regions (9) used to report activity on Schedule F are as follows:

Central America and the Caribbean

> Includes Antigua & Barbuda, Aruba, Bahamas, Barbados, Belize, Cayman Islands, Costa Rica, Cuba, Dominica, Dominican Republic, El Salvador, Grenada, Guadeloupe, Guatemala, Haiti, Honduras, Jamaica, Martinique, Nicaragua, Panama, St. Kitts & Nevis, St. Lucia, St. Vincent & the Grenadines, Trinidad & Tobago, Turks & Caicos Islands, and Virgin Islands

East Asia and the Pacific

> Includes Australia, Brunei, Burma, Cambodia, China (including Hong Kong), East Timor, Fiji, Indonesia, Japan, Kiribati, Korea, Laos, Malaysia, Marshall Islands, Micronesia, Mongolia, Nauru, New Zealand, North Korea, Palau, Papua New Guinea, Philippines, Samoa, Singapore, Solomon Islands, South Korea, Taiwan, Thailand, Timor Leste, Tonga, Tuvalu, Vanuatu, and Vietnam.

Europe (including Iceland and Greenland)

> Includes Albania, Andorra, Austria, Belgium, Bosnia & Herzegovina, Bulgaria, Croatia, Czech Republic, Denmark, Estonia, Finland, France, FYR Macedonia, Germany, Greece, Greenland, Holy See, Hungary, Iceland, Italy, Ireland, Kosovo, Latvia, Liechtenstein, Lithuania, Luxembourg, Macedonia,

(Continued)

Monaco, Montenegro, the Netherlands, Norway, Poland, Portugal, Romania, San Marino, Serbia, Slovakia, Slovenia, Spain, Switzerland, Turkey, and the United Kingdom (England, Northern Ireland, Scotland, and Wales).

Middle East and North Africa

Includes Algeria, Bahrain, Djibouti, Egypt, Iran, Iraq, Israel, Jordan, Kuwait, Lebanon, Libya, Malta, Morocco, Oman, Qatar, Saudi Arabia, Syria, Tunisia, United Arab Emirates, West Bank & Gaza, and Yemen.

North America (including Canada and Mexico, but not the United States)

Russia and the newly Independent States

Includes Armenia, Azerbaijan, Belarus, Georgia, Kazakhstan, Kyrgyzstan, Moldova, Russia, Tajikistan, Turkmenistan, Ukraine, and Uzbekistan.

South America

Includes Argentina, Bolivia, Brazil, Chile, Colombia, Ecuador, French Guiana, Guyana, Paraguay, Peru, Suriname, Uruguay, and Venezuela.

South Asia

Includes Afghanistan, Bangladesh, Bhutan, India, Maldives, Nepal, Pakistan, and Sri Lanka.

Sub-Saharan Africa

Includes Angola, Benin, Botswana, Burkina Faso, Burundi, Cameroon, Cape Verde, Central African Republic, Chad, Comoros, Congo, Dem. Rep. (DRC), Congo Rep., Côte d'Ivoire, Equatorial Guinea, Eritrea, Ethiopia, Gabon, Gambia, Ghana, Guinea, Guinea Bissau, Kenya, Lesotho, Liberia, Madagascar, Malawi, Mali, Mauritania, Mauritius, Mozambique, Namibia, Nigeria, Rwanda, Sao Tome & Principe, Senegal, Seychelles, Sierra Leone, Somalia, South Africa, Sudan, Swaziland, Tanzania, Togo, Uganda, Zambia, and Zimbabwe.

When an organization's activities involve a country not listed above, the appropriate region should be selected based on the region of neighboring countries.

Part I **General Information on Activities Outside the United States.** Complete if the organization answered "Yes" to Form 990, Part IV, line 14b.

1 **For grantmakers.** Does the organization maintain records to substantiate the amount of the grants or assistance, the grantees' eligibility for the grants or assistance, and the selection criteria used to award the grants or assistance? . . . . ☐ **Yes** ☐ **No**

2 **For grantmakers.** Describe in Part IV the organization's procedures for monitoring the use of grant funds outside the United States.

3 Activities per Region. (Use Schedule F-1 (Form 990) if additional space is needed.)

(a) Region	(b) Number of offices in the region	(c) Number of employees or agents in region	(d) Activities conducted in region (by type) (i.e., fundraising, program services, grants to recipients located in the region)	(e) If activity listed in (d) is a program service, describe specific type of service(s) in region	(f) Total expenditures in region

This part summarizes the nature of, and expenditures related to, the organization's non-U.S. activity by regions of the world in which it is conducted, including those directly carried out by the organization itself and grants to organizations, governments, and individuals. Details of grants and awards are also reported in Parts II and III. The newly-released instructions to this part have clarified that both directly conducted activities and grants to other organizations are reported in this part.

Lines 1 and 2. Organizations that make grants directly to foreign organizations, governments, or individuals must describe the due diligence steps taken to document the nature of, purpose of, and fulfillment of requirements placed on grants and grantees. Undoubtedly a filer will not want to say ''No'' it did not maintain records to substantiate amounts, eligibility, and selection criteria used for grants. The procedures the organization follows to monitor grants to ensure that the funds are used as intended and not otherwise diverted must be described in Part IV of this schedule. Specific steps similar to those required for Expenditure Responsibility grants[65] made by private foundations are not suggested but could be implemented. The recommendations contained in the Voluntary Best Practices for U.S.-Based Charities[66] can also be studied for suggestions for monitoring grant funds. For example, the organization may describe periodic reports required, field investigations conducted, benchmarks measured. Due to language differences and the fashion in which financial transactions are conducted in a foreign location, photographs evidencing the building that was constructed or children vaccinated might be a suitable method of documenting an activity. The instructions suggest the expected monitoring may not be conducted by the organization itself, but instead by a ''friends of'' organization that it supports.

Line 3. Activities per Region. The information requested in columns (b)–(f) of this part is reported using the nine regions listed in the definitions above for activity conducted at any time during the year. The individual countries within each region are not listed. Each activity conducted in a region is reported on a separate line.

Column (a). The instructions for this line say to identify each region in which the organization conducted activities and lists as examples, grant making, program services, and fund-raising activities matching the title to column (d). Then, another type of activity—unrelated trade or business—is listed as an activity that should be reported.[67]

Column (b). To tally the number of offices for this column requires studying the definition of ''maintaining offices'' above.

Column (c). Organizations that have employees or agents outside the United States list the number of them who regularly work in each region during the tax year here. Though the instructions do not say, it is reasonable to assume both U.S. and foreign citizens are counted. Those employees or agents whose ''only presence in the region is to conduct on-site visits, or persons who serve as volunteers'' are not counted.

Column (d). Each type of activity conducted in the region listed—grant making, fund-raising, unrelated trade or business, or ''program services'' is separately entered on the lines here. Total expense paid for each type of activity is reported in column (f). One begins to see why Schedule F-1 may be needed by many filers conducting activity outside the United States.

Column (e). A description of the type of program services performed is requested. One can readily see some wordsmithing will be needed because of the small space. Child vaccinations, teacher training, agricultural assistance, dig wells for water, and build housing are examples of descriptions that might fit in the space. Hopefully, software companies will program small type for this column. Schedule F is also one of those that includes a part to provide Supplemental Information.

Column (f). Enter the total amount of expenditures, in U.S. dollars, for activities conducted in each listed region. Expenditures include salaries, wages, and other employment-related costs paid to, or for the benefit of, employees located in the region; rent and other costs relating to offices located in the region; grants to recipients located in the region; and payments to agents located in the region. Report expenditures based on the method used to account for them on the organization's financial statements, and describe this method in Part IV.

Totals. The total of all numbers in columns (b), (c), and (f) are input at the bottom of the page. Amounts pertaining to activities reported on Schedule F-1 logically should be included although the instructions do not say so.

Schedule F (Form 990) 2008   Page **2**

Part II   **Grants and Other Assistance to Organizations or Entities Outside the United States.** Complete if the organization answered "Yes" to Form 990, Part IV, line 15, for any recipient who received more than $5,000. Check this box if no one recipient received more than $5,000 . . . . . ▶ ☐ Use Schedule F-1 (Form 990) if additional space is needed.

1	**(a)** Name of organization	**(b)** IRS code section and EIN (if applicable)	**(c)** Region	**(d)** Purpose of grant	**(e)** Amount of cash grant	**(f)** Manner of cash disbursement	**(g)** Amount of non-cash assistance	**(h)** Description of non-cash assistance	**(i)** Method of valuation (book, FMV, appraisal, other)

Line 1. The instructions for most of the columns appearing in Schedule I, Parts II and III for domestic grants are identical to those provided for this part. Preparers should refer to that discussion for purposes of filling out this part. As the shading for Columns (a) and (b) indicates, those columns should not be completed for 2008. The IRS responded to concerns for the safety of the organizations and their staffs in suspending completion of columns (a) and (b) for 2008. There are, however, two additional columns for the non-U.S. grant reporting as follows:

Column (c). The region where the principal office of the grant recipient organization or entity is located is entered following instructions above for Part I, column (a).

Column (f). The manner of cash disbursement, such as by cash payment, money order, electronic fund or wire transfer, check, other charges against funds on deposit at a financial institution, or other. The instructions request a description of all methods that apply for each recipient; the limited space in the column may make this challenging.

2 Enter total number of organizations that are recognized as charities by the foreign country or for which the grantee or counsel has provided a section 501(c)(3) equivalency letter . . . . ▶ ....

3 Enter total number of other organizations or entities . . . . ▶ ....

Schedule F (Form 990) 2008

Line 2. The sum of the recipient foreign organizations listed in line 1 of this part that possess the following attributes is provided on this line. The counted entities are ones that:

- Have a determination by the IRS that they qualify as a tax-exempt organization as described in §501(c)(3),

- Are recognized as a charity by a foreign country, or

- Have an affidavit or opinion of counsel that the grantee is the equivalent of a public charity, or what is called an equivalency letter.

This response may be difficult, or impossible, for the unprepared.

Line 3. The rest, or difference between the total number of foreign recipients and those reported on line 2 because they have some recognition of tax status, is entered on this line.

Schedule F (Form 990) 2008							Page **3**
Part III	**Grants and Other Assistance to Individuals Outside the United States.** Complete if the organization answered "Yes" to Form 990, Part IV, line 16. Use Schedule F-1 (Form 990) if additional space is needed.						
(a) Type of grant or assistance	(b) Region	(c) Number of recipients	(d) Amount of cash grant	(e) Manner of cash disbursement	(f) Amount of non-cash assistance	(g) Description of non-cash assistance	(h) Method of valuation (book, FMV, appraisal, other)

The type (such as food, clothing, or tools) of grants or other assistance paid directly to, or for the benefit of, foreign individual recipients is reported in this part by region. The names of individual recipients are not provided. Grants or other assistance provided to individuals through another organization or entity is not entered here but in Part II. As an example, a payment to a hospital located outside of the United States to cover the medical expenses of a specific foreign individual is reported here; a payment to that hospital for unspecified individuals goes in Part II.

This part, just like Part II, mostly contains the same columns as Schedule I so that a preparer can consult those materials for suggestions. As described above for Part II, two additional columns—one for the region and one for the manner of cash disbursement—must be completed. Because each type of assistance for each region must be entered, some organizations may need to use Schedule F-1 when the space in this part is inadequate. Free form attachments are not permitted.

Schedule F (Form 990) 2008	Page **4**
Part IV **Supplemental Information**	
Complete this part to provide the information required in Part I, line 2, and any other additional information.	

This part must be used for the following supplemental information:

Part I, line 2 should contain description of procedures for monitoring the use of grant funds outside of the United States.

Part I, line 3 reports the method—cash or accrual—used to account for expenditures on the organization's financial statements.

§ 4.7   SCHEDULE G

SCHEDULE G (Form 990 or 990-EZ) Department of the Treasury Internal Revenue Service	**Supplemental Information Regarding Fundraising or Gaming Activities** ▶ Attach to Form 990 or Form 990-EZ. Must be completed by organizations that answer "Yes" to Form 990, Part IV, lines 17, 18, or 19, and by organizations that enter more than $15,000 on Form 990-EZ, line 6a.	OMB No. 1545-0047 Open To Public Inspection

(a)   Background

Many nonprofit organizations hold special events or conduct other fund-raising activities as a means of generating contribution revenue. What some don't realize is that the revenue generated is partly contribution revenue and partly nonexempt function revenue that could be treated as unrelated business income. The unrelated portion represents the value of goods and services provided by the organization—an exchange transaction rather than a gift stemming from generosity. Any profit on the unrelated portion is usually excluded from taxability because the event is irregularly carried on, run by volunteers, or involves the sale of donated items.[68] For *quid pro quo* contributions of $75 or more, the organization is required to disclose the fair market value (''FMV'') of benefits provided.[69] Schedule G provides a way to compare the disclosed FMV with the actual cost of providing the benefits. If this comparison results in a loss, the loss may indicate the organization has undervalued the nondeductible portion of the revenue.

Part I **Fundraising Activities.** Complete if the organization answered "Yes" to Form 990, Part IV, line 17.

1   Indicate whether the organization raised funds through any of the following activities. Check all that apply.
   a ☐ Mail solicitations
   b ☐ Email solicitations
   c ☐ Phone solicitations
   d ☐ In-person solicitations
   e ☐ Solicitation of non-government grants
   f ☐ Solicitation of government grants
   g ☐ Special fundraising events

This part discloses the type of solicitation methods an organization reporting more than $15,000 of professional fund-raising expenses for the year on Core Part IX, line 11e uses. This part is similar to Part VIII, Question 4a of Form 1023 where information is presented about fund-raising activities.

2a   Did the organization have a written or oral agreement with any individual (including officers, directors, trustees or key employees listed in Form 990, Part VII) or entity in connection with professional fundraising services? ☐ **Yes** ☐ **No**
 b   If "Yes," list the ten highest paid individuals or entities (fundraisers) pursuant to agreements under which the fundraiser is to be compensated at least $5,000 by the organization. Form 990-EZ filers are not required to complete this table.

(i) Name of individual or entity (fundraiser)	(ii) Activity	(iii) Did fundraiser have custody or control of contributions?		(iv) Gross receipts from activity	(v) Amount paid to (or retained by) fundraiser listed in col. (i)	(vi) Amount paid to (or retained by) organization
		Yes	No			

The figures input in this part compare amounts paid to fund-raisers with the amounts raised with an apparent IRS intention to determine if the compensation paid is reasonable. The Question 2a inquiry about whether or not there is a written agreement with fund-raisers is again an IRS indication of the type of governance practice they recommend. The instructions suggest engagement of a firm to conduct a feasibility study for a capital campaign or develop strategy for a mailing is a fund-raiser for this purpose. Similarly, a printing and mailing service that also provides planning services is a fund-raiser. The consequence of responding ''No'' is unknown. Once the IRS develops its capability for scanning returns through the electronic filing system, such a question may lead to a follow-up inquiry using their Compliance Check letter. During 2006, such a letter was sent to organizations reporting donations but no fund-raising expenses.

An officer, director, trustee, or employee who conducts professional fund-raising in their capacity as an officer, director, trustee, or employee is not reported in this part. Form 990-EZ filers are not required to complete this table.

If the "Yes" box is checked in column (iii), the organization must describe the custody arrangement. The arrangement should ensure that the organization has sufficient control and ability to monitor the funds. If the fund-raiser has been paid during the year for a fund-raising activity that has not yet generated revenue, it is appropriate to enter -0- in column iv. The organization could conceivably have an explanation in Schedule O referenced to this part if concerned about the comparison.

---

3 List all states in which the organization is registered or licensed to solicit funds or has been notified it is exempt from registration or licensing.

This part serves as a reminder to organizations operating in multiple states that registration and other state filings may be required. Although the National Association of Attorneys General/National Association of State Charity Officials (NAAG/NASCO) has worked to create a Unified Registration Statement ("URS") to aid organizations soliciting in multiple states, not all states accept the form and many require additional information as a supplement to the form. See Appendix 4A for a copy of the most recent version of the URS and a chart describing information required by each state for initial registration and subsequent reporting. Any organization conducting fund-raising outside its state should determine whether it is required to register and or/make annual filings with such states. Those that solicit donations on their website might unexpectedly incur such a filing obligation when donors outside their state of residence send gifts.

Schedule G (Form 990 or 990-EZ) 2008   Page **2**

| Part II | Fundraising Events. Complete if the organization answered "Yes" to Form 990, Part IV, line 18, or reported more than $15,000 on Form 990-EZ, line 6a. List events with gross receipts greater than $5,000. |

(b) Background

A popular fund-raising tool for nonprofits is an event at which food, drink, and entertainment are provided to participants. The ticket price for such an event embodies both a donation and a purchase of the goods and services—called a *quid pro quo*. When an organization provides *quid pro quo* benefits in connection with a solicitation of a payment of more than $75, the value of the benefits must be disclosed either on the invitation or receipt for payment.[70] Penalties are imposed for failure to disclose. Services or goods received are to be valued at their fair market value, which is often difficult to determine. As a rule, the value is that amount a willing buyer would pay a willing seller in the normal market place in which such items are sold with neither party being compelled to buy or sell.[71] The cost of the event is not necessarily determinative of its value. Technically, a payment of less than $75 must also be reduced by benefits (unless *de minimis*)[72] for tax deductibility purposes; the helpful nonprofit makes a valuation disclosure in connection with all solicitations.

		(a) Event #1	(b) Event #2	(c) Other Events	(d) Total Events (Add col. (a) through col. (c))
		(event type)	(event type)	(total number)	
Revenue	1 Gross receipts				
	2 Less: Charitable contributions				
	3 Gross revenue (line 1 minus line 2)				
Direct Expenses	4 Cash prizes				
	5 Non-cash prizes				
	6 Rent/facility costs . . .				
	7 Other direct expenses . .				
	8 Direct expense summary. Add lines 4 through 7 in column (d) . . . . ▶				( )
	9 Net income summary. Combine lines 3 and 8 in column (d) . . . . ▶				

The Revenue section of this part fragments event proceeds into two parts:

Charitable Contribution Portion (line 2): the excess, if any, of the payment over the value of services or goods

Gross Revenue Portion (line 3): the value of services or goods provided

Proceeds of an auction, car wash, cookie sale, dinner, or other event are reported here. When the cost of the goods provided in connection with qualified fund-raising efforts—a T-shirt, coffee cup, or poster, for example—is less than a *de minimis* amount, the item or benefit is treated as having no value. The total payment made to the organization is then treated as a gift. Also, the expenses associated with purchase of the *de minimis* items are reported in Core Part IX as fund-raising expenses, and not on Core Part VIII, line 8b as direct event expenses.

Fund-raising campaign contributions for which donors receive nothing in return for their gifts are totally reported on Core Part VIII, line 1. The instructions direct §501 (c)(3) organizations to keep both their solicitations and the receipts they furnish to participants in events, as well as proof of the method used to determine the noncontribution portion of the proceeds. Schedule G, Part II displays details of the two largest events sponsored during the year along with a total for all other events. The cost of direct benefits (the food, drink, prizes, etc.) provided during the event are added together on line 8 and deducted from line 3 to arrive at the net income. The portion of the administrative and fund-raising department expenses attributable to management of and solicitation for the event is not reported on this line but on the applicable lines of Part IX.

Part III	Gaming. Complete if the organization answered "Yes" to Form 990, Part IV, line 19, or reported more than $15,000 on Form 990-EZ, line 6a.				
		(a) Bingo	(b) Pull tabs/Instant bingo/progressive bingo	(c) Other gaming	(d) Total gaming (Add col. (a) through col. (c))
Revenue	1 Gross revenue . . .				
Direct Expenses	2 Cash prizes				
	3 Non-cash prizes . . .				
	4 Rent/facility costs . .				
	5 Other direct expenses .				
	6 Volunteer labor . . .	☐ Yes _____ % ☐ No	☐ Yes _____ % ☐ No	☐ Yes _____ % ☐ No	
	7 Direct expense summary. Add lines 2 through 5 in column (d) . . . . ▶				( )
	8 Net gaming income summary. Combine lines 1 and 7 in column (d) . . . . ▶				

A similar table of information is requested for gaming event revenue and direct expenses. Gaming includes: "bingo, pull tabs/instant bingo (including satellite and progressive bingo), Texas Hold-Em Poker and other card games, raffles, scratch-offs, charitable gaming tickets, break-opens, hard cards, banded tickets, jar tickets, pickle cards, Lucky Seven cards, Nevada Club tickets, casino nights, Las Vegas nights, and coin-operated gambling devices. Coin-operated gambling devices include slot machines, electronic video slot or line games, video poker, video blackjack, video keno, video bingo, video pull tab games, etc." Presumably, gaming is separated from other charitable fund-raising activities because many states have laws regulating gaming and seek information to determine compliance with such laws.

Note there are tax reporting and withholding rules associated with gaming prizes. It is critical for an organization to obtain tax reporting information and cash required for the associated income tax due before distributing prizes.[73]

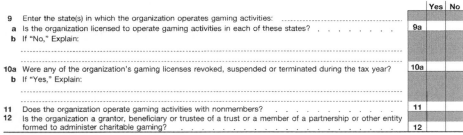

Schedule G (Form 990 or 990-EZ) 2008

Lines 9–10 seek to determine compliance with state rules regulating gaming activities. Explanations are requested from organizations that do not have state licenses to conduct gaming or have had their licenses revoked. Organizations should examine carefully whether they are in compliance with such regulations prior to holding gaming activities.

Line 11 asks whether the organization allows nonmembers to participate in gaming activities. For §501(c)(7) organizations, this is an important question because income from nonmembers is generally considered to be unrelated business income and subject to tax.

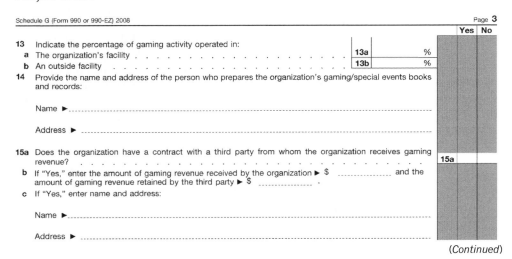

(Continued)

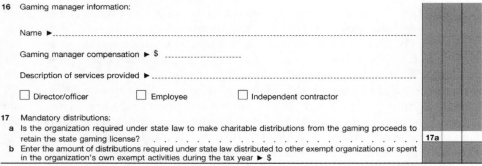

16 Gaming manager information:

Name ▶ ....

Gaming manager compensation ▶ $ ....

Description of services provided ▶ ....

☐ Director/officer ☐ Employee ☐ Independent contractor

17 Mandatory distributions:
a Is the organization required under state law to make charitable distributions from the gaming proceeds to retain the state gaming license? . . . . | 17a |
b Enter the amount of distributions required under state law distributed to other exempt organizations or spent in the organization's own exempt activities during the tax year ▶ $

Schedule G (Form 990 or 990-EZ) 2008

Lines 13–16 seek administrative information, such as the person responsible for keeping the books pertaining to gaming activities. Also, information about third-party conduct of gaming is requested.

Line 17 returns to the theme of compliance with state laws regulating gaming. For most organizations, it should not be difficult to demonstrate that the net income earned from the gaming activity was spent on the organization's charitable programs.

§4.8 SCHEDULE H

SCHEDULE H **(Form 990)** Department of the Treasury Internal Revenue Service	**Hospitals** ▶ To be completed by organizations that answer "Yes" to Form 990, Part IV, line 20. ▶ Attach to Form 990.	OMB No. 1545-0047 **2008** **Open to Public** **Inspection**

(a) Background

Promotion of health as a charitable pursuit is conspicuously absent from the tax code and regulations. The fact that for-profit and not-for-profit hospitals operate in a sometimes indistinguishable fashion complicates this category of exemption. A qualifying hospital must prove it benefits a charitable class rather than the health care professional that created and operates it. Who benefits from the hospital's operations, the sick, or the private doctors and investors who are in control?

The rules have evolved over the years since 1956, when the IRS ruled hospitals had to treat patients not able to pay for their care to the extent of the hospital's financial ability.[74] This charity care position was replaced in 1969, with a *community benefit standard*.[75] To qualify for tax exemption, a nonprofit hospital had to possess most of the following attributes to prove it promoted the community's health:

- Control by a community-based board of directors with no financial interest in the hospital
- Open medical staff with privileges available to all qualified physicians
- Emergency room open to all (unless this duplicates services provided by another institution in the area)
- Acceptance of Medicare and Medicaid patients

- Provision of public health programs and extensive research and medical training
- No unreasonable accumulation of surplus funds
- Limited funds invested in for-profit subsidiaries

The standards above have been refined and expanded since 1969, in IRS examination guidelines, IRS Field Service Advice,[76] and annual articles between 1980 and 1999 in the IRS CPE Technical Instruction Programs. The hospital's communication of its policies to its community has been a factor. More recently, the IRS and the Senate Finance Committee had conducted tax compliance surveys of hospitals. The results of the surveys were posted on the IRS website on 2/12/2009. The general conclusion was that (1) for the most part, executive compensation was supported by rebuttable presumption evidence and (2) the hospitals were all over the map regarding community benefit factors. The IRS intends to review information submitted in Schedule H over the coming years to determine if any change to the standard should or could be implemented. The questions asked in Part I of Schedule H evidence the many factors the IRS will take into account in evaluating a hospital's continuing exempt status. Due to the complexity of information the IRS is seeking, completion of most of the schedule is delayed until 2009. Guidance on hospital tax issues can be found in *The Law of Tax-Exempt Healthcare Organizations, 3rd Edition* by Thomas K. Hyatt, Bruce R. Hopkins, John Wiley & Sons, 2008.

Schedule H must be completed by an organization that operates at least one facility that is, or is required to be, licensed, registered, or similarly recognized by a state as a hospital. An organization that checks Box 3 in Part I of Schedule A, Public Charity Status and Public Support, to report that it is a hospital or cooperative hospital service organization, must complete and attach Schedule H to Form 990 *only* if it meets the following definition of hospital for purposes of Schedule H.

DEFINITION

Hospital (for Sch. H purposes) is "a facility that is, or is required to be, licensed, registered, or similarly recognized by a state as a hospital. This includes a hospital that is operated through a disregarded entity or a joint venture taxed as a partnership. It does not include hospitals that are located outside the United States. It also does not include hospitals that are operated by entities organized as separate legal entities from the organization that are taxable as a corporation for federal tax purposes (except for members of a group exemption included in a group return filed by the organization).

▶ **Transition Period:** *For 2008, organizations are only required to complete Part V, Facility Information.* Hospitals have the option to complete the other Parts of the Schedule voluntarily. A hospital might choose to complete all parts if it has the information available and wishes to promote its transparency.

The one section of Schedule H required to be filed in 2008 is Part V. A list is provided to describe each of the hospital's facilities that are required to be licensed, registered, or similarly recognized as a health care provider under state law, whether it operates it directly or indirectly through a disregarded entity or joint venture. A hospital filing Schedule H must provide the list identifying the following:

Schedule H (Form 990) 2008   Page **3**

| Part V | Facility Information *(Required for 2008)* |

Name and address	Licensed hospital	General medical & surgical	Children's hospital	Teaching hospital	Critical access hospital	Research facility	ER-24 hours	ER-other	Other (Describe)

Schedule H (Form 990) 2008

- Hospitals it directly operates.
- Hospitals operated by disregarded entities of which the organization is the sole member.
- Other facilities or programs of the hospital or the first two entities above, even if provided by a facility that is not a hospital or if provided separately from the hospital's license.
- Hospitals operated by any joint venture taxed as a partnership, to the extent of the organization's proportionate share of the joint venture.

When a group return is filed, the above-listed facilities of all members of the group would be listed. Members of the group filing separate returns would also submit the consolidated Schedule H. Members of a hospital system comprised of organizations holding separate determination letters and using separate employer identification numbers would each file their own Schedule H with their returns.

Foreign hospitals located outside the United States are not reported in Parts I, II, III, or V, but information about foreign joint ventures and partnerships is reported in Part IV. Information concerning foreign hospitals and facilities may be described in Part VI. Though the instructions do not say so, operation of a foreign hospital logically would be reported on Schedule F.

Name of the organization			Employer identification number	

Part I   **Charity Care and Certain Other Community Benefits at Cost** *(Optional for 2008)*

				Yes	No
1a	Does the organization have a charity care policy? If "No," skip to question 6a		**1a**		
b	If "Yes," is it a written policy?		**1b**		

2 If the organization has multiple hospitals, indicate which of the following best describes application of the charity care policy to the various hospitals.

☐ Applied uniformly to all hospitals   ☐ Applied uniformly to most hospitals
☐ Generally tailored to individual hospitals

3 Answer the following based on the charity care eligibility criteria that applies to the largest number of the organization's patients.

a	Does the organization use Federal Poverty Guidelines (FPG) to determine eligibility for providing *free* care to low income individuals? If "Yes," indicate which of the following is the family income limit for eligibility for free care: . . . . ☐ 100% ☐ 150% ☐ 200% ☐ Other _____ %	**3a**
b	Does the organization use FPG to determine eligibility for providing *discounted* care to low income individuals? If "Yes," indicate which of the following is the family income limit for eligibility for discounted care: . . . . ☐ 200% ☐ 250% ☐ 300% ☐ 350% ☐ 400% ☐ Other _____ %	**3b**
c	If the organization does not use FPG to determine eligibility, describe in Part VI the income based criteria for determining eligibility for free or discounted care. Include in the description whether the organization uses an asset test or other threshold, regardless of income, to determine eligibility for free or discounted care.	

			Yes	No
4	Does the organization's policy provide free or discounted care to the "medically indigent"?	**4**		
5a	Does the organization budget amounts for free or discounted care provided under its charity care policy?	**5a**		
b	If "Yes," did the organization's charity care expenses exceed the budgeted amount?	**5b**		
c	If "Yes" to line 5b, as a result of budget considerations, was the organization unable to provide free or discounted care to a patient who was eligible for free or discounted care?	**5c**		
6a	Does the organization prepare an annual community benefit report?	**6a**		
b	If "Yes," does the organization make it available to the public?	**6b**		

Complete the following table using the worksheets provided in the Schedule H instructions. Do not submit these worksheets with the Schedule H.

7   Charity Care and Certain Other Community Benefits at Cost

Charity Care and Means-Tested Government Programs	(a) Number of activities or programs (optional)	(b) Persons served (optional)	(c) Total community benefit expense	(d) Direct offsetting revenue	(e) Net community benefit expense	(f) Percent of total expense
a Charity care at cost (from *Worksheets 1 and 2*) . . .						
b Unreimbursed Medicaid (from *Worksheet 3, column a*) . . .						
c Unreimbursed costs—other means-tested government programs (from *Worksheet 3, column b*) . . .						
d **Total** Charity Care and Means-Tested Government Programs						
Other Benefits						
e Community health improvement services and community benefit operations (from Worksheet 4) .						
f Health professions education (from Worksheet 5)						
g Subsidized health services (from Worksheet 6)						
h Research (from Worksheet 7) . .						
i Cash and in-kind contributions to community groups (from Worksheet 8)						
j **Total** Other Benefits						
k **Total** (line 7d and 7j)						

For Privacy Act and Paperwork Reduction Act Notice, see the Instructions for Form 990.   Cat. No. 50192T   Schedule H (Form 990) 2008

| Part II | **Community Building Activities** Complete this table if the organization conducted any community building activities. *(Optional for 2008)* | | | | | |

		(a) Number of activities or programs (optional)	**(b)** Persons served (optional)	**(c)** Total community building expense	**(d)** Direct offsetting revenue	**(e)** Net community building expense	**(f)** Percent of total expense
1	Physical improvements and housing						
2	Economic development						
3	Community support						
4	Environmental improvements						
5	Leadership development and training for community members						
6	Coalition building						
7	Community health improvement advocacy						
8	Workforce development						
9	Other						
10	**Total**						

| Part III | **Bad Debt, Medicare, & Collection Practices** *(Optional for 2008)* |

Section A. Bad Debt Expense

		Yes	No
1	Does the organization report bad debt expense in accordance with Healthcare Financial Management Association Statement No. 15? **1**		
2	Enter the amount of the organization's bad debt expense (at cost) **2**		
3	Enter the estimated amount of the organization's bad debt expense (at cost) attributable to patients eligible under the organization's charity care policy. **3**		
4	Provide in Part VI the text of the footnote to the organization's financial statements that describes bad debt expense. In addition, describe the costing methodology used in determining the amounts reported on lines 2 and 3, or rationale for including other bad debt amounts in community benefit.		

Section B. Medicare

5	Enter total revenue received from Medicare (including DSH and IME) **5**		
6	Enter Medicare allowable costs of care relating to payments on line 5 . . . . . . **6**		
7	Enter line 5 less line 6—surplus or (shortfall) **7**		
8	Describe in Part VI the extent to which any shortfall reported in line 7 should be treated as community benefit and the costing methodology or source used to determine the amount reported on line 6, and indicate which of the following methods was used:		
	☐ Cost accounting system ☐ Cost to charge ratio ☐ Other		

Section C. Collection Practices

9a	Does the organization have a written debt collection policy? **9a**		
b	If "Yes," does the organization's collection policy contain provisions on the collection practices to be followed for patients who are known to qualify for charity care or financial assistance? Describe in Part VI . . . **9b**		

| Part IV | **Management Companies and Joint Ventures** *(Optional for 2008)* | | | |

	(a) Name of entity	**(b)** Description of primary activity of entity	**(c)** Organization's profit % or stock ownership %	**(d)** Officers, directors, trustees, or key employees' profit % or stock ownership %	**(e)** Physicians' profit % or stock ownership %
1					
2					
3					
4					
5					
6					
7					
8					
9					
10					
11					
12					
13					
14					

| Part VI | **Supplemental Information** (*Optional for 2008*) |

Complete this part to provide the following information.

1   Provide the description required for Part I, line 3c; Part I, line 6a; Part I, line 7g; Part I, line 7, column (f); Part I, line 7; Part III, line 4; Part III, line 8; Part III, line 9b, and Part V. See Instructions.

2   **Needs assessment.** Describe how the organization assesses the health care needs of the communities it serves.

3   **Patient education of eligibility for assistance.** Describe how the organization informs and educates patients and persons who may be billed for patient care about their eligibility for assistance under federal, state, or local government programs or under the organization's charity care policy.

4   **Community information.** Describe the community the organization serves, taking into account the geographic area and demographic constituents it serves.

5   **Community building activities.** Describe how the organization's community building activities, as reported in Part II, promote the health of the communities the organization serves.

6   Provide any other information important to describing how the organization's hospitals or other health care facilities further its exempt purpose by promoting the health of the community (e.g., open medical staff, community board, use of surplus funds, etc.).

7   If the organization is part of an affiliated health care system, describe the respective roles of the organization and its affiliates in promoting the health of the communities served.

8   If applicable, identify all states with which the organization, or a related organization, files a community benefit report.

Schedule H (Form 990) 2008

§4.9   SCHEDULE I

| SCHEDULE I
(Form 990)

Department of the Treasury
Internal Revenue Service | **Grants and Other Assistance to Organizations,
Governments, and Individuals in the U.S.**
▶ Complete if the organization answered "Yes," on Form 990, Part IV, lines 21 or 22.
▶ Attach to Form 990. | OMB No. 1545-0047

Open to Public
Inspection |

(a) Background

Though it is not mentioned specifically on the form or the instructions, an organization's selection and eligibility process for awards must be designed to provide funds to organizations and individuals that meet criteria designed to avoid discrimination against applicants based on race, color, or creed and the organization's insiders. A tax-exempt organization has a responsibility to operate to benefit what is referred to as an *exempt class of persons*, rather than a select few. This schedule is required if an organization has paid >$5,000 in grants or assistance and begins in Part I with a request of due diligence–type information to evidence the exempt purpose of grants and assistance awarded.

Schedule I is required for organizations that make grants of more than $5,000 to organizations, governments, and/or individuals in the United States.[77] Grant activities conducted by the organization directly or indirectly through a disregarded entity, or through a joint venture taxed as a partnership are reported on this schedule. Grants and awards paid to individuals living and residing outside the United States, organizations and governments located outside the United States (at the time of payment) are reported on Schedule F rather than here.

Grants and other assistance include awards, prizes, allocations, stipends, scholarships, fellowships, research grants, and similar payments and distributions. The term *grants or other assistance* does not include salaries or other compensation to employees or other grant management expenses. Grants or other assistance also does not include grants provided by the filing organization to affiliates that are not organized as separate legal entities, or its branch offices, accounts, or employees located in the United States. An organization using an accrual basis of accounting would report pledged grants not yet paid and omit payments on grants pledged and reported in a prior year.

Part I	General Information on Grants and Assistance

1 Does the organization maintain records to substantiate the amount of the grants or assistance, the grantees' eligibility for the grants or assistance, and the selection criteria used to award the grants or assistance? · □ Yes □ No
2 Describe in Part IV the organization's procedures for monitoring the use of grant funds in the United States.

Part I requests due diligence–type information when Question 1 asks if the organization can substantiate the charitable, or exempt-purpose nature of its grant program both as to amounts awarded and its process for choosing recipients. Question 2 asks a grant-making organization to describe its policies and procedures regarding its monitoring of grantees' use of funds awarded. Required periodic reports or field investigations are suggested as the type of tools to use to monitor grantees. The former 990 only asked §501(c)(3) organizations, on Schedule A, Part III, to attach such information. Instead of attaching their grant application as many did in the past, this new schedule provides all descriptive information regarding eligibility, selection criteria, and documentation processes used for grants in Part IV, Supplemental Information.

Though it is not mentioned specifically, an organization's selection and eligibility process for awards should be designed to provide funds to organizations and individuals that meet criteria designed to avoid discrimination against applicants based on race, color, or creed and which serve to advance the organization's nonprofit mission.

Part II	Grants and Other Assistance to Governments and Organizations in the United States. Complete if the organization answered "Yes" on Form 990, Part IV, line 21, for any recipient that received more than $5,000. Check this box if no one recipient received more than $5,000. Use Part IV and Schedule I-1 (Form 990) if additional space is needed ▶ ☐							
1 (a) Name and address of organization or government	(b) EIN	(c) IRC section if applicable	(d) Amount of cash grant	(e) Amount of non-cash assistance	(f) Method of valuation (book, FMV, appraisal, other)	(g) Description of non-cash assistance	(h) Purpose of grant or assistance

Importantly, this part starts with a check box on the right for an organization to say "No," it did not report any grants on line 1 of Core Part IX of more than $5,000 to any one recipient. When the organization has more than twelve grantees, Schedule I-1 is to be completed. The columns in this part are mostly self-explanatory, but some may be a burden for the ill-prepared. Formerly, the information in columns (a), (combined total of d & e), (f), (g), and (h) were submitted in an attachment.

Column (b) requests the recipient's Employer Identification Number (EIN), a fact seldom obtained in the past. Following the practice of private foundations, grant-making public charities will need to request a copy of the grantee's IRS determination letter, look the grantee up on Guidestar.org, or add a blank for this information to its grant request forms.

Column (c) requests the section of the Internal Revenue Code under which the organization receiving the assistance is tax-exempt, such as §501(c)(3) for a church, school, or community campaign or §501(c)(4) for a civic association. The instructions also list a social club described in §501(c)(7) as a potential grantee reminding one that this schedule is filed for non–(c)(3) entities that make such a grant. If a recipient is a government entity, that designation is entered. If a recipient is neither a tax-exempt organization, nor a government entity, (c) should be blank.

Column (d). The total amount of any cash grants paid during the tax year is entered here separately from noncash property distributed. Cash grants include grants and allocations paid by cash, checks, money orders, electronic fund or wire transfers, and other charges against funds on deposit at a financial institution.

Columns (e) and (f). The fair market value of noncash property granted to the recipient, plus a description of the method of valuation, is requested. The value should be based on the price for which the property sells in the normal market place where it is sold. For marketable securities registered and listed on a recognized securities exchange, market value is measured by the average of the highest and lowest quoted selling prices or the average between the bona fide bid and asked prices, on the date the property is distributed to the grantee. For new items sold in a retail store, the store price would be used. For used items, a resale shop value might be used. For items purchased in wholesale quantities, the price paid would be used. For items, such as real estate, for which fair market value cannot be readily determined, an appraisal might be suitable.

Column (g). Though the space provided will make it a challenge, this column requests a description of noncash property or assistance, such as medical supplies or equipment, pharmaceuticals, food, blankets, books, or other educational supplies. Hopefully, software providers may address this problem with small type. If not, the description is to be entered as supplemental information in Part IV.

Column (h). The purpose or ultimate use of the grant funds, rather than broad generic terms such as charitable, educational, religious, or scientific is requested. Specific descriptions suggested include general support, payments for nursing services, or laboratory construction, medical or dental assistance, or free care for indigent hospital patients. For disaster assistance, the information provided should include a description of the particular disaster, such as Hurricane Ike, and the assistance provided (such as food, shelter, and clothing).

This schedule has a continuation Schedule I-1 for those organizations whose grant recipients exceed the space provided. As many supplemental schedules as needed may be submitted.

2	Enter total number of section 501(c)(3) and government organizations . . . . ▶	....
3	Enter total number of other organizations . . . . ▶	

For Privacy Act and Paperwork Reduction Act Notice, see the Instructions for Form 990.   Cat. No. 50055P   Schedule I (Form 990) 2008

Lines 2. For this line, the following total number of the three types of grantees listed below is entered.

- Grantees listed in this part that have been recognized by the IRS as §501(c)(3) tax-exempt organizations.

- §501(c)(3) organizations not required to seek recognition including churches, synagogues, temples, and mosques, integrated auxiliaries of churches and conventions or associations of churches, and any organization that (previously) has gross revenues not more than $5,000.

- Government units or entities in the United States.

Line 3. On this line, the total number of grantees that are not included on line 2 or those exempt under other §501(c) sections and recipients that are not tax exempt is entered. Though at first this count seems difficult, this information needed to determine the number is also required to be displayed in column (c).

Schedule I (Form 990) 2008   Page **2**

Part III **Grants and Other Assistance to Individuals in the United States.** Complete if the organization answered "Yes" on Form 990, Part IV, line 22.
Use Schedule I-1 (Form 990) if additional space is needed.

(a) Type of grant or assistance	(b) Number of recipients	(c) Amount of cash grant	(d) Amount of non-cash assistance	(e) Method of valuation (book, FMV, appraisal, other)	(f) Description of non-cash assistance

Grants or other assistance paid or provided directly to, or for the benefit of, individual recipients are reported in this Part, rather than grants or assistance to another organization to provide such assistance, which is reportable in Part II. No names are entered.

Column (a). Each type of aid is entered on a separate line with a description of the type(s) of assistance provided, or the purpose or use, of grant funds. The instructions say, "Do not use broad terms such as charitable, educational, religious, or scientific." Rather, use more specific descriptions, such as scholarships for students attending school in a particular county or attending a particular school; provision of books or other educational supplies; food, clothing, and shelter for indigents or direct cash assistance to indigents, and so forth is suggested. In the case of specific disaster assistance, the type of assistance provided and identification of the disaster should be described such as "food, shelter, and clothing for immediate relief for Hurricane Katrina disaster victims."

Column (b). The number of aid recipients receiving each type of assistance is requested. Some types of aid, such as crates of food and clothing sent to a community center after a flood, may make it impossible to actually count the number of persons receiving aid. The instructions provide no comment about the estimation process. Presumably, the recommendation for estimating the number of volunteers serving the organization in Core Part I can be followed. For such purposes, a "reasonable basis" for determining an estimate would be used. An explanation of the process should be entered in Part IV.

Column (c). The aggregate dollar amount of cash grants for each type of grant or assistance is entered. Cash grants include only grants and allocations paid by cash, checks, money orders, electronic fund or wire transfers, and other charges against funds on deposit at a financial institution.

Columns (d) and (e). The fair market value of noncash property and a description of the method of valuation are entered. Property with a readily determinable market value (such as market quotations for securities) is to be entered at its fair market value. For marketable securities registered and listed on a recognized securities exchange, the measure of market value is the average of the highest and lowest quoted selling prices or the average between the bona fide bid and asked prices, on the date the property is distributed to the grantee. When fair market value cannot be readily determined, an appraised or reasonably estimated value can be used.

Column (f). For noncash grants or assistance, a description of the property provided to aid recipients is requested. The instructions suggest "all that apply" should be listed, meaning that the space provided may be a challenge. Examples of noncash assistance include, but are said not to be limited to, medical supplies or equipment, pharmaceuticals, blankets, and books or other educational supplies.

Part IV **Supplemental Information.** Complete this part to provide the information required in Part I, line 2, and any other additional information.

This part has 11 lines for use in providing the narrative description of the organization's grant-making policies and procedures requested in Part I, line 2. Specifically, that part asks how the organization monitors each grantee's use of the money granted.

This part is also used when additional room is needed to provide a description of the method of valuation of noncash grants in Part II, column (f) or Part III, column (e). The method used by the organization to estimate the number of aid recipients is explained here, as well as a description of noncash assistance for Part III, column (f). The instructions suggested this part may be duplicated if more space is needed.

§4.10 SCHEDULE J

SCHEDULE J
(Form 990)

Department of the Treasury
Internal Revenue Service

Compensation Information

For certain Officers, Directors, Trustees, Key Employees, and Highest
Compensated Employees
▶ Attach to Form 990. To be completed by organizations
that answered "Yes" to Form 990, Part IV, line 23.

OMB No. 1545-0047

Open to Public
Inspection

(a) Background

Readers should study the introduction to Core Part VII to review the private benefit/
inurement rules that inspire the questions in this schedule. Tax-exempt organizations
under many categories of §501 must operate to benefit their exempt constituents
rather than those that manage and control them. Excessive compensation is deemed
to provide impermissible benefit. The information gathered on this schedule allows
the IRS to make an analysis of the reasonableness of the elements of the compensation
paid to those persons receiving reportable compensation in excess of $150,000.

The "Overview" in the instructions reports, "Part I asks questions regarding certain
of the organization's compensation practices." In a rather confusing roundabout fashion,
careful reading indicates that lines 1, 2, 7, and 8 answers pertain to the filing organization,
but not related ones. Lines 3–6 require information for both the filer and its related entities. Additionally, lines 5–8 are only completed by §501(c)(3) and (c)(4) organizations.

Part I	**Questions Regarding Compensation**			
			Yes	No
1a	Check the appropriate box(es) if the organization provided any of the following to or for a person listed in Form 990, Part VII, Section A, line 1a. Complete Part III to provide any relevant information regarding these items.			
	☐ First-class or charter travel	☐ Housing allowance or residence for personal use		
	☐ Travel for companions	☐ Payments for business use of personal residence		
	☐ Tax indemnification and gross-up payments	☐ Health or social club dues or initiation fees		
	☐ Discretionary spending account	☐ Personal services (e.g., maid, chauffeur, chef)		
b	If line 1a is checked, did the organization follow a written policy regarding payment or reimbursement or provision of all of the expenses described above? If "No," complete Part III to explain	**1b**		
2	Did the organization require substantiation prior to reimbursing or allowing expenses incurred by all officers, directors, trustees, and the CEO/Executive Director, regarding the items checked in line 1a? .	**2**		
3	Indicate which, if any, of the following the organization uses to establish the compensation of the organization's CEO/Executive Director. Check all that apply.			
	☐ Compensation committee	☐ Written employment contract		
	☐ Independent compensation consultant	☐ Compensation survey or study		
	☐ Form 990 of other organizations	☐ Approval by the board or compensation committee		

Line 1 clearly implies that the IRS believes first-class air travel, chauffeurs, and other
executive perks listed are benefits that could result in persons receiving excessive compensation. The reason one of the eight boxed items is provided can be explained in Part III,
Supplemental Information. For example, first-class travel is allowed for flights more than
five hours in duration or for cross-country or overseas flights. The important factor is
whether the benefit is included in compensation reported in Part II. In evaluating reasonableness of compensation, all forms of direct and indirect payments are taken in account.

Lines 1b and 2 should preferably not be answered "No" to indicate lack of oversight over what the IRS considered to be perks in view of the enhanced emphasis on
governance.

Line 3 is essentially a governance question that goes beyond those asked in Core
Part VI. Checkmarks in all of the boxes will be preferable. At a minimum the bottom

two—Form 990 of other organizations and approval by the board or compensation committee—should apply.

4 During the year, did any person listed in Form 990, Part VII, Section A, line 1a:		
a Receive a severance payment or change of control payment?	4a	
b Participate in, or receive payment from, a supplemental nonqualified retirement plan? . . .	4b	
c Participate in, or receive payment from, an equity-based compensation arrangement?	4c	
If "Yes" to any of lines 4a–c, list the persons and provide the applicable amounts for each item in Part III.		
Only 501(c)(3) and 501(c)(4) organizations must complete lines 5–8.		
5 For persons listed in Form 990, Part VII, Section A, line 1a, did the organization pay or accrue any compensation contingent on the revenues of:		
a The organization?	5a	
b Any related organization?	5b	
If "Yes" to line 5a or 5b, describe in Part III.		
6 For persons listed in Form 990, Part VII, Section A, line 1a, did the organization pay or accrue any compensation contingent on the net earnings of:		
a The organization?	6a	
b Any related organization?	6b	
If "Yes" to line 6a or 6b, describe in Part III.		
7 For persons listed in Form 990, Part VII, Section A, line 1a, did the organization provide any non-fixed payments not described in lines 5 and 6? If "Yes," describe in Part III	7	
8 Were any amounts reported in Form 990, Part VII, paid or accrued pursuant to a contract that was subject to the initial contract exception described in Regs. section 53.4958-4(a)(3)? If "Yes," describe in Part III	8	

For Privacy Act and Paperwork Reduction Act Notice, see the Instructions for Form 990.   Cat. No. 50053T   Schedule J (Form 990) 2008

Line 4 delves deeper into the types of compensation the IRS wants to scrutinize. The type of compensation in 4a, for example, is included on the W-2 and therefore already presented in the total compensation amount. The same would be true in 4b and 4c if the amounts were actually paid and reported on a W-2.

Lines 5–8 seek information about incentive compensation based on revenues or profits. Though such a payment method is not prohibited by the tax rules, it is thought to evidence an unhealthy motivation for an organization the purpose of which is not to make a profit. As a general rule, the IRS expects that incentive compensation must be *capped*, or limited to an amount of total compensation that is shown to be reasonable.[78]

Schedule J (Form 990) 2008   Page **2**

Part II   Officers, Directors, Trustees, Key Employees, and Highest Compensated Employees. Use Schedule J-1 if additional space is needed.

For each individual whose compensation must be reported in Schedule J, report compensation from the organization on row (i) and from related organizations, described in the instructions, on row (ii). Do not list any individuals that are not listed on Form 990, Part VII.

Note. The sum of columns (B)(i)–(iii) must equal the applicable column (D) or column (E) amounts on Form 990, Part VII, line 1a.

(A) Name		(B) Breakdown of W-2 and/or 1099-MISC compensation			(C) Deferred compensation	(D) Nontaxable benefits	(E) Total of columns (B)(i)–(D)	(F) Compensation reported in prior Form 990 or Form 990-EZ
		(i) Base compensation	(ii) Bonus & incentive compensation	(iii) Other reportable compensation				
	(i)							
	(ii)							
	(i)							
	(ii)							
	(i)							
	(ii)							
	(i)							
	(ii)							
	(i)							
	(ii)							
	(i)							
	(ii)							
	(i)							
	(ii)							
	(i)							
	(ii)							
	(i)							
	(ii)							
	(i)							
	(ii)							
	(i)							
	(ii)							
	(i)							
	(ii)							

Schedule J (Form 990) 2008

This part of Schedule J only reports (1) those persons with reportable compensation exceeding $150,000 from the filer and its related organizations; (2) former officers, key employees, or highest compensated employees with reportable compensation exceeding $100,000 from the filer and its related organizations; and (3) former directors or trustees with reportable compensation exceeding $10,000 from the filer and its related organizations. As a guide to proper inclusion in the columns of this Part, Figure 2 (the table for compensation types) should be followed.

Who from Part VII Is Reported on Schedule J, Part II

- Former officer or director with reportable compensation >$10,000

- Former officer, key employee, or highest compensated employee with reportable compensation >$100,000

- Any other individual with reportable compensation >$150,000

Column B reflects compensation for any individual paid by both the filing organization and a related entity on two lines. Column B reflects compensation differently from Core Part VII by distinguishing between base (Bi), bonus & incentive compensation (Bii), and other reportable compensation (Biii). These three amounts should, however, agree with the amount in Column (D) for the filing entity and amount in column (E) for a related entity.

Column C reflects all current-year deferrals of compensation, whether under a qualified or nonqualified retirement or other plan, that is established, sponsored, or maintained by or for the organization or a related organization. The annual increase in actuarial value, if any, of a defined benefit plan is also reported.

If the payment of an amount of deferred compensation requires the employee to perform services for a period of time, the amount is treated as accrued and earned ratably over the course of the service period, even though the amount is not funded and may be subject to a substantial risk of forfeiture until the service period is completed. Do not report any amounts included in reportable compensation as defined in Core Part VII. Reasonably estimated amounts can be reported if actual numbers are not readily available.

Column D includes those nontaxable benefits excluded from taxation under §119, including value of housing provided by the employer, educational assistance, health insurance, medical reimbursement programs, life and long-term care insurance, and other benefits listed in the table on page 78.

Benefits that are excluded from gross income under §132[79] and are disregarded for purposes of §4958 are not reported in column (D), including no-additional cost service, qualified employee discount, working condition fringes, qualified transportation and moving expense reimbursement, qualified retirement planning services, and qualified military base realignment and closure fringe.

Column F discloses the amount of compensation reported in a 2007 return based on a noncalendar fiscal year that is being reported in this return following the new method of reporting compensation on a calendar year according to the Form W-2 or 1099.

§ 4.11   SCHEDULE K

| SCHEDULE K
(Form 990)

Department of the Treasury
Internal Revenue Service | **Supplemental Information on Tax-Exempt Bonds**

▶ Attach to Form 990. To be completed by organizations that answered "Yes" to Form 990, Part IV,
line 24a. Provide descriptions, explanations, and any additional information on Schedule O (Form 990). | OMB No. 1545-0047

2008

Open to Public
Inspection |

(a)   Background

Charitable organizations exempt under §501(c)(3) are able to issue bonds to acquire buildings and equipment used in their exempt activities. To encourage such financing, the tax code exempts the interest paid on such bonds from income tax. Due to the tax-free status of interest paid, the rate a charity must pay to its bond purchasers is customarily lower than other lending sources.

Issuers of tax-exempt bonds must adhere to rather complex standards and typically engage specialists referred to as bond counsel to assist in the process. The extensive information requested in Schedule K reflects the standards imposed on bond issuers and the special terms and nomenclature used to govern the bonds when they are issued and throughout the life of the obligation.

Of primary concern to the IRS is compliance with rules governing the use of bond proceeds. The IRS Tax Exempt Bonds and the Exempt Organizations Compliance Area initiated a joint effort in 2007, to evaluate the policies and procedures used by §501(c)(3) exempt organizations to ensure the post-issuance tax compliance of their tax-exempt debt obligations. The project used compliance check questionnaires sent to more than 200 exempt organizations indicating an outstanding balance of tax-exempt liabilities on their 2005 Form 990. The preliminary result indicated that only 15 percent of bond issuers had sufficient procedures in place to monitor compliance with the rules.[80] The schedule should be prepared in concert with an organization's advisors who are conversant with the terms, such as defeasance escrow, refunding escrow, and private business use, and the many IRS rulings and procedures cited in the instructions.

Part I	Bond Issues *(Required for 2008)*							
	(a) Issuer name	(b) Issuer EIN	(c) CUSIP #	(d) Date issued	(e) Issue price	(f) Description of purpose	(g) Defeased	(h) On behalf of issuer
							Yes | No	Yes | No
A								
B								
C								
D								
E								

Schedule K is submitted by an organization that files Form 990 to provide certain information on its outstanding liabilities associated with tax-exempt bond issues. For the first time, evidence of compliance with the requirements must be submitted on Form 990. *Only Part I is required to be completed for 2008.* The threshold for completion of this schedule is the existence of an outstanding tax-exempt bond issue that both had an outstanding principal amount in excess of $100,000 as of the last day of the tax year and was issued after December 31, 2002. Up to five separate outstanding tax-exempt liabilities can be reported on each Schedule K. Schedule K may be duplicated, if needed, to report more than five liabilities. If the organization is not required to file Form 990, it is not required to file Schedule K.

Part II	**Proceeds** *(Optional for 2008)*	A		B		C		D		E	
1	Total proceeds of issue										
2	Gross proceeds in reserve funds										
3	Proceeds in refunding or defeasance escrows										
4	Other unspent proceeds										
5	Issuance costs from proceeds										
6	Working capital expenditures from proceeds										
7	Capital expenditures from proceeds										
8	Year of substantial completion										
		Yes	No	Yes	No	Yes	No	Yes	No	Yes	No
9	Were the bonds issued as part of a current refunding issue?										
10	Were the bonds issued as part of an advance refunding issue?										
11	Has the final allocation of proceeds been made?										
12	Does the organization maintain adequate books and records to support the final allocation of proceeds?										

Part III	**Private Business Use** *(Optional for 2008)*	A		B		C		D		E	
		Yes	No	Yes	No	Yes	No	Yes	No	Yes	No
1	Was the organization a partner in a partnership, or a member of an LLC, which owned property financed by tax-exempt bonds?										
2	Are there any lease arrangements with respect to the financed property which may result in private business use?										
3a	Are there any management or service contracts with respect to the financed property which may result in private business use?										
b	Are there any research agreements with respect to the financed property which may result in private business use?										
c	Does the organization routinely engage bond counsel or other outside counsel to review any management or service contracts or research agreements relating to the financed property?										
4	Enter the percentage of financed property used in a private business use by entities other than a section 501(c)(3) organization or a state or local government ▶		%		%		%		%		%
5	Enter the percentage of financed property used in a private business use as a result of unrelated trade or business activity carried on by your organization, another section 501(c)(3) organization, or a state or local government . ▶		%		%		%		%		%
6	Total of lines 4 and 5		%		%		%		%		%
7	Has the organization adopted management practices and procedures to ensure the post-issuance compliance of its tax-exempt bond liabilities?										

Part IV	**Arbitrage** *(Optional for 2008)*	A		B		C		D		E	
		Yes	No	Yes	No	Yes	No	Yes	No	Yes	No
1	Has a Form 8038-T, Arbitrage Rebate, Yield Reduction and Penalty in Lieu of Arbitrage Rebate, been filed with respect to the bond issue?										
2	Is the bond issue a variable rate issue?										
3a	Has the organization or the governmental issuer identified a hedge with respect to the bond issue on its books and records?										
b	Name of provider										
c	Term of hedge										
4a	Were gross proceeds invested in a GIC?										
b	Name of provider										
c	Term of GIC										
d	Was the regulatory safe harbor for establishing the fair market value of the GIC satisfied?										
5	Were any gross proceeds invested beyond an available temporary period?										
6	Did the bond issue qualify for an exception to rebate?										

For Privacy Act and Paperwork Reduction Act Notice, see the Instructions for Form 990.   Cat. No. 50193E   Schedule K (Form 990) 2008

An organization with bond issues that need to be reported should study the detailed information in these parts to prepare itself for 2009 when Parts II, III, and IV must be completed.

§4.12 SCHEDULE L

SCHEDULE L (Form 990 or 990-EZ) Department of the Treasury Internal Revenue Service	**Transactions With Interested Persons** ▶ Attach to Form 990 or Form 990-EZ. ▶ To be completed by organizations that answered "Yes" on Form 990, Part IV, line 25a, 25b, 26, 27, 28a, 28b, or 28c, or Form 990-EZ, Part V, line 38a or 40b.	OMB No. 1545-0047 2008 Open To Public Inspection

(a) Background

Organizations exempt under most categories of §501 must meet two separate tests in order to retain exemption. The first test, called the *organizational* test, ensures that the entity's assets are permanently devoted to qualifying exempt purposes and essentially no one owns or uses an exempt organization for their private purposes as discussed in the introduction to Schedule J. A second standard, called the *operational test* applies to the organization's actual activity and measures who benefits. Exempt organizations of all categories must continually operate "exclusively" for their particular exempt purposes, whether charitable, agricultural, or advancement of a line of business. An exempt organization (EO) must not devote itself to benefiting private individuals. In 2007, a 990 filer was asked if "any officers, directors, trustees key employees . . . were related to each other through family or business relationships." Schedule A delved deeper for §501(c)(3) organizations and asked for specific information about financial transactions with related parties.

▶ Preparers must pay close attention to details in this part. For Parts I, II and III, all transactions are reported regardless of amount. Individual and aggregate reporting thresholds below which reporting is not required with respect to an interested person are provided for Part IV. Parts III and IV contain separate "reasonable effort" instructions, which essentially expect the organization to make annual inquiries to its officials in a best effort to identify relationships and which the organization may rely on to satisfy reporting requirements for those Parts. There is a separate definition of interested person for each Part of the Schedule, so a person who is an interested person for one Part may not be an interested person for other Parts of the Schedule. See Appendix 4B for a matrix of the list of potential interested parties by Schedule L part and organization type (such as supporting organization).

Part I	**Excess Benefit Transactions** (section 501(c)(3) and section 501(c)(4) organizations only).		
	To be completed by organizations that answered "Yes" on Form 990, Part IV, line 25a or 25b, or Form 990-EZ, Part V, line 40b.		(c) Corrected?
1	**(a)** Name of disqualified person	**(b)** Description of transaction	Yes	No

Part I applies only to a §501(c)(3) or (4) organization that engaged in an excess benefit transaction with a disqualified person (DP) as a result of which penalties called *Intermediate Sanctions* can be imposed. Unlike the sanctions on self-dealing with a private foundation, the only recourse available to the IRS before 1996, to punish a public charity paying excessive salaries to its key employees was to revoke its exemption. IRC §4958 now imposes a nondeductible excise tax on disqualified persons who receive excess benefits, requires that the excess be returned, and imposes penalties on the managers approving the transaction. An excess benefit exists when the organization provides an economic benefit beyond the fair market value to a DP in a transaction such as compensation for services rendered, as rent for a facility, or for purchase price of an organizational asset.

Interested Parties for this Part—Disqualified Persons

Groups A, B, and C are interested parties for this part. Groups D and E are not interested parties for this part.

Group A. Persons in control of the organization are treated as disqualified by virtue of the fact that they have voting powers and responsibilities of the sort included in the following list:

- Persons serving on the governing body who are entitled to vote (evidence that one did not participate in a decision may be important);

- Presidents, chief executive officers, or chief operating officers;

- Treasurers and chief financial officers; and

- Persons with a material financial interest in a provider-sponsored[81] organization.

Ex-officio, advisory, emeritus, or other organizational officials not entitled to vote are not treated as disqualified persons unless they are a member of Group B. The absence of title, or the actual title, for a person in a position of control is not determinative, if the person actually has or shares responsibility for managing the organization's finances.

Group B. A person not listed in Group A may still be treated as a disqualified person based upon the facts and circumstances of his or her relationship to the organization. The following facts tend to indicate a person has substantial influence:

- The person founded the organization;

- The person is a substantial contributor;

- The person's compensation is based on revenues derived from activities of the organization that he or she controls;

- The person has authority to control or determine a significant portion of the organization's capital expenditures, operating budget, or compensation for employees (such as a school headmaster);

- The person has managerial authority or serves as a key advisor to a person with managerial authority; or

- The person owns controlling interest in a corporation, partnership, or trust that is a disqualified person.

Group C. A person is a disqualified person with respect to a transaction if the person is a member of the family of the person with substantial influence. Members of the family and related businesses are defined for this purpose as the following "statutory categories of disqualified persons":

- Family members (spouses, ancestors, children, grandchildren, great-grandchildren, and siblings and their spouses).

- A 35 percent controlled entity meaning corporations in which disqualified persons own more than 35 percent of the combined voting power and partnerships, trusts, and estates in which disqualified persons own more than 35 percent of the profits or beneficial interest.

Group D. Persons deemed not to have substantial influence include:

- Another organization tax exempt under §501(c)(3) or (c)(4) as it regards a (c)(3) organization. A (c)(4) organization can only receive excess benefits from another (c)(4).

- An employee that receives economic benefits in an amount less than that used to define highly compensated employees for pension plan purposes so long as they are not substantial contributors or in a position of control.[82]

Group E. Facts tending to indicate a person does not have control over an organization include the following:

- The person has taken a bona fide vow of poverty as an employee or agent of a religious organization.

- The person is an independent contractor, such as an attorney, accountant, or investment manager, unless such person stands to economically benefit with respect to transactions.

- The direct supervisor of the person is not a disqualified person.

- The person does not participate in any management decisions affecting the organization as a whole or a discrete segment or activity of the organization.

- The person receives preferential treatment commensurate with other comparable contributors in a solicitation that is a part of a program designed to attract a substantial number of donors.

Line 1: The information submitted in this part is pretty self-explanatory. What is particularly important is the check box that asks if the problem has been addressed. Excess benefit transactions must be "corrected." Correction of the transaction occurs when the person repays the excess benefits or otherwise financially restores the organization. The transaction must be corrected or undone to the extent possible. Whatever steps are needed to place the organization in a financial position no worse than would have existed had the person dealt with it under the highest fiduciary standards must be taken. Restoration must be made in cash or cash equivalents, not a promissory note. The organization can choose, or not, to accept a return of property that was involved subject to restitution for any decline in value of the property. An increase in value can be returned to the disqualified person. Conversely, if the property is worth less than its value at the time of original transfer, the difference must be repaid to the organization. Interest at a rate that equals or exceeds the applicable federal rate, compounded annually, for the period between the month of the transaction and return of the cash or property is due.

Line 2. The amount of taxes imposed under §4958 on organization managers and/or disqualified persons, whether or not assessed by the IRS, unless abated is entered here. If transactions resulting in excessive amounts have occurred, Form 4720 is filed to report and pay the tax on excess.

Part II	**Loans to and/or From Interested Persons.** To be completed by organizations that answered "Yes" on Form 990, Part IV, line 26, or Form 990-EZ, Part V, line 38a.									
(a) Name of interested person and purpose	(b) Loan to or from the organization?		(c) Original principal amount	(d) Balance due	(e) In default?		(f) Approved by board or committee?		(g) Written agreement?	
	To	From			Yes	No	Yes	No	Yes	No

Loans outstanding between the organization and an interested person at the end of the taxable year are reported here. The term *loans* include salary advances, expense allowances not made under an accountable plan, and other receivables from lending money or selling property. Loans originally made between the organization and a third party or between an interested person and a third party that were later transferred so as to become a debt outstanding between the organization and an interested person must also be reported.

The following receivables are *not* treated as loans:

- Pledges to make charitable contributions
- Amounts owed for dues or member assessments
- Accrued but unpaid compensation owed by the organization
- Receivables created in the ordinary course of the organization's exempt activities on the same terms as offered to the public, such as for medical services provided by a hospital to an officer of the hospital

---

Interested Parties for this Part

- For all filers, officials reported in Core Part VII, Section A
- For §501(c)(3) and (4) entities, disqualified persons in the box above
- For §509(a)(3) supporting organizations, persons listed in Part III box

---

Column (a). The name and the interested person, whether a debtor or a creditor, is listed plus the purpose for engaging in the transaction, such as "compensation package" or loan to purchase residence. The space provided for the information may be challenging.

Column (b), (c), (f), and (g) are self explanatory.

Column (d) must include, as of the end of the year, the sum of the outstanding principal, accrued interest, and any applicable penalties and collection costs. The amounts in this column should agree with the total of Core Part X, lines 5 and 6, in column (B) (for amounts owed to the organization), and line 22, column (B) (for amounts owed by the organization).

Column (e). When any payment by the debtor is past due as of the end of the organization's tax year, or if the debtor otherwise is in default under the terms and conditions of the loan, a "Yes" check is indicated.

Part III	Grants or Assistance Benefitting Interested Persons.	
	To be completed by organizations that answered "Yes" on Form 990, Part IV, line 27.	
(a) Name of interested person	(b) Relationship between interested person and the organization	(c) Amount of grant or type of assistance

Scholarships, fellowships, internships, prizes, awards, and other types of financial assistance benefiting an interested party are entered in this part. A grant includes the gift portion of a part-sale, part-gift transaction. Grants or assistance provided "to an interested person as a member of the charitable class or other class (such as a member of a section 501(c)(5), (c)(6), or (c)(7) organization) that the organization intends to benefit in furtherance of its exempt purpose, if provided on similar terms as provided to other members of the class, such as short-term disaster relief or trauma counseling," are not reported. Grants for travel, study, or other similar purposes such as to achieve a specific objective, produce a report or other similar product, or improve or enhance a literary, artistic, musical, scientific, teaching, or other similar capacity, skill, or talent of the grantee like those described in §4945(d)(3) are not excluded from reporting under this exception.

Interested Parties for this Part
<ul><li>Officials reported in Core Part VII, Section A</li><li>Substantial contributors reported in Schedule B of this year</li><li>Related persons, including a member of the organization's grant selection committee, a family member of officials listed in Core Part VII, Part A, or of substantial contributors, or of members of the organization's grant selection committee</li><li>A 35 percent controlled entity of persons in this list above</li><li>Employee or child of employee of a substantial contributor or of a 35 percent controlled entity of a substantial contributor *if* the person receives the grant at the direction or advice of such person</li></ul>

▶ An organization is expected to use reasonable efforts to identify any grants to be reported in this part. Distribution of an annual questionnaire to each current or former official and each member of a grant selection committee exemplifies such an effort. See Appendix 3A for a sample questionnaire that could be used to identify this information. The instructions contain examples to study if the organization suspects such grants may have occurred. Many award-granting organizations adopt a policy that prohibits awards to such interested parties. In an academic setting, however, tuition remission programs may result in such a benefit to an official's child. Except for a private foundation, there is no absolute prohibition against such transactions unless they constitute *private inurement*.[83]

Column (a). The name of the interested person that benefited from the grant or assistance is entered, except for substantial contributors who should not be listed by name, but designated as a substantial contributor.

Column (b). The relationship between the interested person and benefit recipient, such as "spouse of Director John Smith" or "daughter of Vice President Jones" is entered. The words "substantial contributor" are entered when such a person is involved.

Column (c). The title for this column may cause confusion when it asks for the "amount of grant or type of assistance." The instructions say, "State the total dollar amount of grants provided to the interested person during the organization's tax year. Also describe the type of assistance and estimate its value. The space provided may be challenging. If the organization needs additional space to explain the nature of the aid, details can be presented in Schedule O.

Part IV	**Business Transactions Involving Interested Persons.** To be completed by organizations that answered "Yes" on Form 990, Part IV, line 28a, 28b, or 28c.					
(a) Name of interested person	**(b)** Relationship between interested person and the organization	**(c)** Amount of transaction	**(d)** Description of transaction	**(e)** Sharing of organization's revenues?		
				Yes	No	

Business transactions with an interested person for which payments were made during the organization's tax year are reported here when they exceed the following thresholds:

- All payments during the year between the organization and interested person exceeded $100,000.

- All payments during the year from a single transaction between such parties exceeded the greater of $10,000 or 1 percent of the filing organization's total revenues.

- Compensation payments by the organization paid to a family member of certain persons exceeded $10,000.

Business transactions include, but are not limited to, contracts of sale, lease, license, and performance of services, whether initiated during the organization's tax year or ongoing from a prior year. Business transactions also include joint ventures, whether new or ongoing, in which either the profits or capital interest of the organization and of the interested person each exceeds 10 percent. Charges for membership dues to its officers, directors, and so on are not considered such business transactions. An organization is expected to make the "reasonable effort" described above for Part III to identify business relationships.

Interested Parties for this Part

- Officials listed in Form 990, Part VII, Section A

- Family member of such officials

- Entity more than 35 percent owned, directly or indirectly, individually or collectively, by persons listed above

- Entity (other than a tax-exempt organization under section 501(c)) of which a current or former official was serving at the time of the transaction as officer, director, trustee, key employee, partner or member with an ownership interest in excess of 5 percent in the entity, or shareholder with an ownership interest in excess of 5 percent in a professional corporation

---

Special rules that apply for this part follow:

- Transactions with a management company more than 35 percent of which is owned directly or indirectly by a person that was an official within the past five years are reportable.

- Ownership is measured by stock ownership (voting power or value, whichever is greater) of a corporation, profits or capital interest (whichever greater) in a partnership or limited liability company, beneficial interest in a trust, or control of a nonprofit organization.

- Ownership includes indirect ownership, such as ownership in an entity that has ownership in the entity doing business with the organization, possibly through a multiple tiers of entities applying the constructive ownership rules of §267(c).

The instructions contain very useful examples to use in applying the thresholds and identifying reportable transactions as follows:

Example (1). T, a family member of an officer of the organization, serves as an employee of the organization and receives during the organization's tax year compensation of $15,000, which is not more than 1 percent of the organization's total revenue. The organization is required to report T's compensation as a business transaction in Schedule L, Part IV because T's compensation to a family member of an officer exceeds $10,000, unless T's compensation was already reported in Form 990, Part VII.

Example (2). X, the child of a current director is a first-year associate at a law partnership that the organization pays $150,000 during the organization's tax year. Given that X has no ownership interest in the law firm and is not an officer, director, trustee, or key employee of the firm, the organization is not required to report this business transaction in spite of X's employment relationship to the law firm.

Example (3). Same facts as in Example (2), except that X is a partner of the law firm and has an ownership interest in the law firm of 5.25 percent of the profits. The organization must report the business transaction due to X's greater than 5 percent ownership interest in the law firm and the dollar amount in excess of the $100,000 aggregate threshold.

Example (4). Same facts as in Example (3), except that the law firm entered into the transaction with the organization before X's parent became a director of the organization. The organization must report all payments made during its tax year to the law firm for the transaction.

Example (5). Same facts as in Example (3), except that X is the child of a former director listed in Form 990, Part VII, Section A. The organization is required to report the business transaction, as family members of former directors listed in Part VII are interested persons.

Example (6). Same facts as in Example (3), except that the organization pays $75,000 in total during the organization's tax year for 15 separate transactions to collect debts owed to the organization. None of the transactions involves payments to the law partnership in excess of $10,000. The organization is not required in this instance to report the business transaction, because the dollar amounts do not exceed either the $10,000 transaction threshold or the $100,000 aggregate threshold.

Example (7). Same facts as in Example (6), except that the organization pays $105,000 instead of $75,000. Because the aggregate payments for the business transactions exceed $100,000, the organization must report all the business transactions. The organization may report the transactions on an aggregate basis or list them separately.

Column (a). The name of the interested person involved in the direct or indirect business relationship with the organization is entered.

Column (b). The relationship between the interested person and the organization, such as key employee of the organization, family member of Freda Jones, former director, or entity more than 35 percent owned by Freda Jones, former director, is entered.

Column (c). The dollar amount of the transaction, meaning the cash and/or fair market value of other assets and services provided by the organization during the tax year, net of reimbursement of expenses, is entered.

Column (d). The type of transaction, such as employment or independent contractor arrangement, rental of property, or sale of assets is entered.

Column (e). Enter "Yes" if all or part of the consideration paid by the organization is based on a percentage of revenues of the organization. For instance, state "Yes" if a management fee is based on a percentage of revenues, or a legal fee owed to outside attorneys by a public interest law firm is a percentage of the amount collected.

§4.13   SCHEDULE M

SCHEDULE M (Form 990) Department of the Treasury Internal Revenue Service	NonCash Contributions ▶ To be completed by organizations that answered "Yes" on Form 990, Part IV, lines 29 or 30. ▶ Attach to Form 990.	OMB No. 1545-0047 Open To Public Inspection

(a)   Background

Unlike cash contributions, gifts of property raise questions about the amount of a contribution and the character of its deductibility for the donor. Importantly, the organization may have additional forms to file regarding the contribution. For gifts of tangible personal property, the amount deductible on the donor's income tax return is directly related to how the organization intends to use the property. If the organization retains the property and uses it in its exempt function activities, then the donor can claim a deduction equal to the fair market value of the property.[84] Otherwise, the deduction is limited to the donor's cost basis.[85] Form 8283 is signed by the organization to indicate the intended use of the property and attached to the donor's tax return. If the organization has signed Form 8283 and sells the property within three years of receipt, it must file Form 8282 within 125 days to report the sale. This form only applies to items that have a value over $5,000 and are not publicly-traded securities. A $10,000 penalty can be imposed on an organization that fraudulently identifies property as being used for its exempt purposes when in fact it was not. Another concern about gifts of property is whether the donor's entire interest in the property has been transferred to the organization. Special rules apply to conservation easements.[86] Gifts of patents and other intellectual property generate a deduction in the year of donation and each year in which income is generated from the property. Form 8899 is filed by the charity to report such income. Two types of property identified separately here are also asked about in Schedule D: works of art/historical treasures and conservation easements. An organization is required to complete Schedule M when it receives either of those types of gifts even if it has not recorded revenue relating to the donation. Noncash contributions do not include donations of services or use of facilities.

Part I   **Types of Property**

	(a) Check if applicable	(b) Number of contributions	(c) Revenues reported on Form 990, Part VIII, line 1g	(d) Method of determining revenues
1 Art—Works of art				
2 Art—Historical treasures . .				
3 Art—Fractional interests . .				
4 Books and publications . .				
5 Clothing and household goods				
6 Cars and other vehicles . .				
7 Boats and planes				
8 Intellectual property				
9 Securities—Publicly traded .				
10 Securities—Closely held stock .				
11 Securities—Partnership, LLC, or trust interests				
12 Securities—Miscellaneous .				
13 Qualified conservation contribution (historic structures)				
14 Qualified conservation contribution (other)				
15 Real estate—Residential . .				
16 Real estate—Commercial . .				
17 Real estate—Other				
18 Collectibles				
19 Food inventory				
20 Drugs and medical supplies .				
21 Taxidermy				
22 Historical artifacts				
23 Scientific specimens . . .				
24 Archeological artifacts . . .				
25 Other ▶ (........................)				
26 Other ▶ (........................)				
27 Other ▶ (........................)				
28 Other ▶ (........................)				

Twenty-four distinct types of property are identified here with a request that the organization, for each type, report the number of gifts it received, the revenue reported in connection with the gift(s), and the method by which the gift was valued. Organizations that report gifts of books and publications or clothing and household goods are not required to quantify the number of items received for 2008 (note shading in column (b), presumably because they were not given sufficient time to develop reporting systems to properly quantify the numbers). For organizations that receive many noncash gifts, tracking this information becomes very important.

Line 1. Works of art include paintings, sculptures, prints, drawings, ceramics, antiques, decorative arts, textiles, carpets, silver, photography, film, video, installation and multimedia arts, rare books and manuscripts, historical memorabilia and other similar objects. Collectibles are not reported here but instead on line 18.

Line 2. A historical treasure is a building, structure, area, or property with recognized cultural, aesthetic, or historical value that is significant in the history, architecture, archeology, or culture of a country, state, or city.

Line 3. A contribution of a fractional interest in art is a contribution of an undivided portion of a donor's entire interest in a work of art. A contribution of the donor's entire interest must consist of a part of each and every substantial interest or right the donor owns in such work of art and must extend over the entire term of the donor's interest in the property. A gift generally is treated as a gift of an undivided portion of a donor's entire interest in property if the donee is given the right, as a tenant in common with the donor, to possession, dominion, and control of the property for a portion of each year appropriate to its interest in such property. For each work of art or item, report in column (b) the fractional interest for each year an interest is received with respect to the underlying work of art or item. IRC §170(o) provides the rules with regard to the deductions allowed for fractional gifts.

Line 4. Enter information about contributions of all books and publications. Do not include rare books and manuscripts reported on line 1, collectibles that are reported on line 18, and archival records that are reported on lines 25–28.

Line 5. Enter information about clothing items and household goods that were in good used condition or better. Clothing items and household goods that were not in good used condition or better are to be reported as a separate type in "other" beginning with line 25. No income tax deduction is allowed for such items.

Lines 6 and 7. On line 6 include only contributions of motor vehicles manufactured primarily for use on public streets, roads, and highways. Do not include in lines 6 or 7 contributions of the donor's stock in trade or property held by the donor primarily for sale to consumers in the ordinary course of a trade or business. Presumably, cars considered to be collectibles would be reported on line 18 rather than line 6. The organization is required to file Form 1098-C with the donor and the IRS for certain of such contributions reported on these lines. Programs under which a charity acknowledged the gift of a vehicle at its blue book value, but sold it at a much reduced price to a car wholesaler inspired a change in the rules governing the deduction for such gifts.[87]

Line 8. Intellectual property ("IP") is any patent, copyright (other than a copyright held by the taxpayer who created it),[88] trademark, trade name, trade secret, know-how, software (other than computer software that is readily available for purchase by the general public),[89] or similar property. As mentioned in the Background section, the income tax deduction for the gift of such property to a charity is limited to the revenue produced by the intellectual property.

Line 9. Publicly traded securities include securities for which (as of the date of the contribution) market quotations are readily available on an established securities market.

For each security, treat each separate gift (rather than each share received) as a contribution for this purpose. Include on this line interests in publicly traded partnerships, limited liability companies or trusts, as well as publicly traded corporations.

Line 10. "Closely held stock" means shares of stock issued by a corporation that is not publicly traded. For lines 10–12 treat each separate gift (rather than each share received) as a contribution for this purpose. The IRS has special interest in such donations because their value is not readily available and can be difficult to correctly assess.

Line 11. Information about contributions of interests in a partnership, limited liability company, or trust, which is not publicly traded is entered. The same troublesome valuation issues as described for line 10 stock exists.

Line 12. Information about contributions of securities that are not publicly traded securities, closely held stock, or partnership, limited liability company, or trust interests, reported on lines 9–11 are entered here. Same lines 10–11 valuation issues exist.

Lines 13–14. A qualified conservation contribution is a contribution of a qualified real property interest exclusively for conservation purposes. A *"qualified real property interest"*[90] means any of the following interests in real property:

- The entire interest of the donor
- A remainder interest
- A restriction (such as an easement), granted in perpetuity, on the use which may be made of the real property

A "conservation purpose"[91] means:

- The preservation of land areas for outdoor recreation by, or the education of, the general public
- The protection of a relatively natural habitat of fish, wildlife, plants, or similar ecosystems
- The preservation of open space (including farmland and forest land) where such preservation is for the scenic enjoyment of the general public or is in accordance with governmental conservation policy
- The preservation of an historically important land area or a certified historic structure[92]

Line 13. Information about contributions of a qualified real property interest subject to a restriction with respect to the exterior of a certified historic structure is reported here. A certified historic structure is any building or structure listed in the National Register of Historic Property as well as any building certified as being of historic significance to a registered historic district.[93]

Line 14. Information about qualified conservation contributions, other than those entered on line 13, is entered here. This includes conservation easements to preserve land areas for outdoor recreation by or for the education of the general public, to protect a relatively natural habitat or ecosystem, to preserve open space, or to preserve a historically important land area.

Line 15. On this line enter information about contributions of residential real estate. Include information about contributions (not in trust) of a remainder interest in a personal residence that was not the donor's entire interest in the property. The term *personal residence* includes any property used by the donor as a personal residence but is not limited to the donor's principal residence. The term *personal residence* also includes stock owned by the donor as a tenant-stockholder in a cooperative housing corporation if the dwelling the donor is entitled to occupy as a tenant-stockholder is used by the donor as a personal residence.

Line 16. Information about contributions of commercial real estate, such as a commercial office building goes here. Also include information about contributions (not in trust) of a remainder interest in a farm that was not the donor's entire interest in the property. The term *farm* refers to land used for the production of crops, fruits, or other agricultural products or for the maintenance of livestock. A farm includes the improvements located on the farm property.

Line 17. Information about real estate interests not reported on lines 15 or 16 is entered here.

Line 18. Collectibles reported on this line include autographs, sports memorabilia, dolls, stamps, coins, books (other than books and publications reported on line 4), gems, and jewelry (other than costume jewelry reportable on line 5), but not art reported on lines 1–3 or historical artifacts or scientific specimens reported on line 22 or line 23.

Line 19. Details about food items, including food inventory contributed by corporations and other businesses, go on this line.

Line 20. Statistical information about drugs, medical supplies, and similar items contributed by corporations and other businesses that manufactured or distributed such items is reported here.

Line 21.*Taxidermy property* means any work of art that is the reproduction or preservation of an animal, in whole or in part; is prepared, stuffed, or mounted to recreate one or more characteristics of the animal, and contains a part of the body of the dead animal.[94] The IRS has expressed concern for inflated donation deductions claimed for such gifts.

Line 22. The number and value of historical artifacts received as donations during the year, such as furniture, fixtures, textiles and household items of an historic nature, are reported here. Works of art or historical treasures reported on lines 1–3 and archeological artifacts reported on line 24 are not included.

Line 23. "Scientific specimens," including living plant and animal specimens and objects or materials that are examples of natural and physical sciences, such as rocks and minerals, or that relate to, or exhibit, the methods or principles of science go here.

Line 24. Archeological and ethnographical artifacts, other than works of art or historical treasures reported on lines 1–3 and historical artifacts reported on line 22 go here. An archaeological artifact is any object that is over 250 years old and is normally discovered as a result of scientific excavation, clandestine or accidental digging for exploration on land or under water. Ethnological artifacts are objects that are the product of a tribal or nonindustrial society, and important to the cultural heritage of a people because of their distinctive characteristics, comparative rarity, or their contribution to the knowledge of the origins, development, or history of that people.

Lines 25–28. Lines 25–28 are used to separately report other types of property that are not described above or reportable on previous lines. This includes items that did not satisfy specific charitable deduction requirements applicable to the contribution of such type of property, but which were contributed to the organization, such as clothing and household goods that were not in good used or better condition, and conservation easements that the organization knows do not constitute qualified conservation contributions. Self-created items, such as art works and personal papers and manuscripts, including archival records, are to be listed separately as a type. Donations of items used by the organization at a charitable auction, (other than goods sold by the charity at the auction) such as food served at the event may be separately reported on these lines.

The instructions provide some clarification about completion of column (b), "Number of Contributions." They state that the organization may either report the number of contributions or the number of items contributed, determined in accordance with the organization's recordkeeping practices. The organization must explain in Part II which method it is using or whether it is using a combination of both methods. For example, an organization receiving a donation of 500 cans of food from a single donor could report either 1 (to indicate the number of contributions) or 500 (to indicate the number of items) in column (b) of line 19.

				Yes	No
29	Number of Forms 8283 received by the organization during the tax year for contributions for which the organization completed Form 8283, Part IV, Donee Acknowledgement	**29**			
30a	During the year, did the organization receive by contribution any property reported in Part I, lines 1–28 that it must hold for at least three years from the date of the initial contribution, and which is not required to be used for exempt purposes for the entire holding period?		**30a**		
b	If "Yes," describe the arrangement in Part II.				
31	Does the organization have a gift acceptance policy that requires the review of any non-standard contributions?		**31**		
32a	Does the organization hire or use third parties or related organizations to solicit, process, or sell noncash contributions?		**32a**		
b	If "Yes," describe in Part II.				
33	If the organization did not report revenues in column (c) for a type of property for which column (a) is checked, describe in Part II.				

For Privacy Act and Paperwork Reduction Act Notice, see the Instructions for Form 990. Cat. No. 51227J Schedule M (Form 990) 2008

Line 29. The number of Forms 8283 received by the organization from donors during the year for contributions for which the organization completed Part IV (that is, certified whether the organization intended to use the property or not) is reported. The instructions provide that if the organization does not keep complete records of such forms, it should not provide an estimate but rather leave line 29 blank. As a good practice, the organization should maintain a copy of all Forms 8283 it completes on behalf of donors in case there are some questions posed to the organization or its donors, or so that it may track and be aware of when it needs to file Form 8282.

Line 30a–b. Answering "Yes," the organization received during the year a noncash contribution that it must hold for at least three years and that is not required to be used for exempt purposes for the entire holding period, may mean the organization is enabling a donor to receive a more favorable deduction than he may otherwise be entitled to. An organization that answers "Yes" must describe the arrangement in Part II.

Line 31. A nonstandard contribution includes an item that is not reasonably expected to be used to further the organization's exempt purpose (aside from the need of such organization for income or funds) and for which (a) there is no ready market to sell it and (b) the value of the item is highly speculative or difficult to ascertain. The example provided in the instructions (the contribution of a taxpayer's successor member interest) as a nonstandard contribution is also a transaction listed as a "transaction of interest" due to its potential for tax avoidance. Clearly, a gift acceptance policy is important to protect the organization from abuse.

Line 32a–b. An organization that answers "Yes" to line 32a must describe these arrangements in Part II.

Line 33. If applicable, describe in Part II why the organization did not report revenue in column (c) for a type of property for which column (a) is checked. Museums and similar organizations that are not required to capitalize their collections will need to provide information here when they receive such gifts.

Schedule M (Form 990) 2008 | Page **2**

Part II	**Supplemental Information.** Complete this part to provide the information required by Part I, lines 30b, 32b, and 33. Also complete this part for any additional information.

(Continued)

Part II **Supplemental Information.** Complete this part to provide the information required by Part I, lines 30b, 32b, and 33. Also complete this part for any additional information.

_____

_____

_____

_____

_____

_____

_____

_____

_____

_____

_____

_____

_____

_____

_____

_____

_____

_____

_____

_____

_____

_____

_____

_____

Use Part II to provide narrative information required in Part I, lines 30b, 32b, and 33 and to provide other narrative explanations and descriptions, as needed. Identify the specific line number that the response supports.

§ 4.14 SCHEDULE N

SCHEDULE N
(Form 990 or 990-EZ)

Department of the Treasury
Internal Revenue Service

Liquidation, Termination, Dissolution, or Significant Disposition of Assets

To be completed by organizations that answer "Yes" to Form 990, Part IV, lines 31 or 32; or Form 990-EZ, line 36.
► Attach certified copies of any articles of dissolution, resolutions, or plans.
► Attach to Form 990 or 990-EZ.

OMB No. 1545-0047

2008

Open to Public
Inspection

(a) Background

The organizational documents of a qualifying tax-exempt organization dedicate its assets permanently to its exempt mission, including on its demise. For a §501(c)(3) organization, the charter or trust provisions must require that all of its assets upon dissolution be distributed for charitable purposes or transferred to another §501(c)(3) entity. Similarly a civic association (c)(4)'s assets upon dissolution would be transferred or spent for social welfare purposes. Other categories of §501(c) exempt organizations may be allowed to return funds to their members, such as a social club or fraternal society. This schedule addresses complete dissolutions and dispositions of a significant portion of the organization's assets. The facts about the nature of the assets distributed, expenses paid, market value of and method of valuing those assets are reported by recipient. Importantly, the name, address, EIN, and tax classification of the recipient are reported. This information will allow the IRS to scrutinize the destination of the assets—and determine whether they are still being dedicated to the exempt purposes for which they were originally held.

Part I	Liquidation, Termination, or Dissolution. Complete this part if the organization answered "Yes" to Form 990, Part IV, line 31, or Form 990-EZ, line 36. Use Schedule N-1 if additional space is needed.						
1	(a) Description of asset(s) distributed or transaction expenses paid	(b) Date of distribution	(c) Fair market value of asset(s) distributed or amount of transaction expenses	(d) Method of determining FMV for asset(s) distributed or transaction expenses	(e) EIN of recipient	(f) Name and address of recipient	(g) IRC section of recipient(s) (if tax-exempt) or type of entity

An organization that has liquidated, terminated, dissolved, or simply spent down its assets and ceased operations, completes Part I. Partial contractions or distributions of more than 25 percent, but less than all assets, referred to as significant dissolutions, are reported in Part II.

▶ A certified copy of the articles of dissolution or merger, resolutions, and plans of dissolution or merger should be attached to the return plus any other relevant documents. If an IRS ruling was sought, the IRS letter should be attached.

Column (a). A list of the assets, aggregated into categories, that were transferred in the liquidation, termination, dissolution, or merger is presented. What are called transaction expenses are detailed if they equal at least $10,000, including attorney, accountant, or other professional fees paid in connection with winding down the activities. Brokerage fees should be taken into account in the fair market value figure in column (c). Note this column presents assets by recipient organization entered in column (f) *or* simply expenses.

Column (b) asks for the "date of distribution." If the transactions took place over a period of time, this might be the date the last transaction took place. If formal dissolution papers have been received from the state, the date approved can be entered.

Column (c). The fair market value of the asset distributed (determined by the method described in column (d) *or* if this line reports expenses, the actual expenses paid.

Column (d). The method of valuation for the asset distributed is entered. IRS examples of methods of valuation include appraisals, comparables, book value, actual cost (with or without depreciation), and outstanding offers (among other methods). For transaction expenses, the method for determining the amount of the expense, such as an hourly rate or fixed fee, is requested.

Columns (e) and (f). The name, address, and EIN of each recipient of assets distributed or transaction expenses paid is required. For membership organizations that transfer assets to individual members, the names of individual members need not be reported. Rather, the members may be aggregated into specific classes of membership, or they may be aggregated into one group, if there is only one class of membership.

Column (g). The Internal Revenue Code section under which the transferee is tax-exempt, if it is so exempt, is requested. For recipients that are not tax-exempt, the type of entity is entered, such as a governmental entity or limited liability corporation, Report ''individual'' if the recipient is not an entity. The answer in this column should be carefully considered with view to the dissolving entity's own tax status keeping in mind the background materials above.

		Yes	No
2	Did or will any officer, director, trustee, or key employee of the organization:		
a	Become a director or trustee of a successor or transferee organization?	2a	
b	Become an employee of, or independent contractor for, a successor or transferee organization?	2b	
c	Become a direct or indirect owner of a successor or transferee organization?	2c	
d	Receive, or become entitled to, compensation or other similar payments as a result of the organization's liquidation, termination, or dissolution? . . .	2d	
e	If the organization answered "Yes" to any of the questions in this line, provide the name of the person involved and explain in Part III. ▶		

For Privacy Act and Paperwork Reduction Act Notice, see the Instructions for Form 990. Cat. No. 50087Z Schedule N (Form 990 or 990-EZ) 2008

Line 2a–e asks a series of questions the import of which is clear. The issue is whether officials of the dissolving organization will be involved in the recipient entity and how their involvement will be constituted. In responding, the ''dedication of asset'' concepts discussed in the background materials should be considered. While there is no prohibition against the type of involvement listed in the questions, the IRS wishes to scrutinize any private benefit or inurement that might result in what the instructions call ''involvement (or expectation of involvement) in the successor or transferee organization by governing, controlling, or having a financial interest in that organization.''[95] The name of the person involved plus an explanation of the nature of the person's relationship with the successor or transferee organization and the type of benefit received or to be received by the person is entered in Part III of this schedule.

		Yes	No
	Note. If the organization distributed all of its assets during the tax year, then Form 990, Part X, column (B) should equal -0-.		
3	Did the organization distribute its assets in accordance with its governing instrument(s)? If "No," describe in Part III	3	
4a	Did the organization request or receive a determination letter from EO Determinations that the organization's exempt status was terminated?	4a	
b	(If "Yes," provide the date of the letter. ▶ . . . .)		
5a	Is the organization required to notify the attorney general or other appropriate state official of its intent to dissolve, liquidate, or terminate?	5a	
b	If "Yes," did the organization provide such notice?	5b	
6	Did the organization discharge or pay all liabilities in accordance with state laws?	6	
7a	Did the organization have any tax-exempt bonds outstanding during the year?	7a	
b	Did the organization discharge or defease tax-exempt bond liabilities in accordance with the Internal Revenue Code and state laws?	7b	
c	If "Yes," describe in Part III how the organization defeased or otherwise settled these liabilities. If "No," explain in Part III.		

Line 3. Here is the important question. Check ''Yes'' if the organization's assets were distributed in accordance with its governing instrument.

Line 4. This is either a good or bad question depending upon the genesis of the exemption termination. A ''Yes'' check applies if the organization requested or received a determination letter from EO Determinations that the organization's exempt status was terminated or it is no longer exempt under §501(a). A copy of the organization's request and if applicable, a copy of the EO Determinations response, is to be attached and the date entered in line 4b.

Line 5a. Check ''Yes'' if the organization is required to notify a state attorney general or other appropriate state official of the organization's intent to dissolve, liquidate, or terminate. In Texas, such notice is not required, and some advisors recommend retention of state incorporation of a dormant entity to provide for unexpected subsequent events.

Line 5b. Check "Yes" if the organization provided the notice described in line 5a.

Line 6. Check "Yes" if the organization discharged or paid all of its liabilities in accordance with state law.

Line 7a–7c. Check "Yes" for 7a and complete line 7b if the organization had any tax-exempt bonds outstanding during the year. Check "Yes" on line 7b and complete line 7c if tax-exempt bond liabilities were discharged or defeased during the year. A Part III explanation is requested the liability was discharged, defeased, or otherwise settled other than in accordance with the Code or applicable state law. If assets were transferred to another §501(c)(3) organization, subject to the obligation, the name of the transferees of such assets, the CUSIP number of the bond issue(s), and a description of the terms of such arrangements, are requested in Part III.

Part II	Sale, Exchange, Disposition, or Other Transfer of More Than 25% of the Organization's Assets. Complete this part if the organization answered "Yes" to Form 990, Part IV, line 32, or Form 990-EZ, line 36. Use Schedule N-1 if additional space is needed.						
1	(a) Description of asset(s) distributed or transaction expenses paid	(b) Date of distribution	(c) Fair market value of asset(s) distributed or amount of transaction expenses	(d) Method of determining FMV for asset(s) distributed or transaction expenses	(e) EIN of recipient	(f) Name and address of recipient	(g) IRC section of recipient(s) (if tax-exempt) or type of entity

This part contains the same columns as Part I and is completed when the organization has a partial dissolution by transferring or otherwise disposing of more than 25 percent of its assets (means total assets less liabilities). The threshold of 25 percent is based on the fair market value of net assets at the beginning of the year and might include a series of transactions. Such a significant disposition of the organization's net assets includes one or more sale, exchange, disposition, or other transfer during the year, regardless of whether the organization received full and adequate consideration. The IRS says, "Whether a significant disposition occurred through a series of related dispositions or events depends on the facts and circumstances in each case." The instructions provide the following examples of the types of transactions required to be reported in Part II as significant:

- Sale or exchange—for cash or other consideration—of a social club's land or other exempt organization's assets it had used to further its exempt purposes;

- Sales, contributions, or other transfers of assets to establish or maintain a partnership, joint venture or a corporation (for-profit or nonprofit) regardless of whether such sales or transfers are governed by §721 or §351, and whether or not the transferor receives an ownership interest in exchange for the transfer;

- Sales of assets by a partnership or joint venture in which the organization has an ownership interest;

- Transfers of assets pursuant to a reorganization in which the organization is a surviving entity;

- A contraction of net assets resulting from a grant or charitable contribution of assets to another organization described in §501(c)(3) [or such transfers by any other category of §501(c) entity].

The following types of situations are not required to be reported in Part II:

- Change in composition of publicly traded securities held in an exempt organization's passive investment portfolio [Did the IRS anticipate the market collapse in late 2008?];

- Asset sales made in the ordinary course of business, such as gross sales of inventory;

- Decrease in the value of net assets due to market fluctuations in the value of assets held by the organization;

- Transfers to a disregarded entity of which the organization is the sole member.

See comments for lines 2a–e of Part I for discussion of the import of answers to these questions.

§ 4.15 SCHEDULE O

SCHEDULE O (Form 990)	**Supplemental Information to Form 990**	OMB No. 1545-0047
Department of the Treasury Internal Revenue Service	▶ Attach to Form 990. To be completed by organizations to provide additional information for responses to specific questions for the Form 990 or to provide any additional information.	Open to Public Inspection

This schedule consists of blank lines and its purpose is to serve as a coordinated place for narrative descriptions requested in Core Form 990, Schedule G, Schedule K, Schedule L, and Schedule R. Freeform attachments are no longer permitted.[96] Instead, any information the organization is requested to provide (or voluntarily chooses to provide) that is not specifically otherwise designated to be reported in another place goes here. Each response should be clearly prefaced by the part to which it pertains, for example, "Core Part III, Line 2." Additionally, the responses should be presented in the same order in which the form appears. As many continuation sheets of Schedule O are needed to report information may be included. A summary of items to be reported in this Schedule follows:

RELEVANT SECTION/CIRCUMSTANCE	WHAT TO DESCRIBE
The organization is filing its return late.	Reason for not filing on time
Page 1, Item B, Amended Return	List each Part (or Schedule) and line item that is being amended and describe the amendments
Page 1, Item C, Name	If the organization has multiple "dba" names that will not fit, report additional names here
Core Part I, Line 6	Organizations may provide an explanation for how the number of volunteers was determined and the types of services/benefits provided by volunteers
Core Part III, Line 2 if "Yes"	Describe any significant new programs undertaken. If the programs are described in Part III, the organization may reference that description rather than repeating it here

Core Part III, Line 3 if "Yes"	Describe any significant changes (or discontinuance) of programs
Core Part III, Line 4d	If the organization has more than three programs to describe in Part III, or needs more space to describe its programs, the additional information is reported here
Core Part V, Line 3b if "No"	Describe why the organization has not filed Form 990-T when it has indicated the need to do so on line 3a
Core Part VI, Line 1a	If the organization's governing body does not all have the same voting rights, explain material differences
Core Part VI, Line 1a	If the organization's governing body delegated authority to act on its behalf to an executive committee, describe the composition of the committee, whether any of the committee's members are not on the governing body, and the scope of the committee's authority (For this purpose, audit committees, investment committees, and similar committees that are limited in scope are not reported here.)
Core Part VI, Line 2 if "Yes"	For each family and business relationship, identify the persons and describe their relationship ("family" or "business" may be used rather than greater detail)
Core Part VI, Line 3 if "Yes"	Describe the circumstances, process, or change in policy to delegate management to a management company
Core Part VI, Line 4 if "Yes"	Describe significant changes but do not attach a copy of the amendments or amended documents
Core Part VI, Line 5 if "Yes"	Explain the nature of the diversion, amounts or property involved, corrective actions taken to address the matter, and pertinent circumstances. Do not identify the person involved by name.
Core Part VI, Line 6 if "Yes"	Describe the classes of members or stockholders
Core Part VI, Line 7a if "Yes"	Describe the classes of such persons and the nature of their rights
Core Part VI, Line 7b if "Yes"	Describe the classes of such persons, the decisions that require their approval, and the nature of their voting rights
Core Part VI, Line 8a if "No"	Explain the organization's practices or policies regarding documentation of meetings and written actions of its governing body
Core Part VI, Line 8b if "No"	Explain the organization's practices or policies regarding documentation of meetings and written actions of committees acting on behalf of its governing body
Core Part VI, Line 9b if "No"	Explain how the organization ensures the activities of its subordinates are consistent with its own
Core Part VI, Line 10	Describe the process by which any of the organization's officers, directors, trustees, board committee members, or management reviewed the prepared Form 990, whether before or after it was filed with the IRS, including specifics such as who conducted the review, when they conducted it, and the extent of any such review
Core Part VI, Line 11	State the mailing addresses of officers, directors, trustees, and key employees who cannot be reached at the organization's address
Core Part VI, Line 12c if "Yes"	Describe the organization's practices for monitoring proposed or ongoing transactions for conflicts of interest and dealing with potential or actual conflicts, whether discovered before or after

(Continued)

Relevant Section/Circumstance	What to Describe
	the transaction has occurred. The description should include which persons are covered under the policy, the level at which determinations of whether a conflict exists are made, and the level at which actual conflicts are reviewed. Also explain any restrictions placed on persons with a conflict, such as prohibiting them from participating in the governing body's deliberation/decision regarding the transaction.
Core Part VI, Line 15a if "Yes"	Describe the process for determining compensation, identify the offices/positions for which the process was used to establish compensation of the persons who served in those offices/positions, and state the year in which the process was last undertaken for each such person
Core Part VI, Line 15b if "Yes"	Describe the process for determining compensation, identify the offices/positions for which the process was used to establish compensation of the persons who served in those offices/positions, and state the year in which the process was last undertaken for each such person
Core Part VI, Line 17	If additional space is needed to list the states with which a copy of the organization's Form 990 is required to be filed
Core Part VI, Line 18 if all boxes are blank	Explain why the organization does not make publicly available any of the listed forms, if such disclosure is required by law
Core Part VI, Line 19	Describe whether, and if so how, the mentioned documents are made available to the public
Core Part XI, Line 1	Explain if (1) the organization changed its method of accounting from a prior year or (2) checked the other box
Core Part XI, Line 2a if "No"	If the answer is "No" because the organization was included in a consolidated audit but not audited separately, the organization may explain that here
Core Part XI, Line 2c	Describe if the process has changed from the prior year
Core Part XI, Line 3b if "No"	Explain why the organization has not undergone any required audits and describe any steps taken to undergo such audits
Schedule G, Part I, Line 2b, Col (iii)	Describe the custody or control arrangement
Schedule G, Part I, Line 2b Col (v)	If the arrangement provides for the payment of fees and other fundraising expenses (such as supplies) the organization must report such amounts paid and describe how the agreement distinguishes payments for services from reimbursed expenses. Also describe whether the organization entered into any agreements with fundraisers under which the organization made payments exclusively for such expenses but not for services.
Schedule G, Part III, Line 9b	If additional space is needed
Schedule G, Part III, Line 10b	If additional space is needed
Schedule G, Part III, Line 15b	If space is needed to list additional third parties
Schedule G, Part III, Line 15c	If space is needed to list additional third parties
Schedule G, Part III, Line 16	If space is needed to list additional gaming managers

Schedule G, Part III, Line 17b	Provide a breakdown of required distributions by state
Schedule K	Provide additional information (if needed) to describe assumptions used if records do not support information provided
Schedule K, Part I, Col (e)	If the issue price is not identical to the amount listed on Form 8038, explain the difference
Schedule K, Part I, Col (f)	If additional space is needed
Schedule L	If additional space is needed to provide explanation or detailed information
Schedule R	If additional space is needed to provide responses (Schedule R-1 is used instead to list information about additional organizations)

§4.16   SCHEDULE R

| SCHEDULE R
(Form 990)

Department of the Treasury
Internal Revenue Service | **Related Organizations and Unrelated Partnerships**

▶ Attach to Form 990. To be completed by organizations that answered "Yes" to Form 990, Part IV, line 33, 34, 35, 36, or 37.
▶ See separate instructions. | OMB No. 1545-0047
2008
Open to Public
Inspection |

(a)   Background

Commonly, separate entities are created to perform functions for an organization. Sometimes an LLC is formed to protect assets such as real estate from activities involving the general public that could bring liabilities. A separate corporation might be formed in another state. A new entity might be formed to function in concert with another organization. Whatever the reason for its formation, the concept addressed in this schedule is one of consolidation. Similar to standards for issuing consolidated financial statements for entities with common economic interests and governance, this schedule provides information about relationships to such separate entities.

Schedule R is used by an organization to provide information on related organizations, on certain transactions with related organizations, and on certain unrelated partnerships through which the organization conducts significant activities. Schedule R is a multifaceted combination of former Part IX, "Taxable Subsidiaries and Disregarded Entities," and Part XI, "Transfers To and From Controlled Entities," of Form 990, and Part VII of Schedule A that was entitled "Information Regarding Transfers, Transactions, and Relationships with Other Organizations."

The original Schedule A, Part VII, now morphed into Part V of this schedule, was added in 1988, in response to a congressional mandate to the IRS to search for connections between public charities and non–501(c)(3) organizations. Particularly in regard to organizations that lobby or enter the political arena, the IRS is scouting for relationships that allow benefits to flow from a charity to a noncharitable organization. This part looks for the use of exempt organization assets to benefit non–(c)(3) organizations and asks the exempt organization to report any financial transactions, such as sales, transfers, or rentals of assets to or from another organization. The reportable transactions are those with affiliated or related organizations. The instructions are extensive and very specific and should be consulted if transactions are to be reported.

This part indicates yet another type of special records an exempt organization might need to maintain in order to accurately complete annual IRS reports. To answer this part correctly, an organization having the described relationship will want to establish subcodes or new departments in its chart of accounts to tabulate the answers.[97] The important definitions applicable in this part follow.

Relationships: An organization is a related organization to the filing organization if it stands in one or more of the following relationships to the filing organization:

- Parent—an organization that controls the filing organization
- Subsidiary—an organization controlled by the filing organization
- Brother/Sister—an organization controlled by the same person or persons that control the filing organization
- Supporting/Supported—a organization that is (or claims to be) at any time during the organization's tax year (i) a supporting organization of the filing organization within the meaning of §509(a)(3), if the filing organization is a supported organization within the meaning of §509(f)(3), or (ii) a supported organization, if the filing organization is a supporting organization

Definition of control. In the case of nonprofit organizations and other organizations without owners or persons having beneficial interests, whether such organization is taxable or tax-exempt, control means:

- In the case of a parent/subsidiary relationship between nonprofit organizations:
  - Power to remove and replace or to appoint or elect a majority of the nonprofit organization's or other organization's directors or trustees, or
  - Management or board overlap where a majority of the subsidiary organization's directors or trustees are trustees, directors, officers, employees, or agents of the parent organization.
- In the case of a brother/sister relationship between nonprofit organizations if the same persons constitute a majority of the members of the governing body of both organizations.
- In the case of stock corporations and other organizations with owners or persons having beneficial interests, whether such organization is taxable or tax-exempt, control means any of the following relationships:
  - Ownership of more than 50 percent of the stock (by voting power or value) of a corporation;
  - Ownership of more than 50 percent of the profits or capital interest in a partnership;
  - Ownership of more than 50 percent of the profits or capital interest in a limited liability company (LLC) taxed as a partnership, regardless of the designation under state law of the ownership interests as stock, membership shares, or otherwise under state law;
  - Being a managing partner or managing member in a partnership or LLC taxed as a partnership which has three or fewer managing partners or managing members (regardless of which partner or member has the most actual control);

- Being a general partner in a limited partnership which has three or fewer general partners (regardless of which partner has the most actual control); or

- Being the sole member of a disregarded entity, or ownership of more than 50 percent of the beneficial interests in a trust.

Indirect control. Control can be indirect. For example, if the filing organization controls entity A, which in turn controls (under the definition of control above) Entity B, the organization will be treated as controlling Entity B. To determine indirect control through constructive ownership of a corporation, rules under §318 shall apply; similar principles shall apply for purposes of determining constructive ownership of another entity (a partnership or trust). If an entity (X) controls an entity taxed as a partnership by being one of three or fewer partners or members, then an organization that controls X also controls the partnership. The instructions contain examples of this concept.

Part I	Identification of Disregarded Entities					
(A) Name, address, and EIN of disregarded entity		(B) Primary activity	(C) Legal domicile (state or foreign country)	(D) Total income	(E) End-of-year assets	(F) Direct controlling entity

Part I requests the identifying information of any organization that is treated for federal tax purposes as a disregarded entity (DE). The sole member's Employer Identification Number can be entered for a DE that has no individual EIN. After January 1, 2009, the disregarded entity must file separate employment tax returns and use its own EIN on such returns.

Part II	Identification of Related Tax–Exempt Organizations					
(A) Name, address, and EIN of related organization		(B) Primary activity	(C) Legal domicile (state or foreign country)	(D) Exempt Code section	(E) Public charity status (if section 501(c)(3))	(F) Direct controlling entity

Part II requires the identifying information of related tax-exempt organizations. When the number of related entities exceeds seven, others are listed in Schedule R-1. Central organizations and subordinate organizations of a group exemption are not required to be listed as related organizations in this part. The detailed listing of subordinates is provided in connection with Core Form, page one, item H(b). The central organization must list in Schedule R the related organizations of each subordinate organization other than (1) related organizations that are included within the group exemption, or (2) related organizations that the central organization knows to be included in another group exemption.

Schedule R (Form 990) 2008 Page **2**

Part III	Identification of Related Organizations Taxable as a Partnership									
(A) Name, address, and EIN of related organization	(B) Primary activity	(C) Legal domicile (state or foreign country)	(D) Direct controlling entity	(E) Predominant income (related, investment, unrelated)	(F) Share of total income	(G) Share of end-of-year assets	(H) Disproportionate allocations?	(I) Code V—UBI amount in box 20 of Schedule K-1 (Form 1065)	(J) General or managing partner?	
							Yes | No		Yes | No	

Part III requires the identifying information of any related organization that is treated for federal tax purposes as a partnership. When a partnership is related to the filing organization by reason of being its parent or brother/sister and the filing organization is not a partner or member in the partnership, complete only columns (A), (B), and (C) and state "NA" in columns (D), (E), (F), (G), (H), (I), and (J).

Part IV	Identification of Related Organizations Taxable as a Corporation or Trust							
(A) Name, address, and EIN of related organization	(B) Primary activity	(C) Legal domicile (state or foreign country)	(D) Direct controlling entity	(E) Type of entity (C corp, S corp, or trust)	(F) Share of total income	(G) Share of end-of-year assets	(H) Percentage ownership

Part IV requires the identifying information of any related organization that is treated for federal tax purposes as a C or S corporation or trust. If the corporation or trust is related to the filing organization as its parent or as a brother/sister organization, and the filing organization does not have an ownership interest in the corporation or trust, complete only columns (A), (B), (C), and (E) and state "NA" in columns (D), (F), (G), and (H). Do not report trusts described within §401(a).

Schedule R (Form 990) 2008   Page **3**

Part V	Transactions With Related Organizations

Note. Complete line 1 if any entity is listed in Parts II, III, or IV.

		Yes	No
1	During the tax year, did the organization engage in any of the following transactions with one or more related organizations listed in Parts II–IV?		
a	Receipt of **(i)** interest **(ii)** annuities **(iii)** royalties **(iv)** rent from a controlled entity	1a	
b	Gift, grant, or capital contribution to other organization(s)	1b	
c	Gift, grant, or capital contribution from other organization(s)	1c	
d	Loans or loan guarantees to or for other organization(s)	1d	
e	Loans or loan guarantees by other organization(s)	1e	
f	Sale of assets to other organization(s)	1f	
g	Purchase of assets from other organization(s)	1g	
h	Exchange of assets	1h	
i	Lease of facilities, equipment, or other assets to other organization(s)	1i	
j	Lease of facilities, equipment, or other assets from other organization(s)	1j	
k	Performance of services or membership or fundraising solicitations for other organization(s)	1k	
l	Performance of services or membership or fundraising solicitations by other organization(s)	1l	
m	Sharing of facilities, equipment, mailing lists, or other assets	1m	
n	Sharing of paid employees	1n	
o	Reimbursement paid to other organization for expenses	1o	
p	Reimbursement paid by other organization for expenses	1p	
q	Other transfer of cash or property to other organization(s)	1q	
r	Other transfer of cash or property from other organization(s)	1r	
2	If the answer to any of the above is "Yes," see the instructions for information on who must complete this line, including covered relationships and transaction thresholds.		

(A) Name of other organization(s)	(B) Transaction type (a–r)	(C) Amount involved
(1)		
(2)		
(3)		
(4)		
(5)		
(6)		

Schedule R (Form 990) 2008

Check "Yes" in the appropriate boxes of line 1 of this part if the filing organization engaged in any of the transactions listed in Part V with any of the related organizations listed in Parts II through IV. A "transfer" includes any conveyance of funds or property not described in lines 1a–1p, whether or not for consideration, such as a merger with a related organization.

Transactions of the same type with a particular organization, such as line a(i) transactions, line a(iv) transactions, line b transactions, and so on can be aggregated. Transactions of a particular type (lines (a)(i)–(r)) between two organizations where the aggregate amounts involved during the tax year do not exceed $50,000, except for receipt of interest, annuities, royalties, or rent from a controlled entity, which are to be reported regardless of amount. Enter the details of each related organization on a separate line of the table.

Schedule R (Form 990) 2008   Page **4**

Part VI	Unrelated Organizations Taxable as a Partnership

Provide the following information for each entity taxed as a partnership through which the organization conducted more than five percent of its activities (measured by total assets or gross revenue) that was not a related organization. See instructions regarding exclusion for certain investment partnerships.

(A) Name, address, and EIN of entity	(B) Primary activity	(C) Legal domicile (state or foreign country)	(D) Are all partners section 501(c)(3) organizations?		(E) Share of end-of-year assets	(F) Disproportionate allocations?		(G) Code V—UBI amount in box 20 of Schedule K-1 (Form 1065)	(H) General or managing partner?	
			Yes	No		Yes	No		Yes	No

Part VI requires information about an unrelated organization taxable as a partnership through which the organization conducted more than 5 percent of its activities as measured by its total assets as of the end of its tax year or gross revenue for its tax year (whichever percentage—total assets or gross revenue—is greater), through the unrelated partnership.

Unrelated partnerships that meet both of the following conditions are not reported:

- 95 percent or more of the filing organization's gross revenue from the partnership for the partnership's tax year ending with or within the organization's tax year is interest, dividends, royalties, rents, and capital gains (including unrelated debt-financed income); and

- The primary purpose of the filing organization's investment in the partnership is the production of income or appreciation of property and not the conduct of a §501(c)(3) charitable activity such as program-related investing.

To calculate the percentage of the filing organization's activities as measured by its total assets, use the amount reportable on Form 990, Part X, line 16 as the denominator, and the filing organization's ending capital account balance for the partnership tax year ending with or within the filing organization's tax year as the numerator (the amount reported on Schedule K-1 may be used). In determining the percentage of the filing organization's activities as measured by its gross revenue, use the amount reportable on Form 990, Part VIII, line 12 as the denominator, and the filing organization's proportionate share of the partnership's gross revenue for the partnership tax year ending with or within the filing organization's tax year as the numerator. Some of the information requested below is derived from Schedule K-1 of Form 1065 issued to the organization. If the Schedule K-1 is not available, provide a reasonable estimate of the required information.

■ 199 ■

Guide to New Required Information by Type of Related Organization

INFORMATION	TAX-EXEMPT ORG	PARTNERSHIP	CORP/TRUST
Primary Activity	YES	YES	YES
Legal Domicile	YES	YES	YES
Exempt Code Section	YES	N/A	N/A
Public Charity Status	YES if above is (c)(3)	N/A	N/A
Direct Controlling Entity	YES	If relationship 4 applies or 1, 2 and org is also a ptr	If relationship 4 applies or 1, 2 and org is also an owner
Character of income	N/A	If relationship 4 applies or 1, 2 and org is also a ptr	
Share of income	N/A	If relationship 4 applies or 1, 2 and org is also a ptr	If relationship 4 applies or 1, 2 and org is also an owner
Share of assets	N/A	If relationship 4 applies or 1, 2 and org is also a ptr	If relationship 4 applies or 1, 2 and org is also an owner
UBI amount	N/A	If relationship 4 applies or 1, 2 and org is also a ptr	N/A
Gen/Mg Partner	N/A	If relationship 4 applies or 1, 2 and org is also a ptr	N/A
Type of entity	N/A	N/A	YES
% ownership	N/A	N/A	If relationship 4 applies or 1, 2 and org is also an owner

Types of related organizations:
(1) Parent/Subsidiary—power to remove and replace a majority of board or board overlap of a majority of board members of both organizations
(2) Brother/Sister—same persons constitute a majority of the members of the governing body of both organizations
(3) Supporting/Supported—an organization that either claims to support the filing organization or that the filing organization claims to support
(4) Stock Corps/Other—ownership > 50% of stock, profits/capital interest, managing partner in LLC/Partnership with less than 4 managing partners, general partner in a limited partnership with less than 4 general partners

NOTES

1. Reg. §1.170A-9 and §1.509(a)-3T.
2. IRS introduction to revised regulations says, "An organization that uses the accrual method will not be able to use the support information reported on Form 990 for prior years to compute its public support for the current year, and instead must report all support for the computation period on the accrual method."

3. See J. Blazek, *Tax Planning and Compliance* (Hoboken, N.J.: John Wiley & Sons, 2008), Ch. 11, for a detailed discussion of these rules.
4. See Differences Between §509(a)(1) and §509(a)(2) below.
5. See Blazek, *Tax Planning and Compliance*, Ch. 3, for an discussion of these distinctions.
6. See Blazek, *Tax Planning and Compliance*, Ch. 5, for an exploration of the complex definitions of the various types of educational organizations.
7. Reg. §1.170A-9(d).
8. See Blazek, *Tax Planning and Compliance*, Ch. 10, for a description of the criteria for this classification.
9. Reg. §1.170A-9T.
10. Reg. §1.509(a)-3T.
11. See Blazek, *Tax Planning and Compliance*, Ch. 11 for an overview of the complex tests that have to be satisfied for an organization to gain the SO classification.
12. IRS Memorandum from Robert Choi, dated 9/24/2007 (found at http://www.irs.gov/pub/irs-tege/509a3guidesheetchoimemo.pdf).
13. §509(a)(3)(B)(i).
14. §509(a)(3)(B)(ii).
15. §509(a)(3)(B)(iii).
16. See Regs. §1.509(a)-4(i)(3)(ii) and Notice 2006–109, 2006–51 I.R.B. 1121 for further information.
17. Reg. §1.170A-9(e)(7).
18. IRC §170(e).
19. Reg. §1.170A-9(e)(7)(iii).
20. Rev. Rul. 75–435. 1975–2 C.B. 215.
21. As discussed in Chapter 2 according to SFAS 136.
22. Reg. §1.170A-9(e)(6)(i) and (v).
23. IRS Priv. Ltr. Rul. 9203040.
24. Reg. §1.170A-9T(f)(3).
25. See IRS Publication 4421-PC.
26. Reg. §1.170A-9T(f)(6)(ii).
27. See Chapter 2 for accounting rules defining contributions.
28. Reg. §1.509(a)-3(h).
29. Rev. Rul. 83–153, 1983–2 C.B. 48; Rev. Rul. 75–387, 1975–2 C.B. 216.
30. 2008–4, 2008–1 IRB 121,134; see also IRS Publication 4221-PC.
31. Regs. §1.170A-9(e)(5)(iii) and §1.509(a)-3(c)(iii).
32. The process of terminating private foundation status is discussed in Blazek, *Tax Planning and Compliance*, Ch. 12.4.
33. Regs. §1.170A-9(e)(4) and §1.509(a)-3(c); see also discussion in 3.4 for Questions 2 and 3.
34. IRC §4946.
35. See Blazek, *Tax Planning and Compliance*, Ch. 23 for details of the rules with full citations to historical cases and rulings.
36. Rev. Rul. 2007–41, 2007–25 I.R.B. (June 18, 2007).
37. Though the instructions contain a sentence that reminds §501(c)(3) filers that exemption can be lost when the 4-year lobbying limits are exceeded.
38. Under rules provided in Regulations §1.527–6(e).
39. See Chapter 5.5, Proxy Tax.
40. As a practical matter, the specific §4911 definitions are often used by nonelecting charities.
41. Reg. §56.4941–4(c).
42. The penalty is 5 percent of the lobbying expenditures.
43. http://www.irs.gov/newsroom/article/0,,id=124196,00.html.
44. IRC §4966(d)(2).
45. IRC §4966(d)(1).

46. See Internal Revenue Manual 7.20.8 for the Exempt Organizations Determination Letter Program, Donor-Advised Funds Guide Sheet for more information about requirements of donor-advised funds.
47. Excess business holdings (IRC §4943(e)), taxable distributions (IRC §4966) and certain distributions to disqualified persons (IRC §4967).
48. http://www.irs.gov/charities/article/0,id=137244,00.html.
49. For more information see Notice 2004–41, 2004–28 I.R.B. 3.
50. IRC §170(h)(2).
51. IRC §170(h)(4)(A).
52. IRC § 170(c)(4)(B)(i) and (ii).
53. Go to http://www.fasb.org/st/ to access SFAS and other financial pronouncements made by the Financial Accounting Standards Board (FASB).
54. IRC §170(e)(1)(B).
55. IR-2006–80, May 15, 2006.
56. IR-2006–74, May 4, 2006.
57. Core Part IV, Question 10, says to complete this part of Schedule D "if the organization, a related organization, or an organization formed and maintained exclusively to further one or more exempt purposes of the organization . . . held assets in . . . endowment funds at any time during the year, regardless of whether the organization" reports endowments on line 29 or 32 of Core Part X.
58. http://en.wikipedia.org/wiki/Derivative_(finance).
59. Section 506 of Division C of the Emergency Economic Stabilization Act of 2008, which was signed into law on Oct. 3, 2008, effectively reversed the amendment to IRC §6694 made effective May 25, 2007, by P.L. 110–28. The 2007 amendment had moved the tax return preparer's standard for a nondisclosed position on a return from "realistic possibility of being sustained on its merits" to "a reasonable belief that the position would more likely than not be sustained on its merits." Now, effective on the same May 25, 2007, the standard moves to "substantial authority," which is the same as the §6662 standard for the taxpayer to avoid the substantial underpayment penalty for a nondisclosed position.
60. FASB Interpretation No. 48, Section 4.
61. IRC §170(e).
62. Rev. Proc. 75–50, 1975–2 C.B. 587, gives guidelines and recordkeeping requirements for determining whether private schools that are recognized as exempt from tax have racially nondiscriminatory policies toward their students. The 2008–2009 IRS Priority Guidance Plan promises an update of this procedure.
63. Unrelated business activity is discussed in Chapter 5.
64. See Blazek, *Tax Planning and Compliance*, Ch. 24.
65. See Blazek, *Tax Planning and Compliance*, Ch. 17.
66. Issued by the U.S. Treasury Department in its Anti-Terrorist Financing Guidelines.
67. See text accompanying note 64.
68. See Chapter 5.2, The Volunteer Exception
69. See Blazek, *Tax Planning and Compliance*, Ch. 24.4(c) of Tax Planning & Compliance.
70. IRC §6115; Core Part V, Question 7b asks if the organization has made this disclosure.
71. See Blazek, *Tax Planning and Compliance*, Ch. 24.2(b).
72. For guidance on valuation issues, see preceding note 70.
73. See Blazek, *Tax Planning and Compliance*, Ch. 24.3.
74. Rev. Rul. 56–185, Rev. Rul. 56–185, 1956–1 C.B. 202.
75. Rev. Rul. 69–545, 1969–2 C.B. 117, amplified by Rev. Rul. 83–157 to remove the open emergency room requirement.
76. FSA 200110030.
77. Organizations in the United States include nonprofits or other exempt organizations, partnerships, corporations, or other business entities that are created or organized in the

United States or under the laws of the United States or of any State, the Commonwealth of Puerto Rico, the Commonwealth of the Northern Mariana Islands, Guam, American Samoa, and the United States Virgin Islands, and an estate or trust other than a foreign estate or trust.

78. See Blazek, *Tax Planning and Compliance*, Ch. 20.3(b).

79. Also as described in Reg. §53.4958–4(a)(4).

80. The compliance questions can be found at www.irs.gov under Qualified 501(c)(3) Bonds Compliance Project.

81. Reg. §53.4958–3(c)(4).

82. For 2008, this amount is $100,000. The number is the inflation-adjusted amount above which one is treated as highly compensated for pension plan purposes. Reg. §53.4958–3 (d)(3) refers to IRC §414(q)(1)(B)(i).

83. See Blazek, *Tax Planning and Compliance*, Ch. 20.10.

84. Referred to as the 'to or for the use of rule'' provided in §170(c).

85. Under §170(e) that also limits the deduction for ''ordinary income'' property primarily including self-produced artworks, such as a painting or a composition.

86. See remarks for Schedule D, Part II.

87. GAO report to the Senate Committee on Finance, ''Vehicle Donations—Benefits to Charities and Donors, but Limited Program Oversight,'' November 2003.

88. IRC §1221(a)(3) or §1231(b)(1)(C).

89. IRC § 197(e)(3)(A)(i).

90. IRC §170(h)(2).

91. IRC §170(h)(4).

92. See IRC §170(h) for additional information, including special rules with respect to the conservation purpose requirement for buildings in registered historic districts. Additional information reported in Schedule D, Part II.

93. See IRC §170(h)(4)(B) for special rules that apply to contributions made after August 17, 2006.

94. IRC §170(e)(1)(iv) provides that a donor of self-prepared taxidermy property will be limited to his basis or fair market value of the property, whichever is lower.

95. See Blazek, *Tax Planning and Compliance*, Ch. 20.1.

96. The only exceptions to this are (1) when a group exemption holder files a group return for some (but not all) of the subordinates covered under the group exemption. In that circumstance, an attachment showing the name, address, and EIN of all the subordinates that are included is to be attached to the return rather than reported in Schedule O and (2) when the organization legally changes its name, it must attach a copy of its amended organizing documents evidencing the change. The instructions (as of August 2008) do not mention how to provide requested statements for Schedule E. The form itself says ''attached statement.'' One presumes it would be acceptable to provide such information in Schedule O.

97. See Blazek, *Tax Planning and Compliance*, Ch. 22.

APPENDIX 4A: STATE UNIFIED REGISTRATION STATEMENT

Unified Registration Statement (URS) for Charitable Organizations© (v. 3.10)

☐ **Initial registration**   ☐ **Renewal/Update**

This URS covers the reporting year which ended (day/month/year) _____

Filer EIN _____

State _____   State ID _____

1. Organization's legal name _____

   If changed since prior filings, previous name used _____

   All other name(s) used _____

2. **(A)** Street address _____

   City _____   County _____

   State _____   Zip Code _____

   (B) Mailing address (if different) _____

   City _____   County _____

   State _____   Zip Code _____

3. Telephone number(s) _____   Fax number(s) _____

   E-mail _____   Web site _____

4. Names, addresses (street & P.O.), telephone numbers of other offices/chapters/branches/affiliates (*attach list*).

5. Date incorporated _____   State of incorporation _____

   Fiscal year end: day/month _____

6. If not incorporated, type of organization, state, and date established _____

   _____

7. Has organization or any of its officers, directors, employees or fund raisers:

   A. Been enjoined or otherwise prohibited by a government agency/court from soliciting?   Yes ☐ No ☐

   B. Had its registration denied or revoked?   Yes ☐ No ☐

   C. Been the subject of a proceeding regarding any solicitation or registration?   Yes ☐ No ☐

   D. Entered into a voluntary agreement of compliance with any government agency or in a case before a court or administrative agency?   Yes ☐ No ☐

   E. Applied for registration or exemption from registration (but not yet completed or obtained)?   Yes ☐ No ☐

   F. Registered with or obtained exemption from any state or agency?   Yes ☐ No ☐

   G. Solicited funds in any state?   Yes ☐ No ☐

   If "yes" to 7A, B, C, D, E, *attach explanation.*

   If "yes" to 7F & G, *attach list* of states where registered, exempted, or where it solicited, including registering agency, dates of registration, registration numbers, any other names under which the organization was/is registered, and the dates and type (mail, telephone, door to door, special events, etc.) of the solicitation conducted.

8. Has the organization applied for or been granted IRS tax exempt status?   Yes ☐ No ☐

   If yes, date of application _____ OR date of determination letter _____.

   If granted, exempt under 501(c) _____.   Are contributions to the organization tax deductible?   Yes ☐ No ☐

APPENDIX 4A: STATE UNIFIED REGISTRATION STATEMENT

9. Has tax exempt status ever been denied, revoked, or modified?   Yes ☐ No ☐

10. Indicate all methods of solicitations:

    Mail ☐   Telephone ☐   Personal Contact ☐   Radio/TV Appeals ☐
    Special Events ☐   Newspaper/Magazine Ads ☐   Other(s) ☐ (specify) _____

11. List the NTEE code(s) that best describes your organization   _____, _____, _____

12. Describe the purposes and programs of the organization and those for which funds are solicited *(attach separate sheet if necessary).*

    _____
    _____
    _____
    _____

13. List the names, titles, addresses, (street & P.O.), and telephone numbers of officers, directors, trustees, and the principal salaried executives of organization *(attach separate sheet).*

14. (A) (1) Are any of the organization's officers, directors, trustees or employees related by blood, marriage, or adoption to: (i) any other officer, director, trustee or employee OR (ii) any officer, agent, or employee of any fundraising professional firm under contract to the organization OR (iii) any officer, agent, or employee of a supplier or vendor firm providing goods or services to the organization?   Yes ☐ No ☐
    (2) Does the organization or any of its officers, directors, employees, or anyone holding a financial interest in the organization have a financial interest in a business described in (ii) or (iii) above OR serve as an officer, director, partner or employee of a business described in (ii) or (iii) above?   Yes ☐ No ☐
    (If yes to any part of 14A, *attach sheet* which specifies the relationship and provides the names, businesses, and addresses of the related parties).
    (B) Have any of the organization's officers, directors, or principal executives been convicted of a misdemeanor or felony? *(If yes, attach a complete explanation.)*   Yes ☐ No ☐

15. *Attach separate sheet listing names and addresses (street & P.O.) for all below:*

    Individual(s) responsible for custody of funds.   Individual(s) responsible for distribution of funds.

    Individual(s) responsible for fund raising.   Individual(s) responsible for custody of financial records.

    Individual(s) authorized to sign checks.   Bank(s) in which registrant's funds are deposited (*include account number and bank phone number*).

16. Name, address (street & P.O.), and telephone number of accountant/auditor.

    Name _____
    Address _____
    City _____ State _____ Zip Code _____ Telephone _____
    Method of accounting _____

17. Name, address (street & P.O.), and telephone number of person authorized to receive service of process. *This is a state-specific item. See instructions.*

    Name _____
    Address _____
    City _____ State _____ Zip Code _____ Telephone _____

■ 205 ■

FORM 990, SCHEDULES A THROUGH R

18.(A) Does the organization receive financial support from other nonprofit organizations (foundations, public charities, combined campaigns, etc.)?   Yes ☐ No ☐

(B) Does the organization share revenue or governance with any other non-profit organization?   Yes ☐ No ☐

(C) Does any other person or organization own a 10% or greater interest in your organization OR does your organization own a 10% or greater interest in any other organization?   Yes ☐ No ☐

(If "yes" to A, B or C, *attach an explanation* including name of person or organization, address, relationship to your organization, and type of organization.)

19. Does the organization use volunteers to solicit directly?   Yes ☐ No ☐

Does the organization use professionals to solicit directly?   Yes ☐ No ☐

20. If your organization contracts with or otherwise engages the services of any outside fundraising professional (such as a "professional fundraiser," "paid solicitor," "fund raising counsel," or "commercial co-venturer"), *attach list* including their names, addresses (street & P.O.), telephone numbers, and location of offices used by them to perform work on behalf of your organization. Each entry *must include* a simple statement of services provided, description of compensation arrangement, dates of contract, date of campaign/event, whether the professional solicits on your behalf, and whether the professional at any time has custody or control of donations.

21. Amount paid to PFR/PS/FRC during previous year: $ _____

22.(A) Total contributions: $ _____

(B) Program service expenses: $ _____

(C) Management & general expenses: $ _____

(D) Fundraising expenses: $ _____

(E) Total expenses: $ _____

(F) Fundraising expenses as a percentage of funds raised: _____%

(G) Fundraising expenses plus management and general expenses as a percentage of funds raised: _____%

(H) Program services as a percentage of total expenses: _____%

Under penalty of perjury, we certify that the above information and the information contained in any attachments or supplement is true, correct, and complete.

Sworn to before me on (or signed on) _____, 20 _____

_____
Notary public (if required)

_____   _____
Name (printed)   Name (printed)

_____   _____
Name (signature)   Name (signature)

_____   _____
Title (printed)   Title (printed)

Consult the state-by-state appendix to the URS to determine whether supporting documents, supplementary state forms or fees must accompany this form. Before submitting your registration, *make sure you have attached or included everything required by each state to the respective copy of the URS.*

Attachments may be prepared as one continuous document or as separate pages for each item requiring elaboration. In either case, please number the response to correspond with the URS item number.

APPENDIX 4A: STATE UNIFIED REGISTRATION STATEMENT

Alabama

Governing law: Al. Code Sec. 13A-9-70 et seq.
Exemptions: Educational institutions and their related foundations; religious organizations; political organizations; fraternal, social, educational, alumni, heath care foundation, historical and civil rights organizations; civic leagues and civic organizations which solicit solely from their membership; any charitable organization that does not intend to solicit and receive and does not actually receive contributions in excess of $25,000 during the fiscal year, provided all of its fundraising functions are carried out by volunteers; veterans organizations provided all fundraising activities are carried out by volunteers.
Fees: $25
Check payable to: "Office of the Attorney General."
Period covered: Indefinite.
Renewal Due date: No renewal of registration but financial reports are due annually within 90 days of Fiscal Year end.
Required signatures: Two. President or other authorized Officer and the Chief Fiscal Officer.
Notarized signature required: Yes.
Fundraiser contracts: No.
Certificate/Articles of Incorporation: Yes.
Bylaws: Yes.
IRS Form 990: No.
IRS Determination Letter: Yes.
Resident/Registered Agent required: No.
Audit: No.
State forms additional to URS: None.
Mailing address: Ofc. of the Atty General, Consumer Affairs Division, 11 S. Union St., Montgomery, AL 36130-2103
Info. telephone & contact: 334-242-7320, Rhonda Lee Barber
Web: www.ago.state.al.us/consumer/charities.cfm

Alaska

Governing law: AS 45.68.010 et seq. and 9 AAC 12.010 et seq.
Exemptions: Religious organizations; an organization that does not intend to or does not receive contributions, excluding government grants, in excess of $5,000 or that does not receive contributions from more than ten persons during fiscal year and 1) all functions, including solicitation, are carried on by volunteers and 2) an officer or member of the organization is not paid or does not otherwise receive all or part of the assets or income of the organization.
Fees: $40
Check payable to: "State of Alaska."
Period covered: One year.
Due Date: September 1st.
Renewal Due date: September 1st.
Required signatures: One.
Notarized signature required: No.
Fundraiser contracts: Yes.
Certificate/Articles of Incorporation: No.
Bylaws: No.
IRS Form 990: Yes or may submit most recent audited financial statement.
IRS Determination Letter: No.
Resident/Registered Agent required: No.
Audit: Yes.
State forms additional to URS: None.
Mailing address: Alaska Department of Law, Attorney General, 1031 W. 4th Ave. Suite 200, Anchorage, AK 99501-1994
Info. telephone & contact: 907-269-5200, Daveed Schwartz
Web:http://www.law.state.ak.us/department/civil/consumer/cp_topics.html#charity

Arizona

Governing law: ARS 44-6551_44-6561.
Exemptions: 1. This state or any counties or municipalities of this state or their agencies, 2. Political parties, candidates for federal, state or local office and campaign committees required to file financial information with federal, state or local election agencies.
Fees: None.
Check payable to: N/A.
Period covered: One year.
Renewal Due date: Between September 1 through 30.
Required signatures: Two. President (or equivalent) and Secretary/Treasurer (or equivalent).
Notarized signature required: Yes.
Fundraiser contracts: No.
Certificate/Articles of Incorporation: No.
Bylaws: No.
IRS Form 990: Yes.
IRS Determination Letter: On initial registration.
Resident/Registered Agent required: No.
Audit: No.
State forms additional to URS: None
Mailing address: Secretary of State, Charities Division, 1700 W. Washington, 7th Floor, Phoenix, AZ 85007-2808.
Information telephone and contact: 602-542-6187, Karie Pesserillo.
Web: www.azsos.gov/business_services/Charities

Arkansas

Governing law: Ark. Code Ann. § 4-28-401 *et seq.*
Exemptions: Nonprofits raising less than $25,000 per year with no paid staff or fundraisers; religious organizations; parent-teacher associations; accredited educational institutions; nonprofit hospitals; political candidates and organizations; and government instrumentality's.
Fees: None.
Check payable to: N/A.
Period covered: One year.
Renewal Due date: Anniversary of initial registration.
Required signatures: One. An authorized officer, director, or an incorporator.
Notarized signature required: Yes.
Fundraiser contracts: Yes.
Certificate/Articles of Incorporation: No.
Bylaws: No.
IRS Form 990: Yes.
IRS Determination Letter: Yes.
Resident/Registered Agent required: No, but related state Form required. See below.
Audit: Yes, if gross revenue exceeds $500,000.
State forms additional to URS: One: "Irrevocable Consent for Service: Charitable Organization."
Mailing address: Ofc. of Atty. General, Consumer Prot. Div., 323 Center St #200, Little Rock, AR 72201-2610
Info. telephone & contact: 501-682-6150, Lisa Gaddy, Charitable Registration Specialist.
Web: www.ag.state.ar.us/index_high.htm

California

Governing law: Cal. Govt Code §§ 12580-12596; Cal. Code of Regulations, Title 11 §§ 300-310, 999.1-999.4; Bus. & Prof. Code Sec. 17510-17510.85; 22930; Cal. Corp Code Sec. 5250.
Exemptions: Government agencies; religious corporations; political committees; religious organizations and hospitals; corporate trustees subject to the jurisdiction of other California state and federal agencies; any charity organized in another state that is not "doing business" or holding property in California.
Fees: $25 (if assets or revenues are in excess of $100,000) due annually with State Form RRF-1 (obtain on-line or from state office)
Check payable to: "Office of the Attorney General."
Period covered: One year.

FORM 990, SCHEDULES A THROUGH R

Renewal Due date: Within four and a half months of Fiscal Year end. Extensions granted by the IRS for filing a copy of From 990, Form 990PF, or Form 990EZ will be honored; however, no extensions will be granted for filing the RRF-1.
Required signatures: One. Any authorized officer or director.
Notarized signature required: No.
Fundraiser contracts: No.
Certificate/Articles of Incorporation: Yes.
Bylaws: Yes.
IRS Form 990: Yes.
IRS Determination Letter: Yes.
Resident/Registered Agent required: No.
Audit: Yes, if gross revenue exceeds $2 million (exclusive of grants from, and contracts for services with, governmental entities for which the entity requires an accounting of the funds received).
State forms additional to URS: One. RRF-1.
Mailing address: Registry of Char. Trusts, Ofc. of Atty. General, P.O. Box 903447, Sacramento, CA 94203-4470
Info. telephone: 916-445-2021
Web: http://ag.ca.gov/charities/

Connecticut
Governing law: C.G.S. §21A-175, et seq.
Exemptions: (from registration and financial filing requirements): Organizations that solicit contributions within Connecticut and (one of the following) (1) are a religious corporation, institution or society, (2) are a parent teacher association or an accredited educational institution, (3) are a nonprofit hospital, (4) are a governmental unit or instrumentality, (5) solicit solely for the benefit of 1 through 4 above, or (6) normally receives less than $50,000 in contributions annually. Exemption must be claimed, using Connecticut Form CPC-54, available on the website
Fees: $50
Check payable to: "Dept. of Consumer Protection."
Period covered: One year.
Renewal Due date: Within five months of Fiscal Year end. Extensions of 180 days may be granted upon written request.
Required signatures: Two, any authorized officers.
Notarized signature required: No.
Fundraiser contracts: No.
Certificate/Articles of Incorporation: No.
Bylaws: No.
IRS Form 990: Yes.
IRS Determination Letter: No.
Resident/Registered Agent required: No.
Audit: Yes, if gross revenue exceeds $200,000 (excluding government grants and fees, and trust revenues).
State forms additional to URS: None.
Mailing address: Public Charities Unit, c/o Ofc. of Atty. General, 55 Elm St., P.O. Box 120, Hartford, CT 06141-0120
Info. telephone: 860-808-5030
Web: http://www.cslib.org/attygenl/mainlinks/tabindex8.htm

District of Columbia
Governing law: D.C. Code §44-1701 (2001 ed.)
Exemptions: Organizations receiving less than $1,500 in gross total receipts in a calendar year, provided all functions, including fundraising, are carried out by individuals who are unpaid; for educational purposes; for a church or a religious corporation or an organization under the control of a church or religious corporation; by American Red Cross; exclusively among the membership of the soliciting agency. Organizations seeking exemption must file "Form 164."
Fees: $80* (now rolled into a consolidated fee - See Below)
Check payable to: "DC Treasurer."
Period covered: One year.
Renewal Due date: September 1.

Required signatures: Two. President or Vice President, and Secretary or Assistant Secretary.
Notarized signature required: Yes.
Fundraiser contracts: Yes.
Certificate/Articles of Incorporation: Yes.
Bylaws: Yes.
IRS Form 990: Yes.
IRS Determination Letter: Yes.
Resident/Registered Agent required: Yes. May use Item #17 on URS. *Audit*: No.
State forms additional to URS: See Below.
Mailing address: Dept. of Consumer & Reg. Affairs, 941 N. Capital St. NE, Room 7211, Washington, DC 20002-4259
Info. telephone: 202-442-4513
*In addition to the URS, DC requires charities to obtain a basic business license. Further information on licensing is included in the Supplementary Forms section of this packet. The two-year license costs $208, plus a $35 application fee and $10 endorsement fee. DC accepts the URS, but it does so as a required replacement for DC's previous reporting form (not as an optional substitute for it). Moreover, DC has elected to treat out-of-state nonprofits just as it does DC-located organizations. Effectively imposing a host of local licensure requirements having no logical (nor, perhaps, legal) application to organizations outside DC whose sole contact with DC is sending mail or emails (or making calls) to DC residents.

Georgia
Governing law: O.C.G.A. §43-17-1, et seq.
Exemptions: Organizations with less than $25,000 in annual revenues; organizations recognized as religious under IRC 501(c)(3) and not required to file IRS Form 990; nonprofit educational institutions and their agencies; political parties, candidates, and political action committees; national charities with registered Georgia affiliates.
Fees: $25 initial. $10 renewal.
Check payable to: "Secretary of State."
Period covered: One year.
Renewal Due date: Anniversary of initial registration.
Required signatures: One. Any authorized executive officer.
IMPORTANT NOTE: By signing the URS, the signer irrevocably appoints the Secretary of State as the organization's agent for service of process for any action arising from the Solicitation Act [this condition replaces a separate Georgia form for that purpose].
Notarized signature required: Yes.
Fundraiser contracts: No.
Certificate/Articles of Incorporation: No.
Bylaws: No.
IRS Form 990: Yes.
IRS Determination Letter: Yes.
Resident/Registered Agent required: No.
Audit: Yes, if gross revenue over 1 million; CPA review for organizations with revenue between $500,000 and $1 million. Financial report when revenue is less than $500,000.
State forms additional to URS: One: "Georgia Supp. to URS".
Mailing address: Securities and Business Regulation, 2 Martin Luther King, Jr. Dr. #802 W. Tower, Atlanta, GA 30303-9000
Info. telephone & contact: 404-656-3920; Martha Ann Elliot
Web: www.sos.state.ga.us/securities/default.htm

Illinois
Governing Law: 760 ILCS 55/1; 225 ILCS 460/1
Exemptions: This Act does not apply to the United States, any State, territory or possession of the United States, the District of Columbia, the Commonwealth of Puerto Rico, or to any of their agencies or to any governmental subdivision; or to a corporation sole, or other religious corporation, trust or organization which holds property for religious, charitable, hospital or educational purposes or for the purpose of operating cemeteries or a home or

APPENDIX 4A: STATE UNIFIED REGISTRATION STATEMENT

homes for the aged; nor to any agency or organization, incorporated or unincorporated, affiliated with and directly supervised by such a religious corporation or organization; or to an officer, director or trustee of any such religious corporation, trust or organization who holds property in his official capacity for like purposes; or to a charitable organization foundation, trust or corporation organized for the purpose of and engaged in the operation of schools or hospitals.
Fees: $15
Check payable to: "Illinois Charity Bureau Fund."
Period covered: Indefinite.
Renewal Due date: No renewal of registration but financial reports are due annually within six months of Fiscal Year end.
Required signatures: Two. President and Chief Financial Officer.
Notarized signature required: No.
Fundraiser contracts: Yes.
Certificate/Articles of Incorporation: Yes.
Bylaws: Yes.
IRS Form 990: Yes.
IRS Determination Letter: Yes.
Resident/Registered Agent required: Yes. May use Item #17 on URS.
Audit: Yes, if over $150,000 in gross revenue.
State forms additional to URS: None.
Mailing address: Office of the Illinois Attorney General, Charitable Trust & Solicitations Bureau, 100 W. Randolph St., 3rd fl., Chicago, IL 60601-3175
Info. telephone: 312-814-2595
Web: www.ag.state.il.us/charitable/charity.html

Kansas
Governing law: KSA 17-1760 et seq.
Exemptions: Any religious corporation, trust or organization; Accredited educational institutions or any of their foundations; Any other educational institution confining its solicitation to the student body, alumni, faculty and trustees; Fraternal, social, alumni organizations and historical societies when solicitation is confined to their membership; Any organization which does not receive contributions in excess of $10,000 per year.
Fees: $35
Check payable to: "Secretary of State."
Period covered: One year.
Renewal Due date: Within 6 months of Fiscal Year end.
Required Signatures: Two. An Authorized Officer and Chief Fiscal Officer.
Notarized signature required: No.
Fundraiser contracts: No.
Certificate/Articles of Incorporation: Yes.
Bylaws: No.
IRS Form 990: Yes.
IRS Determination Letter: Yes.
Resident/Registered Agent required: No.
Audit: Yes if receive contributions more than $500,000.
State forms additional to URS: None.
Mailing address: Ron Thornburgh, Sec. of State, First Floor, Memorial Hall, 120 SW 10th Avenue, Topeka, KS 66612-1594
Info. Telephone: 785-296-4564
Web: www.kssos.org/charity.html

Kentucky
Governing law: K.R.S. §367.650
Exemptions: Religious organizations; solicitations by an organization of its members and their families only; solicitations by an accredited educational institution from alumni, faculty, students and families.
Fees: None.
Check payable to: N/A
Period covered: One year (or until next IRS form is due).

Renewal Due date: "The Form 990 shall be filed with the Attorney General each year in which contributors are solicited in the Commonwealth at the same time the form is filed with the Internal Revenue Service. If a Form 990 is not filed with the Internal Revenue Service, a new notice of intent to solicit shall be filed with the Attorney General." K.R.S. 367.657
Required signatures: One. Any officer.
Notarized signature required: Yes.
Fundraiser contracts: No.
Certificate/Articles of Incorporation: No.
Bylaws: No.
IRS Form 990: Yes.
IRS Determination Letter: No.
Resident/Registered Agent required: No.
Audit: No.
State forms additional to URS: None.
Mailing address: Cynthia Lowe, Ofc. of Atty. General, Consumer Prot. Div., 1024 Capital Center Dr., Frankfort, KY 40601-8204
Info. telephone & contact: 502-696-5479, Cynthia Lowe or 502-696-5300, Elizabeth Natter
Web: www.law.state.ky.us/cp/charity.htm

Louisiana
Governing law: La. R.S. 51:1901-1904; La. Admin. Code, Title 16, Part III, Chapter 5, Sec. 515.
Exemptions: Religious organizations, including exempt from federal income tax under IRC 501(c)(3), if not primarily supported by funds solicited outside its own membership or congregation; educational institutions recognized or approved by the Louisiana Dept. of Education; voluntary health organizations organized under Louisiana or federal law. **VERY IMPORTANT NOTE:** Only those organizations employing "professional solicitors" to raise funds in Louisiana are required to register in the state.
Fees: $25
Check payable to: "Consumer Protection Section."
Period covered: One year.
Renewal Due date: Anniversary of initial registration.
Required signatures: One. Any authorized officer, director or incorporator.
Notarized signature required: No.
Fundraiser contracts: Yes.
Certificate/Articles of Incorporation: Yes.
Bylaws: Yes.
IRS Form 990: Yes.
IRS Determination Letter: No.
Resident/Registered Agent required: No.
Audit: No.
State forms additional to URS: None.
Mailing address: Ofc. of the Attorney General, Consumer Protection Section, 1885 N. 3rd St., Baton Rouge, LA 70802-5146.
Info. telephone & contact: 225-326-6465; Sonja Anderson.
Web: http://ladoj.ag.state.la.us/

Maine
Governing law: 9 M.R.S.A. Chapter 385, Sec. 5001-5016
Exemptions: Organizations established for religious purposes; organizations soliciting primarily within the membership of the organization where solicitation activities are conducted by members; organizations that do not receive contributions from the public in excess of $10,000 or do not receive contributions from more than 10 persons during the calendar year, if fundraising is carried on by volunteers; educational institutions whose curriculum is registered or approved by Dept. of Ed.; nonprofit and charitable hospitals. If claiming exemption, org. must submit an affidavit for exemption, a copy of form letter from IRS and a $10 fee.
Fees: $100 initial (includes license and application fees). $25 renewal.
Check payable to: "Treasurer, State of Maine."

FORM 990, SCHEDULES A THROUGH R

Period covered: One year (or until Nov. 30 following initial registration).
Renewal Due date: November 30.
Required signatures: One. An authorized officer.
Notarized signature required: Yes.
Fundraiser contracts: No.
Certificate/Articles of Incorporation: No.
Bylaws: No.
IRS Form 990: Yes.
IRS Determination Letter: Yes.
Resident/Registered Agent required: No.
Audit: Yes, if gross receipts more than $30,000.
State forms additional to URS: Organizations must indicate (e.g. in a cover letter) the estimated percentage of each dollar contribution that will be expended in Maine. No later than September 30 of each year, the charitable organization must submit an Annual Fundraising Activity Report.
Mailing address: Ofc. of Licensing & Registration, Charitable Solicitation Registration, 35 State House Station, Augusta, ME 04333-0035
Info. telephone & contact: 207-624-8624, Marlene McFadden
Email: marlene.m.mcfadden@state.me.us
Web: www.state.me.us/pfr/olr/categories/cat10.htm

Maryland
Governing law: Ann. Code, Bus. Reg. Art., Sec. 6-101 et seq.
Exemptions: An organization is exempt if it does not employ a professional solicitor and is: a religious organization exempt from federal tax; an organization soliciting only from its members; an organization that does not receive more than $25,000 per year in contributions from the public. Please note: Organizations exempt because they receive less than $25,000 in charitable contributions must file annually "Exempt Organization Fundraising Notice" (Form SS-208), which is available from MD.
Fees: $0 if $0-$24,999.99; $50 if $25,000-$50,000; $75 if $50,001-$75,000; $100 if $75,001-100,000; $200 if $100,001 or more.
Check payable to: "Secretary of State."
Period covered: One year.
Renewal Due date: Within six months of Fiscal Year end.
Required signatures: One. The president, chairman or principal officer.
IMPORTANT NOTE: By signing the URS, the signer (i) consents to the jurisdiction and venue of the Circuit Court of Anne Arundel Co. in actions brought under Title 6 of the Business Regulation Article of the Annotated Code of Maryland and (ii) certifies that all taxes due or due to be collected and paid over to the State, Baltimore City, or a Maryland county have been paid or collected and paid over and (iii) certifies the copy of the IRS Form 990 or 990EZ accompanying the statement is a true copy of the form filed with the IRS.
Notarized signature required: No.
Fundraiser contracts: Yes.
Certificate/Articles of Incorporation: Yes.
Bylaws: Yes.
IRS Form 990: Yes.
IRS Determination Letter: Yes.
Resident/Registered Agent required: No.
Audit: Yes, if gross income from charitable contributions equals or exceeds $200,000 (CPA review if between $100,000 and 200,000).
State forms additional to URS: None.
Mailing address: Office of the Secretary of State, Charitable Organizations Division, State House, Annapolis, MD 21401-1547.
Info. telephone: 410-974-5534.
Web: www.marylandsos.gov

Massachusetts
Governing law: Mass. Gen. Law, Chapters 12 & 68.

Exemptions: Religious corporation, trust, foundation, association, or organization established for religious purposes and agencies and affiliates.
Fees: $50.
Check payable to: "Commonwealth of Massachusetts."
Period covered: Indefinite.
Renewal Due date: No renewal of registration BUT financial reports filed on Mass. Form PC are due annually within four and half months of Fiscal Year end.
Required signatures: Two. The President or other authorized officer and the treasurer or Chief Financial Officer.
Notarized signature required: No.
Fundraiser contracts: No.
Certificate/Articles of Incorporation: Yes.
Bylaws: Yes.
IRS Form 990: No.
IRS Determination Letter: Yes.
Resident/Registered Agent required: No.
Audit: No.
State forms additional to URS: None.
Mailing address: Mass. Office of the Attorney General, One Ashburton Place, Boston, MA 02108-1698
Info. telephone: 617-727-2200 x2101.
Web: http://www.mass.gov/ago. Click on "Regulation of Charities" under the "Non-Profits & Charities" heading to find further information on initial registrations.

Michigan
Governing law: MCLA §400.271
Exemptions: Religious organizations with tax-exempt status; groups receiving $8,000 or less annually, if no one is paid to fundraise and financial statements are available to the public; groups soliciting quarterly or less often from members and their immediate families; educational institutions certified by the state board of education; veterans groups organized under federal law; licensed nonprofit hospitals and their foundations and auxiliaries. Organizations seeking exemption must file "Initial Charitable Trust/Solicitation Questionnaire."
IMPORTANT NOTE: If a parent corp. wishes to include MI chapters in its license _ Must include with URS: IRS group exemption letter or determination letter for each chapter; if foreign corp., MI certificate of authority; listing of names and addresses of MI chapters; a copy of the IRS group return; a financial report for each chapter.
Fees: None.
Check payable to: N/A
Period covered: One year.
Renewal Due date: 30 days prior to license expiration.
Required signatures: One. Trustee or Officer.
Notarized signature required: No.
Fundraiser contracts: Yes.
Certificate/Articles of Incorporation: Yes.
Bylaws: Yes.
IRS Form 990: Yes.
IRS Determination Letter: Yes.
Resident/Registered Agent required: Yes. May use item #17 on URS.
Audit: Yes, if public support is over $250,000. If between $100,000 and $250,000, CPA review required.
State forms additional to URS: None.
Mailing address: Atty. General, Charitable Trust Sec., Williams Bldg., 525 W. Ottawa, 6th fl., Lansing, MI 48933-1067
Info. telephone & contact: 517-373-1152, Marion Gorton, Administrator
Web: www.ag.state.mi.us/

Minnesota
Governing law: Minn. Stats. Chapter 309

APPENDIX 4A: STATE UNIFIED REGISTRATION STATEMENT

Exemptions: Religious organizations and churches which are not required to file the IRS Form 990; organizations receiving $25,000 or less annually and whose functions and activities, including fundraising, are performed wholly by persons who are unpaid for their services; Accredited colleges and secondary schools; fraternal, patriotic, social, educational, alumni, professional, trade, or learned societies that limit solicitations to members. Exempt organizations are asked to file "Verification of Exemption" Form.
Fees: $25.
Check payable to: "State of Minnesota."
Period Covered: One year.
Renewal Due date: Seven months and fifteen days following close of fiscal year. Four month extension available upon written request. NOTE: MN consolidates registration renewal and annual financial reporting. Organizations that submit the "Charitable Organization Annual Report" (the state's annual financial report form) are regarded as having also renewed their registrations. The state will accept the URS in lieu of its own annual financial reporting form (and as a simultaneous renewal of registration) if the filer fulfills the audit requirement attached to annual financial reporting (See the Minn. entry in the "Information on Annual Financial Reporting" section of this Appendix).
Required signatures: Two. Any authorized officer or director or incorporator. **IMPORTANT NOTE**: By signing the URS, the signers certify the registration has been executed and submitted pursuant to a resolution of the board of directors or trustees which has approved the content of the registration statement.
Notarized signature required: No.
Fundraiser contracts: Yes.
Certificate/Articles of Incorporation: Yes.
Bylaws: No.
IRS Form 990: Yes.
IRS Determination Letter: Yes.
Resident/Registered Agent required: No.
Audit: Yes, if revenue exceeds $350,000.
State forms additional to URS: None.
Mailing address: Ofc. of Atty General, Charities Div., 445 Minnesota St #1200 NCL Tower, St. Paul, MN 55101-2130
Info. telephone & contact: 651-296-6172, Cyndi Nelson
Web: www.ag.state.mn.us.

Mississippi
Governing Law: Miss. Code Ann. Sec. 79-11-501, et.seq.
Exemptions: Accredited educational institutions; Educational institutions which solicits solely from its students, alumni, faculty, trustees and families; Fraternal, patriotic, social, educational alumni organizations and historical societies when solicitation of contributions is made solely by their membership; Any charitable organization which does not intend to solicit and receive and does not actually receive contributions in excess of $4,000, provided all of its fundraising functions are carried on by persons who are unpaid for such services. Organizations seeking exemption must file "Form CE."
Fees: $50
Check payable to: "Mississippi Secretary of State."
Period covered: One year.
Renewal Due date: Anniversary of initial registration.
Required signatures: Two. President or authorized officer and Chief Financial Officer.
Notarized signature required: Yes.
Fundraiser contracts: Yes.
Certificate/Articles of Incorporation: Yes.
Bylaws: No.
IRS Form 990: Yes.
IRS Determination Letter: Yes.
Resident/Registered Agent required: Yes. May use item #17 on URS.

Audit: Yes, if gross revenue is more than $100,000. If gross revenue is less than $100,000 file a financial statement and Forrm 990 (if filed). The Secretary has statutory authority to request audits on a case-by-case basis for registrants between $25,000 and $100,000.
State forms additional to URS: One. "Supplement to URS" (includes Annual Financial Reporting form).
Mailing address: Miss. Sec. of State, Charities Registration, P.O. Box 136, Jackson, MS 39205-0136
Info. telephone & contact: 601-359-1633 or (toll free) 888-236-6167, Kathy French
Web: www.sos.state.ms.us/regenf/charities/charities.asp

Missouri
Governing law: Sec. 407.450, et seq., RSMo supp. 1988.
Exemptions: Religious, educational and fraternal organizations; Hospitals, provided fundraising not done by professional fundraiser; all 501(c) 3, 501(c) 7 and 501(c)(8) organizations. A copy of the organization's IRS tax exemption determination letter may be filed with the state to obtain exemption.
Fees: $15. ($50 reinstatement fee).
Check payable: Check or money order to "Merchandising Practices Revolving Fund."
Period covered: One year.
Renewal Due date: Within two and a half months of Fiscal Year end.
Required signatures: One. Any authorized officer.
Notarized signature required: Yes.
Fundraiser contracts: Yes.
Articles of Incorporation: Yes.
Bylaws: No.
IRS Form 990: Yes.
IRS Determination Letter: Yes, if 501(c)(3), (c)(7) or (c)(8).
Resident/Registered Agent required: No.
Audit: No.
State forms additional to URS: One (not a "form," but required attachments. See note following). **IMPORTANT NOTE**: organizations must attach copies of all solicitation materials (including telephone scripts) currently in use.
Mailing Address: Atty. General's Ofc., Consumer Protection Div., P.O. Box 899, Jefferson City, MO 65102-0899
Info. telephone & contact: 573-751-1197, Kimberly Haddix
Web: www.ago.state.mo.us

New Hampshire
Governing law: RSA 7:19
Exemptions: Religious organizations and their integrated auxiliaries; conventions or associations of churches.
Fees: $25 initial. $75 renewal.
Check payable to: "State of New Hampshire."
Period Covered: One year.
Renewal Due Date: Within four and a half months of Fiscal Year end
Required signatures: Two. President or chief presiding officer, and treasurer or custodian of funds.
Notarized signature required: Yes.
Fundraiser Contracts: No.
Certificate/Articles of Incorporation: Yes.
Bylaws: Yes.
IRS Form 990: Yes.
IRS Determination Letter: Yes.
Resident/Registered Agent required: No.
Audit: Yes, if revenue equals $1 million or more.
State forms additional to URS: One (not a "form," but a required attachment. See note following). **IMPORTANT NOTE**: A registering organization must attach to the URS a copy of its conflict-of-interest policy currently in effect.
Mailing address: Department of Justice, Charitable Trust Division, 33 Capitol St, Concord, NH 03301-6397.

Info. telephone & contact: 603-271-3591, Terry Knowles, Registrar
Web: www.state.nh.us/nhdoj/CHARITABLE/char.html

New Jersey
Governing law: NJSA 45:17A, et seq.
Exemptions: Any religious corporation, trust, foundation association or organization, or any agency or organization established for charitable purposes which is operated by, controlled or supervised by a religious organization; any education institution or library supervised by the Dept. of Education.
Fees: Gross contributions less than $10,000 = no fee; less than $100,000 = $60; $500,000 or less = $150; more than $500,000 = $250.
Check payable to: "NJ Division of Consumer Affairs."
Period covered: One year.
Renewal Due date: Within six months of Fiscal Year end.
Required signatures: Two. Any authorized officers, one being the chief fiscal officer.
Notarized signature required: No.
Fundraiser contracts: Yes.
Certificate/Articles of Incorporation: Yes.
Bylaws: Yes.
IRS Form 990: Yes.
IRS Determination Letter: Yes.
Resident/Registered Agent required: No.
Audit: Yes, if over $100,000 in Gross Revenue.
State forms additional to URS: None.
Mailing address: N.J. Division of Consumer Affairs, Charities Registration Section, P.O. Box 45021, Newark, NJ 07101-8002.
Info. telephone: 973-504-6215
Web: www.state.nj.us/lps/ca/ocp.htm#charity

New Mexico
Governing law: NMSA 22 §57-22-1, et seq.
Exemptions: Religious organizations as defined by the Act; educational institutions as defined by the Act; and persons soliciting for an individual or group that has suffered a medical or other catastrophe when certain conditions are met.
Fees: None.
Check payable to: N/A
Period covered: Indefinite
Renewal Due date: No renewal of registration but financial reports are due annually within 6 months of Fiscal Year end
Required signatures: One. Chief Financial Officer or other authorized officer (preferably the Treasurer).
Notarized signature required: Yes.
Fundraiser contracts: Yes.
Certificate/Articles of Incorporation: Yes.
Bylaws: No.
IRS Form 990: Yes.
IRS Determination Letter: Yes.
Resident/Registered Agent required: Yes.
Audit: Yes, if total revenue is in excess of $500,000.
State forms additional to URS: None.
Mailing address: Registrar of Charitable Organizations, Ofc. of Atty. General, 111 Lomas Blvd. NW, Suite 300, Albuquerque, NM 87102-2368.
Info. telephone & contact: 505-222-9092, Christie Turner
Web: www.ago.state.nm.us/divs/spcons/spcons.htm

New York
Governing law: Art. 7-A, Executive Law. Please Note: Registrants may also be subject to registration pursuant to the Estates, Powers & Trusts law. See www.oag.state.ny.us or call (212) 416-8400 for instructions.
Exemptions: Religious agencies and organizations and charities operated, supervised, or controlled in connection with a charity organized under the Religious Corporations Law; Educational

institutions confining solicitations to student body, alumni, faculty and trustees and their families; Fraternal, patriotic, social and alumni organizations and historical societies chartered by Board of Regents when soliciting memberships; Organization receiving $250,000 or less and not paying professional fundraisers or commercial coventurers; Local post, camp, chapter or county unit of a veteran's organization; educational institutions or libraries that file annual financial reports with Regents of University of State of New York or with an agency having similar jurisdiction in another state. Organizations seeking exemption must file "Form Char. 006."
Fees: $10 if revenue is below $250,000. $25 if fee is $250,000 or more.
Check payable to: "NYS Department of Law."
Period covered: Indefinite.
Renewal Due date: No renewal of registration but financial reports are due annually within four and a half months of Fiscal Year end.
Required signatures: Two. President and director or chief fiscal officer.
Notarized signature required: No.
Fundraiser contracts: No.
Certificate/Articles of Incorporation: Yes.
Bylaws: Yes.
IRS Form 990: Yes.
IRS Determination Letter: Yes. (Must also submit copy of IRS Form 1023 or 1024).
Resident/Registered Agent required: No.
Audit: Yes, if over $150,000 in revenues (CPA review if between 75,000-$150,000).
State forms additional to URS: None.
Mailing address: Dept. of Law, Charities Bureau, 120 Broadway 3rd fl., New York, NY 10271
Info. telephone & contact: 212-416-8400, Karin K. Goldman, Asst. Attorney General
Web: www.oag.state.ny.us/charities/charities.html

North Carolina
Governing law: Chapter 131 F.
Exemptions: Qualifying religious institutions, government agencies, persons or organizations receiving less than $25,000 in contributions in a calendar year that do not compensate any officer, trustee, organizer, incorporator, fund-raiser or solicitor, educational institutions and foundations, hospitals and hospital foundations, noncommercial broadcast stations, qualified community trusts; volunteer fire departments, rescue squads, emergency medical services; YMCAs or YWCAs; nonprofit continuing care facilities, and certain tax exempt nonprofit fire or emergency medical service organizations involved in the sale of goods or services that do not ask for donations.
Fees: $0 if contributions received for last fiscal year total less than $5,000. $50 if between $5,000 and $100,000. $100 if between $100,001 and $200,000. $200 if $200,001 or more.
Check payable to: "North Carolina Department of Sec. of State."
Period covered: One Year.
Renewal *Due date:* Within four months and fifteen days after Fiscal Year end.
Required signatures: One. Treasurer or Chief Fiscal Officer.
Notarized signature required: Yes.
Fundraiser contracts: No. Certain fundraising disclosures required.
Certificate/Articles of Incorporation: No.
Bylaws: No.
IRS Form 990: Yes. No, if filing NC Annual Financial Report Form.
IRS Determination Letter: For initial filing only, Yes. For renewal filings, No.
Resident/Registered Agent required: No.
Audit: No.
State forms additional to the URS: None. Certain state forms may be required depending on the responses to questions. Please refer to

APPENDIX 4A: STATE UNIFIED REGISTRATION STATEMENT

the web site or statute for specific requirements.
Mailing address: NC Dept. of Secretary of State, Charitable Solicitation Licensing, P.O. Box 29622, Raleigh, NC 27626-0622.
Info. telephone & contact: 919-807-2214. Angelia Boone-Hicks, Licensing and Filing Supervisor.
E-mail: csl@sos.nc.com
Web: http://www.secretary.state.nc.us/csl

North Dakota
Governing law: No.Dak. Century Code, Chapter 50-22.
Exemptions: An organization using volunteer fundraisers and soliciting funds for a political subdivision, government entity, or for a civic or community project in which the contributions received are used solely for the project; a charitable organization or person soliciting contributions for any person specified by name at the time of the solicitation if all the contributions received are transferred within a reasonable time after receipt to the person named or that person's parent, guardian or conservator with no restrictions on their expenditure and with no deduction; religious organizations; institutions of higher learning; a private or public elementary or secondary school; any candidate for national, state, or local elective office or political party or other committee required to file information with the federal election committee, a state election commission, or an equivalent office or agency.
Fees: $25 initial. $10 renewal.
Check payable to: "Secretary of State."
Period covered: One Year.
Renewal Due date: September 1.
Required signatures: One. Any party authorized by the corporation.
Notarized signature required: Yes.
Fundraiser contracts: Yes.
Certificate/Articles of Incorporation: Yes.
Bylaws: No.
IRS Form 990: Yes.
IRS Determination Letter: Yes.
Resident/Registered Agent required: Yes (see below for required form).
Audit: No.
State forms additional to URS: Two. "Certificate of Authority " (SFN 13100), with an additional $125 fee and "Registered Agent" (SFN 7974), with an additional $10 fee.
Mailing address: Sec. of State, State of North Dakota, 600 E. Boulevard. Ave., Dept. 108 Bismarck, ND 58505-0500
Info. telephone & contact: 701-328-3665 or 800-352-0867 ext.83665
Web: www.nd.gov/sos/nonprofit/registration

Ohio
Governing law: OHIO REV CODE Chapt. 1716
Exemptions: (A) Any religious agencies and organizations, and charities, agencies, and organizations operated, supervised, or controlled by a religious organization; (B) Any charitable organization that meets all of the following requirements: (1) It has been in continuous existence in this state for a period of at least two years; (2) It has received from the internal revenue service a determination letter that is currently in effect, stating that the charitable organization is exempt from federal income taxation under subsection 501(a) and described in subsection 501(c)(3) of the IRS; (3) It has registered with the attorney general as a charitable trust pursuant to section 109.26 of the Revised Code; (4) It has filed an annual report with and paid the required fee to the attorney general pursuant to section 109.31 of the Revised Code. (C) Any educational institution, when solicitation of contributions is confined to alumni, faculty, trustees, or the student membership and their families; (D) Every person other than an individual, when solicitation of contributions for a charitable purpose or on behalf of a charitable organization is confined to its existing membership, present or former employees, or present or former trustees; (E) Any

public primary or secondary school, when solicitation of contributions is confined to alumni, faculty, or the general population of the local school district; (F) Any booster club that is organized and operated in conjunction with and for the benefit of students of public primary or secondary schools; (G) Any charitable organization that does not receive gross revenue, excluding grants or awards from the government or an organization that is exempt from federal income taxation under section 501(a) and described in section 501(c)(3) of the IRS, in excess of $25,000 during its immediately preceding fiscal year, if the organization does not compensate any person primarily to solicit contributions. If the gross revenue, excluding grants or awards from the government or an organization that is exempt from federal income taxation under section 501(a) and described in section 501(c)(3) of the IRS, of any charitable organization received during any fiscal year exceeds $25,000, the charitable organization, within 30 days after the receipt of the revenue, shall file a registration statement with the attorney general pursuant to section 1716.02 of the Revised Code.
Fees: $0-$4999.99: $0; $5000-$24,999.99: $50; $25,000-$49,999.99: $100; $50,000+: $200
Check payable to: "Treasurer of the State of Ohio."
Period covered: One year.
Renewal Due date: Within four and a half months of Fiscal Year end.
Required signatures: One. Treasurer or Chief Fiscal Officer.
Notarized signature Required: Yes.
Fundraiser contracts: No.
Certificate/Articles of Incorporation: Yes.
Bylaws: Yes.
IRS Form 990: Yes.
IRS Determination Letter: Yes.
Resident/Registered Agent required: No.
Audit: No.
State forms additional to URS: None.
Mailing Address: Atty. General's Ofc., Charitable Law Sect., 150 E. Gay St., 23rd fl., Columbus, OH 43215-3130.
Info. telephone & contact: 614-466-3180; Public Information Unit.
Web: www.ag.state.oh.us/charitab/charitab.htm

Oregon
Governing law: Ore. Rev. Stat. 128.610 - 129.
Exemptions: A religious corporation; Educational institutions that do not hold property in the state or whose solicitations of individuals residing in the state are confined to alumni.
Fees: $10 if $0-$25,000; $25 if $25,000-$50,000; $45 if $50,000-$100,000; $75 if $100,000-$250,000; $100 if $250,000-$500,000; $135 if $500,000-$750,000; $170 if $750,000-$1 million; $200 if 1 million and over. If $50,000-$10 million, subject to percentage rate fee (1.18% of fund balance rounded to whole dollar. If less than .50 than drop but if .50 and higher, round to next dollar.)
Check payable to: "Oregon Department of Justice".
Period covered: Indefinite.
Renewal Due date: No renewal of registration but financial reports are due annually within four and a half months of Fiscal Year end.
Required signatures: One. An authorized trustee, officer or director.
Notarized signature required: No.
Fundraiser contracts: No.
Certificate/Articles of Incorporation: Yes.
Bylaws: Yes.
IRS Form 990: Yes.
IRS Determination Letter: Yes.
Resident/Registered Agent required: No.
Audit: No.
State forms additional to URS: None.
Mailing address: Oregon Dept. of Justice, Charitable Activities, 1515 S.W. 5th Ave. #410, Portland, OR 97201-5446
Info. telephone: 503-229-5725
Web: http://www.doj.state.or.us/ChariGroup/welcome2.htm

FORM 990, SCHEDULES A THROUGH R

Pennsylvania

Governing law: 10 P.S. §162.1 et seq.

Exemptions: Religious institutions and separate groups or corporations that form an integral part that are tax exempt and primarily supported by fees charged for services rendered, government grants or contracts, or solicitations from their own memberships, congregations, or previous donors; Accredited educational institutions; hospitals subject to regulation by the Dept. of Health or Dept. of Public Welfare and any foundation which is an integral part; Nonprofit libraries filing an annual fiscal report with the state library system; Senior citizen centers and nursing homes that are nonprofit, charitable and tax exempt, and have all fundraising activities carried out by volunteers; Organizations raising $25,000 or less annually that do not compensate anyone; Local post, camp, or chapter of any veterans organization chartered under federal law and any service foundations recognized in their by-laws.

Fees: $15 if $25,000 or less; $100 if $25,001-$100,000; $150 if $100,001-$500,000; $250 if $500,001 and over.

Check payable to: "Commonwealth of Pennsylvania."

Period covered: One year.

Renewal Due date: 135 days after end of Fiscal Year.

Required signatures: Two authorized officers.

Notarized signature required: No.

Fundraiser contracts: No.

Certificate/Articles of Incorporation: Yes.

Bylaws: Yes.

IRS Form 990: Yes.

IRS Determination Letter: Yes.

Resident/Registered Agent required: No.

Audit: Yes, if gross contributions exceed $125,000 (CPA review $50,000 to $125,000).

State forms additional to URS: None.

Mailing address: Dept. of State, Bureau of Charitable Orgs., 207 North Office Building, Harrisburg, PA 17120-0103.

Info. telephone & contact: 717-783-1720, Karl Emerson, Dir.

Web: www.dos.state.pa.us/charity/index.html

Rhode Island

Governing law: R.I.G.I. Title 5, Chapter 53.1

Exemptions: Churches and religious organizations operated, supervised or controlled by a religious organization; institutions indirectly affiliated with any religious organization that maintain and operate homes for the aged, orphans or unwed mothers; Accredited educational institutions; Organizations raising $25,000 or less in a calendar year, whose fundraising activities are carried on by volunteers; Nonprofit hospitals; Organizations soliciting exclusively from their membership; Public libraries; Veterans organizations and their auxiliaries; Public art museums.

Fees: $75

Check payable to: "General Treasurer of Rhode Island."

Period covered: One year.

Renewal Due date: Anniversary of initial registration.

Required signatures: Two authorized officials, one of who must be a director or trustee.

Notarized signature required: Yes.

Fundraiser Contracts: Yes.

Certificate/Articles of Incorporation: Yes.

Bylaws: No.

IRS Form 990: Yes.

IRS Determination Letter: Yes.

Resident/Registered Agent required: No.

Audit: Yes, if annual gross budget exceeds $500,000.

State forms additional to URS: Either (1) a copy of Form 990 and additional information including organization's address, percentage of contribution spent for fund raising and administration, and whether organization or officers have been enjoined from fund raising or convicted or found liable for fraudulent activities; or 2) financial statements comprising a statement of activities and statement of financial position. **IMPORTANT NOTE:** An organization must list the names and compensation of the organization's five most highly compensated individuals in excess of the amount specified as requiring disclosure by IRS Form 990.

Mailing address: Dept of Business Regulation, Securities Division, 233 Richmond St. #232, Providence, RI 02903-4232

Info. telephone & contact: 401-222-1754; Alicia Mildner

Web: www.dbr.state.ri.us/

South Carolina

Governing law: §33-56-10 South Carolina

Exemptions: Religious organizations or groups affiliated with and forming an integral part. The following are exempt provided they do not raise funds through professional solicitors: Educational institutions that solicit contributions only from students and their families, alumni, faculty, friends, and other constituencies; Charitable organizations that do not solicit and receive more than $5,000 per calendar year; Organizations that solicit exclusively from their members; any veterans organization that has a congressional charter.

Fees: $50

Check payable to: "Secretary of State"

Period covered: One year.

Renewal Due date: July 1.

Required signatures: Two. Chief Executive Officer and Treasurer.

Notarized signature required: Yes.

Fundraiser contracts: Yes.

Certificate/Articles of Incorporation: No.

Bylaws: No.

IRS Form 990: Yes.

IRS Determination Letter: No.

Resident/Registered Agent required: No.

Audit: No.

State forms additional to URS: None.

Mailing address: Public Charities Section, Office of the Secretary of State, PO Box 11350, Columbia, SC 29211-1350

Info. telephone: 803-734-1790

Web: www.scsos.com/charities.htm

Tennessee

Governing law: TCA 48-101-501 et seq.

Exemptions: Religious groups and their integrated auxiliaries which are not subject to federal income tax and are not required to file an IRS From 990 and which are not primarily supported by funds solicited outside their own membership or congregation; Organizations which do not intend to solicit and receive and do not actually receive gross contributions from the public in excess of $30,000; Accredited educational institutions, including organizations of parents, students and others operated in support of the institutions; Volunteer fire departments, rescue squads or local civil defense organizations.

Fees: $50 initial. Renewal: 0-48,999.99: $100; $49,000-$99,999.99: $150; $100,000-$249,999.99: $200; $250,000-$499,999.99: $250; $500,000+: $300

Check payable: "Secretary of State"

Period covered: One year.

Renewal Due date: Within 6 months of Fiscal Year end.

Required signatures: Two authorized officers of the organization, one of whom must be the Chief Fiscal Officer.

Notarized signature required: Yes.

Fundraiser contracts: Yes.

Certificate/Articles of Incorporation: Yes.

Bylaws: Yes.

IRS Form 990: Yes.

APPENDIX 4A: STATE UNIFIED REGISTRATION STATEMENT

IRS Determination Letter: Yes (and if the determination is still pending, a copy of the application OR the IRS letter acknowledging the application's receipt).
Resident/Registered Agent required: No.
Audit: Yes if gross revenue over $300,000.
State forms additional to URS: Two: "Summary of Financial Activities" and "Supplemental Registration Form"
Mailing address: Div. of Charitable Solicitations, 312 Eighth Ave. North, 8th fl., William Snodgrass Tower, Nashville, TN 37243
Info. telephone: 615-741-2555
Web: www.state.tn.us/sos/charity.htm

Utah

Governing law: UCA 13-22-1 et. seq.
Exemptions: (a) A solicitation that an organization conducts among its own established and bona fide membership exclusively through the voluntarily donated efforts of other members or officers of the organization; (b) a bona fide religious, ecclesiastical, or denominational organization if: (i) the solicitation is made for a church, missionary, religious, or humanitarian purpose; and (ii) the organization is either: (A) a lawfully organized corporation, institution, society, church, or established physical place of worship, at which nonprofit religious services and activities are regularly conducted and carried on; (B) a bona fide religious group: (I) that does not maintain specific places of worship; (II) that is not subject to federal income tax; and (III) not required to file an IRS Form 990 under any circumstance; or (C) a separate group or corporation that is an integral part of an institution that is an income tax exempt organization under 26 U.S.C. Sec. 501(c)(3) and is not primarily supported by funds solicited outside its own membership or congregation; (c) a solicitation by a broadcast media owned or operated by an educational institution or governmental entity, or any entity organized solely for the support of that broadcast media; (d) except as provided in Subsection **13-22-21**(1), a solicitation for the relief of any person sustaining a life-threatening illness or injury specified by name at the time of solicitation if the entire amount collected without any deduction is turned over to the named person; (e) a political party authorized to transact its affairs within this state and any candidate and campaign worker of the party if the content and manner of any solicitation make clear that the solicitation is for the benefit of the political party or candidate; (f) a political action committee or group soliciting funds relating to issues or candidates on the ballot if the committee or group is required to file financial information with a federal or state election commission; (g) any school accredited by the state, any accredited institution of higher learning, or club or parent, teacher, or student organization within and authorized by the school in support of the operations or extracurricular activities of the school; (h) a public or higher education foundation established under Title 53A or 53B; (i) a television station, radio station, or newspaper of general circulation that donates air time or print space for no consideration as part of a cooperative solicitation effort on behalf of a charitable organization, whether or not that organization is required to register under this chapter; (j) a volunteer fire department, rescue squad, or local civil defense organization whose financial oversight is under the control of a local governmental entity; and (k) any governmental unit of any state or the United States.
Fees: $100.
Check payable to: "State of Utah _ Div. of Consumer Protection."
Period covered: One Year.
Renewal Due date: One year from Jan. 1, April 1 or Oct. 1.
Required signatures: Two. Charity officers.
Notarized signature required: Yes.
Fundraiser contracts: Yes.
Certificate/Articles of Incorporation: Yes.
Bylaws: Yes.
IRS Form 990: Yes.
IRS Determination Letter: Yes.

Resident/Registered Agent required: Yes, but not required to reside in the State of Utah.
Audit: No.
State forms additional to URS: One: "Utah Supplement to URS".
Mailing address: Dept. of Commerce, Div. of Consumer Protection, 160 East 300 South, Box 146704, Salt Lake City, UT 84114-6704.
Info. telephone and contact: 801-530-6601. Francine Giani.
Web: www.commerce.utah.gov/dcp/registration/index.html

Virginia

Governing law: §57-48 to 57-69, Code of Virginia
Exemptions (from the law): Any church or convention or association of churches; American Red Cross and any of its local chapters; Political parties or action committees that register with an election commission or board. Exemption from annual registration upon request: Accredited educational institutions or related foundations, and any other educational institution confining its solicitation of contributions to its students, alumni, faculty and trustees, and their families; Organizations that do not, in a calendar year or the three preceding years, receive contributions from the public in excess of $5,000, all of whose functions are carried out by volunteers; Organizations that solicit only within their membership; Organizations that have no office within the Commonwealth and solicit within the state, solely by means of telephone, telegraph, direct mail or advertising in national media **and** have a registered Virginia chapter, branch or affiliate; 501(c)(3) tax-exempt health care institutions licensed by their state Dept. of Health or Mental Health and any supporting foundation, free clinics and clinics certified by HCFA; Civic organizations such as a local service club, veterans' post, fraternal society or association, volunteer fire or rescue group, or local civic league or association; trade associations, and labor organizations; nonprofit debt counseling agencies licensed by the Virginia State Corporation Commission; 501(c)(3) organizations that solicit solely through grant proposals. $10 exemption application fee. Organizations seeking exemption must file "Form 100" as applicable.
Fees: $100 initial surcharge, plus sliding scale: 0-$25,000 = $30; 25,001-$50,000 = $50; 50,001-$100,000 = $100; 100,001-$500,000 = $200; 500,001-$1,000,000 = $250; $1,000,000+ = $325.
Check payable to: "Treasurer of Virginia." (Please take note that the following information must be included on the face of the check: (1) the Employer Identification Number (EIN) and (2) code "910-02184" if the check is for the initial registration fee or code "910-02619" if the check is for a renewal registration).
Period covered: One year.
Renewal Due date: Within four and a half months of Fiscal Year end.
Required signatures: Two. Chief fiscal officer and President or another authorized official. **IMPORTANT NOTE:** *By signing the URS, the signers certify, on behalf of the organization, that "No funds have been or will knowingly be used, directly or indirectly, to benefit or provide support, in cash or in kind, to terrorists, terrorist organizations, terrorist activities, or the family members of any terrorists."*
Notarized signature required: No.
Fundraiser contracts: Yes.
Certificate/Articles of Incorporation: Yes.
Bylaws: Yes.
IRS Form 990: Yes or may submit audited financial statement.
IRS Determination Letter: Yes.
Resident/Registered Agent required: Optional. May use Item #17 on URS.
Audit: Yes if revenue $25,000 or more. This requirement may be fulfilled by filing IRS Form 990.
State forms additional to URS: None.
Mailing address: Ofc. of Consumer Affairs, Dept. of Agriculture & Consumer Services, PO Box 1163, Richmond, VA 23218-0526

FORM 990, SCHEDULES A THROUGH R

Info. telephone & contact: 804-786-1343, J. Michael Wright, Manager of Regulatory Programs
Web: http://www.vdacs.virginia.gov/consumers/registrations.shtml

Washington

Governing law: Chapt. 19.09 *et seq.* RCW
Exemptions: Religious and political activities are exempt from the definition of "charitable activity." Those activities (1) under direction of a religious organization entitled to receive tax-exempt status for religious purposes, or (2) subject to the reporting requirements of the State Public Disclosure Act or the Federal Elections Campaign Act are not subject to the Charitable Solicitations Act. An organization's sole purpose must be religious to claim exemption from registration; other purposes or activities may require registration under the Act. Organizations raising less than $25,000 in any accounting year are exempt, if all the activities of the organization are carried out by people who are unpaid for their services (volunteers). The use of a Commercial Fundraiser is considered a paid service and therefore cannot be considered "exempt." Organizations seeking an exemption from registration under the Charitable Solicitations Act should file an "Optional Statement for Exempt Organization" in lieu of the URS. There is a $20 filing fee for the statement.
Fees: $20 initial. $10 renewal.
Check payable to: "The State of Washington"
Period covered: One Year.
Renewal Due date: Within four months and fifteen days after Fiscal Year end (state provides an <u>automatic</u> 6 _ month extension).
Required signatures: One. The President, Treasurer, or comparable officer of the organization.
Notarized signature required: No.
Fundraiser contracts: Yes, but only for contracts with 1) solicitors - "commercial fundraisers" or 2) "commercial coventurers" under WA law. Those contracts must be submitted with a "Fundraising Service Contract Registration Form" (WA form) and a $10 fee.
Certificate/Articles of Incorporation: No.
Bylaws: No.
IRS Form 990: Yes. **IMPORTANT NOTE:** A charity must ensure that its board has reviewed and accepted any financial report that it is required to file with the state and may be subjected to civil fines if there is a material error in the financial information filed.
IRS Determination Letter: Yes (one-time submission).
Resident/Registered Agent required: No.
Audit: No.
State forms additional to URS: One: "Washington URS Addendum".
Mailing address: Office of the Secretary of State, Charities Program P.O. Box 40234, 801 Capitol Way South, Olympia, WA 98504-0234
Info. telephone: 800-332-4483 (toll-free in WA only) or 360-753-0863
Email: charities@secstate.wa.gov
Web address: www.secstate.wa.gov/charities

West Virginia

Governing law: Sec. 29-19-5 et. seq.
Exemptions: Educational institutions, the curriculums of which in whole or in part are registered or approved by the state board of education, either directly or by acceptance of accreditation by an accrediting body and any auxiliary associations, foundations and support groups which are directly responsible to any such educational institutions; Persons requesting contributions for the relief of any individual specified at the time of solicitation when all of the contributions collected without any deduction are turned over to the named beneficiary; Hospitals which are nonprofit; Organizations which solicit only within the membership of the organization by members thereof: provided the term "membership" shall not include those persons who are granted membership upon

making a contribution as the result of solicitation; churches, synagogues, associations or conventions of churches, religious orders or religious organizations that are an integral part of a church which qualifies as tax exempt under 501(c)(3); Organizations such as local youth athletic organizations, community service clubs, fraternal organizations, volunteer fireman or auxiliaries are exempt if they do not employ a professional solicitor or fund-raiser or do not intend to solicit or receive contributions in excess of $10,000 during the calendar year.
Fees: $15 if gross contributions received is less than $1 million. $50 of gross contributions is more than $1 million.
Check payable to: "West Virginia Secretary of State."
Period covered: One Year.
Renewal Due date: Anniversary of initial registration
Required signatures: One. An authorized officer.
Notarized signature required: Yes.
Fundraiser contracts: Yes.
Certificate/Articles of Incorporation: No.
Bylaws: No.
IRS Form 990: Yes.
IRS Determination Letter: Yes.
Resident/Registered Agent required: No.
Audit: Yes, if contributions more than $50,000.
State Forms Additional to URS: One: "State of West Virginia Unified Registration State Supplement".
Mailing address: Secretary of State, State Capitol, Room 157-K, Charleston, WV, 25305.
Info. telephone & contact: 304-558-6000, Catherine Ferotte
Web: www.wvsos.com/charity/

Wisconsin

Governing law: Chapter 440, Subchapter III, stats; Chapter RL5, Wis. Admin. Code.
Exemptions: Candidate for national, state or local office or a political party or other committee or group required to file financial information with the federal elections commission; Organizations that do not raise or receive contributions of $5,000; Fraternal, benevolent, patriotic or social organizations that solicit contributions solely from their membership; Veterans organizations; Nonprofit post-secondary educational institutions; A person soliciting contributions for relief of a named individual if all contributions are given to the named individual.
Fees: $15
Check payable to: "Department of Regulation & Licensing."
Period covered: One year.
Renewal Due date: July 31st.
Required signatures: Two. The president or an authorized Officer and the Chief Fiscal Officer.
Notarized signature required: Yes.
Fundraiser contracts: No.
Certificate/Articles of Incorporation: Yes.
Bylaws: Yes.
IRS Form 990: Yes, may file Wisconsin form #308 instead of IRS Form 990.
IRS Determination Letter: Yes (and if determination is still pending, a copy of the IRS tax exemption form #1023).
Resident/Registered Agent required: No.
Audit: Yes, if charitable organizations receive contributions in excess of $100,000, but increases to $175,000 if $75,000 or more comes from one contributor.
State forms additional to URS: One: Form 1952 (if filing IRS form 990 instead of Wisconsin form #308.)
Mailing address: Department of Regulation & Licensing, Charitable Organizations, P.O. Box 8935, Madison, WI 53708-8935.
Info. telephone: (608) 266-2112/Hearing and Speech impaired only: TTY# (608) 267-2416
(608) 266-2112
Email: web@drl.state.wi.us
Web: http://drl.wi.gov

■ 216 ■

States Requiring Registration but NOT Accepting the URS

Colorado   Oklahoma
Florida

PLEASE NOTE: The following registration information for the above states is to assist users in independently registering with states that do NOT accept the URS. The URS cannot be used for registration in any of these states.

Colorado

Governing law: Colo. Rev. Stat. § 6-16-101 *et seq.* Exemptions: Organizations exempt from filing a Form 990; Political parties, candidates for federal or state office, and political action committees required to file financial information with federal or state elections commissions; and Charitable organizations that do not intend to and do not actually raise or receive gross revenue (excluding grants) in excess of $25,000 during a fiscal year *or* do not receive contributions from more than ten persons during a fiscal year. Fees: $10. Check payable to: Checks will not be accepted except to establish a prepaid account. Otherwise Visa, MasterCard, or American Express will be accepted. Period covered: One year. Due date: Prior to raising funds in Colorado. Required signatures: Two. Charity Officer and Charity Chief Fiscal Officer. Notarized signature required: No. Fundraiser contracts: Yes. Certificate/Articles of Incorporation: No. Bylaws: No. IRS Form 990: No. IRS Determination Letter: Yes. (Only the date of the letter is required.) Resident/Registered Agent required: No. Mailing address: (See note following.) Charitable Solicitations Program, Ofc. of the Secretary of State, 1560 Broadway, Ste. 200, Denver, CO 80202. IMPORTANT NOTE: All filings must be made electronically via the Secretary of State's web site. Info. telephone & contact: 303-894-2200, ext. 6407, Chris Cash. Web: http://www.sos.state.co.us/pubs/bingo_raffles/charitable.htm.

Florida

Governing law: F.S. 496.405 et seq. Exemptions: Religious organizations; an organization which limits solicitation to its membership. Fees: $10 if gross revenue is less than $5000; $75 if between $5000 and $100,000; $125 if between $100,001 and $200,000; $200 if between $200,001 and $500,000; $300 if between with $500,001 and $1 million; $350 if between $1,000,001 and $9,999, 999; $400 if $10 million or more. Note: If $25,000 or less and no paid professional, the fee is $10. Check payable to: "Florida Department of Agriculture and Consumer Services." Period covered: One Year. Due date: Anniversary date. Required signatures: One. Treasurer or Chief Fiscal Officer. Notarized signature required: Yes. Fundraiser contracts: Yes. Certificate/Articles of Incorporation: No. Bylaws: No. IRS Form 990: Yes. IRS Determination Letter: Yes. Resident/Registered Agent required: No. Audit: No. Mailing address: Florida Department of Agriculture & Consumer Services, 407 S. Calhoun, Tallahassee, FL 32399-0800. Information telephone and contact: 850-922-2966, Rudy Hamrick. Annual Reporting information: NO REPORTING APART FROM REGISTRATION. Web: http://doacs.state.fl.us/onestop/cs/solicit.html

Oklahoma

Governing law: Title 18 O.S. § 552 et seq. *Exemptions:* Religious organizations; educational institutions that have a faculty and regularly enrolled students when solicitations are limited to students and their families, alumni, faculty, and trustees; fraternal organizations, when soliciting from their own members, and patriotic and civic organizations, when solicitations are confined to membership and managed by membership without paid solicitors; organizations raising less than $10,000. *Fees:* $15 *Check payable to:* "Secretary of State." *Period covered:* One year. *Due date:* Anniversary of initial registration. *Required signatures:* One. An authorized officer. *Notarized signature required:* No. *Fundraiser contracts:* Yes. *Certificate/Articles of Incorporation:* No. *Bylaws:* No. *IRS Form 990:* Yes. *IRS Determination Letter:* No. *Resident/Registered Agent required:* No. *Audit:* No. *Mailing address:* Office of the Secretary of State, 2300 N. Lincoln, #101, Oklahoma City, OK 73105-4897 *Info. telephone & contact:* 405-521-3049; Darlene Adams. *Web:* http://www.sos.state.ok.us/forms/FORMS.HTM#Charity

FORM 990, SCHEDULES A THROUGH R

Information on Annual Financial Reporting

As noted throughout the URS, most states requiring registration also require annual financial reporting. Although the URS CAN NOT BE USED FOR THIS PURPOSE, basic information on annual financial reporting for the URS cooperating states is presented below:

Alabama:
Due Date: Within 90 days of Fiscal Year end.
Fee: $25
IRS 990: No.
Financial Report: Yes, this requirement may be met by submitting a copy of IRS Form 990.
Audit: No

Arizona
Due Date: Within one year of filing.
Fees: None.
IRS 990: Yes
Financial Report: Yes. Form 990.
Audit: No

Arkansas:
Due Date: By May 15th. If Fiscal Year other than calendar year, may file within six months after Fiscal Year end, upon request.
Fee: None.
IRS 990: Yes, if required to file with the IRS.
Financial Report: Yes, if no Form 990 to file and receive more than $10,000.
Audit: Yes, for organizations with gross revenue more than $500,000.

California:
Due Date: Within 4_ months of Fiscal Year end.
Fee: $25 for organizations with assets or revenue exceeding $100,000 during Fiscal Year. Such organizations must submit Form RRF-1 due Within 4_ months after the close of the organization's fiscal or calendar accounting period.
IRS 990: Yes. (Note: Due within 4_ months of the close of the organization's fiscal or calendar accounting period. Extensions granted by the IRS will be honored)
Financial Report: Yes.
Audit: Yes, if gross revenue exceeds $2 million (exclusive of grants from, and contracts for services with, governmental entities for which the entity requires an accounting of the funds received).

Connecticut:
Due Date: Last day of the fifth month following the close of the organization's Fiscal Year end. Extensions of 180 days may be granted upon written request.
Fee: $25 if postmarked on or before the due date or extended due date, $50 if postmarked after the due date or extended due date.
IRS 990: Yes.
Financial Report: Yes.

Audit: Yes, if gross revenue exceeds $200,000 (excluding government grants and fees, and trust revenues).

District of Columbia:
Due Date: September 1
Fee: $80
IRS 990: Yes.
Financial Report: Yes.
Audit: No.

Georgia:
Due Date: Within one year of filing but if Fiscal Year has ended within 90 days prior to date of filing, report may be dated as of end of preceding FY.
Fee: $10
IRS 990: Yes.
Financial Report: Independent CPA review required for proceeds between $500,000 and $1 million; Form 990 if proceeds are less than amount required by IRS.
Audit: Yes, if revenue over $1 million.

Illinois:
Due Date: Within 6 months of Fiscal Year end.
Fee: $15 ($100 late fee if registration expires)
IRS 990: Yes.
Financial Report: Yes. (state form)
Audit: Yes, if gross revenue over $150,000 or professional fundraiser used and contributions exceed $25,000.

Kansas:
Due Date: Within 6 months of Fiscal Year end.
Fee: $20
IRS 990: Yes.
Financial Report: Yes. May be submitted instead of IRS Form 990.
Audit: Yes, if contributions in excess of $500,000.

Kentucky:
Due Date: Within 4 1/2 months of Fiscal Year end.
Fee: None.
IRS 990: Yes, unless Form 990 has not yet been filed with the IRS.
Financial Report: No.
Audit: No.

Louisiana:
Due Date: Anniversary of initial registration.

Fee: $25
IRS 990: Yes.
Financial Report: No
Audit: No.

Maine:
Due Date: September 30.
Fee: $50 plus $50 if raised more than $30,000
IRS 990: Yes.
Financial Report: Yes. May be submitted instead of 990.
Audit: Yes, if gross receipts are more than $30,000.

Maryland:
Due Date: Within 6 months of Fiscal Year end.
Fee: No fee if gross income from charitable contributions is less than $25,000; $50 if $25,000-$50,000; $75 if $50,001-$75,000; $100 if $75,001-$100,000; $200 if $100,001 or more.
IRS 990: Yes.
Financial Report: Yes, must be reviewed by an independent CPA if revenue is between $100,000 and $200,000.
Audit: Yes, if gross income equals or exceeds $200,000.

Massachusetts:
Due Date: Within 4 1/2 months of Fiscal Year end.
Fee: $35 if revenue under $100,000; $70 if $100,001-$250,000; $125 if $250,001-$500,000; $250 if over $500,000.
IRS 990: Yes.
Financial Report: Yes (Mass. Form PC),
Audit: Yes, if revenue exceeds $500,000. If revenue over $100,000 and not more than $500,000, CPA review required.

Michigan:
Due Date: 30 days prior to license expiration.
Fee: None.
IRS 990: Yes.
Financial Report: Yes.
Audit: Yes, if public support $250,000 or more. If between $100,000 and $250,000, reviewed financial statements required.

Minnesota:
FILERS MAY USE the URS in lieu of the state's own annual report FORM if the filer fulfills the audit requirement, below (See the Minnesota entry on Page 4 of this Appendix for further information).
Due Date: If Fiscal Year ends December 31st, due on or before July 15th. Otherwise, due on or before the 15th day of the seventh

APPENDIX 4A: STATE UNIFIED REGISTRATION STATEMENT

month following the close of its fiscal year. Attorney General may extend the time for filing the annual report for a period not to exceed four months. File extension request in writing prior to due date.
Fee: $25 ($50 late fee)
IRS 990: Yes. Accepted in lieu of separate financial statement if it fulfills the requirements of Minnesota Statutes section 309.53 (2000).
Audit: Yes, if revenue exceeds $350,000. (Audit must be prepared in accordance with generally accepted accounting principles. Cash basis audit not acceptable)

Mississippi:
FILERS MUST USE THE URS AND CAN, WITH A SINGLE FILING, BOTH RENEW REGISTRATION AND EFFECT ANNUAL FINANCIAL REPORTING
Due Date: Anniversary of registration
Fee: $50.
IRS 990: Yes.
Financial Report: Yes.
Audit: Yes, if the organization received contributions over $100,000; or engaged the services of a professional fund-raiser. Secretary has statutory authority to request audits on a case-by-case basis for registrants between $25,000-$100,000.

Missouri:
Due Date: Within 2 _ months of Fiscal Year end.
Fee: $15
IRS 990: Yes.
Financial Report: Yes.
Audit: No.

New Hampshire:
Due Date: Within 4 1/2 months of Fiscal Year end.
Fee: $75
IRS 990: Yes.
Financial Report: Yes.
Audit: Yes, if revenue equals $1 million or more.

New Jersey:
Due Date: Within 6 months of Fiscal Year end.
Fee: No fee if short form filer and less than $10,000; $30 if short form filer and more than $10,000. $60 if long form filer and less than $100,000; $150 if long form filer and $100,000- $500,000; $250 if long form filer and more than $500,000. ($25 late fee if submitted more than 30 days after due date)
IRS 990: Yes.
Financial Report: Yes and certified by authorized officer of organization if revenue under $100,000.
Audit: Yes, if revenue $100,000 and over.

New Mexico:
Due Date: Within 6 months of Fiscal Year end.
Fee: None.

IRS 990: Yes.
Financial Report: Yes.
Audit: Yes, if total revenue is in excess of $500,000.

New York:
Due Date: Within 4 1/2 months of Fiscal Year end.
Fee: $10 if revenue is below $250,000. $25 if fee is $250,000 or more.
IRS 990: Yes.
Financial Report: Yes. Must be reviewed by CPA if revenue $75,000-$150,000.
Audit: Yes, if revenue $150,000 and over.

North Carolina:
Due Date: Within 4 months and 15 days after Fiscal Year end.
Fee: $50 if revenue is under $100,000. $100 if revenue $100,001-$200,000. $200 if revenue $200,001 or more.
IRS 990: Yes.
Financial Report: Yes. May be submitted instead of 990.
Audit: No.

North Dakota:
Due Date: September 1.
Fee: $10.
IRS 990: Yes.
Financial Report: Yes.
Audit: No.

Ohio:
Due Date: Within 4 1/2 months of Fiscal Year end.
Fee: $50 if revenue $5,000-$24,999.99; $100 if $25,000-$49,999.99; $200 if $50,000 or more.
IRS 990: Yes or financial report.
Financial Report: Yes (on Attorney General Form).
Audit: No.

Oregon:
Due Date: Within 4 1/2 months of Fiscal Year end.
Fee: $10 if $0-$25,000; $25 if $25,000-$50,000; $45 if $50,000-$100,000; $75 if $100,000-$250,000; $100 if $250,000-$500,000; $135 if $500,000-$750,000; $170 if $750,000-$1 million; $200 if 1 million and over. If $50,000-$10 million, subject to percentage rate fee (1.18% of fund balance rounded to whole dollar. If less than .50 than drop but if .50 and higher, round to next dollar.) ($20 late fee)
IRS 990: Yes.
Financial Report: Yes.
Audit: No.

Pennsylvania:
Due Date: Within 4.5 months of Fiscal Year end.
Fee: $15 if $25,000 or less; $100 if $25,001-$100,000; $150 if $100,001-$500,000; $250 if $500,001 and over.
IRS 990: Yes.
Financial Report: Yes. Must be reviewed by CPA if contributions $50,000-$125,000.
Audit: Yes, if gross contributions are $125,000 or more.

Rhode Island:
Due Date: Anniversary of initial registration.
Fee: $75
IRS 990: Yes.
Financial Report: Yes
Audit: Yes, if annual gross budget exceeds $500,000.

South Carolina:
Due Date: Within 4 1/2 months of Fiscal Year.
Fee: $50.
IRS 990: Yes.
Financial Report: Yes. May be submitted instead of 990.
Audit: No.

Tennessee:
Due Date: Within 6 months of Fiscal Year end.
Fee: $0-48,999.99: $100; $49,000-$99,999.99: $150; $100,000-$249,999.99: $200; $250,000-$499,999.99: $250; $500,000+: $300
IRS 990: Yes, if revenue between $25,000 and $100,000. Organizations with more than $100,000 in revenue must submit audited financial statements.
Financial Report: Yes, audited statements required when revenue is more than $100,000.
Audit: Yes if gross revenue exceeds $300,000.

Utah:
Utah requires initial registration and annual renewal of registration only.

Virginia:
Due Date: Within 4 1/2 months of Fiscal Year end.
Fee: $30 if revenue less than $25,000; $50 if revenue is $25,000-$50,000; $100 if $50,000-$100,000; $200 if $100,000-$500,000; $250 if $500,000-$1 million; $325 if 1 million or more. ($100 late filing fee)
IRS 990: Yes, or may submit audited financial statement. Certified treasurer's report for proceeds less than $25,000.
Financial Report: Yes.
Audit: Yes if revenue $25,000 or more. This requirement may be fulfilled by filing IRS Form 990.

FORM 990, SCHEDULES A THROUGH R

Washington:
Due Date: Within four months and fifteen
days after Fiscal Year end (state provides an
automatic 6 _ month extension).
Fee: $10.
IRS 990: Yes.
Financial Report: Yes. (WA also requires
the following state form: "Solicitation
Report")
Audit: No.

West Virginia:
Due date: Anniversary of registration.
Fees: $15 if gross revenue is less than $1
million; $50 if gross contributions $1 million
or more.
IRS 990: Yes.
Audit: Yes if contributions exceed $50,000.

Wisconsin:
Due date: 6 months of Fiscal Year end.
Fee: $15
IRS 990: Yes, plus Wisconsin supplement,
Form 1952, or may file Wisconsin form
#308 instead of IRS Form 990.
Financial Report: Yes. If contributions from
Wisconsin amount to more than $5,000
organizations must file either Wisconsin
form #308 or IRS Form 990.
Audit: Yes, if charitable organizations
receive contributions in excess of $100,000,
but increases to $175,000 if $75,000 or more
comes from one contributor.

Checklist for Initial Registrations©
(URS v. 3.10)

	Fee	State Forms	IRS Det. Lttr	FR Contracts	Bylaws	Cert/Arts Inc	Form 990	Audit	Notarized
Alabama	✓		✓		✓	✓			✓
Alaska	✓						✓	✓	
Arizona		✓	✓	✓			✓	✓	✓
Arkansas		✓	✓	✓			✓	✓	✓
California	✓				✓		✓	✓	
Connecticut	✓				✓	✓	✓		
D.C.	✓	✓	✓	✓	✓	✓	✓	✓	✓
Georgia	✓	✓	✓	✓	✓	✓	✓	✓	✓
Illinois	✓		✓				✓	✓	
Kansas	✓		✓			✓	✓	✓	
Kentucky									✓
Louisiana	✓			✓	✓		✓	✓	
Maine	✓		✓					✓	✓
Maryland	✓		✓	✓	✓	✓	✓	✓	
Massachusetts	✓		✓		✓		✓	✓	
Michigan			✓	✓	✓		✓	✓	
Minnesota	✓		✓	✓	✓		✓		
Mississippi	✓	✓	✓	✓			✓	✓	✓
Missouri	✓	See Appendix	✓	✓	✓	✓	✓	✓	✓
New Hampshire	✓	See Appendix	✓		✓	✓	✓	✓	✓
New Jersey	✓		✓	✓	✓	✓	✓	✓	
New Mexico			✓	✓		✓	✓		
New York	✓	See Appendix	✓	See Appendix	✓	✓	✓	✓	
North Carolina	✓	See Appendix	✓	See Appendix		✓	✓		✓
North Dakota	✓	✓	✓	✓		✓	✓		✓
Ohio	✓		✓		✓	✓	✓		
Oregon	✓		✓		✓	✓	✓		
Pennsylvania	✓		✓		✓	✓	✓	✓	
Rhode Island	✓		✓	✓		✓	✓	✓	✓
South Carolina	✓		✓	✓		✓	✓		✓
Tennessee	✓	✓	✓	✓	✓	✓	✓	✓	
Utah	✓	✓	✓	✓	✓		✓		✓
Virginia	✓		✓	✓	✓	✓	✓	✓	
Washington	✓	See Appendix	✓	✓			✓		
West Virginia	✓		✓	✓		✓	✓	✓	✓
Wisconsin	✓		✓		✓		✓	✓	✓

Distribution Sites for Unified Registration Statement (URS)

The listed organizations have each agreed to provide free copies of the current version of the URS and its attachments. Each reserves the right to require reimbursement for its out-of-pocket expenditures for shipping or postage and duplication costs. Check with the respective organization for its requirements.

DMA Nonprofit Federation
1615 L Street NW, Suite 1100
Washington, DC 20036-3603
202-628-4380
nonprofitfederation@the-dma.org
www.nonprofitfederation.org

National Council of Nonprofit Associations
1030 15th St., NW #870
Washington, DC 20005-1525
202-962-0322
www.ncna.org

Association of Fundraising Professionals
Rita Keener, Manager
AFP Fundraising Resource Center
4300 Wilson Blvd #300
Arlington, VA 22203
703-519-8495
Rkeener@afpnet.org

Multi-State Filer Project (MFP)
Robert Tigner, General Counsel
1612 K St., NW #510
Washington, DC 20006-2802
202-463-7980
mfpdc@msn.com

Please also note that the complete URS form and packet can be viewed and downloaded from the Internet at this address:

http://www.multistatefiling.org

APPENDIX 4B: INTERESTED PARTY BY PART AND TYPE

Schedule L
Interested Parties by Part and Organization Type

Organization Type	Part I	Part II	Part III	Part IV
501(c)(3)	B	A & B	D, E, & F	F & G
Supporting Organization	B & C	A, B, & C	D, E, & F	F & G
501(c)(4)	B	A & B	D, E, & F	F & G
Other than 501(c)(3) or (4)	N/A	A	D, E, & F	F & G

Group A	Current or former officers, directors, trustees, key employees, five highest compensated employees
Group B Disqualified persons	Any person during the past 5-year period who was in a position to exercise substantial influence over the affairs of the organization, a member of the family of such person, (C) an entity controlled by such persons by at least 35%, any person mentioned previously who has such a relationship with a supporting organization that supports this organization. If a donor advised fund is involved, disqualified persons also include donors, donor advisors, investment advisors, and their family members or entities controlled by such persons by at least 35%.
Group C Additional DPs for SOs	Substantial contributor, member of the family of such person, and entities controlled by such persons by at least 35%.
Group D Substantial contributor	A person who contributed at least $5,000 during the tax year and is required to be reported in Schedule B for such year.
Group E Related person	A member of the organization's grant selection committee or their family member, a family member of any person in Group D or F, a 35% controlled entity of any of the above individuals, or an employee (or child of an employee) of a substantial contributor or of a 35% controlled entity of a substantial contributor, but only if the person received the grant or assistance by the direction or advice of the substantial contributor or 35% controlled entity, or pursuant to a program funded by the substantial contributor that was intended primarily to benefit such employees (or their children).
Group F	Current or former officers, directors, trustees, key employees
Group G	A family member of a person in Group F, an entity more than 35% owned by members of Group F and/or their family members, an entity (other than a tax-exempt organization under section 501(c)) of which a member of Group F was serving at the time of the transaction as (1) an officer, (2) a director, (3) a trustee, (4) a key employee, (5) a partner or member with an ownership interest in excess of 5% if the entity is treated as a partnership, or (6) a shareholder with an ownership interest in excess of 5% if the entity is a professional corporation.

CHAPTER FIVE

Form 990-T: Exempt Organization Business Income Tax Return

Form **990-T**	**Exempt Organization Business Income Tax Return** (and proxy tax under section 6033(e))	OMB No. 1545-0687
Department of the Treasury Internal Revenue Service	For calendar year 2008 or other tax year beginning ...., 2008, and ending , 20 . ► See separate instructions.	**2008** Open to Public Inspection for 501(c)(3) Organizations Only

Proper preparation of Form 990-T is partly a matter of remembering that an exempt organization is a normal taxpayer subject to all of the federal income tax code provisions applicable to a for-profit taxpayer when it earns income that is unrelated to the accomplishment of its exempt purpose. Careful attention to the rules defining taxable unrelated business income yields a labyrinth of exceptions and modifications that allow a wide range of unrelated income to be excluded from tax and not reported on Form 990-T.

Tax-exempt organizations receive two types of income: earned and unearned. Unearned income—income for which the organization gives nothing in return—comes from grants, membership fees, and voluntary donations. One can think of it as *one-way-street* money. The motivation for giving the money is gratuitous and/or of a nonprofit character with no expectation of gain on the part of the giver. Such gifts are made with intent to donate and are specifically excluded from income tax.[1]

In contrast, an organization furnishes services/goods or invests its capital in return for earned income: an opera is seen, classes are attended, hospital care is provided, or credit counseling is given, for example. The purchasers of the goods and services do intend to receive something in return; they expect the street to be *two-way*. An investment company holding the organization's money expects to have to pay reasonable return for using the funds. In these examples, the organization receives earned income. The important issue this chapter considers is how to report and calculate the tax when earned income, referred to as trade or business income, becomes taxable unrelated business income. The rules that govern how earned income becomes unrelated business income (UBI) are complex. The fact that the business profits are used to pay for programs that accomplish the exempt organization's mission, referred to as the destination of the income, does not create an exclusion from tax. The activity that produces revenue must be connected to the program to be treated as related income—students pay tuition to be educated or people buy tickets to concerts, for example. To understand these rules, it is useful to remember that the rationale for the unrelated business income tax (UBIT) is to eliminate unfair competition that results if a nonprofit organization escapes tax when it conducts the same activity as a for-profit.

Tax planning of the sort practiced by a good businessperson is in order for organizations receiving UBI. The best method for reducing the tax is to keep good records. The accounting system must support the desired allocation of deductions for personnel and facilities with time records, expense usage reports, auto logs, documentation reports, and so on.[2] Minutes of meetings of the board of directors or trustees should reflect discussion of relatedness of any project claimed to accomplish an exempt purpose. Contracts and other documents concerning activities that the organization wants to prove are related to its exempt purposes should contain appropriate language to reflect the project's exempt purposes. An organization's original purposes can be expanded and redefined to broaden the scope of potential activities or to justify some proposed activity as related. Such evolved or expanded purposes can be reported to the IRS to justify the relatedness of a new activity. If loss of exemption[3] is a strong possibility because of the extent and amount of unrelated business activity planned, a separate for-profit organization[4] can be formed to shield the exempt organization from a possible loss of exemption due to excessive business activity.

§5.1 WHAT IS UNRELATED BUSINESS INCOME?

Unrelated business taxable income is defined as the gross income derived from any *unrelated trade or business regularly carried on*, less the *deductions connected* with the carrying on of such trade or business, computed with *modifications and exceptions*.[5] The italicized terms are key to identifying UBI.

A *trade or business* is any activity carried on for the production of income from selling goods or performing services. Accounting theory refers to trade or business income earned by a nonprofit organization as *exchange revenue:* The street is two-way—money is paid, and the organization gives something in return. To identify a trade or business, a "sweat test" can be applied. Purchasing a share of stock or a certificate of deposit to reap a return for allowing someone else to use its assets is not considered to be a trade or business; interest and dividend income is not treated as business income. The concepts identifying income that is taxed as capital gain versus ordinary income to for-profit taxpayers are somewhat analogous. If the nonprofit uses personnel (including volunteers), buys inventory and supplies, and otherwise gets its hands dirty performing services and handling products, a business exists.

An *unrelated trade or business* is defined by the tax code to include any trade or business, the conduct of which is not substantially related (aside from the need of such organization for income or funds or the use it makes of the profits derived) to the exercise or performance by such organization of its charitable, educational, or other purpose or function constituting the basis for its exemption.[6] The most important question is whether the income-producing activity contributes importantly to, aids in accomplishing, or has a nexus to the organization's mission. There are countless examples of activities generating unrelated business income that nonprofit organizations conduct, which are deemed to benefit society and thereby are suitable for a tax-exempt organization. Identifying related activity is not always simple, however, because some nonprofit organizations conduct activities similar to those of for-profit organizations, such as schools, hospitals, theaters, and bookstores. The following list of revenue-producing activities that the IRS has found are related to a nonprofit mission illustrate the concept of relatedness:

- Sale of products made by handicapped workers or trainees[7]
- Sale of educational materials[8]
- Fees for use of college golf course by students and faculty[9]
- Monthly charges for secretarial and telephone answering service that is a training program for indigent and homeless persons[10]
- Revenue from operation of diagnostic health devices, such as computed tomographic scans or magnetic resonance imaging machines by a hospital or health care organization[11]
- Sale of online bibliographic data from central databases[12]

(a)   The Fragmentation Rule

Sometimes, a nonprofit has facilities that are dually used—for activities that embody both an exempt purpose as well as those that are nonexempt or unrelated. Revenue received in an activity that *combines* related and unrelated aspects must be identified, or fragmented, into the respective parts. An activity does not lose its identity as a trade or business merely because it is carried on within a larger group of similar activities that may or may not be related to the exempt purposes of the organization. If dual-use facilities are partly debt financed and partly paid for, the debt-financed income rules might also apply.[13]

Take, for example, a museum shop. The shop itself is clearly a trade or business, often established with a profit motive and operated in a commercial manner. Items sold in such shops, however, often include both educational items, such as books and reproductions of art works, and souvenirs. The fragmentation rule requires that all items sold be analyzed to identify:

- The educational, or related, items (the profit from which is not taxable)
- The unrelated souvenir items that do produce taxable income

The standards applied to identify museum objects as related or unrelated are well documented in IRS rulings.[14]

(b)   Consequences of Receiving Unrelated Income

There are several potentially unpleasant consequences of earning unrelated business income.

(i) *Payment of Unrelated Income Tax.* Unrelated net income may be taxed at corporate or trust rates with estimated tax payments required as discussed later in this chapter. Social clubs, homeowner associations, and political organizations also pay the UBI tax on certain passive investment income in addition to the unrelated business income.

(ii) *Exempt Status Revocation.* A nonprofit organization can run a business as a significant part of its activities, but not as its primary purpose.[15] Thus, its tax-exempt status could be revoked and all of its net income taxed, if the unrelated business activity is found to be its primary activity. As a rule, the tax code requires a nonprofit organization to be both organized and operated exclusively for an exempt purpose, although *exclusively* does not mean 100 percent.[16] In evaluating the amount of unrelated business activity that is permissible, not only the amount of gross revenue, but other factors as well, may be taken into consideration. Nonrevenue aspects of the activity, such as staff time devoted or value of donated services, are factors that might be determinative. The basic issue is whether the operation of the business subsumes, or is inconsistent with, the organization's exempt activities.

A complex of nonexempt activity caused the IRS to revoke the exemption of the Orange County Agricultural Society.[17] Its UBI averaged between 29 and 34 percent of its gross revenue. Private inurement was also found because the Society was doing business with its board of directors. In another context, the IRS privately ruled that a 50–50 ratio of related to unrelated income was permitted for a day care center raising funds from travel tours.[18] An organization with unrelated income in excess of 15 to 20 percent of its gross revenue must be prepared to defend its exempt status.

(iii) *Excess Business Holdings.* A private foundation may not operate a business and is limited in the ownership percentage it can hold in a separate business entity.[19]

§ 5.2 EXCEPTIONS AND MODIFICATIONS FROM TAX

The concepts of UBI are vague and contain many exceptions that have been carved out by special interest groups to allow nonprofit organizations to generate revenue free of tax. The exceptions and modifications are outlined below.

(a) The Irregular Exception

Profits from a business conducted irregularly are excluded from tax. A business is *regularly carried on* if it is operated with a frequency and continuity comparable to for-profit entities that conduct the same trade or business. Operation of a sandwich stand at the annual county fair is an example of a periodic and discontinuous business. A café that is open daily, by comparison, is a regular activity. A five-day antique show is an irregular business when compared to an antique store open five days each week. Taxpayers and the IRS argue about whether the preparation time involved in conducting a revenue-raising activity must be counted in measuring the irregular factor. Year-round sales efforts for ads in a labor organization's yearbook, in the IRS's eyes, meant the activity was regularly carried on. The facts indicated that the yearbook had relevance to the members throughout the year and "the vast majority of advertisements carried a definitely commercial message."[20]

(b) The Volunteer Exception

Any business in which substantially all the work is performed without compensation is excluded from UBI. *Substantially*, for this purpose, means at least 80 to 85 percent of the total work performed, measured normally by the total hours worked. A paid manager or executive, administrative personnel, and all sorts of support staff can manage the business if most of the work is performed by volunteers. This rule is one of the reasons that the countless boxes of candy, coupon books, and other items sold by school children to raise funds for parent-teacher organizations do not result in un-related business income to the school or PTA.

In most cases, the number of hours worked, rather than relative value of the work, is used to measure the percent test. This means that the value of volunteer time need not necessarily be quantified for comparison to monetary compensation paid. In the case of a group of volunteer singing doctors, the value of the doctors' time was considered. Because the doctors were the stars of the records producing the income, their time was counted by the court at a premium, which offset administrative personnel whose time was compensated modestly.[21] Having 77 percent of its labor donated by volunteers, however, was not enough to allow a bingo operation to avail itself of this exception. The 23 percent compensated workforce ratio was substantial enough to cause the Elks Lodge to pay tax on its bingo profits.[22]

Expense reimbursements, in-kind benefits, and prizes are treated as compensation if they are compensatory in nature. In the case that expense reimbursements enable the volunteers to work longer hours and serve the convenience of the organization, the payments need not be counted in measuring this exception. However, solicitors for a religious organization that traveled in vans and lived a "very Spartan life" were not unpaid volunteers, as the organization had claimed, because their livelihood was provided for by the organization. Similarly, when food, lodging, and other living expenses were furnished to sustain members of a religious group, the members working for the group's businesses were not treated as volunteers.[23]

(c) The Donated Goods Exception

The selling of merchandise, substantially all of which is received by the nonprofit as donations, is not treated as a taxable activity. Thrift and resale shops selling donated goods are afforded a special exception from UBI for donated goods they sell. A shop selling goods on consignment as well as donated goods must distinguish between the two types of goods. Under the fragmentation rules,[24] the consigned good sales would be separated, or fragmented, from the donated goods and any net profit from those sales included in UBI. Consignment sales by volunteer-run resale shops might be excluded under the volunteer exception.

(d) The Convenience Exception

For §501(c)(3) organizations only, a cafeteria, bookstore, residence, or similar facility used in the organization's programs and operated for the convenience of patients, visitors, employees, or students is specifically excepted from UBI.[25] The rationale for this exception says recovery of patients is hastened when family and friends visit or stay with them in the hospital, and the cafeteria facilitates the visits. Museum visitors can spend more time viewing art if they can stop to rest their feet and have a cup of coffee. When the café, shop, dorm, or parking lot is also open to the general public, the revenue produced by public use is unrelated income. It is thought by some that the whole facility becomes subject to UBIT if the facility's entrance is on a public street. At best, the income from a facility used by both qualified visitors and the disinterested public off the street is fragmented. The taxable and nontaxable revenue is identified and tabulated, and the net taxable portion is calculated under the dual-use rules.[26]

(e) The Passive Income Modification

For all §501(c) organizations other than social clubs (7), voluntary employee benefit associations (9), supplemental unemployment plans (17), and group legal service plans (20), specified types of investment income are modified, or excluded, from UBI unless the underlying property is subject to debt. IRC §512(b) excludes "all dividends, interest, royalties, rents, payments with respect to security loans, and annuities, and all deductions connected with such income." Passive income of a sort not specifically listed is not necessarily modified or excluded from UBI. Amounts distributed to a tax-exempt organization from a partnership retain their character as either nontaxable passive or active business taxable income. Distributions from a subchapter S corporation, however, are fully taxed with no modifications available.

Dividends and interest paid on amounts invested in savings accounts, certificates of deposit, money market accounts, bonds, loans, preferred or common stocks, payments in respect to security loans, annuities, and the net of any allocable deductions are excluded from UBI.

Rental income is considered a passive type of investment income that is modified (excluded) from unrelated business income, except:

- Personal property rentals are taxable unless they are rented incidentally (not more than 10 percent of rent) with real property.

- A fluctuating rental agreement that calculates the rent based on net profits from the property is unrelated income (however, rent based upon gross revenue is *not* UBI).

- When substantial services are rendered in connection with rentals, such as a theater complete with staff or a hotel room complete with room service, the rental is not considered passive.[27]

Royalties, whether measured by production or by the gross or taxable income from a property, are modified.[28] The fact that the term *royalties* is not defined under the Code or regulations pertaining to unrelated income has caused significant controversy. The IRS insisted that a royalty must be received in an activity that is passive in order to qualify. The Tax Court instead found that a royalty paid for the use of intangible property rights can be modified, or not taxed. The battle focused on licensing of mailing lists, exempt organization logos, and associated issuance of affinity cards; the IRS conceded defeat in December 1999.[29] Income from an oil and gas working interest, for which the exempt organization is responsible for its share of development costs, is not modified or excluded from UBI.[30]

Research income is generally excluded from UBI unless the work is performed for private for-profit purposes, such as drug testing for a pharmaceutical company. Research conducted for the federal government and its agencies, states, municipalities, and their subdivisions is excluded from UBI. Fundamental research (and in practice applied research), the results of which are made available to the general public, are also excluded.[31] Research of all types conducted by a college, university, or hospital is excluded.

Gains from the sale, exchange, or other disposition of property is classified as UBI dependent upon the character of the property sold. Generally, the normal income tax rules of §§1221 and 1231 for identifying capital versus ordinary income property apply to identify property covered by this exception. Sales of stock in trade or other inventory-type property, or of property held for sale to customers in the ordinary course of a trade or business, produces UBI. Net capital loss from the sale or other disposition of assets used in an unrelated trade, business, or debt-financed property is not allowed to offset other UBI reported by a tax-exempt corporation. An exempt trust, however, can deduct a $3,000 net capital loss. Form 4797 is attached to Form 990-T to report sales of business property.

Social clubs can possibly achieve a tax-free sale of club property if another site is acquired within one year before, or three years after, a sale.[32] There is an exception to the general rule that a club is taxed on all of its investment income: Some clubs choose *not* to seek tax-exempt status in order to offset club activity losses against investment income. Care must be exercised in converting a club from tax-exempt to for-profit status. Appreciation inherent in the club's assets—often substantial—is taxed upon conversion to a for-profit status.[33]

For-profit subsidiary payments in the form of rent, interest, royalties, or other deductible expenses are not eligible to be modified and are instead taxable to a tax-exempt parent that owns more than 50 percent (by vote or value) of the subsidiary stock, partnership, or other beneficial interest.

Other special exceptions to classification as an unrelated business are provided in the tax code for public fairs and conventions, bingo games permitted under state law, certain low-cost articles distributed in connection with a fund-raising campaign, and exchanges of certain mailing lists.

§ 5.3   UNRELATED DEBT-FINANCED INCOME

The modifications exempting passive investment income, such as dividends and interest, from the UBIT do not apply to the extent that the investment is made with borrowed funds, called *acquisition indebtedness*. Debt-financed property is defined as including property held for the production of income that was acquired or improved with borrowed funds and has a balance of acquisition indebtedness attributable to it during the year.[34] The classic examples are a margin account held against the nonprofit's endowment funds or a mortgage financing the purchase of a rental building.

(a)   Properties Subject to Debt-Financed Rules

Real or other tangible or intangible property used 85 percent or more of the time it is actually devoted to and actually used directly in the organization's exempt or related activities is exempt from these rules.[35] Assume that a hospital borrows money and builds an office tower for its projected staff needs over a 20-year period. If less than 85 percent of the building is used by its staff and a net profit is earned, the non–hospital-use portion of the building income is unrelated business income. Special exceptions apply for schools.[36]

Income included in UBI for some other reason, such as hotel room rentals or a 100 percent–owned subsidiary's royalties, is specifically excluded by the code and is not counted twice because the property is debt financed.[37] Conversely, an indebted property used in an unrelated activity that is excluded from UBI because it is managed by volunteers, is for the convenience of members, or is a facility for sale of donated goods, is not treated as unrelated debt-financed property.[38] Research property producing income otherwise excluded from the UBIT is not subject to the acquisition indebtedness taint.

Future-use land (not including buildings) acquired and held by a nonprofit for use within 10 years (churches get 15 years) from the date it is acquired, and located in the *neighborhood* in which the organization conducts a program, is exempt from this provision. This exception applies until the plans are abandoned; after five years, the organization's plans for use must be "reasonably certain."[39]

The tax status of the tenant or user is not determinative. Rental of an indebted medical office building used by staff physicians can be related to a hospital's purposes.[40] Although their restoration served a charitable purpose, the rental of restored historic properties to private tenants was deemed not to serve an exempt purpose where the properties were not open to the public.[41] Regulations suggest that all facts and circumstances of property usage will be considered.

Although investment of a pension fund is admittedly inherent in its exempt purposes, debt-financed investments made by such a fund (or most other exempt organizations) are not inherent in a fund's purposes.[42] For that reason, the Southwest Texas Electric Cooperative's purchase of Treasury notes with Rural Electrification Administration (REA) loan proceeds represented a debt-financed investment. Though the loan proceeds had to be used to pay construction costs, the cooperative's cash flow allowed it to pay part of the construction costs with operating funds. To take advantage of a more than 4 percent spread in the REA loan and prevailing Treasury note rates, the cooperative deliberately "drew down" on the REA loan. The Tax Court agreed with the IRS that the interest income was taxable debt-financed income.[43]

Indebted property producing no recurrent annual income, but held to produce appreciation in underlying value, or capital gain, is subject to this rule.[44] A look-back rule prevents deliberate payoff prior to sale to avoid the tax. The portion of the taxable gain is calculated using the highest amount of indebtedness during the 12 months preceding the sale as the numerator.[45]

Schools and their supporting organizations, certain pension trusts, and §501(c)(25) title holding companies may have a special exception for indebted real property. If the property is purchased in a partnership with for-profit investors, profit-and-loss–sharing ratios must have substantial economic effect and not violate the disproportionate allocation rules.[46]

(b) Acquisition Indebtedness

Acquisition indebtedness is the unpaid amount of any debt incurred to purchase or improve property or any debt "reasonably foreseen" at the time of acquisition that would not have been incurred otherwise.[47] Securities purchased on margin are debt financed; payments on loans of securities already owned are not. The formula for calculation of income subject to tax is:

$$\frac{\text{Income from property} \times \text{Average acquisition indebtedness}}{\text{Average adjusted basis}}$$

The average acquisition indebtedness equals the arithmetic average of each month or partial month of the tax year. The average adjusted basis is calculated by averaging the adjusted basis on the first and last tax day of the year, and only straight-line depreciation is allowed. The proportion-of-use test applied to identify property used for exempt and nonexempt purposes can be based on a comparison of the number of days used for exempt purposes with the total time the property is used, on the basis of square footage used for each, or on relative costs.[48]

Debt placed on property by a donor (prior to donating) will be attributed to the organization only when the exempt organization agrees to pay all or part of the debt or makes any payments on the equity.[49] Property that is encumbered and subject to existing debt at the time it is received by bequest is not treated as acquisition-indebted property for 10 years from its acquisition if there is no assumption or obligation to pay the debt by the organization. Gifted property subject to debt is similarly excluded, if the donor placed the mortgage on the property over five years prior to gift and had owned the property over five years, unless there is an assumption or payment on the mortgage by the nonprofit. A life estate does not constitute a debt. When some other individual or organization is entitled to income from the property for life or another period of time, a remainder interest in the property is not considered to be indebted.[50]

Federal funding provided or insured by the Federal Housing Administration, if used to finance purchase, construction, or rehabilitation of residential property for low-income persons, is excluded.

Charitable gift annuities issued as the sole consideration in exchange for property worth more than 90 percent of the value of the annuity is not considered acquisition indebtedness. The annuity must be payable over the life (not for a minimum or maximum number of payments) of one or two persons alive at the time. The annuity must not be measured by the property's (or any other property's) income.

(c) Calculation of Taxable Portion

Only that portion of the net income of debt-financed property attributable to the debt is classified as UBI.[51] Each property subject to debt is calculated separately, with the resulting income or loss netted to arrive at the portion to include in UBI. A planning opportunity arises for an organization that intends to buy a dual-use building. The nontaxable exempt function portion of the property could purposefully be purchased with debt and the unrelated part of the facility purchased with cash available. Or separate notes could be executed, with the taxable and unrelated property's debt being paid off first. Expenses directly connected with the property are deducted from gross revenue in the same proportion. The formula for calculating capital gain or loss is different in one respect than in the one used above: The highest amount of indebtedness during the year preceding sales is used as the numerator. The formula can be better understood by studying Schedule E of Form 990-T.

§ 5.4 WHO FILES FORM 990-T?

All domestic and foreign nonprofits, including churches, state colleges and universities, trusts, individual retirement accounts, medical savings plans, and other tax-exempt organizations not required to file Forms 990, must file Form 990-T illustrated later in § 5.7. This Exempt Organization Business Income Tax Return[52] is filed to report gross income from UBI over $1,000 that is not excluded for one of the reasons outlined in Chapter 5.2.[53] Gross income for this purpose means gross receipts less cost of goods sold but before reduction for selling and administrative expenses. The tax on UBI applies to all organizations exempt from tax under §501(c) other than corporations created by an act of Congress and municipalities of the government. It also applies to:

- Tax-exempt employee trusts described in IRC §401, including individual retirement accounts
- State and municipal colleges and universities and the corporations they own
- Qualified state tuition programs described in IRC §529
- Education individual retirement accounts described in IRC §530 and medical savings accounts described in IRC §220(d)

Since 1989, Form 990 has identified revenues according to their character as related, unrelated but subject to an exclusion or modification, and taxable unrelated revenue.[54] Unrelated business income that is subject to tax is reported in Core Part VIII, column C, giving the IRS a red flag indicating that Form 990-T must be filed. Correspondingly, it is important to coordinate amounts reported on the 990-T with Column C of Core Part VIII. The front page of the Core Form 990 now reflects the gross unrelated revenue and the net taxable amount on line 7 and in addition, Question 3a of Core Part V has a check box if $1,000 or more of UBI was received during the year), so that the IRS is alerted as to when to expect the tax to be paid.

§5.5 DUE DATES, TAX RATES, AND OTHER FILING ISSUES

(a) Due Date

Most Forms 990-T are due to be filed on the same day as the other Forms 990—the 15th day of the 5th month following the close of the organization's fiscal year (it used to be the third month). Trusts, employee trusts, and IRAs file by the 15th day of the 4th month following the close of the organization's fiscal year. Nonprofits that are corporations may obtain an automatic six-month extension of this time to file by submitting Form 8868, "Application for Extension of Time to File an Exempt Organization Return." Others (usually trusts) also use Form 8868, to obtain an automatic three-month extension but must also file the second page of Form 8868 to obtain an additional (not automatic) three-month extension. The extension of time to file does not allow an extension of time to pay any tax due.

(b) Payment of Tax

The tax liability is paid in advance through the quarterly estimated tax system if the annual tax is in excess of $500. Estimated tax deposits are due the 15th day of the 5th, 6th, 9th, and 12th month of the tax year. Payments are made either using Form 8109, "Federal Tax Deposit Coupon," or through electronic funds transfer.[55] Exempt organization taxpayers with taxable income of $1 million or more must use the actual method and pay tax for its 2nd through 4th quarters based on actual income earned for the year, rather than basing the payment on the prior year. The tax rates applicable to nonexempt corporations and trusts are applied to calculate the tax.

Although the impact may be reduced by the charitable deduction (using §170 individual limitations), the significantly higher tax rate imposed on trusts reflects a need for good planning by a tax-exempt trust. For this reason, such a trust might create a for-profit subsidiary from which to conduct unrelated business activity. See Appendix 5A for an analysis of the differences between trusts and corporations for 990-T purposes. Affiliated exempt organizations that are commonly controlled corporations must combine their incomes. The 15 percent bracket applies only to the first $50,000 of their combined income; the 25 percent applies to the next $25,000, and so on. The affiliates can apportion the tax brackets among themselves as they please, or they can share the lower brackets equally.[56] An apportionment plan must be signed by all members and attached to their Form 990-T.

(c) Credits and Alternative Minimum Tax

Because an exempt organization earning UBI is taxed just like for-profit corporations and trusts, the general business and foreign tax credits and alternative minimum taxes (AMT) may apply.[57] The AMT was repealed (effective 1998) for corporations with average gross receipts of $5 million or less for the past three years. A discussion of these tax rules is beyond the scope of this book; a prudent organization should seek the help of competent consultants in this regard.

(d) Proxy Tax

Expenses of attempts to influence legislation—lobbying—are not deductible in arriving at taxable income. A civic association, labor union, or business league that has lobbying activity has a choice of either informing its members of the portion of their dues so expended or paying a tax of 35 percent of its lobbying expenses.[58] The amount of the proxy tax is reported on a single line in the tax calculation on Part III of Form 990-T.

(e) Interest and Penalties

Several different charges are imposed when a return is filed late. The failure-to-file penalty of 5 percent of the tax due per month the return is late (up to a maximum of 25 percent) is imposed,[59] unless the organization can show reasonable cause for the delay. In the authors' experience, the Ogden Service Center is often lenient toward first-time filers who voluntarily submit Forms 990-T and pay the tax. The IRS, however, has suggested penalties should be more frequently imposed in the future. For the late filing and paying penalties to be abated, the failure to file cannot be due to willful neglect; ordinary business care and prudence must have been used to ascertain the requirement.[60] An explanation seeking abatement should be attached to the return requesting relief and explaining why the return was filed late, particularly if the organization regularly engages independent accountants who failed to advise it of its obligation to do so. Late receipt of an unexpected Form K-1 might be a good excuse. Next, a penalty of 0.5 percent of the unpaid tax may be assessed for failure to pay (that is, an annual rate of 6 percent up to a maximum of 25 percent of the amount due). Additionally, a penalty may be due for failure to pay the tax in advance through the estimated tax system described above. Form 2220 is used to calculate this penalty, which is assessed on a daily basis at the prevailing federal rate.

(f) Statute of Limitations

The statute of limitations for assessment of the unrelated business income tax on Form 990-T is three years and begins when the 990 contains sufficient facts (shown in Part VII) from which the UBIT can be determined.[61] Say, for example, an organization lists an amount for shop sales on its year 2005 Form 990, Part VII, column D, identifying it with the #2 exclusion code as being run by volunteers. Assume the IRS examines the organization in 2008 and finds, in their opinion, that less than the requisite 85 percent of labor was provided by volunteers. If the organization acted in good faith without intent to defraud the IRS or evade tax, tax cannot be assessed for returns filed before 2005. Note that substantial underpayment penalties might be assessed for the open years.[62]

(g) Why File to Report Losses

Form 990-T is due to be filed when gross income exceeds $1,000, even when the deductions an organization is entitled to claim result in a loss from the unrelated business activity. The statute of limitations for IRS examination of the issue begins to toll, and net operating losses can be carried over for up to 20 years to offset net unrelated income in subsequent years. An operating loss may also be carried back by filing an amended Form 990-T for the two immediately preceding tax years if income tax was paid.

(h) Consolidated Returns

As a rule, each nonprofit organization is required to file its own separate Form 990, except for subordinate members included in a group return.[63] A consolidated Form 990-T can be filed if (1) the 80 percent control requirements of IRC §1504 are satisfied, (2) all members are tax exempt under §501(a), (3) at least one member of the group is a title-holding company, and (4) all other members of the group are entitled to receive income from the title-holding company.

(i) Refund Claim

Payers of dividends, interest, and other types of income must do backup withholding of income tax if Form W-9 is not furnished in order to indicate that no tax withholding is required by them. A tax-exempt organization files Form 990-T to claim a refund for any such tax. A tax-exempt organization investing in a regulated investment company might also have had some taxes paid by the company on its behalf for which it can claim a tax credit on Form 990-T.

§5.6 NORMAL INCOME TAX RULES APPLY

(a) Accounting Methods and Periods

Taxable income is calculated using the method of accounting regularly used in keeping the exempt organization's books and records.[64] Organizations with more than $5 million of annual gross receipts must use the accrual method for reporting taxable income.[65] Also, an organization selling merchandise or goods that are accounted for piece by piece must maintain inventory records and also use the accrual method.[66] Any change in method results in *§481 adjustments*. Form 3115 is filed to seek permission for the change and to spread the effect of the change over five years (from the effective date of the change).[67]

(b) "Ordinary and Necessary" Criteria

Deductions claimed against the unrelated income must be "ordinary and necessary" in conducting the activity and must meet the other standards of IRC §162 for business deductions. *Ordinary* means common and accepted for the type of business operated; *necessary* means helpful and appropriate, and not indispensable. Ordinary does not necessarily mean required, but can mean appropriate or customary. Thus, an organization can deduct expenses commonly claimed by commercial businesses operating similar businesses.[68]

(c) Profit Motive

For an expenditure to be deductible, the motivation for making it must be the production of income. The activity must be operated for the purpose of making a profit to be considered a business.[69] IRC §183 specifically prohibits the deduction of hobby losses, or those activities losing money for more than two years out of every five. In the social club arena, the IRS and the clubs battled for several years over the deductibility of nonmember activity losses against investment income. Ultimately, the clubs lost. The exploitation rule[70] disallows the deduction of related activity expenses against UBI, partly because exempt activities are not conducted with a profit motive.

(d) Depreciation

Equipment, buildings, vehicles, furniture, and other properties that are used in the business are deductible over their useful lives through the depreciation system. As a simple example, one-third of the cost of a computer that is expected to become obsolete within three years is deductible each year for three years. Unfortunately, Congress uses these calculation rates and methods as political and economic tools, and the revenue code prescribes rates and methods that are not simple. IRC §§167, 168, and 179 apply and must be studied to properly calculate allowable deductions for depreciation.

(e) Inventory

If the organization keeps an inventory of items for sale, such as books, drugs, or merchandise of any sort, it must use an inventory method to deduct the cost of such goods. The concept is one of matching the cost of the item sold with its sales proceeds. If the organization buys 10 widgets for sale and at the end of a year only five have been sold, the cost of the five is deductible and the remaining five are capitalized as an asset to be deducted when in fact they are sold. Again, the system is far more complicated than this simple example, and an accountant should be consulted to ensure use of proper reporting and tabulation methods. IRC §§263A and 471 through 474 apply.

(f) Capital and Nondeductibles

A host of nondeductible items contained in §§261 through 280H might apply to disallow deductions either by total disallowance or required capitalization of permanent assets. Again, all the rules applicable to for-profit businesses apply, such as the luxury automobile limits, travel and entertainment substantiation requirements, and 50 percent disallowance for meals.

(g) Dividend Deduction

The dividends-received deductions provided by §§243 through 245 for taxable non-exempt corporations are not allowed. Normal corporations are allowed to exclude 70 percent of their investment dividends; exempt organizations are not. Note that this rule presents a problem only for dividends received from investments that are debt financed and thereby taxable. Most dividends received by exempts are excluded from the UBI under the *Modifications* for passive income.[71] For certain thinly capitalized subsidiaries, IRC §163(j) can remove the passive income exception.

(h) Charitable Deduction

Up to 10 percent of an exempt corporation's and 20 to 50 percent of a trust's unrelated taxable income, before the deduction, is deductible for contributions paid to another charitable organization.[72] Note that the deduction is not allowed for an organization's internal project expenditures or gifts to a controlled subsidiary. In addition, similar to the substantiation rules for individuals, the organization must have a contemporaneous receipt from the donee acknowledging any donation of $250 or more in order to claim a deduction for such donation. Contributions in excess of allowable amounts are eligible for a five-year carryover. Social clubs, voluntary employee business associations, unemployment benefit trusts, and group legal service plans can take a 100 percent deduction for direct charitable gifts and qualified set-asides for charitable purposes.[73]

(i) Net Operating Losses

A net operating loss (NOL) can be applied to offset income on which income tax was paid for the two tax years preceding the loss by filing a carryback claim. The preferable way to file a carryback claim is to amend Form 990-T for each prior year to which the loss can be carried to offset income previously reported. The instructions direct the preparer to consult IRS Publication 536, which pertains to individual NOLs. Apparently since both nonprofit corporations and trusts file the 990-T, there is no form prescribed particularly for nonprofit organizations. The IRS technical assistors in Cincinnati say there is no specific guidance on this issue. Any remaining losses can be carried forward to offset net income for 20 years following the loss year.[74] Thus, it can be important for an exempt to file Form 990-T to establish a loss potentially available to offset future income.

§5.7 THE UNIQUE DESIGN OF THE 990-T

Form 990-T has evolved over the years to accommodate the unique fashion in which deductions against certain types of income are claimed. The sequence of lines is somewhat different from other tax forms with special schedules for rentals, debt-financed UBI, payments from controlled subsidiaries, exploited exempt activities, and advertising. The form is designed to enforce the general concept that no portion of the organization's underlying mission-related expenses is deductible.

Form 990-T

Exempt Organization Business Income Tax Return
(and proxy tax under section 6033(e))

OMB No. 1545-0687

2008

Department of the Treasury
Internal Revenue Service

For calendar year 2008 or other tax year beginning ...., 2008, and ending ...., 20 .... ► See separate instructions.

Open to Public Inspection for 501(c)(3) Organizations Only

A ☐ Check box if address changed

Name of organization (☐ Check box if name changed and see instructions.)

B Exempt under section
☐ 501( )( )
☐ 408(e) ☐ 220(e)
☐ 408A ☐ 530(a)
☐ 529(a)

Print or Type

Number, street, and room or suite no. If a P.O. box, see page 9 of instructions.

City or town, state, and ZIP code

D Employer identification number
(Employees' trust, see instructions for Block D on page 9.)

E Unrelated business activity codes
(See instructions for Block E on page 9.)

C Book value of all assets at end of year

F Group exemption number (See instructions for Block F on page 9.) ►

G Check organization type ► ☐ 501(c) corporation ☐ 501(c) trust ☐ 401(a) trust ☐ Other trust

H Describe the organization's primary unrelated business activity. ►

I During the tax year, was the corporation a subsidiary in an affiliated group or a parent-subsidiary controlled group? ► ☐ Yes ☐ No
If "Yes," enter the name and identifying number of the parent corporation. ►

J The books are in care of ► _____ Telephone number ► ( )

Part I   **Unrelated Trade or Business Income**

			(A) Income	(B) Expenses	(C) Net
1a	Gross receipts or sales				
b	Less returns and allowances _____ **c** Balance ►	**1c**			
2	Cost of goods sold (Schedule A, line 7)	**2**			
3	Gross profit. Subtract line 2 from line 1c	**3**			
4a	Capital gain net income (attach Schedule D)	**4a**			
b	Net gain (loss) (Form 4797, Part II, line 17) (attach Form 4797)	**4b**			
c	Capital loss deduction for trusts	**4c**			
5	Income (loss) from partnerships and S corporations (attach statement)	**5**			
6	Rent income (Schedule C)	**6**			
7	Unrelated debt-financed income (Schedule E)	**7**			
8	Interest, annuities, royalties, and rents from controlled organizations (Schedule F)	**8**			
9	Investment income of a section 501(c)(7), (9), or (17) organization (Schedule G)	**9**			
10	Exploited exempt activity income (Schedule I)	**10**			
11	Advertising income (Schedule J)	**11**			
12	Other income (See page 11 of the instructions; attach schedule.)	**12**			
13	**Total.** Combine lines 3 through 12	**13**			

Part II   **Deductions Not Taken Elsewhere** (See page 11 of the instructions for limitations on deductions.)
(Except for contributions, deductions must be directly connected with the unrelated business income.)

14	Compensation of officers, directors, and trustees (Schedule K)	**14**	
15	Salaries and wages	**15**	
16	Repairs and maintenance	**16**	
17	Bad debts	**17**	
18	Interest (attach schedule)	**18**	
19	Taxes and licenses	**19**	
20	Charitable contributions (See page 13 of the instructions for limitation rules.)	**20**	
21	Depreciation (attach Form 4562)	**21**	
22	Less depreciation claimed on Schedule A and elsewhere on return	**22a**	**22b**
23	Depletion	**23**	
24	Contributions to deferred compensation plans	**24**	
25	Employee benefit programs	**25**	
26	Excess exempt expenses (Schedule I)	**26**	
27	Excess readership costs (Schedule J)	**27**	
28	Other deductions (attach schedule)	**28**	
29	**Total deductions.** Add lines 14 through 28	**29**	
30	Unrelated business taxable income before net operating loss deduction. Subtract line 29 from line 13	**30**	
31	Net operating loss deduction (limited to the amount on line 30)	**31**	
32	Unrelated business taxable income before specific deduction. Subtract line 31 from line 30	**32**	
33	Specific deduction (Generally $1,000, but see line 33 instructions for exceptions.)	**33**	
34	**Unrelated business taxable income.** Subtract line 33 from line 32. If line 33 is greater than line 32, enter the smaller of zero or line 32	**34**	

For Privacy Act and Paperwork Reduction Act Notice, see instructions.   Cat. No. 11291J   Form **990-T** (2008)

FORM 990-T: EXEMPT ORGANIZATION BUSINESS INCOME TAX RETURN

Part III　Tax Computation

35	**Organizations Taxable as Corporations.** See instructions for tax computation on page 15. Controlled group members (sections 1561 and 1563) check here ▶ ☐ **See instructions** and:			
a	Enter your share of the $50,000, $25,000, and $9,925,000 taxable income brackets (in that order): **(1)** $\|\ \ \ \ \ \ \|$　**(2)** $\|\ \ \ \ \ \ \|$　**(3)** $\|\ \ \ \ \ \ \|$			
b	Enter organization's share of: **(1)** Additional 5% tax (not more than $11,750)　$\|\ \ \ \ \ \|$			
	(2) Additional 3% tax (not more than $100,000) . . . . $\|\ \ \ \ \ \|$			
c	Income tax on the amount on line 34 . . . . ▶	35c		
36	**Trusts Taxable at Trust Rates.** See instructions for tax computation on page 16. Income tax on the amount on line 34 from: ☐ Tax rate schedule or ☐ Schedule D (Form 1041) . . . ▶	36		
37	**Proxy tax.** See page 16 of the instructions . . . . ▶	37		
38	Alternative minimum tax	38		
39	**Total.** Add lines 37 and 38 to line 35c or 36, whichever applies	39		

Part IV　Tax and Payments

40a	Foreign tax credit (corporations attach Form 1118; trusts attach Form 1116) .	40a			
b	Other credits (see page 17 of the instructions)	40b			
c	General business credit. Check here and indicate which forms are attached: ☐ Form 3800　☐ Form(s) (specify) ▶	40c			
d	Credit for prior year minimum tax (attach Form 8801 or 8827)	40d			
e	**Total credits.** Add lines 40a through 40d		40e		
41	Subtract line 40e from line 39		41		
42	Other taxes. Check if from: ☐ Form 4255 ☐ Form 8611 ☐ Form 8697 ☐ Form 8866 ☐ Other (attach schedule)		42		
43	**Total tax.** Add lines 41 and 42		43		
44a	Payments: A 2007 overpayment credited to 2008	44a			
b	2008 estimated tax payments	44b			
c	Tax deposited with Form 8868	44c			
d	Foreign organizations: Tax paid or withheld at source (see instructions) .	44d			
e	Backup withholding (see instructions)	44e			
f	Other credits and payments: ☐ Form 2439 _____ ☐ Form 4136 _____ ☐ Other _____ Total ▶	44f			
45	**Total payments.** Add lines 44a through 44f		45		
46	Estimated tax penalty (see page 4 of the instructions). Check if Form 2220 is attached . ▶ ☐		46		
47	**Tax due.** If line 45 is less than the total of lines 43 and 46, enter amount owed . . . . ▶		47		
48	**Overpayment.** If line 45 is larger than the total of lines 43 and 46, enter amount overpaid . . ▶		48		
49	Enter the amount of line 48 you want: **Credited to 2009 estimated tax ▶** 　　Refunded ▶		49		

Part V　Statements Regarding Certain Activities and Other Information (see instructions on page 18)

		Yes	No
1	At any time during the 2008 calendar year, did the organization have an interest in or a signature or other authority over a financial account (bank, securities, or other) in a foreign country? If YES, the organization may have to file Form TD F 90-22.1, Report of Foreign Bank and Financial Accounts. If YES, enter the name of the foreign country here ▶		
2	During the tax year, did the organization receive a distribution from, or was it the grantor of, or transferor to, a foreign trust? . If YES, see page 5 of the instructions for other forms the organization may have to file.		
3	Enter the amount of tax-exempt interest received or accrued during the tax year ▶ $		

Schedule A—Cost of Goods Sold. Enter method of inventory valuation ▶

1	Inventory at beginning of year	1			6	Inventory at end of year	6		
2	Purchases	2			7	**Cost of goods sold.** Subtract line 6 from line 5. Enter here and in Part I, line 2	7		
3	Cost of labor	3							
4a	Additional section 263A costs (attach schedule)	4a							
					8	Do the rules of section 263A (with respect to property produced or acquired for resale) apply to the organization?		Yes	No
b	Other costs (attach schedule)	4b							
5	**Total.** Add lines 1 through 4b	5							

Sign Here

Under penalties of perjury, I declare that I have examined this return, including accompanying schedules and statements, and to the best of my knowledge and belief, it is true, correct, and complete. Declaration of preparer (other than taxpayer) is based on all information of which preparer has any knowledge.

▶ _____ ▶ _____

Signature of officer　　　　　　Date　　　Title

May the IRS discuss this return with the preparer shown below (see instructions)? ☐ Yes ☐ No

Paid Preparer's Use Only	Preparer's signature ▶		Date	Check if self-employed ☐	Preparer's SSN or PTIN
	Firm's name (or yours if self-employed), address, and ZIP code ▶			EIN	
				Phone no. ( )	

Form **990-T** (2008)

Schedule C—Rent Income (From Real Property and Personal Property Leased With Real Property)
(see instructions on page 19)

1 Description of property

(1)

(2)

(3)

(4)

2 Rent received or accrued		**3(a)** Deductions directly connected with the income in columns 2(a) and 2(b) (attach schedule)
(a) From personal property (if the percentage of rent for personal property is more than 10% but not more than 50%)	**(b)** From real and personal property (if the percentage of rent for personal property exceeds 50% or if the rent is based on profit or income)	
(1)		
(2)		
(3)		
(4)		
Total	Total	

(c) Total income. Add totals of columns 2(a) and 2(b). Enter here and on page 1, Part I, line 6, column (A) . . . ▶

(b) Total deductions.
Enter here and on page 1,
Part I, line 6, column (B) ▶

Schedule E—Unrelated Debt-Financed Income (see instructions on page 19)

1 Description of debt-financed property	**2** Gross income from or allocable to debt-financed property	**3** Deductions directly connected with or allocable to debt-financed property	
		(a) Straight line depreciation (attach schedule)	**(b)** Other deductions (attach schedule)
(1)			
(2)			
(3)			
(4)			

4 Amount of average acquisition debt on or allocable to debt-financed property (attach schedule)	**5** Average adjusted basis of or allocable to debt-financed property (attach schedule)	**6** Column 4 divided by column 5	**7** Gross income reportable (column 2 × column 6)	**8** Allocable deductions (column 6 × total of columns 3(a) and 3(b))
(1)		%		
(2)		%		
(3)		%		
(4)		%		
			Enter here and on page 1, Part I, line 7, column (A).	Enter here and on page 1, Part I, line 7, column (B).

Totals . . . . ▶

Total dividends-received deductions included in column 8 . . . . ▶

Schedule F—Interest, Annuities, Royalties, and Rents From Controlled Organizations (see instructions on page 20)

		Exempt Controlled Organizations			
1 Name of controlled organization	**2** Employer identification number	**3** Net unrelated income (loss) (see instructions)	**4** Total of specified payments made	**5** Part of column 4 that is included in the controlling organization's gross income	**6** Deductions directly connected with income in column 5
(1)					
(2)					
(3)					
(4)					

Nonexempt Controlled Organizations

7 Taxable Income	**8** Net unrelated income (loss) (see instructions)	**9** Total of specified payments made	**10** Part of column 9 that is included in the controlling organization's gross income	**11** Deductions directly connected with income in column 10
(1)				
(2)				
(3)				
(4)				
			Add columns 5 and 10. Enter here and on page 1, Part I, line 8, column (A).	Add columns 6 and 11. Enter here and on page 1, Part I, line 8, column (B).

Totals . . . . ▶

Form **990-T** (2008)

FORM 990-T: EXEMPT ORGANIZATION BUSINESS INCOME TAX RETURN

Schedule G—Investment Income of a Section 501(c)(7), (9), or (17) Organization (see instructions on page 21)

1 Description of income	2 Amount of income	3 Deductions directly connected (attach schedule)	4 Set-asides (attach schedule)	5 Total deductions and set-asides (col. 3 plus col. 4)
(1)				
(2)				
(3)				
(4)				
Totals ▶	Enter here and on page 1, Part I, line 9, column (A).			Enter here and on page 1, Part I, line 9, column (B).

Schedule I—Exploited Exempt Activity Income, Other Than Advertising Income (see instructions on page 21)

1 Description of exploited activity	2 Gross unrelated business income from trade or business	3 Expenses directly connected with production of unrelated business income	4 Net income (loss) from unrelated trade or business (column 2 minus column 3). If a gain, compute cols. 5 through 7.	5 Gross income from activity that is not unrelated business income	6 Expenses attributable to column 5	7 Excess exempt expenses (column 6 minus column 5, but not more than column 4).
(1)						
(2)						
(3)						
(4)						
Totals ▶	Enter here and on page 1, Part I, line 10, col. (A).	Enter here and on page 1, Part I, line 10, col. (B).				Enter here and on page 1, Part II, line 26.

Schedule J—Advertising Income (see instructions on page 21)

Part I   Income From Periodicals Reported on a Consolidated Basis

1 Name of periodical	2 Gross advertising income	3 Direct advertising costs	4 Advertising gain or (loss) (col. 2 minus col. 3). If a gain, compute cols. 5 through 7.	5 Circulation income	6 Readership costs	7 Excess readership costs (column 6 minus column 5, but not more than column 4).
(1)						
(2)						
(3)						
(4)						
Totals (carry to Part II, line (5)) ▶						

Part II   Income From Periodicals Reported on a Separate Basis (For each periodical listed in Part II, fill in columns 2 through 7 on a line-by-line basis.)

1 Name of periodical	2 Gross advertising income	3 Direct advertising costs	4 Advertising gain or (loss) (col. 2 minus col. 3). If a gain, compute cols. 5 through 7.	5 Circulation income	6 Readership costs	7 Excess readership costs (column 6 minus column 5, but not more than column 4).
(1)						
(2)						
(3)						
(4)						
(5) **Totals from Part I**						
Totals, Part II (lines 1-5) ▶	Enter here and on page 1, Part I, line 11, col. (A).	Enter here and on page 1, Part I, line 11, col. (B).				Enter here and on page 1, Part II, line 27.

Schedule K—Compensation of Officers, Directors, and Trustees (see instructions on page 22)

1 Name	2 Title	3 Percent of time devoted to business	4 Compensation attributable to unrelated business
		%	
		%	
		%	
		%	
Total. Enter here and on page 1, Part II, line 14 . . . ▶			

Part I of Form 990-T contains a column to present the direct expenses alongside gross income, for which supporting schedules are completed. This display is said to reflect an IRS intention to evaluate deductible expenses. However, for line 1 income, the direct expenses other than cost of goods sold are deducted in Part II and may cause some confusion, particularly in relation to lines called Excess Exempt and Excess

Readership Expenses. The suggestions for this part will therefore be presented according to the various types of UBI, rather than line by line. For Form 990 and 990-PF filers, line 13 should generally equal the total on line 15, column (b) of Form 990-T.

(a) Part II, Deductions Not Taken Elsewhere

On Form 990-T, expenses are deducted either in Part I or Part II, not due to the nature of particular types of expenses, but strictly according to the form's design and the type of income. As the title implies, allocable expenses not deducted in Part I are claimed here. The IRS instructions for this part contain guidance for preparation. Modest organizations whose gross unrelated income does not exceed $10,000 need not play the line game; the total UBI expense is entered on line 29.

Helpful schedules designed to apply the different limitations for certain types of deductions flow into both Parts I and II and serve the following functions:

- Schedule A reports cost of goods sold for those organizations required to maintain inventories. There is no Schedule B or H.

- Schedule C calculates the portion of taxable personal property rentals.

- Schedule D calculates capital gain attributable to UBI. This is not contained within the body of Form 990-T. The Schedule D used by a taxable corporation (or trust) is used.

- Schedule E calculates the taxable portion of revenue attributable to debt-financed income.

- Schedule F calculates the taxable portion of revenue from controlled subsidiaries.

- Schedule G calculates the taxable income of social clubs, voluntary employee benefit associations, and supplemental employee benefit trusts setting aside part of their income for charitable purposes.

- Schedule I applies a deduction limitation for unrelated income exploited from an exempt activity, such as green fees paid by nonstudents to play on a school's golf course or commissions for nonmember insurance.

- Schedule J applies the deduction limitations and income allocations necessary to arrive at taxable advertising revenue.

- Schedule K reports officer, director, and trustee compensation attributable to unrelated business income.

§5.8 CATEGORIES OF DEDUCTIONS

The complexity of Form 990-T goes beyond the task of understanding the income tax system. Exempt organizations, in their efforts to raise funds, have devised creative methods to make money by utilizing their tangible and intangible assets and their staff. In the words of the regulations, such money-making schemes "exploit" the organization's exempt functions. People and things can be mingled and used for both exempt and income-producing purposes. Whatever method is used to arrive at the deductible expenses, including overhead or general and administrative costs, the method must not permit the amalgamation of for-profit and nonprofit activities.[75] If followed consistently from year to year, an organization can apply the method it uses for financial statement purposes as a reasonable basis for claiming UBI deductions. Regarding joint costs, the accounting profession says, "The cost allocation methodology used should be rational and systematic, it should result in an allocation of joint costs that is reasonable, and it should be applied consistently given similar facts and circumstances."[76] The UBI sections of the code "do not specifically address how expenses are to be allocated when exempt organizations are computing their UBI."[77] The regulations provide three specific types of deductible expenses.[78]

- Type 1: Expenses attributable solely to unrelated business activities
- Type 2: Dual-use property or project expenses
- Type 3: Exploited activity expenses

(a) Type 1

Expenses attributable solely to unrelated business activities are fully deductible.[79] Such expenses are those reasonably allocable under good accounting theory consistently applied using a method that evidences their connection with the production of unrelated gross income.[80] Two classic business expense deduction concepts are applied:

1. A "proximate and primary relationship" between the expense and the activity is the standard for deduction.[81] Proximate means near, close, or immediate, such as the full-time personnel devoted solely to the business.

2. A "but for" test can be applied by asking the question, "Would the expense be incurred if the unrelated activity was not carried on?"

(b) Type 2

A portion of dual-use or shared employees, facilities, equipment, and other overhead expenses is also deductible. Shared costs are allocated between related and unrelated activities on a reasonable basis. The only example given in the IRS regulations allocates 10 percent of an organization president's salary to the business activity to which he devotes 10 percent of his time.[82] This type of allocation presents a classic chicken-and-egg or tail-wagging-the-dog situation. Is the UBI activity an afterthought, or was a facility built to be dually used? When the exempt activity would be carried on regardless of the UBI funds and essentially came first, the exploitation rule (Type 3) rather than the dual-use type of expense allocation applies. A mailing list developed and maintained for a symphonic society's ticket sales instead might be dual-use property.

It is sometimes difficult to decide whether the Type 2 or 3 category should apply. It is important to note in making this choice that the exploitation method often yields a higher level of expense deduction. Conceivably, 100 percent of an exploited activity's expenses are allocable to the unrelated income, but subject to an income limitation. As discussed later, to make cost allocations, the denominator of the formulas can significantly influence the result.

(c) Type 3

The third type is an allocated portion of a program-related or exempt function activity's expense that produces income from an unrelated aspect (such as the sale of advertising), and is said to exploit the exempt activity. Under specific conditions that depend on the character of the exploited activity, the deduction of exempt function cost is allowed but may be limited by the income generated. The general rule is expressed negatively and disallows such deductions because they are not considered to have a proximate and primary relationship to the revenue. Nonetheless, to the extent of the revenue earned, a portion of this Type 3 expense is deductible. The deductible portion of a Type 3 expense is calculated through a series of steps in Schedules I and J of Form 990-T that do not allow a loss from an exploited activity to be deducted. To compute UBI, no expense attributable to the conduct of the exempt activity is deductible, except in specified circumstances and with limitation.[83] To be deductible, all three conditions must be satisfied:

- *Condition 1:* The unrelated trade or business activity is of a kind carried on for profit by taxable organizations, and the exempt activity exploited by the business is a type of activity normally conducted by taxable organizations in pursuance of such business.

- *Condition 2:* Expenses, depreciation, and similar items attributable to the exempt activity exceed the income (if any) derived from or attributable to the exempt activity.

- *Condition 3:* The allocation of such expenses to the unrelated trade or business activity does not result in a loss from such unrelated trade or business activity.[84]

Fundraising activity in pursuit of voluntary contributions is a good example of a revenue activity that is not normally considered businesslike.[85] Generally, the cost of maintaining an organization's contributor or member lists is not deductible against the proceeds of sales of the list. The IRS says the regulation "is somewhat helpful in trying to decide whether the sale of a mailing list is a dual related/unrelated use or an exploitation of an exempt function."[86] The IRS admits that there seems to be "a significant question of whether exempt function expenses that exceed exempt function income may be deducted."

Type 3 (exploitation) deductions can be financially valuable. Essentially, program service costs, also known as exempt function costs, of an inherently businesslike exempt activity can be deducted for UBI purposes, despite the general rule that they cannot be. When the allocation is permitted, the organization essentially earns tax-free income to cover its exempt function costs. Treating expenses as a Type 3 may result in a higher deduction than a Type 2 that allows for only a calculated portion of the exempt function costs. Type 2 (dual-use) expenses may be advantageous in some circumstances because the Type 3 allocable expense must first be reduced by exempt function revenue. Also, a loss deductible against other UBI cannot result from Type 3 expenses,[87] whereas a dual-use facility loss may be deducted against other types of UBI.

Publications are less troublesome. The rules anticipate that periodicals are businesslike, and the exploited activity costs can be deducted.[88] A framework for allocating exempt function, or readership, costs against the advertising revenue is reported on Schedule J. Reportable income is calculated in two parts. First, any advertising revenue is offset by the direct cost of producing, selling, and presenting the ads in the publication. Second, revenue from the direct sale of the publication plus an imputed portion of member dues, if any, is tallied and offset by other costs referred to as *readership costs*.

Advertising revenue produces UBI. An advertisement contains words printed or aired to recognize a sponsor that are "qualitative and quantitative."[89] Words like "XYZ is the best" or "buy XYZ products" taint the revenue. Recognition of business sponsors with a listing of their name, address (including their Internet address without a link), and logo is not treated as an advertisement. The standard is rather broad and has been established by sponsor recognition allowed on public television and radio by the Federal Communication Commission. The sponsorship regulations add other types of advertising revenue. Revenue received for permitting exclusive distribution of a company's products to an organization's participants is also deemed to be taxed under the proposed regulations. The exploitation method is used to allocate and report expenses attributable to this sort of revenue, and in the authors' opinion such revenue may be reported in either Part I or Part J of Form 990-T, dependent on whether a publication is involved.

Sales of merchandise or products, scientific research, health care service, and many other categories of revenue production are conducted by both tax-exempts and for-profit businesses. Some activities, such as education and cultural performances (dance and theater), are conducted primarily by exempts but also by businesses, and technically qualify under Condition 1.

§ 5.9 COST ALLOCATIONS

The UBI code sections "do not specifically address how a dual-use or exploited expense is to be allocated when exempt organizations are computing UBI."[90] The IRS Manual instructs examining agents that any reasonable method resulting in identifying relationship of the expenses to revenue produced is acceptable.[91] Different allocation methods are available, but once a method is chosen it must be consistently followed from year to year and for all purposes.[92] The choice of method depends on the organization's complexity and the nature of its activities. The AICPA (American Institute of Certified Public Accountants) and the NACUBO (National Association of College and University Business Officers), in response to the time spent and controversies resulting from IRS examinations, suggest the adoption of standards of cost allocations for UBI purposes.

The IRS has prescribed the fashion in which a §501(c)(4), (5), or (6) organization allocates its expenses to compute the cost of its lobbying activity.[93] Two simplified methods—a direct gross-up of labor costs (take total salaries and add 175 percent for indirect costs) and a ratio method (take total costs and allocate them based on number of hours personnel spend on various functions)—are suggested in addition to the complex rules of IRC §263A. Those rules should be carefully studied as a harbinger of future IRS rules. The AICPA Tax Exempt Organizations Resource Panel and the NACUBO have suggested that this sort of guidance be issued. Whatever method an exempt organization chooses to follow to allocate costs, the method should clearly reflect the economic realities of the organization and the UBI it receives, and should be evidenced by suitable documentation. Actual time records must be maintained by all personnel and professional advisors to reflect the effort devoted to related versus unrelated activities. Absent time records, an allocation based on relative gross income produced might be used. Direct and indirect expenses must be distinguished.

Direct expenses are those that increase proportionately with the usage of a facility or the volume of activity, and are also called *variable expenses*. For example, the number of persons attending an event influences the number of ushers or security guards and represents a direct cost, or, in other words, a cost attributable to that specific use that would not have been incurred *but for* the particular event. *Indirect costs* are incurred without regard to usage or frequency of participation, and are also called *fixed expenses*. An organization's building acquisition costs or annual audit fees, for example, do not necessarily vary with usage. Management and general expenses are normally of this character.

A *gross income method* of cost allocation is sometimes used to calculate cost of goods sold when costs bear a relationship to the revenue produced from exempt and nonexempt factors. The regulations say, "Such allocations based on receipts from exempt activities may not be reasonable since such receipts are not normally reflective of cost."[94]

A proration based on the number of participants might be suitable in some circumstances. This type of formula is used in calculating allocations for social clubs charging different prices to members and nonmembers. The hours a facility is used might be applied. The proper denominator of the fraction used to calculate costs allocable to UBI is also significant in reducing or increasing allowable deductions. Arguably, no fixed costs of a property used for exempt purposes should be allocated to UBI, but to date the courts have allowed allocation among both the exempt and nonexempt functions that benefit from building use. In a football stadium case, for example, the court allowed the following:[95]

$$\frac{\text{Number of hours or days used for unrelated purposes}}{\text{Total number of hours or days in use}}$$

The IRS argued that fixed costs were allocated (produces a much smaller number) by:

$$\frac{\text{Number of hours or days used for unrelated purposes}}{\text{Total number of hours or days in entire year}}$$

The IRS has said it prefers a system that allocates costs to all activities similar to a generally accepted accounting principles (GAAP) functional expense statement. One commentator suggests reference to the foreign tax credit allocation rules for guidance in allocating dual-use facility costs.[96] Take, for example, a hospital pharmacy. A portion of the revenue is generated from sales to patients and is considered as related income. The nonpatient sales are instead classified as unrelated income. The objective is to assign the expenses of the pharmacy operation to the appropriate category of revenue. The easy way is to apportion the expenses using the relative percentages of related and unrelated revenue. Revenue, however, can be dissected and leveled for market and other differences. If the patient sales, for example, are made at a 20 percent discount below that of the amount charged over the counter, patient sales would be grossed back up, or the nonpatient revenue discounted, before calculating the ratio. This example follows the fragmentation rules, which require that unrelated sales be segregated from related sales in an activity that embodies both. Readers should be alert to developments on this topic.

§ 5.10 IN-KIND DONATIONS

Three different types of in-kind donations are quantified and reported as revenue and corresponding expense by tax-exempt nonprofits—donated services, facility use, and material goods. Statement of Financial Accounting Standards (SFAS) No. 116 contains specific standards for valuing and reporting such gifts.[97] Donations of the first two types are not reported for Form 990 purposes,[98] presumably to remind taxpayers that donations of services and facilities are not deductible. Tangible goods, however, are reported and may be deductible.[99]

Donated services and use of facilities (as well as tangible goods), in the authors' opinion, are reportable as deductions for UBI purposes. This tax planning opportunity can be significant. Booking the in-kind donations does not produce taxable gross income if they are voluntary gifts not subject to income tax.[100] The corresponding expense, to the extent that it is directly associated with or can be partly allocated to an unrelated business activity, can result in alleviating UBIT.

NOTES

1. IRC §102.
2. Discussed in Chapter 1.3.
3. Discussed in Chapter 5.1(b).
4. See J. Blazek, *Tax Planning and Compliance* (Hoboken, N.J.: John Wiley & Sons, 2008), Ch. 22, "Relationships with Other Organizations and Businesses."
5. IRC §512(a)(1).
6. IRC §513(a); Reg. §1.513–1(b). The term is defined in reference to IRC §162.
7. Rev. Rul. 73–128, 1973–1, C.B. 222; Priv. Ltr. Rul. 9152039.
8. See Blazek, *Tax Planning and Compliance*, Ch. 21.15, for a compendium of factors to use in determining when a publication program will be considered a business.
9. Usage by spouses, alumni, and donors was not considered as related in Priv. Ltr. Rul. 9645004.
10. IRS Priv. Ltr. Rul. 9009038.
11. IRS Priv. Ltr. Rul. 9017028.
12. Discussed in Chapter 5.3.
13. Rev. Ruls. 73–104 and 105, 1973–1 C.B. 258–265; Priv. Ltr. Ruls. 8303013, 8326003, 8236008, and 8328009 and Tech. Adv. Memo. 9550003.
14. Reg. §1.501(c)(3)-1(e)(1).
15. See Chapter 2.
16. *Orange County Agricultural Soc'y, Inc. v. Commissioner*, 90.1 USTC ¶50.076 (2d Cir. 1990), aff'g 55 T.C.M. 1602 (1988).
17. IRS Priv. Ltr. Rul. 9521004.
18. See Blazek, *Tax Planning and Compliance*, Ch. 16, for rules defining impermissible excess business holdings for private foundations.
19. IRS Priv. Ltr. Rul. 9304001; see also Priv. Ltr. Rul. 9417003; *Suffolk County Patrolmen's Benevolent Ass'n Inc. v. Commissioner*, 77 T.C. 1314 (1981), acq. 1984–1 C.B. 2; and *National College Athletic Ass'n v. Commissioner*, 914 F.2d 1417 (10th Cir. 1990).

20. *Greene County Med. Society Found. v. United States*, 345 F. Supp. 900 (W. D. Mo. 1972).
21. *Waco Lodge No. 166, Benevolent & Protective Order of Elks v. Commissioner*, T. C. Memo. 1981–546, aff'd per curiam, 696 F.2d 372 (5th Cir. 1983).
22. *Shiloh Youth Revival Ctrs. v. Commissioner*, 88 T.C. 579 (1987).
23. Discussed in Chapter 5.1(a).
24. IRC §513(a)(2).
25. Discussed in Chapter 5.9.
26. While agreeing there was some educational benefit from the site, a museum renting its exhibition halls for private receptions provided substantial services to its tenants that caused the usage fees to be unrelated income in Priv. Ltr. Rul. 9702003.
27. IRC §512(b)(2).
28. *Sierra Club v. Commissioner*, T. C. Memo. 1999–86 on remand from the 9th Circuit Court; *Planned Parenthood Federation of America v. Commissioner*, T. C. Memo. 1999–206 (June 1999); *Texas Farm Bureau v. United States*, 53 F.3rd 120 (5th Cir. 1995).
29. Reg. §1.512(b)-1(b).
30. IRC §512(b)(7); Priv. Ltr. Rul. 7924009.
31. See Blazek, *Tax Planning and Compliance*, Ch. 21.10(b), for a consideration of the special rules attributable to sales of social club properties.
32. Reg. §1.337(d)-4.
33. IRC §514.
34. Reg. §1.514(b)-1.
35. IRC §514(c)(9).
36. Reg. §1.514(b)-1(b)(2)(ii).
37. IRC §514(b)(1)(B) and (C).
38. IRC §514(b)(3)(A)-(E).
39. Reg. §1.514(b)-1(c)(1); Rev. Rul. 69–464, 19969–2 C. B. 132; Tech. Adv. Memo. 8906003.
40. Rev. Rul. 77–47, 1977–1 C. B. 156; Tech. Adv. Memo. 9017003.
41. §514(c)(4); *Elliot Knitwear Profit Sharing Plan v. Commissioner*, 71 T. C. 765 (1979), aff'd, 614 F.2d 347 (3d Cir. 1980).
42. *Southwest Tex. Electric Coop., Inc. v. Commissioner*, 68 T. M. Dec. 50,008(M), T. C. Memo. 1994–363.
43. Reg. §1.514(b)-1(a).
44. Reg. §1.514(a)-1(a)(1)(v).
45. IRC §§168(h)(6), 514(c)(9), and 704(b)(2); Reg. §1.514(c)-2.
46. IRC §514(c).
47. Reg. §1.514(b)-1(b)(ii), §1.512(b)-1(b)(iii), Example 2; Priv. Ltr. Ruls. 8030105 and 8145087.
48. Reg. §1.514(c)-1(b).
49. Reg. §1.514(b)-1(c)(3).
50. IRC §514(a)(1).
51. See Appendix 5A.
52. Reg. §1.6012–2(e); Reg. §1.61–3.
53. See 2008 Core Part VIII and 2007 Form 990, Part VII.
54. The depositing method used is the same as the organization's payroll tax payment method.
55. Reg. §1.1561–3(b).
56. IRC §§27, 28, 29, 38–44, 51, 55–59, and 59A.
57. IRC §6033(e)(2); see Blazek, *Tax Planning and Compliance*, Ch. 6, §4, for a discussion of alternative methods of allocating an organization's administrative costs to lobbying activities.
58. IRC §6651. When the return is delinquent over 60 days, the minimum tax for failure to file is the smaller of the actual tax or $100.
59. Reg. §301.6651–1(c) explains the acceptable excuses.

60. Rev. Rul. 69–247,1969–1 C. B. 303, modifying Rev. Rul. 62–10,1962–1 C. B. 305 and reflecting the Tax Court decision in *California Thoroughbred Breeders Ass'n*, 47 T. C. 335, Dec. 28, 225 (acq).
61. IRC §6662.
62. Discussed in Chapter 1.2(e).
63. IRC §446(a).
64. IRC §448(c).
65. IRC §§263A and 471.
66. Rules pertaining to seeking approval for a change in method are presented in Chapter 6, §4.
67. See Chapter 2 for discussion of accounting terms and expense allocation issues.
68. IRC §162; Reg. §1.512(a)-1(b); *Iowa State Univ. of Science & Tech. v. United States*, n. 51; *Commissioner v. Groetzinger*, 480 U.S. 23 (1987); Reg. §1.513–1(4)(d)(iii); *Portland Golf Club v. Commissioner*, 497 U.S. 154 (1990).
69. See discussion later for Type 3 expenses.
70. IRC §512(b).
71. IRC §512(b)(10 and 11).
72. IRC §§170(b)(2), 512(a)(3)(B)(i), and 642(c).
73. IRC §172(b).
74. *Iowa State University of Science and Technology v. Portland Golf Club v. Commissioner*, 110 S. Ct. 2780, 500 F.2d 508 (Ct. Cl. 1974).
75. Statement of Position 98–2, Accounting for Costs of Activities of Not-for-Profit Organizations and State and Local Governmental Entities That Include Fund Raising, issued March 11, 1998, as an amendment to the AICPA Audit and Accounting Guide.
76. 1991 Exempt Organizations Continuing Professional Education Technical Instruction Program, at page 20.
77. Reg. 1.512(a)-1.
78. 121 IRC §512(a)(1); Reg. §1.512(a)-1(b).
79. *Iowa State Univ. of Science and Tech. v. United States*, 500 F.2d 508 (Ct. Cl. 1974).
80. Reg. §1.512(a)-1(a).
81. Reg. §1.512(a)-1(c).
82. Reg. §1.512(a)-1(d)(1).
83. Reg. §1.512(a)-1(d)(2).
84. Reg. §1.513–1(c)(iii) says, "Income derived from the conduct of an annual dance or similar fund-raising event for charity would not be income from trade or business regularly carried on." In *United States v. American Bar Endowment*, 477 U.S. 105 (1986), an insurance sales program, the profit (which reportedly was dependent on member generosity) was determined to be a taxable business, not a fund-raising effort. The "donated" portion of the member premium was not voluntary, and the program was conducted with the intention of producing a profit. Note that because of this decision, the ABA's total cost in relation to the insurance program would be deductible.
85. 1992 Exempt Organizations Continuing Professional Education Technical Instruction Program (published annually and ordered from the IRS Reading Room in Washington, DC, or the IRS Web site), at 74, in discussion of the example found in Reg. §1.512(a)-1(e).
86. Reg. §1.512(a)-1(d)(1); *West Va. Med. Ass'n v. Commissioner*, 882 F.2d 123 (4th Cir. 1989).
87. Reg. §1.512(a)-1(f).
88. Prop. Reg. §513–4(c)(1) and (2); readers should be alert for new developments.
89. 1991 Exempt Organizations Continuing Professional Education Technical Instruction Program, at page 20.
90. *Exempt Organizations Examination Guidelines Handbook, Internal Revenue Manual*, §720(7).
91. *Portland Golf Club*, supra n.112.
92. Reg. §1.162–28.

93. Reg. §1.512(a)-1(f)(6).

94. *Rensselaer Polytechnic Institute v. Commissioner*, 732 F.2d 1058 (2d Cir. 1984), aff'g 79 T. C. 967 (1982).

95. Special report of L. Kalish, "Allocation of Expenses—Foreign Solution," *Exempt Organization Tax Review* (Feb. 1995): 283.

96. See Blazek, *Tax Planning and Compliance*, Ch. 27.3(b).

97. There is no published precedent for this position. An IRS exempt organization specialist's informal opinion was that there could be no deduction because no cash changed hands. There are several precedents in the tax code for imputed income. Under IRC §482, income can be allocated between related companies, essentially on paper. Interest income is imputed to certain below-market rate loans under IRC §7872. Although the analogy is not perfect (because it is not an exchange transaction in which the exempt organization earns its side of the donated services), the value of goods or services received in a barter transaction is reportable income as outlined in IRS Publication 525, "Taxable and Nontaxable Income."

98. IRC §170(e).

99. IRC §102.

APPENDIX 5A: ANALYSIS OF CORPORATION VERSUS TRUST 990-T ISSUES

<u>Analysis of Form 990-T Issues</u>

	Corporation	**Trust**
Form 8868	One automatic 6 month extension. *See IRC Reg. 1.6081-9(a).*	One automatic 3 month extension and one additional 3 month extension. *See IRC Reg. 1.6081-9(a).*
Contribution deduction	10% of taxable income. *See IRC 170(b)(2)(A) and 512(b)(10).*	20-50% of taxable income. *See IRC 512(b)(11) and IRC 170(b)(1)(A) and (B).*
Unused contribution carryover	Allowed to be carried forward for five years. *See IRC 170(d)(2)(A).*	Allowed to be carried forward for five years. *See IRC 512(b)(11) and IRC 170(b)(1)(B).*
Capital loss deduction	Deduction for capital losses limited to capital gains. The loss can be carried back three years and forward five years. *See IRC 1212(a)(1).*	Allowed a deduction for capital losses up to $3,000. Any remaining losses are carried forward indefinitely until used up. *See IRC 1211(b) and 1212(b)(1).*
Net operating loss deduction	The loss can be carried back two years and forward for twenty years. *See IRC 172(b)(1)(A).*	The loss can be carried back two years and forward for twenty years. *See IRC 172(b)(1)(A).*
2007 Tax rates on ordinary income	<$50,000 (15%) 50,000-75,000 (25%) 75,000-100,000 (34%) 100,000-335,000 (39%) 335,000-10,000,000 (34%) 10,000,000-15,000,000 (35%) 15,000,000-18,333,333 (38%) 18,333,333 + (35%) *See IRC 511(a)(1) and IRC 11(b).*	< $2,150 (15%) 2,150-5,000 (25%) 5,000-7,650 (28%) 7,650-10,450 (33%) 10,450 + (35%) *See IRC 511(b)(1) and IRC 1(e)(2).*
2007 Tax rates on long term capital gains	Same as above.	If the trust's overall taxable income puts it in the 15% tax bracket, capital gains are taxed at 5%. Otherwise, capital gains are taxed at 15%. *See IRC 1(h)(1)(B) & (C).*
Required to provide preparer's identification number on Form 990-T	Yes. *See IRC 6109(a)(4) and 6696(e)(1).*	Yes. *See IRC 6109(a)(4) and 6696(e)(1).*

CHAPTER SIX

The Private Foundation Return

Form **990-PF**	**Return of Private Foundation** or Section 4947(a)(1) Nonexempt Charitable Trust Treated as a Private Foundation	OMB No. 1545-0052
Department of the Treasury Internal Revenue Service	**Note.** The foundation may be able to use a copy of this return to satisfy state reporting requirements.	2008

In addition to reporting financial activity for the year, the 13-page Form 990-PF enables the IRS to evaluate a private foundation's compliance with the special sanctions and limitations on activities of foundations. The significance the IRS places on Form 990-PF is indicated by the fact that all private foundations, even those with few, if any, assets, are technically required to file the form annually. Equally important, private foundations, just like public charities, are required to make the form available for inspection by anyone who asks to see it or is willing to pay for a copy of the return. The returns are posted on the Internet site of Guidestar.org. Additionally, the form must be furnished to any and all states in which the foundation is registered or qualified to operate. Therefore this chapter is devoted to explaining part by part and, sometimes, line by line the why and how of completing this important form.[1]

Readers should watch for a revised Form 990-PF by 2010 or 2011 following the format of the significant Form 990 revisions. The authors were commissioned by Foundation Financial Officers Group to redesign the Form 990-PF in 2006.

§ 6.1 SUCCESSFUL COMPLETION OF FORM 990-PF

Before one can successfully prepare Form 990-PF, the definitions of the following terms must be understood:

- *Private foundation:* A nonprofit organization qualifying as an IRC §501(c)(3) organization that does not meet the definitions for public charities in IRC §509(a) (1),(2), or (3) outlined in Chapter 4.1.

- *Disqualified person:* A substantial contributor, a foundation manager, owners of more than 20 percent of a business owned by a substantial contributor, a family member of those three persons (spouse, children, spouses of children, grandchildren, ancestors, but not siblings or aunts and uncles), and a corporation or partnership owned more than 35 percent by a disqualified person. Financial transactions between the foundation and its disqualified persons are generally prohibited by the self-dealing rules.

- *Substantial contributor:* A person who has donated an aggregate amount of more than 2 percent of the total contributions and bequests received by the private foundation before the close of the year, or $5,000, whichever is higher. Once one becomes a disqualified person, he or she remains so forever as a general rule.

- *Foundation manager:* A director, trustee, officer, or other individual having similar powers or responsibilities are the foundation's managers. Managers have authority to make administrative and policy decisions; for public charities, these persons are also called *key employees.*

- *Self-dealing:* A private foundation is not allowed to have financial transactions with its disqualified persons. Even if the transaction benefits the foundation— say the founder sells property worth $1 million to the foundation for $100,000—it is prohibited. Disqualified persons can be paid reasonable compensation for the services they render for the foundation and, with limitations, a foundation can share office space and personnel. If any money changes hands between the foundation and its disqualified persons, IRC §4941 should be very carefully studied.[2]

- *Mandatory payout:* IRC §4942 requires that a private foundation make grants for charitable and administrative purposes that equal at least 5 percent of the fair market value of its investment assets for the past year, less any excess distributions carried over from a prior year.

- *Taxable expenditure:* A private foundation is penalized under IRC §4945 if it makes an expenditure for noncharitable purposes, for lobbying or electioneering, for scholarship grants (unless prior IRS plan approval is in place), and certain grants to other private or foreign organizations.[3]

- *Jeopardizing investments:* A foundation's managers are penalized under IRC §4944 if the foundation's assets are invested in a fashion that violates the prudent investor rules. Purchasing stocks on margin and buying and selling puts and calls are among the examples provided in the regulations that were written in 1972 and have not been updated for contemporary investing practices.[4]

- *Excess business holdings:* A private foundation, when its holdings are combined with those of its disqualified persons, may not own more than 20 percent of a business—whether it is a corporation, partnership, or investment trust. Excess holdings that are acquired by gift can be disposed of over a five-year period. Purchased holdings creating an excess are taxed under IRC §4943 and must be disposed of immediately.[5]

Form 990-PF is designed to accomplish a number of purposes. First, the basic financial information—the revenues, disbursements, assets, and liabilities—is classified into meaningful categories to allow the IRS to statistically evaluate the scope and type of foundation activity, to measure the foundation's taxable investment income, and to tally those disbursements counted in meeting the foundation's 5 percent payout requirement. Second, the form has special parts with information and questions that fish for failures to comply with the federal requirements for maintenance of tax-exempt status for private foundations. The issues addressed by the information presented include, among many others, matters such as:

- Are the officers' salaries reported in Part VIII reasonable in relation to the foundation's resources and scope of activity, and if not, has prohibited self-dealing occurred?

- Does Part XIII or Part XIV show that the foundation has made the required amount of qualifying distributions by the end of the year?

- Is the foundation required to pay its investment income tax in quarterly installments because the liability shown in Part VI exceeds $500? Or must the foundation calculate its excise tax liability on a quarterly basis because its net investment income during one of the past three years exceeded $1 million?

- Does the difference between the book value and the fair market value of the assets reported in Part II indicate that the foundation may have made jeopardizing investments?

- Do the programs described in Part IX-A constitute direct charitable activity? For a private operating foundation, do the descriptions indicate that the programs are directly carried out by the foundation? Or, similarly, do the program-related investments described in Part IX-B serve a charitable purpose?

Respective parts of Form 990-PF appear as each part is discussed and illustrate the depth and girth of information provided with the form. The instructions for the 2008 Form 990-PF alone are 32 pages long and exemplify the complexity of reporting and compliance requirements for a private foundation.[6]

Form 990-PF has evolved over the past 40 years as the law of private foundations has developed, retaining original concepts and adding new ones. Certain interdependent calculations do not follow in logical order. The most efficient order in which to prepare the form is the following:

Order in Which Form 990-PF Must Be Completed

1. Part IV	8. Part XIII, lines 1–4
2. Parts I & II	9. Parts V & VI
3. Heading	10. Part XII, lines 5–6
4. Part III	11. Part XI
5. Part VII-A	12. Part XIII
6. Part VIII	13. Part VII-B
7. Parts IX-A—X	14. Parts XIV-XVII

§ 6.2   THE PART I COLUMNS

Part I of Form 990-PF may be the most challenging and difficult part because some discretion is involved in presenting the information, particularly the expenses. The instructions for this part, in a very helpful fashion, begin by informing the preparer that the three right-hand columns may not necessarily equal the total amount of expenses shown in the leftmost column. Each column in Part I serves a different purpose in the IRS regulatory scheme for private foundations. Deciding what goes where, and why, is not a logical process. Different accounting methods are used for reporting information in the columns, and some items are included in more than one column, while others are not. A good accounting system, which applies the concepts presented in Chapter 2 is critical to the accurate preparation of this part.

(a) Column (a): Revenue and Expenses per Books

This column agrees with the financial reports prepared for the board and for public dissemination by the organization, except that in-kind contributions of services or the use of property or facilities are not included. Either the cash or accrual method of accounting is permitted following the system regularly used to prepare financial statements for other purposes. While the change is essentially automatic, Form 3115 must be filed to seek IRS approval for changing the tax reporting method from either a cash to an accrual basis or vice versa. A foundation that adopts the accounting literature set out in Statement of Financial Accounting Standard (SFAS) No. 116 for reporting contributions received and paid out need not seek permission for the change.

(b) Column (b): Net Investment Income

- Each and every private foundation and wholly charitable trust is required to pay an excise tax on certain investment income. Column (b) reports the four specific types of designated taxable income—interest, dividends, rents, and royalties—plus capital gain, less associated deductions used to arrive at income subject to the excise tax. Gain from sale of exempt function assets is now included.[7]

Column (b) does not include:

- Unrelated business income separately reported on Form 990-T
- Program service revenue received from performing an exempt function
- Profits from fund-raising events
- A net loss from the sale of investment assets
- Unrealized investment gains or losses recognized under SFAS No. 124

(c) Column (c): Adjusted Net Income

This column became obsolete for most private foundations in 1976, but it is still important for two types of foundations. Private operating foundations must spend 85 percent of their adjusted net income on charitable projects they conduct directly. This column calculates what is called *adjusted gross income* by adding up investment income plus net short-term capital gains in excess of losses (a net loss is not entered) and unrelated business income, less expenses attributable to producing the includible income. The bottom line carries to Part XIV to calculate ongoing qualification.

Private nonoperating foundations receiving program service revenue use column (c) to report the income from the performance of their exempt functions. Such revenues, except for dividends, interest, rents and royalties, are typically not reported in column (b) because they are not taxable. This column is basically used to reduce charitable disbursements by any income generated by a program so that only the excess expenses over the revenues from program services are reported in column (d).

(d) Column (d): Disbursements for Charitable Purposes

The cash method must be used for this column. Under SFAS No. 116, foundations following generally accepted accounting principles ("GAAP") report grants approved or pledged for future payment when the promise is made, rather than when the grant is actually disbursed. Such foundations must maintain a parallel accounting system that can prepare a report of grants paid on both the cash (for column (d)) and the accrual basis (for column (a)). For foundations with expenses for the conduct of active programs, the same type of dual reporting is required.

As the title of this column indicates, the total of this column is significant because it is carried to Part XII to tally up qualifying distributions for measuring satisfaction of the mandatory charitable payout rules. As a basic concept, any expenses claimed as allocable to investment income would not also be reportable in this column. Direct charitable expenditures such as medical care, food, clothing, or cash to indigents or other members of a charitable class, books for a literacy program, printing expenses for producing the books, or other expenses associated with direct program activities are included here. Grants paid to other charitable organizations, fund-raising costs, and administrative expenses not allocable to investment income or to adjusted gross income are reported in this column.

§ 6.3 LINE-BY-LINE INSTRUCTIONS FOR REVENUES

Part I Analysis of Revenue and Expenses (The total of amounts in columns (b), (c), and (d) may not necessarily equal the amounts in column (a) (see page 11 of the instructions).)	(a) Revenue and expenses per books	(b) Net investment income	(c) Adjusted net income	(d) Disbursements for charitable purposes (cash basis only)
1 Contributions, gifts, grants, etc., received (attach schedule)				
2 Check ► ☐ if the foundation is **not** required to attach Sch. B				
3 Interest on savings and temporary cash investments				
4 Dividends and interest from securities				
5a Gross rents				
b Net rental income or (loss)				
6a Net gain or (loss) from sale of assets not on line 10				
b Gross sales price for all assets on line 6a				
7 Capital gain net income (from Part IV, line 2)				
8 Net short-term capital gain				
9 Income modifications				
10a Gross sales less returns and allowances				
b Less: Cost of goods sold				
c Gross profit or (loss) (attach schedule)				
11 Other income (attach schedule)				
12 Total. Add lines 1 through 11				

(a) Line 1: Contributions, Gifts, and Grants Received

The total amount of voluntary donations the foundation receives during the year is reported on this line. The name, address, amount, date, and, in the case of property other than cash, a description of such property for gifts of $5,000 or more must be reported on Schedule B.[8] The present value of pledges for future support reported in accordance with SFAS No. 116 are reported on this line. Distributions from split-interest trusts are included here for column (a) purposes. In-kind donations of time, services, or the use of property are not reported[9] as support on page 1. They are not reported even if the services are recorded for financial reporting purposes in accordance with GAAP.

The instructions to this line remind the foundation it must adhere to certain disclosure rules if it solicits contributions of more than $75 for which it gives the donor in return something of value (note that such a transaction might constitute self-dealing as described earlier). Similarly, to enable its donors to claim a charitable contribution deduction for gifts to it, the foundation must provide a receipt acknowledging all gifts of $250 or more and indicating whether or not it provided goods and services to the contributor.

(b)   Line 3: Interest on Savings and Temporary Cash Investments

This line is mostly self-explanatory. The interest on a bank checking, savings, money market, or other investments of the type reported on line 2 of the balance sheet is reported on this line; interest on a money market mutual fund reported on line 10b might instead be reported on line 4. Interest earned on a program-related investment, on a note receivable from the sale of a foundation asset, or on an employee loan would be reported as other income on line 11.

(c)   Line 4: Dividends and Interest from Securities

Income payments from investments in stocks, bonds, security loans, and other financial instruments regulated by state or federal securities law (of the type reported on line 10 of the balance sheet) are reported here. Dividends paid by a subsidiary operated as a program-related investment would be reported on line 11. Capital gain dividends paid by a mutual fund are reported on line 6. Amounts received on tax-exempt government obligations are included only in column (a) and (c), not in (b).

(d)   Line 5: Gross and Net Rental Income

Gross rents received from investment real or personal property of the type reported on line 11 of the balance sheet is reported on this line in columns (a), (b), and (c). Rents produced through exempt function programs, such as low-income housing, and rents received from rental of office space to other unaffiliated exempt organizations is reported on line 11. Expenses directly connected with the rental income are deducted on lines 13 through 23.

(e)   Line 6: Net Gain (Loss) from Sale of Assets

The gains or losses reported by the foundation for financial purposes from sales or other dispositions of all types of capital assets, including those held for investment, those held for exempt purposes, and those that produce unrelated business income, are reported on line 6 in column (a) only. By comparison, line 7 reports, in column (b) only, the gain subject to excise tax on investment income. The details of sales reported also on line 7 are not reported here. In 2008, the only gains not reportable in Part IV would come from nontaxable exchanges and property donated to another charity. For sales of assets other than publicly traded securities, a detailed schedule is attached reflecting the date acquired and sold, gross sales price and selling expenses, cost basis, and any depreciation. Unrealized gains reported for financial statement purposes under SFAS No. 124 are not included here but instead are shown as a reconciling item in Part III.

(f) Line 7: Capital Gain Net Income

The tax code, effective for fiscal years beginning after August 17, 2006, defines net capital gains subject to the excise tax broadly and essentially says most capital gains are taxed, including those resulting from the sale of exempt function assets. In a negative fashion the tax code simply says: "There shall not be taken into account any gain or loss from the sale or other disposition of property to the extent that such gain or loss is taken into account for purposes of computing the tax imposed by section 511."[10] A second exception provides for a nontaxable exchange by saying:

> Under rules similar to the rules of section 1031, no gain or loss shall be taken into account with respect to any portion of property used for a period of not less than 1 year for a purpose or function constituting the basis of the private foundation's exemption if the entire property is exchanged immediately following such period solely for property of like kind which is to be used primarily for a purpose or function constituting the basis for such foundation's exemption.
>
> For tax years 2006 and before, only gains from the sale of property that ordinarily produced interest, dividends, royalties, or rents was taxed, even if the property produced no current income.

The capital loss deduction limitation still applies. Net losses from sales or other dispositions of property are only allowed to the extent of gains from such sales or other dispositions, and no capital loss carryovers or carrybacks are allowed.[11] This loss limitation requires the prudent foundation to review its current year investment results prior to its year end so as to take steps, if possible, to avoid loss of the tax benefit from any capital losses. Gain from property used in an unrelated trade or business, if it is subject to the unrelated business income tax, is not taxed again under these rules.[12] Mutual fund capital gain dividends, both short and long term, are classified as capital gain, not dividends.[13] Certain types of gains will continue to be excluded from tax:

- Gain inherent in appreciated property distributed as a grant to another charity.[14] The reason is that distribution of property for charitable purposes is not considered a sale or other disposition for purposes of this tax.

- Gain from disposition of excess business holdings held on December 31, 1969 (or received as a bequest under a trust irrevocable on May 26, 1969) and sold to or redeemed by a disqualified person to reduce the holdings pursuant to the excess business holdings rules.[15]

- Gain realized in a merger or corporate reorganization ruled to be tax free.[16]

- Distributions of capital gains from a charitable lead trust.[17]

For planning purposes, it is important to note that property received by the foundation as a donation retains the donor's basis.[18] Since the wealth of a foundation's creator often comes from business interests that are highly appreciated, the foundation receiving such wealth through gifts ends up paying tax on its contributor's gains, albeit at a much lower rate. If such property is distributed to the foundation's grant recipients, rather than cash from sale of the property, the gain is not taxed. See §6.9 for ideas about reducing the foundation's tax rate from 2 to 1 percent.

Even though the foundation is instructed to follow its book method of reporting income and expense in column (a), the tax rules require different reporting in certain respects for tax purposes. The basis of property the foundation received as a donation may be different for tax purposes than for financial purposes, as reflected in the discussion for lines 6 and 7. Thus, the capital gains shown in column (a) calculated using "book basis" may be different than those shown in columns (b) and (c) using the "tax basis."

(g)   Line 8: Net Short-Term Capital Gains

Foundations that complete column (c) separately report net short-term capital gains. The gain increases the "adjusted net income" of a private operating foundation that may be required to be spent on active charitable programs. If line 27c of column (c) is less than line 6 of Part X, adjusted net income determines the required distributions for a private operating foundation.

(h)   Line 9: Income Modifications

This line also pertains exclusively to column (c) and mostly affects the required distributions for private operating foundations: repayments of amounts previously treated as qualifying distributions; proceeds of sales of assets, the purchase of which were treated as qualifying distributions; and the unused portion of funds previously set aside and claimed as funds must be added. Essentially such recouped funds must be redistributed. Nonoperating foundations make similar adjustments in Part XI.

(i)   Line 10: Gross Sales

This line is used by a foundation conducting a self-initiated project(s) that generates sales of inventory, such as an educational bookstore or handicapped worker factory. Because the excess business holdings rules generally prohibit a foundation's operation of a business, it is important that such revenues be identified as program-related business income. The gross profit reported in column (c) should be reported in Part XVI-A in column (e). Such revenue also increases a private operating foundation's annual distribution requirement. This income is not entered into column (b) because it is not investment income subject to the excise tax. The instructions suggest reporting of inventory items sold during fund-raising events (contribution portion is reported on line 1) on this line.

(j)   Line 11: Other Income

All other types of income are reported on this line. Examples of such income include mineral royalties; interest on student or economic development loans not reported on line 3 or 4; rentals from low-cost housing or historic property; and distributable amounts reported on Form K-1 when the foundation is a partner of a partnership or a Subchapter S shareholder.

Other kinds of income that are not subject to the investment income tax are also entered on line 11, but only in columns (a) and possibly (c). Fees for services generated in an exempt activity, such as student tuition, testing fees, and ticket sales for cultural events, are good examples of this type of income. This type of income is entered in column (e) of Part XVI-A, and its relationship to the foundation's exempt activities must be explained. Unrealized gains or losses on investments carried at market value are reported in Part III, not here.

§ 6.4 LINE-BY-LINE INSTRUCTIONS FOR EXPENDITURES

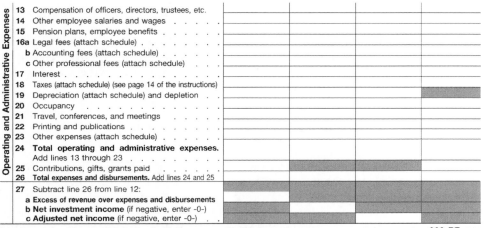

For Privacy Act and Paperwork Reduction Act Notice, see page 30 of the instructions.   Cat. No. 11289X   Form **990-PF** (2008)

Good accounting is the key to successful completion of the expense columns on page 1 of Form 990-PF. Proper identification of those expenses directly attributable to management of the foundation affairs in general, its investments, and its grant-making and active charitable programs is a significant aspect of preparing Form 990-PF. Since foundations must pay a 1 to 2 percent tax rate on investment income and normal tax rates on unrelated business income, expenditure allocations can be important. Proper identification of allocable expenses is the goal. Documentation and cost accounting records should be developed to capture revenues and costs in categories and to report them by function. A foundation often incurs expenses that support both its investment and charitable activities, such as the salary of its executive director, administrative staff, and office space. The portion of the compensation and fees paid to those persons is allocable to each function they perform. A foundation must develop techniques that provide verifiable bases on which expenses may be related to its grant-making and active charitable programs, its investment management activity, and its support service functions. To maintain such a functional classification of expenses, a foundation needs to study the cost accounting rules and allocation concepts discussed in Chapter 2.

The ordinary and necessary expenses of managing, accounting for, and reporting on investments producing taxable investment income are deductible in column (b) to arrive at net investment income subject to the excise tax. Basically, the rules are the same as the tax code provisions pertaining to deductible business and investment expenses.[19] In an ideal situation, foundation personnel should keep track of the time they spend performing different functions so that directly attributable expenses can be entered into the respective columns. At a minimum, a foundation can report a reasonable portion, such as one-fourth to one-half of the total expense of its personnel and advisors, as attributable to its investment income in column (b). The other three-quarters or half is reflected in column (d) and adds to the amount of the foundation's qualifying distributions for the year. Upon examination, the IRS will request substantiation of such allocations.

(a) Line 13: Compensation of Officers, Directors, Trustees, etc.

Column (a) of this line must agree with the detailed information in column (c) of line 1 of Part VIII reporting compensation paid to each and every officer, trustee, director, and foundation manager. The foundation has a burden to prove that amounts on this line are reasonable and do not result in self-dealing.

(b) Lines 14–15: Other Employee Salaries and Wages and Pension Plans, Employee Benefits.

The amounts paid for compensation on lines 13 through 15 must be apportioned between that paid in connection with managing and collecting investment income (column (b)) and managing the foundation's charitable programs (columns (c) and (d)). The names, addresses, and compensation paid to employees other than officers and directors are also detailed in Part VIII for those paid more than $50,000.

(c) Line 16: Legal, Accounting, and Other Professional Fees

Fees paid for professional services to outside consultants that are not employees are entered here. Management fees paid to investment or property managers, writers, researchers, or other independent contractors typically are reported on these lines. An attachment describing the type of service performed for the foundation and amount of expense for each is requested and, in addition, the name and address plus description in amount is entered again on Part VIII for those contractors paid in excess of $50,000.

(d) Line 17: Interest

A private foundation that borrows money for any purpose reports the interest on this line. Allocation of the interest to columns is a challenge and depends on the reason why the PF borrowed money. The unrelated debt-financed rules[20] make interest used to acquire investment property an expense of unrelated business income reportable only in column (a), as is the corresponding income. The net income from the indebted property is subject to normal income tax and is, therefore, not reported in column (b). A foundation that borrows money to pay its operating expenses would report the interest in columns (b), (c), and (d) and possibly face a challenge regarding its motivation for the borrowing. The self-dealing rules prohibit interest payments to the foundation's insiders.

(e) Line 18: Taxes

All types of taxes are reported in column (a), including excise taxes on investment income, property taxes on real estate, unrelated business income tax (UBIT), and state taxes. Payroll taxes for employees are reported on line 15 rather than here. Only taxes paid in regard to investment property are reported in column (b). Private operating foundations include both excise taxes and taxes paid on investment property in column (c). Only taxes paid to employees performing exempt functions and property used for those charitable programs are reported in column (d). For nonoperating foundations, the excise tax reduces the foundation's distributable amount in Part XI, line 2a so it should only be reflected in column (a) on line 18.

(f) Line 19: Depreciation

Depreciation is reported in column (a) using the same method the foundation follows for financial reporting purposes. Columns (b) and (c) depreciation must be calculated using the straight-line method and for mineral properties, cost, but not percentage, depletion is allowed. The basis of property for this purpose is the same as that for calculating gain. Depreciation is entered in columns (b) and (c) only for the depreciation attributable to investment properties, the income of which is reported in the column.

Depreciation cannot be entered in column (d). The total acquisition cost of an asset used in conducting the foundation's charitable programs is treated as a qualifying distribution in the year in which the asset is acquired. The purchase price of exempt function assets is reported in Part XII, line 2, and adds to amounts treated as qualifying distributions for the year.

(g) Line 21: Travel, Conferences, and Meetings

Transportation fares, hotels, meals, and other costs of officers, employees, or others participating in meetings and conferences is reported here. Other costs of sponsoring a conference, including materials, planning meetings, promotion, and the like go here too. Honoraria or other fees paid to persons for services rendered in connection with such meetings should be reported on line 13, 14, or 16, not here. Only 50 percent of the cost of meals paid in connection with investment income management activities is deductible in columns (b) and (c), a limitation that parallels the income tax rules for deductible meals.

A foundation incurring travel expenses should use a system of documentation designed to prove the travel's exempt or investment-related purpose. Expense vouchers reflecting the programmatic nature of the expenditures and evidence of the absence of any personal expenses are desirable. Staff members using a foundation's vehicles or being reimbursed for use of a personal auto should maintain a mileage log to prove that auto usage is devoted to foundation affairs. Auto allowances for officers, directors, managers, and key and highly paid employees are included in column (e) of Part VIII.

(h) Line 25: Contributions, Gifts, Grants Paid

The total contributions or grants paid to other charitable organizations are reported on this line and in column (d) if the payments are qualifying distributions. A detailed report of grant recipients, their addresses, the purpose for each grant, and other information is entered in Part XV, line 3, as explained later. Grants or other payments that are not counted in calculating the foundation's qualifying distributions are not reported in column (d), such as those paid to a controlled organization, another private foundation,[21] a nonfunctionally integrated supporting organization, and certain pass-through grants. The following types of grant transactions are also excluded from column (d):

- Returned grant funds are not entered as a reduction, but added back in calculating required qualifying distributions for the year in Part XI.
- Set-asides are entered in Part XII.
- Write-off (reduction of asset value or declaration of a bad debt) of a program-related investment is also omitted because such investments are reported in Part XII in the year the investments are made.

For column (a) of this line, the foundation reports contributions and grants on the accounting method used for financial purposes. Column (d) must be prepared on a cash basis. As a result of the SFAS No. 116 accounting standards, some foundations now book unconditional pledges of support to other organizations in the year the pledge is made; consequently, such foundations may now have a significant difference between columns (a) and (d).

(i) Line 26: Total Expenses and Disbursements

The total disbursements for charitable purposes shown in column (d) are transferred to Part XII, line 1a, to measure compliance with the minimum distributions requirement test.

(j) Line 27a: Excess of Revenues over Expenses and Disbursements

The difference between revenues and expenses reported for financial purposes shown here is carried to Part III, the analysis of changes in net assets or fund balances.

(k) Line 27b: Net Investment Income

The amount shown in column (b) is the foundation's taxable income that is carried to Part VI to calculate the excise tax.

(l) Line 27c: Adjusted Net Income

Generally, only private operating foundations reflect an amount in this box. This number, if it is more than the amount shown on line 6 of Part X, is carried to Part XIV, line 2a, to determine satisfaction of the income test.

§6.5 PART II: BALANCE SHEETS

Part II	Balance Sheets	Attached schedules and amounts in the description column should be for end-of-year amounts only. (See instructions.)	Beginning of year (a) Book Value	End of year (b) Book Value	End of year (c) Fair Market Value
Assets	1	Cash—non-interest-bearing			
	2	Savings and temporary cash investments			
	3	Accounts receivable ▶			
		Less: allowance for doubtful accounts ▶			
	4	Pledges receivable ▶			
		Less: allowance for doubtful accounts ▶			
	5	Grants receivable			
	6	Receivables due from officers, directors, trustees, and other disqualified persons (attach schedule) (see page 15 of the instructions)			
	7	Other notes and loans receivable (attach schedule) ▶			
		Less: allowance for doubtful accounts ▶			
	8	Inventories for sale or use			
	9	Prepaid expenses and deferred charges			
	10a	Investments—U.S. and state government obligations (attach schedule)			
	b	Investments—corporate stock (attach schedule)			
	c	Investments—corporate bonds (attach schedule)			
	11	Investments—land, buildings, and equipment: basis ▶			
		Less: accumulated depreciation (attach schedule) ▶			
	12	Investments—mortgage loans			
	13	Investments—other (attach schedule)			
	14	Land, buildings, and equipment: basis ▶			
		Less: accumulated depreciation (attach schedule) ▶			
	15	Other assets (describe ▶)			
	16	**Total assets** (to be completed by all filers—see the instructions. Also, see page 1, item I)			
Liabilities	17	Accounts payable and accrued expenses			
	18	Grants payable			
	19	Deferred revenue			
	20	Loans from officers, directors, trustees, and other disqualified persons .			
	21	Mortgages and other notes payable (attach schedule) . .			
	22	Other liabilities (describe ▶)			
	23	**Total liabilities** (add lines 17 through 22)			
Net Assets or Fund Balances		Foundations that follow SFAS 117, check here ▶ ☐ and complete lines 24 through 26 and lines 30 and 31.			
	24	Unrestricted			
	25	Temporarily restricted			
	26	Permanently restricted			
		Foundations that do not follow SFAS 117, check here ▶ ☐ and complete lines 27 through 31.			
	27	Capital stock, trust principal, or current funds			
	28	Paid-in or capital surplus, or land, bldg., and equipment fund .			
	29	Retained earnings, accumulated income, endowment, or other funds .			
	30	**Total net assets or fund balances** (see page 17 of the instructions)			
	31	**Total liabilities and net assets/fund balances** (see page 17 of the instructions)			

Both the book value of the foundation assets and liabilities and the ending fair market value are presented in Part II. The total in column (c), line 16, must agree with item I on page 1, top left side. A considerable amount of detail is requested. The instructions should be read carefully for the following lines on the balance sheet:

Line 6	Insider receivables
Line 10	Investments—securities
Line 11	Investments—land, buildings, and equipment
Line 13	Investments—other

Line 14	Land, buildings, and equipment (devoted to exempt purposes)
Line 15	Other assets
Line 19	Support and revenue designated for future periods
Line 20	Loans from officers, directors, trustees, or other disqualified persons
Line 21	Mortgages and other notes payable

Certain lines in this part alert the IRS to problem issues, and in those cases detailed schedules are requested. For most loans receivable by or payable by the foundation, 10 detailed items of information are required: borrower's name and title, original amount, balance due, date of note, maturity date, repayment terms, interest rate, security provided by borrower, purpose of the loan, and description and fair market value of consideration furnished by the lender. This information is submitted to enable the IRS to evaluate the presence of self-dealing.

Schedules for depreciable assets should be prepared to coordinate with the information required to be attached for Parts I and II. Likewise, payable information should bear a reasonable relationship to the amount reported on line 17 of Part I for interest expense.

The same method used by the foundation for maintaining its normal accounting books and records is followed in completing this part. The fair market value for each category of asset is reported in column (c) for all foundations with total assets of $5,000 or more at any time during the year. Only a total is entered on line 16 for a foundation that had less than $5,000 of assets for the entire year. If detailed schedules are requested, they need only be furnished for the year-end numbers. The instructions for this part are quite good and need not be repeated here. Foundations following SFAS No. 124[22] that mark their assets up or down to market value may essentially have identical numbers in columns (b) and (c).

§6.6 PART III: ANALYSIS OF CHANGES IN NET WORTH OR FUND BALANCES

Part III	Analysis of Changes in Net Assets or Fund Balances		
1	Total net assets or fund balances at beginning of year—Part II, column (a), line 30 (must agree with end-of-year figure reported on prior year's return)	1	
2	Enter amount from Part I, line 27a	2	
3	Other increases not included in line 2 (itemize) ▶	3	
4	Add lines 1, 2, and 3	4	
5	Decreases not included in line 2 (itemize) ▶	5	
6	Total net assets or fund balances at end of year (line 4 minus line 5)—Part II, column (b), line 30	6	

Form **990-PF** (2008)

The information reported on page 1 for Form 990-PF purposes is reconciled to the Part II balance sheet in this part. The information in Part II is reported according to the accounting method under which the foundation keeps its financial records, which may not match the tax reporting rules applicable to Part I. Revenues and expenses of this type include:

- Donated services associated with a capitalized asset, such as fees donated by the architects in connection with a foundation building

- Unrealized gain or loss in carrying value of marketable securities and other investment assets under SFAS No. 124

- Change in accounting treatment of charitable pledges receivable or payable as required under SFAS No. 116

- A prior-period accounting adjustment not corrected on an amended return because it is immaterial

Sometimes, a foundation discovers a mistake was made in a prior-year return that requires correction. Depending upon the significance of the mistake, an amended return must be considered. An under- or overreporting of investment income calculated in Part VI signals a need for amendment. As a practical matter, a modest mistake can be adjusted in the currently filed return by increasing or decreasing revenues or expenses. A prior-year mistake that affects a foundation's excess distribution carryover can also be corrected by attaching an explanation of the adjustment to the return and accurately reflecting the carryover in Part XIII. The statute of limitations for purposes of correcting a prior mistake in the payout calculations does not close.[23] A change affecting the income tax on unrelated business income would necessitate the filing of an amended return.

§6.7 PART IV: CAPITAL GAINS AND LOSSES FOR TAX ON INVESTMENT INCOME

Form 990-PF (2008)   Page **3**

Part IV   **Capital Gains and Losses for Tax on Investment Income**

(a) List and describe the kind(s) of property sold (e.g., real estate, 2-story brick warehouse; or common stock, 200 shs. MLC Co.)	(b) How acquired P—Purchase D—Donation	(c) Date acquired (mo., day, yr.)	(d) Date sold (mo., day, yr.)
1a			
b			
c			
d			
e			

(e) Gross sales price	(f) Depreciation allowed (or allowable)	(g) Cost or other basis plus expense of sale	(h) Gain or (loss) (e) plus (f) minus (g)
a			
b			
c			
d			
e			

Complete only for assets showing gain in column (h) and owned by the foundation on 12/31/69

(i) F.M.V. as of 12/31/69	(j) Adjusted basis as of 12/31/69	(k) Excess of col. (i) over col. (j), if any	(l) Gains (Col. (h) gain minus col. (k), but not less than -0-) or Losses (from col. (h))
a			
b			
c			
d			
e			

2 Capital gain net income or (net capital loss)   { If gain, also enter in Part I, line 7   If (loss), enter -0- in Part I, line 7 }   **2**

3 Net short-term capital gain or (loss) as defined in sections 1222(5) and (6):
If gain, also enter in Part I, line 8, column (c) (see pages 13 and 17 of the instructions).
If (loss), enter -0- in Part I, line 8 . . . . }   **3**

The definition of capital gains and losses for excise tax purposes was greatly expanded by the Pension Protection Act in 2006 to include most gains on sales of foundation property, both that held for investment and used in charitable programs. Between 1970 and 2006, only gains resulting from the sale or exchange of property capable of producing interest, dividends, rents, and royalties were subject to the excise tax.

The gain or loss is calculated by subtracting from the amount of sales proceeds the foundation received, the amount the foundation paid to purchase the property, adjusted for depreciation reserves, amortization, and selling expenses.[24] However, basis for property that the foundation received as a gift is equal to the amount the donor paid for the gifted property, or what is called the donor's tax or carryover basis. Property received through a bequest is valued as of the date of death or the alternate valuation date for the decedent.[25]

Only the total capital gain net income is carried from this schedule to column (b) and added to taxable investment income. The short-term portion of the gain is reported only in column (c) and increases the amount of adjusted gross income that affects the amount of direct charitable activity expenditures a private operating foundation is required to pay out for the year. A net capital loss for the year is not carried to Part I and is *not* deductible against other investment income, and no capital loss carryover to a subsequent year is allowed.[26]

§6.8 REPORTS UNIQUE TO PRIVATE FOUNDATIONS

To measure compliance with and enforce the special rules unique to private foundations, Form 990-PF contains 19 parts. The first four, discussed above, essentially report the financial transactions for the year in a financial statement format. The other 15 parts explore particular issues and ask questions that indicate satisfaction of requirements and prompt attachments of additional information. Failure to furnish a complete report regarding an expenditure responsibility agreement, for example, results in a taxable expenditure. Each foundation should seek to clearly reflect its mission in completing these parts. Its charitable programs are described and detailed to furnish the reader a clear picture of the type of grants and activities it supports. Not only is the form available for all to see and request a copy of, the information is widely available in directories—paper and electronic—published throughout the country as an aid to grant seekers.[27] The volume and quality of grant requests the foundation receives is influenced by the manner in which information is presented on its Form 990-PF.

§6.9 PART V: REDUCING THE TAX RATE

Part V	Qualification Under Section 4940(e) for Reduced Tax on Net Investment Income

(For optional use by domestic private foundations subject to the section 4940(a) tax on net investment income.)

If section 4940(d)(2) applies, leave this part blank.

Was the foundation liable for the section 4942 tax on the distributable amount of any year in the base period? ☐ Yes ☐ No
If "Yes," the foundation does not qualify under section 4940(e). Do not complete this part.

1 Enter the appropriate amount in each column for each year; see page 18 of the instructions before making any entries.

(a) Base period years Calendar year (or tax year beginning in)	(b) Adjusted qualifying distributions	(c) Net value of noncharitable-use assets	(d) Distribution ratio (col. (b) divided by col. (c))
2007			
2006			
2005			
2004			
2003			

2 Total of line 1, column (d) . . . . | 2 | |

3 Average distribution ratio for the 5-year base period—divide the total on line 2 by 5, or by the number of years the foundation has been in existence if less than 5 years . . . . | 3 | |

(Continued)

4 Enter the net value of noncharitable-use assets for 2008 from Part X, line 5 . . . . | **4** |

5 Multiply line 4 by line 3 . . . . | **5** |

6 Enter 1% of net investment income (1% of Part I, line 27b) . . . . | **6** |

7 Add lines 5 and 6 . . . . | **7** |

8 Enter qualifying distributions from Part XII, line 4 . . . . | **8** |

If line 8 is equal to or greater than line 7, check the box in Part VI, line 1b, and complete that part using a 1% tax rate. See the Part VI instructions on page 18.

Form **990-PF** (2008)

A private foundation can cut its tax in half (from 2 percent to 1 percent of net investment income) by essentially giving the tax to charity. If the foundation's current-year qualifying distributions (Part XII) exceed a hypothetical number (past five-year average payout percentage times average fair market value of assets for the year of calculation plus 1 percent tax for the current year), the tax is reduced to 1 percent. Achieving this reduction is complicated because the two most important factors are not known until the last day of the taxable year—line 4 (the average month-end value of investment assets) and probably line 8 (qualifying distributions). Except for the most generous foundations whose distributions continually increase year to year, reducing the excise tax requires very careful planning. A newly established private foundation cannot qualify for the reduced tax rate in its first year.[28] Those new foundations that are created late in the year with a donation of highly appreciated property may benefit from delaying the sale of the asset, typically readily marketable securities, and making any grants, until the second tax year.

§ 6.10 PART VI: CALCULATING THE EXCISE TAX

Form 990-PF (2008)   Page **4**

Part VI	Excise Tax Based on Investment Income (Section 4940(a), 4940(b), 4940(e), or 4948—see page 18 of the instructions)		
1a	Exempt operating foundations described in section 4940(d)(2), check here ▶ ☐ and enter "N/A" on line 1. Date of ruling letter: . . . . **(attach copy of ruling letter if necessary—see instructions)**	**1**	
b	Domestic foundations that meet the section 4940(e) requirements in Part V, check here ▶ ☐ and enter 1% of Part I, line 27b		
c	All other domestic foundations enter 2% of line 27b. Exempt foreign organizations enter 4% of Part I, line 12, col. (b)		
2	Tax under section 511 (domestic section 4947(a)(1) trusts and taxable foundations only. Others enter -0-)	**2**	
3	Add lines 1 and 2	**3**	
4	Subtitle A (income) tax (domestic section 4947(a)(1) trusts and taxable foundations only. Others enter -0-)	**4**	
5	**Tax based on investment income.** Subtract line 4 from line 3. If zero or less, enter -0- . .	**5**	
6	Credits/Payments:		
a	2008 estimated tax payments and 2007 overpayment credited to 2008 **6a**		
b	Exempt foreign organizations—tax withheld at source **6b**		
c	Tax paid with application for extension of time to file (Form 8868) **6c**		
d	Backup withholding erroneously withheld **6d**		
7	Total credits and payments. Add lines 6a through 6d	**7**	
8	Enter any **penalty** for underpayment of estimated tax. Check here ☐ if Form 2220 is attached	**8**	
9	**Tax due.** If the total of lines 5 and 8 is more than line 7, enter **amount owed** . . . . . ▶	**9**	
10	**Overpayment.** If line 7 is more than the total of lines 5 and 8, enter the **amount overpaid** . ▶	**10**	
11	Enter the amount of line 10 to be: **Credited to 2009 estimated tax** ▶ Refunded ▶	**11**	

Except for exempt operating foundations, which do not pay tax, generally private foundations pay a tax of 2 percent, or possibly 1 percent, on their net investment income reported in Part I, column (b), line 27b. Foreign foundations that receive more than 15 percent of their investment income from U.S. sources pay a 4 percent tax on such income. A foundation converting itself to a public charity under the 60-month termination rules is excused from paying the excise tax. Such a foundation signs an agreement to extend the statute of limitations for collecting the excise tax in the event that it fails to receive sufficient amounts of public support. A copy of the signed consent agreement is attached to the return each year during the termination period, and Part VI, line 1, should refer to the attachment and state the tax is not applicable.

If the annual tax is under $500, it can be paid with a check accompanying the return as it is filed. If the tax is over $500, it must be paid in advance through the estimated tax system, using the depository receipt system at a banking institution. Form 990-W is used to compute the tax. Foundations with over $1 million of net investment income must make quarterly payments based on actual income earned during the second, third, and fourth quarters, similar to the *large corporation* rules. Penalties are due for failure to pay a sufficient amount by the quarterly due dates.[29] Form 2220 is attached to Form 990-PF to calculate the penalty or to display the annualization of income that results in no penalty. Penalties are also imposed for failure to deposit taxes with a federal tax deposit coupon (Form 8109) at a qualified bank or federal reserve bank.

§ 6.11 PART VII-A: PROOF OF ONGOING QUALIFICATION FOR EXEMPTION

Part VII-A **Statements Regarding Activities**

		Yes	No
1a During the tax year, did the foundation attempt to influence any national, state, or local legislation or did it participate or intervene in any political campaign? **1a**			
b Did it spend more than $100 during the year (either directly or indirectly) for political purposes (see page 19 of the instructions for definition)? **1b**			
*If the answer is "Yes" to **1a** or **1b**, attach a detailed description of the activities and copies of any materials published or distributed by the foundation in connection with the activities.*			
c Did the foundation file **Form 1120-POL** for this year? **1c**			
d Enter the amount (if any) of tax on political expenditures (section 4955) imposed during the year:			
(1) On the foundation. ▶ $ _____ **(2)** On foundation managers. ▶ $ _____			
e Enter the reimbursement (if any) paid by the foundation during the year for political expenditure tax imposed on foundation managers. ▶ $ _____			
2 Has the foundation engaged in any activities that have not previously been reported to the IRS? . . . **2**			
If "Yes," attach a detailed description of the activities.			
3 Has the foundation made any changes, not previously reported to the IRS, in its governing instrument, articles of incorporation, or bylaws, or other similar instruments? *If "Yes," attach a conformed copy of the changes* . . . **3**			
4a Did the foundation have unrelated business gross income of $1,000 or more during the year? **4a**			
b If "Yes," has it filed a tax return on **Form 990-T** for this year? **4b**			
5 Was there a liquidation, termination, dissolution, or substantial contraction during the year? **5**			
If "Yes," attach the statement required by General Instruction T.			
6 Are the requirements of section 508(e) (relating to sections 4941 through 4945) satisfied either:			
• By language in the governing instrument, or			
• By state legislation that effectively amends the governing instrument so that no mandatory directions that conflict with the state law remain in the governing instrument? **6**			
7 Did the foundation have at least $5,000 in assets at any time during the year? *If "Yes," complete Part II, col. (c), and Part XV.* **7**			
8a Enter the states to which the foundation reports or with which it is registered (see page 19 of the instructions) ▶ --			
b If the answer is "Yes" to line 7, has the foundation furnished a copy of Form 990-PF to the Attorney General (or designate) of each state as required by *General Instruction G? If "No,"* attach explanation **8b**			
9 Is the foundation claiming status as a private operating foundation within the meaning of section 4942(j)(3) or 4942(j)(5) for calendar year 2008 or the taxable year beginning in 2008 (see instructions for Part XIV on page 27)? *If "Yes," complete Part XIV* **9**			
10 Did any persons become substantial contributors during the tax year? *If "Yes," attach a schedule listing their names and addresses* **10**			

Form **990-PF** (2008)

(Continued)

11	At any time during the year, did the foundation, directly or indirectly, own a controlled entity within the meaning of section 512(b)(13)? If "Yes," attach schedule (see page 20 of the instructions)	11	
12	Did the foundation acquire a direct or indirect interest in any applicable insurance contract before August 17, 2008?	12	
13	Did the foundation comply with the public inspection requirements for its annual returns and exemption application?	13	
	Website address ▶		
14	The books are in care of ▶.. Telephone no. ▶..................................		
	Located at ▶... ZIP+4 ▶..........................		
15	Section 4947(a)(1) nonexempt charitable trusts filing Form 990-PF in lieu of **Form 1041**—Check here . . . . . ▶ ☐		
	and enter the amount of tax-exempt interest received or accrued during the year . . . . ▶	15	

The information desired by the IRS to evaluate a private foundation's qualification for ongoing tax exemption is solicited by 15 questions in this part and the 7 questions in Part B. Certain answers can cause serious problems for the foundation, as described below. The questions essentially fish, or look for failures to comply with the tax code and regulations and IRS policy rules pertaining to private foundations. The IRS is reportedly guided by the answers to certain questions in choosing suitable candidates for examination. Certain answers must be "No," as described below. Other questions, like 2 and 4, indicate that other filings are required. Attention to the impact of the answer to each question is desirable. The IRS instructions to the form provide no guidance regarding the answers to Questions 2, 4, 5, or 7.

(a)   Line 1: Did the Foundation Intervene in an Election or Conduct Any Lobbying?

Answering any of the three parts of this question "Yes" is tantamount to admitting that the foundation's exempt status should be questioned and certainly that a taxable expenditure has occurred. All §501(c)(3) organizations are strictly prohibited from seeking to influence an election.[30] Though public charities may spend a limited amount of money on lobbying efforts, private foundations may spend nothing to attempt to influence legislation. A PF can conduct research and issue impartial reports that focus on public affairs that could be the subject of legislation so long as it does not make contacts with the general public or legislators. All of the parts of this question, including (c), should be "No."

(b)   Line 2: Did the Foundation Have Activities Not Previously Reported to the IRS?

A "Yes" answer to this question alerts the IRS to review organizational changes that the form instructs the foundation to explain in a detailed attachment. The question is sometimes hard to answer when the foundation's activity has evolved or expanded, but has not necessarily dramatically or totally changed in its focus or overall purpose. As an example, assume a grant-making foundation previously supported soup kitchen programs to feed the poor and has begun to redirect its grants to community garden organizations that teach the poor to raise their own food. If the PF began to operate the gardens itself, the change probably should be reported.

The question requests detailed disclosure for any new foundation activities. A "Yes" response does not constitute a request for IRS approval for the new activity, but is simply a mechanism to keep the IRS informed with a detailed description of the changes that are attached. In fact, a "Yes" answer does not customarily result in an IRS response. If the foundation's board of directors or trustees desire written IRS approval for conduct of the new projects or change in purpose, a formal ruling request must be filed with the Key District Office.[31] Such a submission, however, is not required or encouraged by the IRS.

(c)   Line 3: Have the Organizational Documents Been Changed?

A conformed copy, meaning one accompanied by a foundation official's sworn statement that it is a "true and correct copy of the original," of any nonprofit charter, trust instrument, or bylaw changes must be attached. The same issues regarding a desire for IRS positive approval for such changes, as discussed under line 2, are raised by a "Yes" answer to this question.

(d)   Line 4: Did the Foundation Have More Than $1,000 of Unrelated Business Gross Income?

If question 4(a) is answered "Yes," question 4(b) must also be answered "Yes." The answer to this question should be coordinated with Part XVI-A. If an amount in excess of $1,000 appears in column (b), the answer to this question should be "Yes." This question can be confusing since the investment income private foundations typically earn is technically defined as unrelated trade or business income.[32] Most investment income, however, is "modified" or excluded from unrelated business taxable income, and is not required to be reported on Form 990-T, and should appear in column (d) of Part XVI-A.

(e)   Line 5: Did the Foundation Liquidate, Terminate, Dissolve, or Substantially Contract?

The tax code specifically requires a private foundation to notify the secretary of the treasury of its intention to, and the fashion in which it plans to, cease to operate.[33] A statement explaining the facts and circumstances of any of the four named situations must be attached. For a full liquidation or termination, a certified copy of the plan with a schedule listing the names and addresses of all recipients of assets, along with a description of the nature and value of such assets, is required. According to the IRS instructions, disposition of 25 percent or more of the fair market value of the foundation's assets is a substantial contraction. Prior permission to make a substantial contraction, short of totally terminating the foundation, is not literally required by the tax code or the IRS instructions, although the foundation managers may deem it prudent to seek such approval. Additionally, if the substantial disposition is to another private foundation, certain attributes of the grantor foundation carry over to the recipient foundation.[34]

(f)   Line 6: Does the Foundation's Governing Instrument Satisfy §508(e) Requirements?

This question must be answered "Yes." A private foundation cannot qualify and be recognized as an exempt organization by the IRS unless its governing instruments prohibit its engaging in transactions that would cause it to incur excise taxes for entering into a self-dealing transaction, making taxable expenditures, maintaining excess business holdings, or buying a jeopardizing investment. The requirement can be met in two ways. Many foundations' governing instruments actually contain required language. Instead, some foundations rely on local law. Most states passed legislation in the early 1970s to automatically incorporate the required language for private foundations based in the state.

(g) Line 7: Did the Foundation Have at Least $5,000 in Assets During the Year?

If the answer to this question is "Yes," the foundation must report the fair market value of its assets in Part II by completing column (c). Such a modestly sized foundation is also excused from completing Part XV.

(h) Line 8: Submit Information Regarding State Filings

This question has two parts. The foundation must enter the name(s) of any state(s) to which the foundation reports and in which the foundation is registered as a charitable organization. Note that even if a private foundation is not registered to do business in a particular state, state filings may be required if the foundation has solicited and received donations from persons residing in the state. A foundation with assets of $5,000 or more (answers question 7 "Yes") is required to furnish a copy of Form 990-PF and Form 4720, if any, to the attorney general of:

- Each state listed in the answer to question 8(a)
- The state in which its principal office is located
- The state in which the foundation was incorporated or created

The state copy must be submitted at the same time the federal form is filed. The foundation must also furnish a copy of its Form 990-PF to the attorney general of any state that requests it whether or not it is registered in that state.

(i) Line 9: Is This Organization a Private Operating Foundation?

A "Yes" answer to this question alerts the IRS that the foundation will complete Part XIV, instead of Part XIII, to determine satisfaction of charitable pay-out tests *and* that the foundation must complete column (c) of Part I. A private operating foundation spends its money to conduct its own active programs, rather than granting money to other organizations.

(j) Line 10: Did Any Person(s) Become Substantial Contributors During the Year?

If the answer to this question is "Yes," the foundation is prompted to attach a schedule listing their names and addresses. Note that for those contributing $5,000 or more during the year, the same information plus details regarding the gift are reported in Schedule B.

(k) Line 11(a): At Any Time During the Year, Did the Foundation Own a Controlled Entity Within the meaning of §512(b)(13)?

Control for this purpose is defined as more than 50 percent ownership of the entity in accordance with IRC §318. If so, and the foundation made a loan or other payment to the entity, or received payments from the entity, a detailed schedule is required to be attached. See the instructions for samples.

(l)   Line 11(b): If "Yes" Did the Foundation Have a Binding Written Contract in Effect?

Lines 11a and b appeared for the first time in the 2006 return as a result of the Pension Protection Act, which required this disclosure. The exclusions from unrelated business income for interest, annuities, royalties, and rents, explained earlier in this chapter, may not apply to a payment of these items received by a controlling organization from its controlled organization. The payment is included in the controlling organization's unrelated business taxable income to the extent that it reduced the net unrelated income (or increased the net unrelated loss) of the controlled organization. All deductions of the controlling organization directly connected with the amount included in its unrelated business taxable income are allowed. The Pension Protection Act allows for an exclusion from unrelated business income for payments described above when they are pursuant to a binding contract in effect before August 17, 2006, and the payments are received before January 1, 2008.

(m)   Line 12: Did the Foundation Acquire a Direct or Indirect Interest in Any Applicable Insurance Contract?

An applicable insurance contract is any life insurance, annuity, or endowment contract in which an applicable exempt organization *and* a person other than an applicable exempt organization have directly or indirectly held an interest in the contract (whether or not at the same time). However, an applicable insurance contract does not include any life insurance, annuity, or endowment contract if[35]:

1. All persons directly or indirectly holding any interest in the contract (other than applicable exempt organizations) have an insurable interest in the insured under the contract independent of any interest of an applicable exempt organization in the contract, or

2. The sole interest in the contract of an applicable exempt organization or each person other than an applicable exempt organization is as a named beneficiary, or

3. The sole interest in the contract of each person other than an applicable exempt organization is:

    1. As a beneficiary of a trust holding an interest in the contract, but only if the person's designation as such beneficiary was made without consideration and solely on a gratuitous basis, or

    2. As a trustee who holds an interest in the contract in a fiduciary capacity solely for the benefit of applicable organizations or persons described above in 1, 2, or 3a. An applicable organization is the foundation and any organization to which contributions are deductible for income tax, estate tax, or gift tax purposes and Indian tribal governments.

The import of this question is that a contribution deduction is denied for a payment made by an individual to an organization to pay a premium on his (or his family member's) life insurance contract (or similar). Additionally, Form 8921 may need to be filed regarding such a contract.

(n)   Line 13: Did the Foundation Comply with the Public Inspection Requirements for its Annual Returns and Exemption Application?

The answer to Question 13 should never be "No." A penalty is imposed for failure to comply with the return disclosure rules outlined in Chapter 1, §3.

§ 6.12   PART VII-B: QUESTIONS SEEKING EVIDENCE THAT NO SANCTIONS APPLY

Part VII-B Statements Regarding Activities for Which Form 4720 May Be Required		
File Form 4720 if any item is checked in the "Yes" column, unless an exception applies.		Yes | No
1a During the year did the foundation (either directly or indirectly):		
(1) Engage in the sale or exchange, or leasing of property with a disqualified person? ☐ Yes ☐ No		
(2) Borrow money from, lend money to, or otherwise extend credit to (or accept it from) a disqualified person? ☐ Yes ☐ No		
(3) Furnish goods, services, or facilities to (or accept them from) a disqualified person? ☐ Yes ☐ No		
(4) Pay compensation to, or pay or reimburse the expenses of, a disqualified person? ☐ Yes ☐ No		
(5) Transfer any income or assets to a disqualified person (or make any of either available for the benefit or use of a disqualified person)? ☐ Yes ☐ No		
(6) Agree to pay money or property to a government official? (**Exception.** Check "No" if the foundation agreed to make a grant to or to employ the official for a period after termination of government service, if terminating within 90 days.) ☐ Yes ☐ No		
b If any answer is "Yes" to 1a(1)–(6), did **any** of the acts fail to qualify under the exceptions described in Regulations section 53.4941(d)-3 or in a current notice regarding disaster assistance (see page 20 of the instructions)? Organizations relying on a current notice regarding disaster assistance check here ▶ ☐	**1b**	
c Did the foundation engage in a prior year in any of the acts described in 1a, other than excepted acts, that were not corrected before the first day of the tax year beginning in 2008?	**1c**	
2 Taxes on failure to distribute income (section 4942) (does not apply for years the foundation was a private operating foundation defined in section 4942(j)(3) or 4942(j)(5)):		
a At the end of tax year 2008, did the foundation have any undistributed income (lines 6d and 6e, Part XIII) for tax year(s) beginning before 2008? ☐ Yes ☐ No If "Yes," list the years ▶ 20....., 20....., 20....., 20.....		
b Are there any years listed in 2a for which the foundation is **not** applying the provisions of section 4942(a)(2) (relating to incorrect valuation of assets) to the year's undistributed income? (If applying section 4942(a)(2) to **all** years listed, answer "No" and attach statement—see page 20 of the instructions.)	**2b**	
c If the provisions of section 4942(a)(2) are being applied to **any** of the years listed in 2a, list the years here. ▶ 20...., 20...., 20...., 20.....		
3a Did the foundation hold more than a 2% direct or indirect interest in any business enterprise at any time during the year? ☐ Yes ☐ No		
b If "Yes," did it have excess business holdings in 2008 as a result of **(1)** any purchase by the foundation or disqualified persons after May 26, 1969; **(2)** the lapse of the 5-year period (or longer period approved by the Commissioner under section 4943(c)(7)) to dispose of holdings acquired by gift or bequest; or **(3)** the lapse of the 10-, 15-, or 20-year first phase holding period? (*Use Schedule C, Form 4720, to determine if the foundation had excess business holdings in 2008.*)	**3b**	
4a Did the foundation invest during the year any amount in a manner that would jeopardize its charitable purposes?	**4a**	
b Did the foundation make any investment in a prior year (but after December 31, 1969) that could jeopardize its charitable purpose that had not been removed from jeopardy before the first day of the tax year beginning in 2008?	**4b**	

Form **990-PF** (2008)

(Continued)

Part VII-B	Statements Regarding Activities for Which Form 4720 May Be Required *(continued)*

5a During the year did the foundation pay or incur any amount to:

(1) Carry on propaganda, or otherwise attempt to influence legislation (section 4945(e))? . ☐ Yes ☐ No

(2) Influence the outcome of any specific public election (see section 4955); or to carry on, directly or indirectly, any voter registration drive? . . . . ☐ Yes ☐ No

(3) Provide a grant to an individual for travel, study, or other similar purposes? . . . . ☐ Yes ☐ No

(4) Provide a grant to an organization other than a charitable, etc., organization described in section 509(a)(1), (2), or (3), or section 4940(d)(2)? (see page 22 of the instructions) . . . ☐ Yes ☐ No

(5) Provide for any purpose other than religious, charitable, scientific, literary, or educational purposes, or for the prevention of cruelty to children or animals? . ☐ Yes ☐ No

b If any answer is "Yes" to 5a(1)–(5), did **any** of the transactions fail to qualify under the exceptions described in Regulations section 53.4945 or in a current notice regarding disaster assistance (see page 22 of the instructions)? **5b**

Organizations relying on a current notice regarding disaster assistance check here . . . . . . ▶ ☐

c If the answer is "Yes" to question 5a(4), does the foundation claim exemption from the tax because it maintained expenditure responsibility for the grant? . . . . ☐ Yes ☐ No

If "Yes," attach the statement required by Regulations section 53.4945–5(d).

6a Did the foundation, during the year, receive any funds, directly or indirectly, to pay premiums on a personal benefit contract? . . . . ☐ Yes ☐ No

b Did the foundation, during the year, pay premiums, directly or indirectly, on a personal benefit contract? . . **6b**

If you answered "Yes" to 6b, also file Form 8870.

7a At any time during the tax year, was the foundation a party to a prohibited tax shelter transaction? . ☐ Yes ☐ No

b If yes, did the foundation receive any proceeds or have any net income attributable to the transaction? . . **7b**

A "Yes" answer to a question in this part signals the IRS that the foundation may have violated one of the rules in §§4941 through 4945. An entry in the "Yes" column may require that the foundation file Form 4720 and possibly pay an excise tax for the forbidden act. A "Yes" answer to question 5c requires attachment of an Expenditure Responsibility Report.

The labyrinth of don'ts (but-it-may-be-okay-if-you-do's) regarding self-dealing should be studied carefully if any of the Question 1 answers are "Yes." To avoid an excise tax for self-dealing, the foundation must be able to answer "No" to Question 1b. Similarly, any "Yes" answers to the (a) portions of Questions 2, 3, or 5 need to be followed with a "No" answer in 2b, 3b, and 5b to signal that, though a potential violation of the rules occurred, an exception applied. The answer to both Questions 4a and 4b should be "No." Readers might find it useful to study Chapter 6 of *Private Foundations*[25] to aid in answering Question 2, Chapter 7 for Question 3, Chapter 8 for Question 4, and Chapter 9 for Question 5.

§ 6.13 PART VIII: INFORMATION ABOUT OFFICERS, DIRECTORS, TRUSTEES, FOUNDATION MANAGERS, HIGHLY PAID EMPLOYEES, AND CONTRACTORS

Part VIII	Information About Officers, Directors, Trustees, Foundation Managers, Highly Paid Employees, and Contractors

1 List all officers, directors, trustees, foundation managers and their compensation (see page 22 of the instructions).

(a) Name and address	(b) Title, and average hours per week devoted to position	(c) Compensation (If not paid, enter -0-)	(d) Contributions to employee benefit plans and deferred compensation	(e) Expense account, other allowances

(Continued)

2 Compensation of five highest-paid employees (other than those included on line 1—see page 23 of the instructions). If none, enter "NONE."

(a) Name and address of each employee paid more than $50,000	(b) Title, and average hours per week devoted to position	(c) Compensation	(d) Contributions to employee benefit plans and deferred compensation	(e) Expense account, other allowances

Total number of other employees paid over $50,000 . . . . ▶

3 Five highest-paid independent contractors for professional services (see page 23 of the instructions). If none, enter "NONE."

(a) Name and address of each person paid more than $50,000	(b) Type of service	(c) Compensation

Total number of others receiving over $50,000 for professional services . . . . ▶

Form **990-PF** (2008)

To assist the IRS in detecting self-dealing and private inurement, details of compensation are to be reported. Line 1 of this part must be completed to list all of the foundation's officials, regardless of the number, and indicate whether they receive any compensation or expense allowances. Foundation managers are those persons who have responsibilities or powers similar to those of officers, directors, and trustees. A foundation's executive director and chief financial officer are usually considered managers. The address at which officials would prefer the IRS contact them (can be the foundation's address) is requested.

Some foundations may lack precise time records regarding their volunteer officials. Nonetheless, it is not suitable to note that they spent "part time" attending to foundation affairs; a reasonable time estimate should be entered. For an official that is compensated, the entry in column (b) has another import and should, if possible, be entered with some precision. The relationship between the amount of time spent and the compensation paid could indicate that the foundation has made a taxable expenditure and a self-dealing transaction.

Total compensation paid to persons serving on the governing board, for all services rendered, is to be reported, whether they are employees or independent contractors. For persons serving in more than one position (such as both as a director and officer or staff member), the compensation for each respective position should be separately presented.

§ 6.14   PART IX-A AND B: SUMMARY OF DIRECT CHARITABLE ACTIVITIES AND PROGRAM-RELATED INVESTMENTS

Part IX-A   Summary of Direct Charitable Activities

List the foundation's four largest direct charitable activities during the tax year. Include relevant statistical information such as the number of organizations and other beneficiaries served, conferences convened, research papers produced, etc.	Expenses
1	
2	
3	
4	

Part IX-B   Summary of Program-Related Investments (see page 23 of the instructions)

Describe the two largest program-related investments made by the foundation during the tax year on lines 1 and 2.	Amount
1	
2	
All other program-related investments. See page 24 of the instructions. 3	
Total. Add lines 1 through 3 . . . . ▶	

Form **990-PF** (2008)

In Part IX-A, the foundation has the opportunity to describe the direct charitable programs it conducts that advance its exempt purposes and the achievements of those programs. To describe its accomplishments, the services provided are summarized along with numerical data. How many children were counseled, classes taught, meals served, patients healed, sites restored, books published, conferences convened, research papers produced, or similar data are reported for the foundation's four major projects. This part is similar to Core 990, Part III, and suggestions for that part might be studied in completing this part.

If numerical results are not pertinent or available, the project objectives and the long-range plans can be described. Reasonable estimates can be furnished if the exact number of recipients is not known. A foundation conducting research on heart disease and testing a controlled group of 100 women over a five-year period would say so. Similarly, the foundation that commissions a study of an area's history and expects the project to take 10 years, would say "Four scholars have been hired to annually deliver a minimum of 100 pages each, with citations and appropriate photographic documentation or other archival materials to reflect our area's history. How the documents will be eventually published is not known, so the number of copies and eventual public benefit cannot be measured. However, the research modality can be described to evidence the work's educational nature."

Program-related investments (PRIs) made during the year are reported in Part IX-B. For a foundation with ongoing investments, this report can be coordinated with the balance sheet reporting of the investments in such detail and the expenditure responsibility reporting requirements. Though there are no specific instructions for completion of this part, a PF making such investments can embellish the description of its PRIs in the interest of clearly informing the public that looks at its return of the activity.

§6.15   PART X: MINIMUM INVESTMENT RETURN

Form 990-PF (2008)		Page **8**
Part X Minimum Investment Return (All domestic foundations must complete this part. Foreign foundations, see page 24 of the instructions.)		

1 Fair market value of assets not used (or held for use) directly in carrying out charitable, etc., purposes:		
a Average monthly fair market value of securities	**1a**	
b Average of monthly cash balances	**1b**	
c Fair market value of all other assets (see page 24 of the instructions)	**1c**	
d **Total** (add lines 1a, b, and c)	**1d**	
e Reduction claimed for blockage or other factors reported on lines 1a and 1c (attach detailed explanation) **1e**		
2 Acquisition indebtedness applicable to line 1 assets	**2**	
3 Subtract line 2 from line 1d	**3**	
4 Cash deemed held for charitable activities. Enter 1½ % of line 3 (for greater amount, see page 25 of the instructions)	**4**	
5 **Net value of noncharitable-use assets.** Subtract line 4 from line 3. Enter here and on Part V, line 4	**5**	
6 **Minimum investment return.** Enter 5% of line 5	**6**	

This part calculates the first factor used to determine the foundation's required amount of annual charitable giving—the average fair value of the foundation's investment assets times 5 percent, less a modest "cash deemed held for charitable activities" reserve. Cash and marketable securities for which market quotes are available are valued monthly and averaged for the year. Partnership interests and unlisted securities are valued annually. Land and mineral properties are valued every five years. Assets used in conducting the foundation's charitable programs are not included. Assets held for less than a full year are prorated. The 5 percent rate is also prorated on a daily basis for a foundation filing for less than a full year. Investments placed in a partnership, fund of funds, or other so-called alternative investments, present unique valuation issues.[36]

§6.16   PART XI: DISTRIBUTABLE AMOUNT

Part XI Distributable Amount (see page 25 of the instructions) (Section 4942(j)(3) and (j)(5) private operating foundations and certain foreign organizations check here ▶ ☐ and do not complete this part.)			
1 Minimum investment return from Part X, line 6			**1**
2a Tax on investment income for 2008 from Part VI, line 5	**2a**		
b Income tax for 2008. (This does not include the tax from Part VI.)	**2b**		
c Add lines 2a and 2b		**2c**	
3 Distributable amount before adjustments. Subtract line 2c from line 1			**3**
4 Recoveries of amounts treated as qualifying distributions			**4**
5 Add lines 3 and 4			**5**
6 Deduction from distributable amount (see page 25 of the instructions)			**6**
7 **Distributable amount** as adjusted. Subtract line 6 from line 5. Enter here and on Part XIII, line 1			**7**

This part begins with the calculated minimum investment return from Part X. The excise tax on investment income and income tax on unrelated business income is next allowed to reduce the required charitable payout. Returned grants and sales of assets previously counted as charitable disbursements are added to the requirement. Private operating foundations do not complete this part. The resulting sum is the amount required to be distributed in the next fiscal year that is carried to Part XIII. Line 6 only applies to foundations organized before May 27, 1969.

§6.17 PART XII: QUALIFYING DISTRIBUTIONS

Part XII	**Qualifying Distributions** (see page 25 of the instructions)		
1	Amounts paid (including administrative expenses) to accomplish charitable, etc., purposes:		
a	Expenses, contributions, gifts, etc.—total from Part I, column (d), line 26	1a	
b	Program-related investments—total from Part IX-B	1b	
2	Amounts paid to acquire assets used (or held for use) directly in carrying out charitable, etc., purposes	2	
3	Amounts set aside for specific charitable projects that satisfy the:		
a	Suitability test (prior IRS approval required)	3a	
b	Cash distribution test (attach the required schedule)	3b	
4	**Qualifying distributions.** Add lines 1a through 3b. Enter here and on Part V, line 8, and Part XIII, line 4 . .	4	
5	Foundations that qualify under section 4940(e) for the reduced rate of tax on net investment income. Enter 1% of Part I, line 27b (see page 26 of the instructions)	5	
6	**Adjusted qualifying distributions.** Subtract line 5 from line 4	6	
	Note. The amount on line 6 will be used in Part V, column (b), in subsequent years when calculating whether the foundation qualifies for the section 4940(e) reduction of tax in those years.		

Form **990-PF** (2008)

Finally, in this part, the foundation tallies up the amount of its current-year disbursements that are counted toward its mandatory distribution requirement that is calculated in Part XIII or XIV (for private operating foundations). Expenditures that count for this test are reported in column (d) on page 1, as discussed in Chapter 6, sec. 2, and mostly include grants paid out to other charitable organizations. Certain commitments to spend money in the future, called *set-asides*, may be counted. Acquisition of assets used for charitable purposes and program-related investments are counted. The number on line 4 carries to Part XIII, line 4 (nonoperating foundation) or Part XIV, line 2c (operating foundation).

§6.18 PART XIII: UNDISTRIBUTED INCOME

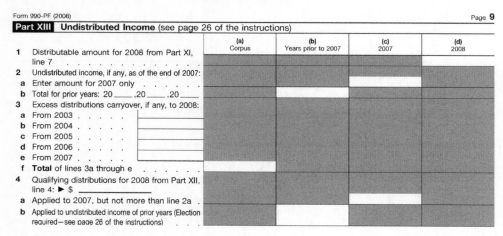

Form 990-PF (2008)   Page **9**

Part XIII	**Undistributed Income** (see page 26 of the instructions)	(a) Corpus	(b) Years prior to 2007	(c) 2007	(d) 2008
1	Distributable amount for 2008 from Part XI, line 7				
2	Undistributed income, if any, as of the end of 2007:				
a	Enter amount for 2007 only				
b	Total for prior years: 20____,20____,20____				
3	Excess distributions carryover, if any, to 2008:				
a	From 2003				
b	From 2004				
c	From 2005				
d	From 2006				
e	From 2007				
f	**Total** of lines 3a through e				
4	Qualifying distributions for 2008 from Part XII, line 4: ▶ $ _____				
a	Applied to 2007, but not more than line 2a .				
b	Applied to undistributed income of prior years (Election required—see page 26 of the instructions) . . .				

(Continued)

	(a) Corpus	(b) Years prior to 2007	(c) 2007	(d) 2008
c Treated as distributions out of corpus (Election required—see page 26 of the instructions)				
d Applied to 2008 distributable amount				
e Remaining amount distributed out of corpus				
5 Excess distributions carryover applied to 2008. *(If an amount appears in column (d), the same amount must be shown in column (a).)*				
6 Enter the net total of each column as indicated below:				
a Corpus. Add lines 3f, 4c, and 4e. Subtract line 5				
b Prior years' undistributed income. Subtract line 4b from line 2b				
c Enter the amount of prior years' undistributed income for which a notice of deficiency has been issued, or on which the section 4942(a) tax has been previously assessed				
d Subtract line 6c from line 6b. Taxable amount—see page 27 of the instructions				
e Undistributed income for 2007. Subtract line 4a from line 2a. Taxable amount—see page 27 of the instructions				
f Undistributed income for 2008. Subtract lines 4d and 5 from line 1. This amount must be distributed in 2009				
7 Amounts treated as distributions out of corpus to satisfy requirements imposed by section 170(b)(1)(F) or 4942(g)(3) (see page 27 of the instructions)				
8 Excess distributions carryover from 2003 not applied on line 5 or line 7 (see page 27 of the instructions)				
9 Excess distributions carryover to 2009. Subtract lines 7 and 8 from line 6a				
10 Analysis of line 9:				
a Excess from 2004				
b Excess from 2005				
c Excess from 2006				
d Excess from 2007				
e Excess from 2008				

Form **990-PF** (2008)

This part surveys five years of grant-making history to determine if the foundation has expended sufficient funds on charitable giving to meet the IRC §4942 tests. If this schedule reflects a balance remaining on line 6(d) or 6(e), Form 4720 must be filed to report and calculate the penalty on underdistributions. The order in which distributions are applied is important, particularly in a deficiency situation.[37]

Qualifying distributions entered on line 4 should be the same as on line 4 of Part XII, but the trick is knowing how to apply the total among the four columns and when a distribution is charged to corpus. As the form's design indicates, current-year distributions are first applied to column (c), the remaining undistributed income from the immediately preceding year. This can create a cash flow problem when a foundation (or the IRS) finds that deficient distributions from the past must be corrected. The current-year required payments must be paid before the correction can be made. Next, corrections of prior-year deficiencies are applied to line 4(b) (not required).

A foundation might choose to apply current-year grants as a distribution out of corpus on line 7, column (a), under certain circumstances. For example, such an application is appropriate for a foundation redistributing a donation for which the contributor desires the maximum deduction. The point is that the private foundation cannot count a gift attributable to a pass-through contribution as part of its qualifying distributions. Other instances in which such treatment is appropriate involve grants paid to a controlled public charity and pass-through grants to another foundation.

§ 6.19 PART XIV: PRIVATE OPERATING FOUNDATIONS

Part XIV	Private Operating Foundations (see page 27 of the instructions and Part VII-A, question 9)				

1a If the foundation has received a ruling or determination letter that it is a private operating foundation, and the ruling is effective for 2008, enter the date of the ruling . . . . ▶

b Check box to indicate whether the foundation is a private operating foundation described in section ☐ 4942(j)(3) or ☐ 4942(j)(5)

		Tax year	Prior 3 years			(e) Total
		(a) 2008	(b) 2007	(c) 2006	(d) 2005	
2a	Enter the lesser of the adjusted net income from Part I or the minimum investment return from Part X for each year listed					
b	85% of line 2a					
c	Qualifying distributions from Part XII, line 4 for each year listed . . .					
d	Amounts included in line 2c not used directly for active conduct of exempt activities . .					
e	Qualifying distributions made directly for active conduct of exempt activities. Subtract line 2d from line 2c . .					
3	Complete 3a, b, or c for the alternative test relied upon:					
a	"Assets" alternative test—enter:					
	(1) Value of all assets					
	(2) Value of assets qualifying under section 4942(j)(3)(B)(i)					
b	"Endowment" alternative test—enter ⅔ of minimum investment return shown in Part X, line 6 for each year listed . . .					
c	"Support" alternative test—enter:					
	(1) Total support other than gross investment income (interest, dividends, rents, payments on securities loans (section 512(a)(5)), or royalties) . .					
	(2) Support from general public and 5 or more exempt organizations as provided in section 4942(j)(3)(B)(iii) . . .					
	(3) Largest amount of support from an exempt organization . . .					
	(4) Gross investment income . .					

Private operating foundations submit information to calculate their ongoing qualification based on four years of their qualifying distributions, income, and assets. The terms and rules applicable to this special type of foundation are somewhat complex and should be carefully studied before this part is completed.[38]

§ 6.20 PART XV: SUPPLEMENTARY INFORMATION (LINES 1–2)

Part XV	Supplementary Information (Complete this part only if the foundation had $5,000 or more in assets at any time during the year—see page 27 of the instructions.)

1 **Information Regarding Foundation Managers:**

a List any managers of the foundation who have contributed more than 2% of the total contributions received by the foundation before the close of any tax year (but only if they have contributed more than $5,000). (See section 507(d)(2).)

b List any managers of the foundation who own 10% or more of the stock of a corporation (or an equally large portion of the ownership of a partnership or other entity) of which the foundation has a 10% or greater interest.

2 **Information Regarding Contribution, Grant, Gift, Loan, Scholarship, etc., Programs:**

Check here ▶ ☐ if the foundation only makes contributions to preselected charitable organizations and does not accept unsolicited requests for funds. If the foundation makes gifts, grants, etc. (see page 28 of the instructions) to individuals or organizations under other conditions, complete items 2a, b, c, and d.

a The name, address, and telephone number of the person to whom applications should be addressed:

b The form in which applications should be submitted and information and materials they should include:

c Any submission deadlines:

d Any restrictions or limitations on awards, such as by geographical areas, charitable fields, kinds of institutions, or other factors:

Form **990-PF** (2008)

Lines 1 and 2 of this part are completed for foundations with assets of $5,000 or more, except those foreign foundations whose U.S. source income is entirely investment income. The name of any foundation manager who has donated more than $5,000 (or 2% of the total contributions received by the foundation) to the foundation is listed. Those foundation managers who own 10 percent or more of the stock of a corporation in which the foundation also has a 10 percent or greater interest are also listed in this part.

The foundation reveals the following information regarding its grant programs: to whom a request is addressed, the form (if any) in which applications should be submitted, what should be attached, the deadlines, and any restrictions and limitations on awards, such as geographic area, subject, kinds of institutions, and so on. Grant seekers use the information submitted in this part to select the PFs to whom they will make applications for funding. Many PFs now post an application form on their website. Because the return is also on the Internet at Guidestar.org, this part should be very carefully prepared. The Foundation Center and other organizations publish books and electronic media that also contain this information. Most often, persons seeking to understand a PF's mission and type of funding it awards look at this and the following part to find out what kind of grants a PF makes.

Foundations that make grants only to preselected charities and do not accept unsolicited requests for funds can check the box on line 2. Because the paper load for some foundations is immense, there is a temptation in some cases to check the box although it does not necessarily apply. There are ongoing philosophical discussions about the pros and cons of the box: Should a private foundation with unrestricted funds close the door to grant applicants by checking the box?

§6.21 PART XV: GRANTS AND CONTRIBUTIONS PAID DURING THE YEAR OR APPROVED FOR FUTURE PAYMENT (LINE 3)

| Form 990-PF (2008) | | | | Page **11** |

Part XV Supplementary Information (Complete this part only if the foundation had $5,000 or more in assets at any time during the year—see page 27 of the instructions.)

3 Grants and Contributions Paid During the Year or Approved for Future Payment

Recipient — Name and address (home or business)	If recipient is an individual, show any relationship to any foundation manager or substantial contributor	Foundation status of recipient	Purpose of grant or contribution	Amount
a Paid during the year				
				(Continued)

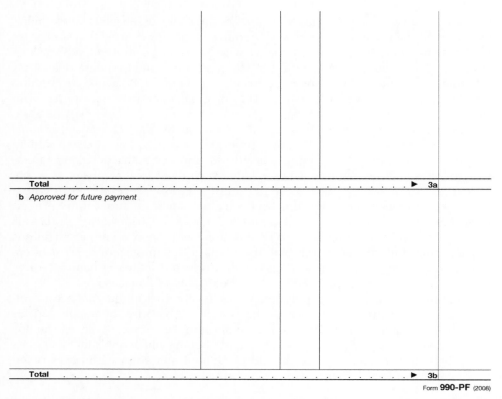

Total . . . . ▶ **3a**

b *Approved for future payment*

Total . . . . ▶ **3b**

Form **990-PF** (2008)

This part lists both grants paid during the year and those approved for future payment. The total under 3a should agree with the amount reported on line 25, column (d). The line 3b total of future grant commitments is provided for public inspection purposes only, and does not necessarily carry to any other part of the form. A foundation following GAAP would reflect a liability on the balance sheet in Part II, line 18, for grants payable with which the number should agree. Note that this amount for SFAS No. 116 financial purposes will be equal to the discounted present value of the pledges, not necessarily the gross face amount of the pledge.

The presentation of this information is extremely important for several reasons. Grant information is contained in the widely circulated local, state, and national directories published for grant seekers, in books and electronic media, and now on the Internet. The foundation has an opportunity to paint a picture of its mission and reflect the scope and depth of its grant making. Organizing the grant payments to arrive at subtotals that reflect the nature of programs the foundation funds, such as feeding the poor, crime prevention, education, culture, and so on, can result in the receipt of improved grant applications. At the same time, it satisfies the IRS request that the purpose of the grant be described in the second-from-the-left column.

From a tax standpoint, the middle column in this part is very important and informs the IRS of the "foundation status of the recipient." What this means is the grantee's classification as a public or private charity under IRC §509, as described for Schedule A in Chapter 4. If the grantee is a public charity (other than a nonfunctionally integrated Type III supporting organization [NFIIISO]), no other information is reported in Form 990-PF concerning the grant. If, instead, the grantee is another private foundation or NFIIIISO, Question 5a(4) in Part VII-B will be answered "Yes." Additionally, the foundation must exercise "expenditure responsibility," answer Question 5a(c) "Yes," and attach a detailed report to the return.

The relationship, if any, between individual grant recipients and any foundation manager or substantial contributor is also revealed. Any answer other than "None" raises several issues. The first question is whether self-dealing might have occurred because a payment was made to a disqualified person. Additionally, payment to related individuals might indicate that the foundation's scholarship payments are not made on the required "objective and nondiscriminatory basis." Finally, a grant to a controlled organization or a private foundation may not be a qualifying distribution.

§6.22 PART XVI-A: ANALYSIS OF INCOME-PRODUCING ACTIVITY

Form 990-PF (2008)   Page **12**

Part XVI-A   Analysis of Income-Producing Activities

Enter gross amounts unless otherwise indicated.

	Unrelated business income		Excluded by section 512, 513, or 514		(e) Related or exempt function income (See page 28 of the instructions.)
	(a) Business code	**(b)** Amount	**(c)** Exclusion code	**(d)** Amount	
1 Program service revenue:					
a					
b					
c					
d					
e					
f					
g Fees and contracts from government agencies					
2 Membership dues and assessments					
3 Interest on savings and temporary cash investments					
4 Dividends and interest from securities					
5 Net rental income or (loss) from real estate:					
a Debt-financed property					
b Not debt-financed property					
6 Net rental income or (loss) from personal property					
7 Other investment income					
8 Gain or (loss) from sales of assets other than inventory					
9 Net income or (loss) from special events					
10 Gross profit or (loss) from sales of inventory					
11 Other revenue: a					
b					
c					
d					
e					
12 Subtotal. Add columns (b), (d), and (e)					

13 **Total.** Add line 12, columns (b), (d), and (e) . . . . 13 _____
(See worksheet in line 13 instructions on page 28 to verify calculations.)

Part XVI-B   Relationship of Activities to the Accomplishment of Exempt Purposes

Line No. ▼	Explain below how each activity for which income is reported in column (e) of Part XVI-A contributed importantly to the accomplishment of the foundation's exempt purposes (other than by providing funds for such purposes). (See page 28 of the instructions.)

(Continued)

Part XVI-B—Relationship of Activities (Continued)

[ruled blank lines]

Form **990-PF** (2008)

At the behest of Congress, Part XVI-A was added to Form 990-PF in 1989, as an audit trail to find unrelated business income. Unrelated income is reported alongside related income in Part I, and this part is designed to fragment the two different types and alert the IRS when Form 990-T should be filed to report and identify. The IRS instructions contain a helpful chart comparing the lines of Part I to the lines for entry on this part. This part was moved to the Statement of Revenue, Core Part IX for 2008. Discussion of the concepts is found in Chapter 5.

§6.23 PART XVII: INFORMATION REGARDING TRANSFERS TO AND TRANSACTIONS AND RELATIONSHIPS WITH NONCHARITABLE EXEMPT ORGANIZATIONS

Form 990-PF (2008)   Page **13**

Part XVII   Information Regarding Transfers To and Transactions and Relationships With Noncharitable Exempt Organizations

		Yes	No
1 Did the organization directly or indirectly engage in any of the following with any other organization described in section 501(c) of the Code (other than section 501(c)(3) organizations) or in section 527, relating to political organizations?			
a Transfers from the reporting foundation to a noncharitable exempt organization of:			
(1) Cash	1a(1)		
(2) Other assets	1a(2)		
b Other transactions:			
(1) Sales of assets to a noncharitable exempt organization	1b(1)		
(2) Purchases of assets from a noncharitable exempt organization	1b(2)		
(3) Rental of facilities, equipment, or other assets	1b(3)		
(4) Reimbursement arrangements	1b(4)		
(5) Loans or loan guarantees	1b(5)		
(6) Performance of services or membership or fundraising solicitations	1b(6)		
c Sharing of facilities, equipment, mailing lists, other assets, or paid employees	1c		

d If the answer to any of the above is "Yes," complete the following schedule. Column **(b)** should always show the fair market value of the goods, other assets, or services given by the reporting foundation. If the foundation received less than fair market value in any transaction or sharing arrangement, show in column **(d)** the value of the goods, other assets, or services received.

(a) Line no.	(b) Amount involved	(c) Name of noncharitable exempt organization	(d) Description of transfers, transactions, and sharing arrangements

(Continued)

■ **286** ■

2a Is the foundation directly or indirectly affiliated with, or related to, one or more tax-exempt organizations
described in section 501(c) of the Code (other than section 501(c)(3)) or in section 527? . . . . . . ☐ Yes ☐ No
b If "Yes," complete the following schedule.

(a) Name of organization	(b) Type of organization	(c) Description of relationship

Under penalties of perjury, I declare that I have examined this return, including accompanying schedules and statements, and to the best of my knowledge and belief, it is true, correct, and complete. Declaration of preparer (other than taxpayer or fiduciary) is based on all information of which preparer has any knowledge.

Sign Here

► Signature of officer or trustee   Date   ► Title

Paid Preparer's Use Only

Preparer's signature ►	Date	Check if self-employed ► ☐	Preparer's identifying number (see **Signature** on page 30 of the instructions)
Firm's name (or yours if self-employed), address, and ZIP code ►		EIN ►	
		Phone no. ( )	

Form **990-PF** (2008)

This part was designed for Form 990, does not apply to many private foundations, and was added in 1988, in response to a congressional mandate that the IRS search for connections between private foundations and non–501(c)(3) organizations. The IRS is scouting for relationships that allow benefits, or the use of a foundation's assets, to flow from the foundation to a noncharitable exempt organization. Instructions for completion of new Schedule L of Form 990 describe relationships that should be disclosed and can be found in Chapter 4.12.

NOTES

1. The technical aspects of the sanctions applied to PFs, found in IRC §4940–4946, are far reaching. Tax Planning and Compliance contains 135 pages presented in Chapters 12 through 17, on the complex rules that can be studied along with the following suggestions for completion of the form. For further study consult *Private Foundations: Tax Law and Compliance*, 3rd edition, Hopkins and Blazek (Hoboken, N.J.: John Wiley & Sons, 2008).
2. See J. Blazek, *Tax Planning and Compliance* (Hoboken, N.J.: John Wiley, 2008), Ch. 14 of Tax for 31 pages of discussion of these rules.
3. See Blazek, *Tax Planning and Compliance*, Ch. 17, for 45 pages of discussion of these rules.
4. See Blazek, *Tax Planning and Compliance*, Ch. 16, for 10 pages of discussion of these rules.
5. See Blazek, *Tax Planning and Compliance*, Ch. 16, for 8 pages of discussion of these rules.
6. The instructions for the 1990 form contained 22 pages—proof that this form is not getting simpler.
7. IRC §4940(c)(4)(D).
8. See Chapter 4.2, the same form is used for Form 990 filers.
9. See Blazek, *Tax Planning and Compliance*, Ch. 14, for 24 pages of discussion of these rules.
10. IRC §4940(c)(4), as revised by the Pension Protection Act of 2006 and §3(f) of the Tax Technical Corrections Act of 2007, P.L. 110–172, 12/29/2007.
11. §4940(c)(4)(C); before revision, the regulations, but not the tax code disallowed carrybacks.
12. A similar rule operates for nonexempt charitable trusts described in IRC §4947 (§3.6); Rev. Rul. 74–497, 1974–2 C.B. 383.
13. Rev. Rul. 73–320, 1973–2 C.B. 385.
14. Reg. §53.4940–1(f)(1); see *Private Foundations: Tax Law and Compliance*, Chapter 10, sec. 2(b).
15. Reg. §53.4940–1(d)(3); Priv. Ltr. Rul. 8214023.

16. IRC §368 or other provision of IRC Subchapter C. E.g., Priv. Ltr. Rul. 8730061.
17. Tech. Adv. Mem. 9724005.
18. Reg. §1.4940–1.
19. IRC §§162 and 212.
20. Discussed in Chapter 5.3.
21. Unless the recipient private foundation has agreed to redistribute the funds in accordance with §4942(g)(3).
22. Discussed in Chapter 2.2.
23. Gen. Coun. Memo 39808.
24. IRC §§1011, 1012, 1014, 1015, and 1016 apply in completing this part. IRC §4940(c)(3)(B).
25. Reg. §53.4940–1(f)(2)(i)(B), which refers to IRC §1015.
26. Reg. §53.4940–1(f)(3).
27. Returns are displayed on Guidestar.org.
28. See Blazek, *Tax Planning and Compliance*, Ch. 13 for illustrations of this important tax savings opportunity.
29. IRC §6655.
30. Discussed in Chapter 4.3.
31. Process and propriety of seeking approval discussed in Chapter 3.4.
32. IRC §513. Chapter 5 defines unrelated income and the many exceptions to taxation for certain types of unrelated income, including indebted investment properties.
33. IRC §507(a). Chapter 13 of Blazek, *Private Foundations* explains the circumstances under which a private foundation can go out of existence either by converting itself to a public charity or distributing its assets to other charitable organizations. Model forms and instructions on this complicated matter are provided.
34. Reg. §1.507–3.
35. IRC §6050V(d)(2)(B)
36. See Blazek, *Tax Planning and Compliance*, Ch. 15.2.
37. The order in which qualifying distributions are applied is illustrated in Blazek, *Tax Planning and Compliance*, Ch.15.6.
38. See Blazek, *Tax Planning and Compliance*, Ch.15.5.

Index

Printed and bound by CPI Group (UK) Ltd, Croydon, CR0 4YY

17/04/2025

14658916-0001